BAR REVIEW

New Jersey
Essay Testing

Table of Contents

Grading Keys

Essay Questions

Essay Answers

Subject Index of New Jersey Essay

THOMSON

BAR/BRI

celebrating over
35 YEARS
of preparing
law students
for the bar exam

ESSAY GRADING KEY

DATE RECEIVED _____

Name _____

Address _____

_____

BAR/BRI ID # _____

ESSAY QUESTION # _____

COURSE LOCATION _____

SESSION: AM / AFT / PM   (circle one)

ESSAY GRADE _____

GRADER NUMBER _____

_____

_____

_____

_____

_____

	GRADER'S COMMENTS

GRADER'S COMMENTS

ESSAY GRADING KEY

DATE RECEIVED _____

Name _____

Address _____

_____

BAR/BRI ID # _____

ESSAY QUESTION # _____

COURSE LOCATION _____

SESSION: AM / AFT / PM   (circle one)

ESSAY GRADE _____

GRADER NUMBER _____

_____

_____

_____

_____

_____

GRADER'S COMMENTS

GRADER'S COMMENTS

BAR REVIEW

ESSAY GRADING KEY

DATE RECEIVED _____

Name _____

Address _____

_____

BAR/BRI ID # _____

ESSAY QUESTION # _____

COURSE LOCATION _____

SESSION: AM / AFT / PM   (circle one)

ESSAY GRADE _____

GRADER NUMBER _____

_____

_____

_____

_____

_____

GRADER'S COMMENTS

GRADER'S COMMENTS

ESSAY GRADING KEY

DATE RECEIVED _____

Name _____

Address _____

_____

ESSAY GRADE _____

BAR/BRI ID # _____

ESSAY QUESTION # _____

COURSE LOCATION _____

SESSION: AM / AFT / PM   (circle one)

GRADER NUMBER _____

_____

_____

_____

_____

_____

_____

GRADER'S COMMENTS

BAR REVIEW

ESSAY GRADING KEY

DATE RECEIVED _____

Name _____

Address _____

_____

ESSAY GRADE _____

BAR/BRI ID #_____

ESSAY QUESTION #_____

COURSE LOCATION _____

SESSION: AM / AFT / PM   (circle one)

GRADER NUMBER _____

GRADER'S COMMENTS

GRADER'S COMMENTS

ESSAY GRADING KEY

DATE RECEIVED _____

Name _____

Address _____

_____

BAR/BRI ID #_____

ESSAY QUESTION #_____

COURSE LOCATION _____

SESSION: AM / AFT / PM   (circle one)

ESSAY GRADE _____

GRADER NUMBER _____

_____

_____

_____

_____

_____

_____

GRADER'S COMMENTS

GRADER'S COMMENTS

BAR REVIEW

NEW JERSEY BAR EXAM SUGGESTED ESSAY FORMAT

1- **Read the call of the question.**

2- Spend the **first 10 minutes outlining** the issues in the essay and framing your answer. Spend the remaining 35 minutes writing your answer.

3- <u>CIRAC</u> **— EACH ISSUE PRESENTED:**
   C - conclusion (start each issue stating your conclusion)
   I - issue (state the issue presented by the facts)
   R - rule (state the applicable rule of law)
   A - analyze (for each element of the rule of law, state the fact(s) which applies or the absence of a fact(s) which makes the rule of law inapplicable)
   C - conclusion (restate your conclusion)

4- **Write concise sentences.** Run-ons, fragments, and dangling participles make it difficult for the grader. Graders should not have to "search" for the answer. Remember, you want the grader to "like" you.

5- **WRITE CLEARLY!** If the grader can't read your paper, the grader can't grade your paper. Using print rather than script and double spacing may make it easier for the grader.

6- **Do <u>not</u> argue both sides** unless the facts warrant. Take a position and stick to it. Follow through with the best support for the argument based upon your knowledge of the applicable law. Being indecisive makes the bar examiners think you don't know the law at all.

7- **ONLY DEAL WITH THE ISSUE(S) PRESENTED.** For example, if you are dealing with one particular hearsay exception, you should not list all the hearsay exceptions. It is not necessary to tell the Bar Examiners what **does not apply** to the facts presented.

8- Do not **OVEREMPHASIZE,** *i.e.,* underlining, capitalizing, etc., too many words so that the effect is lost. **Only "buzz words"** should be set off.

9- Always **complete the discussion of one issue** before jumping to another. Do not combine two or three issues into one paragraph and one thought. Discussion of each issue should be viewed as a "mini essay" and should be able to stand by itself.

10- Develop your analysis fully. A mere conclusion without legal reasoning and fact application is worthless. **FOR EACH ELEMENT OF EACH RULE OF LAW, YOU MUST STATE HOW A FACT (OR THE ABSENCE THEREOF) APPLIES OR DOES NOT APPLY.**
   i.e., There was an entering <u>because</u> he put his hand through the window.
   It's a dwelling <u>because</u> people live there.
   The defendant was armed <u>because</u> he had a gun.

11- **Do not interject your personal opinion** as to how a court should rule based upon your sense of "fairness, justice, and decency" rather than on the applicable legal principles.

12- If a statute is applicable to your answer you should mention the broad name of the statute, *i.e.,* U.C.C., etc. However, **do not mention statute numbers** or case names unless they are extremely significant and recognizable.

13- Lastly, we suggest that you **write on only the right-hand page.** By doing this, if you want to add something as an afterthought all you have to do is draw an arrow to the left-hand page and make your insert. You will be given as many "bluebooks" as you need.

BAR REVIEW

Essay Questions

celebrating over
35 YEARS
*of preparing
law students
for the bar exam*

1.   On January 10, 2002, Lucy voluntarily entered Restlawn, a private mental institution. To assist in forming a psychiatric evaluation, Dr. Beard, a staff psychiatrist, took a history from Lucy, her husband Arthur, and Elderly, her mother. Among the facts elicited, Dr. Beard learned of two recent incidents when Lucy had attempted suicide. Dr. Beard examined Lucy on the following day and ordered appropriate laboratory tests. He also conferred at length with Lucy and learned of facts which assisted him in forming his psychiatric evaluation.

Having diagnosed Lucy's condition as schizophrenia with suicidal tendencies, Dr. Beard instructed a staff nurse to stamp "SUICIDAL" across the face sheet of Lucy's chart in red ink.

Dr. Beard visited Lucy the following morning and recommended extensive therapy at Restlawn, telling her that in his judgment she was potentially dangerous to herself. Lucy angrily shouted, "You can't help me. You psychiatrists are fakers! I'm getting out of this loony bin right now." Dr. Beard replied, "If that's the way you feel, then go." He prepared discharge papers and Lucy signed herself out of Restlawn. Dr. Beard took no steps toward involuntary commitment, although he had frequently done so in similar cases and was familiar with the legal procedure.

Lucy went home to the apartment where she lived with Arthur. Later that day she went shopping in a Fairshake supermarket. She selected several food items from a merchandise shelf and put them into a shopping cart. Suddenly two men, Rack and Pinion, strode roughly up to her and identified themselves as Fairshake's security guards. Each man said he had seen her shoplifting. Rack said, "Make it easy on yourself and take that carton of cigarettes out of your handbag." Lucy denied having any cigarettes. Pinion then said, "We'll have to do it the hard way. Come with us."

Both men walked her to a room which Fairshake provided for questioning suspected shoplifters. The room had a heavy door and contained a stool on which the men seated Lucy. Rack slammed the door shut and told Lucy she would be detained unless she confessed and returned the cigarettes. Lucy continued to protest her innocence and begged to be allowed to leave. She was told, "You're not going anywhere. We're getting the cops."

Lucy was terrified and began to tremble and cry. She dropped her handbag and stood up, crying hysterically, "Poor Lucy! Oh, what's the use." Then she bent forward, ran headlong into the door and fell unconscious.

Rack and Pinion opened Lucy's handbag but found no cigarettes. Rack then summoned an ambulance which took her to a hospital. Her skull was found to be fractured. She died that night of a related brain hemorrhage.

Lucy was 30 years of age at her death. Three days before entering Restlawn she had quit a steady job which had netted her a weekly salary of $100. While working, Lucy had contributed $30 a week for household expenses, and had also given Elderly $10 a week to help with her expenses. Lucy died intestate. All of her funeral expenses were paid by Arthur.

Shortly after the funeral, Arthur and Elderly retained you as their attorney. You are about to file suit in the Superior Court of New Jersey, Law Division, by filing complaints against Restlawn, Dr. Beard, Fairshake, Rack and Pinion.

Arthur qualifies as Lucy's representative and individually asserts claims for his own damages. Elderly claims damages she suffered as the result of Lucy's untimely death. Without drafting the complaint, detail each cause of action you would allege against each defendant. Include in your discussion the legal and factual basis for each cause of action.

2.   Oaner owned a four-acre square-shaped parcel fronting on Forest Avenue in Green Pines, New Jersey. In 1997, Oaner agreed to sell to Byer a two-acre portion of the property which included the entire frontage on Forest Avenue. At that time, Oaner and Byer discussed the reservation of an easement from Forest Avenue to Oaner's remaining land-locked parcel. During the discussion the parties agreed that Oaner would have the right in the future to designate

the location of an easement up to 50 feet in width on the Byer property. There was then no permitted use under the local zoning ordinance which required a right of way greater than 50 feet in width. The deed from Oaner to Byer contained the following provision:

> Grantor reserves to himself, his heirs, successors, and assigns, a right of way over the lands conveyed hereby to Grantee for vehicular and pedestrian traffic between Forest Avenue and the remaining lands of Grantor.

In 2001, Byer contracted to sell his parcel to Uzer. Byer approached Oaner and requested Oaner to designate the location of his easement. Oaner refused to do so and demanded instead that Byer purchase his remaining property at a price which was twice its then fair market value. Byer would not do so and conveyed his parcel to Uzer by bargain and sale deed with covenants against grantor's acts.

Uzer built a plant on the property in 2002 and, for the security of his operations, fenced in the entire perimeter of the property.

Oaner has decided to develop his property as an office building site. This use is permitted by the Green Pines zoning ordinance, but a 60-foot-wide right of way is now required by the ordinance for construction of an office building. The zoning ordinance also permits residential use with a minimum 20-foot-wide right of way to the land-locked parcel.

Oaner has instituted litigation seeking equitable relief designating a 60-foot-wide easement over the property of Uzer which would include Uzer's present 40-foot-wide driveway. Uzer is willing to permit a 20-foot right of way along his boundary line which would not include the driveway.

(a) Discuss the rights and liabilities of Uzer.

(b) Draft the easement that you would have requested on behalf of Oaner if you had represented him at the time of his conveyance to Byer.

3. Frank, age 50, went into E-Z Check Cashing Agency on August 20 and committed an armed robbery. As he was leaving, the police arrived and started shooting. In his haste to escape, Frank pushed Customer out of his way and into the line of police fire. Customer was struck by a police bullet and died instantly. Frank escaped unharmed with $20,000.

One evening while driving with three juvenile passengers, Frank was stopped by the police because one of his headlights was out. All occupants were requested to get out of the car. Policemen soon arrived and asked one of the passengers if the car could be searched. Not knowing what to say, he responded, "I guess so." When the police pulled out the rear seat of the car they found a package of marked bills which had been stolen in the robbery.

Frank and his passengers were then taken into custody and held separately for questioning. Frank was brought into a room by Detective who asked him where he was on August 20. Frank replied, "Okay, okay. I was in the Agency when the job was pulled." Prosecutor was prepared to seek an indictment, but Detective asked him to wait until a lineup could be arranged.

Frank and his passengers were placed in a line-up by themselves. An E-Z employee pointed to Frank and said, "That looks like the guy."

A few days after Frank was indicted for murder and armed robbery, Attorney was appointed to represent him.

During Frank's trial, the marked money and testimony concerning the lineup identification were received in evidence. Frank testified that he was out of the state at the time of the robbery. The prosecutor then asked Frank if he had ever stated that he was present at the scene. Frank denied any such statement. The detective was then called to testify to the statement made to him by Frank. All proper objections were timely made by Attorney.

The court charged the substance of all Requests to Charge submitted by Attorney except one relating to presumption of innocence. Frank was convicted on both counts by a verdict of 5–1. The state court rule permits a jury of six persons in criminal cases and a verdict based on a five-sixths vote.

You are the attorney representing Frank in the appeal of his conviction. Prepare the "Law and Argument" portion of the appellate brief you would submit on behalf of your client. Do not prepare a separate statement of facts, but incorporate into your argument any of the above facts which support your client's position.

4. PART A

Mom and Dad lived together, unmarried, during which time Suzy was born. They lived as a close family unit. In 1998, when Suzy was five years of age, Mom died and Suzy became a ward of the State under a statute which required minor children of unwed fathers to become wards of the State upon the death of the mother. The unwed father's unfitness as a parent was statutorily established so that minor children of unwed parents could be expeditiously placed for adoption upon the death of their mothers and minimal use of court time and facilities would be required. Under the statute, an unwed father was not included in the definition of "parent," although married or divorced persons and unwed mothers were included. These latter classes of persons could be deprived of custody of their children only after a hearing to determine fitness. There was no statutory provision for a fitness hearing for an unwed father.

Without notice to Dad, the court entered an order terminating his parental rights to Suzy, who was then placed in the custody of the Children's Society.

Dad retained you to challenge these actions. He has requested your advice in writing. Please comply with his request.

PART B

In 1999, Dad died intestate. He was survived by Suzy and by Sonny, an adult son by a prior marriage which had terminated in divorce. Sonny has been appointed administrator of Dad's estate. He reported that Dad's estate consisted of a house, a car, and $500 in cash. Sonny has challenged the right of Suzy to share in Dad's estate. He relies upon a statute which provides that an illegitimate child shall be treated as the legitimate child of the mother and shall inherit from her but not from the father.

Based on the facts in Part B, the legislative revision committee has requested you to draft an advisory letter interpreting the statute. Respond to the request.

5. Blood Pressure, Inc. ("BP") manufactured a device which permits an individual to measure blood pressure without a doctor. BP sold the device to retail stores located in New Jersey and New York and attempted to market its product in other states.

On March 31, 1981, Tom Tenser ("Tenser"), the sole owner of BP, conveyed 100% of BP's stock for a price of $3 million to Norm Norvis ("Norvis"). In the stock purchase agreement Tenser, who planned to retire, agreed that for a period of 20 years he would not "directly or indirectly engage in or work for a business which sold blood pressure monitoring equipment anywhere in the United States of America."

On April 1, 1981, BP's long-time sales manager, Willy Loman ("Loman"), signed an employment contract with BP. The contract provided that for 10 years following his termination of employment for any reason Loman would not "indirectly engage in or work for any business which sold blood pressure monitoring equipment in any state east of the Mississippi River." The employment contract was terminable at will by either party on 90 days' notice.

Although Loman was immediately successful in expanding BP's sales into Pennsylvania and Connecticut, Norvis felt he no longer needed Loman's expertise. After giving the required notice, Norvis terminated Loman's employment effective December 31, 1981. During the next two years Loman tried working in an unrelated field, but with little success.

In January 1984, Tenser advised Loman that he had purchased the patent for a new, low-cost blood pressure testing device which was superior to anything else available to consumers. On January 30, 1984, for a royalty based on 5% of all sales, Tenser granted an exclusive license to Loman to manufacture and sell the new device. By July 1984 Loman was enjoying a profitable and growing business, and the product was being sold in all 50 states. BP had not expanded its sales territory after Loman's departure.

Although Norvis was aware of Loman's activities as early as February 1984, his intense dislike of attorneys kept him from consulting a lawyer until February of 1987, when he sought the advice of the senior partner in the law firm where you are employed. Norvis wants to know (1) the chances of BP's success in a suit for an injunction and damages against Tenser and Loman; and (2) the chances of obtaining a preliminary injunction at an early stage in the litigation. Norvis is afraid that BP will be bankrupt if it must wait until the case reaches trial.

Please prepare a memorandum to the senior partner which will enable her to render the advice sought by Norvis.

6.   Dave, a college student with substantial income from a trust fund established by his great grandfather in 1897, was leading a group of young people on a march to the city hall of a medium-sized town where the college was located, in order to protest certain actions of the town council. When it appeared that continuance of the march would result in a confrontation with the local police, Dave climbed to the top of an automobile parked by the curb adjacent to Peter's house and lot. Part of the crowd that collected to hear what Dave had to say gathered on Peter's property, trampled his flower beds and knocked down his fence.

Dave shouted to the crowd: "The mayor of this town is immoral and unfit to hold political office." He then read verbatim portions of the transcript of a divorce action between the mayor and his former wife, Wilma, which described fascinatingly scandalous behavior on the part of both the mayor and Wilma. Some of the matter read from the transcript about the mayor was not true. All of the statements about Wilma were true. Since the divorce, Wilma has become proprietor of a small antique shop and has avoided public activities for more than 10 years.

During Dave's speech, several demonstrators were arrested for narcotics violations committed in the presence of the arresting officers. As a protest against the state narcotics control act, Dave, unnoticed by the arresting officers, climbed into the police van with the prisoners. As soon as the van doors were locked, Dave began pounding on the inside of the van and demanded his release. The arresting officers ignored the pounding and drove the van to the local jail, where, after a count of the prisoners and a short conference, Dave was released.

A suit has been instituted against Dave by Mayor, Wilma, and Peter. Dave has filed suit against the police officers. A motion for consolidation was granted because of the similarity of the events. You are the law clerk for the judge hearing this bench trial. He requests you to draft a memorandum which details each prima facie case and whether each party could meet the burdens of each prima facie case.

7.   Buyer and Seller consult you in your law office and present you with the following facts.

Buyer wishes to purchase from Seller a lot, with a small house on it, for $20,000. Buyer expects to live in the house until he can enlarge it or tear it down and build a larger house. The house currently is occupied by a large and active colony of termites and by a tenant under a month-to-month tenancy. Buyer knows about the tenant, but not about the termites. Seller is aware of the termites.

Seller tells you that she is a widow but plans to remarry soon. Her late husband bought the lot just before their marriage in 1935. In 1940, her late husband built the house, even though a clause in the deed prohibited any structures on the lot. Seller wants to sell because all her children are married and are living far away and because her long-standing dispute with Neighbor over the shared driveway has recently become more bitter. She has also heard that there are new laws that make it hard to remove tenants and she no longer wishes to be a landlord or to make mortgage payments to Bank.

You know that the entire area is zoned residential, that the house has always constituted a violation of the minimum house size requirements of the zoning ordinance and that the Planning Board has just adopted a Master Plan that would place the entire area in a commercial zone and prohibit residential use.

Buyer and Seller have already agreed that Seller will take back a $15,000 purchase money mortgage.

Buyer and Seller ask you to prepare a contract that protects all their legitimate interests and to handle the closing.

What further information do you need to prepare the contract and effectuate transfer of title? State why such information is factually or legally significant.

What contingencies, if any, should be provided for in the contract? What other problems do you anticipate?

8.   On July 10, 1984, Lawyer Sally and Naomi, her secretary, left their office after dark. On the way to their cars, they were attacked by three unarmed men who demanded money. Sally pulled a revolver from her pocket and fired several shots at the attackers. One bullet passed through one attacker, killing him and a passerby. The other bullets wounded a second attacker. The entire attack took less than 30 seconds.

The next day, Naomi could not identify the third attacker from 500 mug shots. On September 10, 1984, Naomi bumped into Detective Rite in the courthouse corridor. Rite said, "I think that's your man in there," pointing to a man known as Brown, who was on the witness stand in an unrelated case. Naomi replied, "Now that you mention it, he does look something like the guy." Subsequently, the police conducted a proper form of lineup and Naomi selected Brown from the group.

Brown was indicted for robbery and murder without a preliminary hearing. The grand jury panel was chosen from that part of the county in which most of the violent crimes were committed.

At the trial, over Brown's lawyer's objection, Naomi identified Brown as one of her attackers.

During a recess, Brown and the jury departed via separate doorways and elevators. Inadvertently, Brown's elevator door opened on the wrong floor in full view of the jury while he was shackled with seven feet of chain. Brown's motion of mistrial based on this incident was denied.

(a)   You are the trial judge's law clerk and he has directed you to draft a memo on:

(1)   The elements of felony murder applicable to this case,

(2)   The legal effect of any pretrial identification, and

(3)   The elevator incident.

(b)   Evaluate any problems which may be raised on appeal by Brown which relate to jury panel selection.

9.   Growe, a farmer, spoke to Dealer and ordered a tractor from him. Dealer said, "The price will be $10,000, C.O.D."

Growe picked up the tractor from Dealer on Nov. 1, 1973, and handed Dealer a check drawn on Bank for $10,000, dated Nov. 2, 1973. Growe knew there was only $200 in the account.

While driving the tractor to his farm, Growe noticed that the motor was working poorly. He immediately stopped payment on the check.

Growe then telephoned Dealer and told him that he wanted Dealer to come out to the farm and take the tractor back and "fix it right"; that although he didn't need the tractor immediately, it was essential that it be working properly for summer harvesting; and that he would "make the check good" as soon as this was done. Dealer said, "Okay."

Dealer worked on the tractor and redelivered it to Growe in February, 1974. Dealer then redeposited the check, but it was returned by the Bank marked "Insufficient Funds." Dealer telephoned Growe about the check, and Growe replied, "I've tried out the tractor and it seems to be okay, but let's wait until harvesting time to see if it really works."

In July 1974, Growe commenced harvesting. The tractor worked but the motor still performed poorly. Growe wrote to Dealer.

> The tractor is still no damn good. The deal is off. But I'm in a bind and
> am going to use it for harvesting as best I can. Come and take it back
> after Labor Day.

Dealer was furious. He paid $100 to Phuzz, a moonlighting town police officer, to repossess the tractor. On July 30, 1974, Phuzz, while off duty but still in uniform, went to Growe's farm and demanded and received the keys to the tractor from Growe's spouse.

While driving the tractor back to Dealer, Phuzz drove into the rear of Innocent's car, and by so doing severely damaged the tractor and injured Innocent.

Draft a letter to Dealer informing Dealer of his rights and liabilities. Include advice on Growe's liability.

10. When Joe Gefallen was expelled from Siwash U., he set off for Pashon Beach, New Jersey, where he rented a nine-room house for the summer months. He then sent word to his former buddies and "coeds" at Siwash that for a modest charge, the "welcome mat would be out for one and all" at his beach place. As soon as exams were over, the rush was on, and they descended on Pashon Beach, where it was "guys and gals together" at Joe's place.

The staid residents of Pashon Beach complained that the house was overcrowded; the uninhibited occupants were excessively noisy at all hours; they were intoxicated in public, engaged in wild parties, immoral acts and lewd and lascivious conduct; and that they created traffic and parking congestion and generally upset the whole community. The residents demanded enforcement of the local ordinance that prohibited "group rentals to two or more unrelated persons."

In another part of town, the senior citizens of the community, all of whom were 62 years of age, were having difficulty in securing rental housing because of their limited finances and the scarcity of rental apartments. They demanded that the zoning ordinance be amended to allow them to occupy trailers and mobile homes in a designated area where such use was prohibited by the local ordinance. They claimed their requests were justified because they were all advanced in years and could not make ends meet on their fixed incomes.

They also demanded that the town council provide a special fund for their benefit by charging nonresidents an additional fee for use of the public beaches, and also help them in securing permanent housing by amending the local zoning ordinance to prohibit conversion of rental apartment houses into condominium ownership. They also urged that they be exempted from the group rental ordinance so that they could reduce the cost of housing by sharing with other, unrelated persons.

You are the town attorney and the mayor and council have consulted you under these circumstances.

Discuss and evaluate the various legal issues and legal alternatives that the municipality might consider.

11.   Dave contracts with the General Housing Administration, a federal agency, to carry bulk building materials to be used in the construction of a federal building between highway points within State X. After entering into the contract, he performs services only for the federal government.

State X's laws require any commercial carrier to obtain a permit from the state's Public Utility Commission, which is granted upon proof of financial responsibility and the safety of the carrier's equipment. Dave never got a permit.

On several occasions while engaged in the performance of his government contract, Dave is arrested by state highway patrolmen, in each case for violating a state statute that prohibits any speed greater than is reasonable or prudent, having due regard for the traffic on, and the surface and width of, the road or highway. On the last such occasion, after Dave had ignored the prior citations, his driver's license is suspended by State's director of motor vehicles, pursuant to statute, pending an administrative hearing that Dave has the right to request. Concurrently therewith, Dave is ordered by the State X Public Utility Commission to cease transportation of all goods until he obtains a permit therefor.

Dave continues to perform his contract without regard to suspension of his driver's license or the required carrier's permit. He is subsequently arrested and charged with violating State X's statutes that make it a crime for any person to drive on state highways or roads while his driver's license is suspended or to carry goods for hire on the highways without a permit therefor.

What constitutional defenses may be raised by Dave to the charges? Discuss.

12.   You are engaged in a non-jury trial in the County District Court. All parties have completed proof as to liability, but will have to come back tomorrow to present their proofs as to damages. The judge has requested counsel to submit a short brief to her in the morning, limited to the issues of liability. The basic facts in evidence are substantially uncontroverted: Mistkill, Inc. manufactured and distributed a weed-killing spray for use by growers of narrow-leaved plants. It was very effective on broad-leaved weeds—and any other broad-leaved plants—but imaginative research and a rigorous system of quality control had eliminated all toxicity to human or animal life. Mistkill sold to Upwind a barrel of its spray that had become contaminated with strychnine. There is no evidence that the contamination was due to any lack of care in the manufacturing process or that it should have been detected by Mistkill or Upwind. Upwind sprayed the contents of the barrel on its crop of rye grass from an airplane in a manner recommended by the Department of Agriculture. A gentle breeze carried a small quantity onto its neighbor Potter's land. Fortunately, this missed Potter's broad-leaved tobacco crop, but unfortunately, some of it was inhaled by Eagle Scout, Potter's valuable stud horse. The inhalation would have caused no more than a mild stomach upset in a normal horse, but Eagle Scout had a very acute and very rare (and hitherto unsuspected) susceptibility to strychnine, and died as a result of inhaling the spray.

Potter sued Mistkill and Upwind for the loss of his horse and (as permitted by local procedure) Upwind cross-claimed for recovery from Mistkill in the event that it should be held liable.

You represent Plaintiff Potter. Prepare the "Law and Argument" portion of the brief you would submit on Potter's behalf. Do not prepare a separate statement of facts, but incorporate into your argument facts which support your client's position.

13.   For 20 years Cliff owned farmland that was not particularly desirable because of its rough terrain. During the past five years, Cliff tried unsuccessfully to sell the land for $10 per

acre. On August 7 he offered it to Bill, but Bill objected to the price. Cliff then lowered his price and convinced Bill to seriously consider buying the land. The two men signed the following paper:

> Cliff Johnson hereby offers to sell his Sections 33, 34, & 35 of Township (location specified) to Bill Benson for $8 per acre. Dated: August 9.

Bill considered the proposition for a day, and on August 10, again conferred with Cliff. Bill wanted assurance that Cliff would not raise the price or sell to someone else while Bill looked at the farm. Cliff finally sent Bill a written memorandum signed by him, stating:

> You examine the land, think about the deal seriously, and I promise that for 30 days I will not revoke the offer, sell the land to anybody else, or raise the price.

Bill replied at once in a written memorandum signed by him, stating:

> Okay, I agree—I will examine it carefully and think about it seriously.

On August 10, Bill took the 30-mile trip to Cape May to look at the land and minutely examined the farm. He returned home on August 13 and borrowed $10,000 to buy Cliff's farm.

On August 14, Bill was on his way to Cliff's home to tell him he accepted the offer when he met Cliff's brother. The brother told Bill that on August 13, Cliff had discovered that a proposed water conservation project on adjoining property would make Cliff's land very desirable for summer cabins, and that on the same day Cliff had conveyed the land to Smith for $30,000. Bill immediately went to a post office and sent Cliff a letter (received by Cliff on August 15) stating:

> I accept your offer to sell the farm for $8 per acre.

Smith was unaware at all times of the dealings between Cliff and Bill. On August 16, Smith reconveyed the same farm to Cliff for $31,000.

You are an associate in the law firm representing Cliff. Bill seeks specific performance and damages. The senior partner asks you to draft a memorandum addressing the relevant issues and Cliff's potential liability.

14. Art, an undercover police agent posing as a hoodlum, is asked by Bob to assist him in murdering Carl. When Art pretends to agree, Bob shows Art a bomb he is making to attach to the starter of Carl's car. At Bob's request, Art helps complete the bomb, but secretly rigs it not to explode. Bob then takes the bomb to Carl's house alone and attaches it to Carl's automobile. The police, having been tipped off by Art, arrive just as Bob finishes and is standing next to the starter. They immediately arrest Bob, remove the bomb, and take him to the nearest police station. The police then return to Carl's house, where they conduct a thorough search of Carl's automobile. Bob's car is parked across the street in a tow-away zone. While writing a ticket for illegal parking, the police officer views a sales receipt for the same kind and amount of explosives used for the bomb in Carl's auto, on the dashboard.

The car is impounded and, according to departmental policy, a list is drawn up of all property found in the interior of the car, including the sales receipt. Neither the trunk nor locked glove compartment were opened.

Bob is charged with attempted murder. At trial the prosecution introduces the bomb and the sales receipt into evidence. Art testifies to Bob's original request that Art help him murder Carl. Art also testifies to a conversation he had with Bob when he visited Bob in jail after his indictment. In the latter conversation, Bob made damaging admissions. At no time did Art advise Bob that he was an undercover police agent. Art testifies that he secretly recorded both pre-arrest and post-arrest conversations on a miniature tape recorder, and the recordings are introduced to corroborate his testimony. The jury finds Bob guilty.

All of Bob's rights have been properly preserved. Bob appeals his conviction for attempted murder. You are the law clerk to the judge hearing the appeal. Draft a memorandum to the judge addressing the legal problems presented by this appeal.

15.   Spaceburger, Inc., operates a nationwide chain of fast food restaurants, all of which have been built to the same futuristic design. On February 1, 1986, Spaceburger signed a 20-year agreement to lease a vacant site ("Blackacre") in Jersey Town from H, on which it plans to build a restaurant. Rent was fixed at $1,000 per month. The lease contained no covenants other than Spaceburger's covenant to pay rent. Spaceburger recorded the lease the day after it was signed.

Just before he signed the lease, Spaceburger's president told H that Blackacre was a somewhat smaller site than those normally used by Spaceburger and that "parking might be a little tight." He responded: "Don't worry, I own a parking lot ("Whiteacre") across the street and your patrons can park there free when the on-site lot is full."

Within two weeks following the lease signing, these events occurred:

Jersey Town amended its zoning ordinance to require all commercial structures to be of "colonial design."

H entered into a written agreement to sell Whiteacre to Department Store for $10,000. Department Store announced plans to build a store which would cover the entire lot.

Immediately after signing the agreement with Department Store, H died. H's will left his entire estate to F, a friend. Prior to his death, H's assets consisted solely of Blackacre, Whiteacre, and a $15,000 savings account. His only debt was to Bank for $20,000.

Two days after H's death, his wife, W, executed an agreement to lease Blackacre to Colonial Furniture Store for 20 years at $1,100 per month. The lease was to commence immediately.

The deed pursuant to which H acquired his interest in Blackacre some 10 years ago read "to H and W, his wife." H paid all the consideration, and W did not learn that H had acquired Blackacre or that her name was on the deed until the day after H's death.

The deed pursuant to which H acquired Whiteacre some five years ago read "to H." Three years ago, H borrowed $25,000 from Bank. H alone signed the note and the mortgage securing the loan on Whiteacre. The mortgage was never recorded. The loan is in default and a balance of $20,000 is still due. Bank would like to collect the $20,000 and, if possible, acquire Whiteacre and locate a branch office on it.

Discuss and evaluate the rights and liabilities of the parties and indicate in what manner Spaceburger could have protected itself against the zoning and title problems.

16.   Ace is a manufacturer of tennis equipment. In 1978, it announced the development of a new oversized tennis racquet called the "Boomer," which had a unique shape and was made of a special composition.

Distor, a wholesale distributor of tennis equipment, ordered 5,000 Boomers from Ace at a price of $50 each and received delivery in March, 1979. Pursuant to the written contract, Distor paid $100,000 upon delivery; the balance of $150,000 was payable on September 1, 1979. The contract also contained the following language:

> Ace guarantees that its price to wholesalers will not drop below the stated
> contract price for 12 months from the date of delivery, and Ace will reim-
> burse Distor for total gross purchases in the event of such a price drop.

Distor gave similar guarantees to retailers covering its prices to them.

Factor Co. had advanced funds to Ace for the development and manufacture of the Boomer. Demand for Boomers did not meet Ace's expectations. In June, 1979, as payment against its indebtedness, Ace transferred to Factor its entire inventory of Boomers. Ace also gave Factor a written assignment of certain accounts receivable, including the balance owed by Distor on the Boomer contract and on purchases of other types of tennis racquets. Factor immediately reassigned the accounts receivable in writing to Bank for value. Factor and Bank gave immediate written notice of the assignments to Distor.

In July 1979, Factor held a distress sale of all the Boomers at prices well below $50 per unit. Distor had already sold 4,000 Boomers to retailers and had 1,000 left. As a result of the distress sale, Distor was only able to sell the remaining 1,000 Boomers at prices far below its cost.

In August 1979, Ace breached a contract with Distor for the sale of tennis balls, for which Distor claimed $50,000 in damages.

In September 1979, after Distor refused Bank's demands for payment, Bank instituted suit against Distor on the accounts receivable.

Discuss and evaluate the rights and liabilities of Distor.

17.   Pete Convict was recently released from State Prison after having served 10 years for distribution and heavy use of narcotics. He had had previous narcotics convictions, and one more conviction of any felony would subject him to life imprisonment under the Multiple Offender Act. Unknown to prison officials, narcotics were available to Convict and he used them throughout his prison term.

Following Convict's release, he was unable to obtain narcotics and he experienced severe withdrawal symptoms. He suffered extreme pain and frequently became delusional.

During the morning of one of these delusional episodes, a friend dropped Convict off at the local medical clinic for treatment. When the doctor stepped out of the examining room, Convict noticed some narcotics in an opened cabinet. He grabbed a handful and swallowed them just as Nurse walked in. Because of his condition, he remained in the clinic the balance of the day.

When Convict was calm and ready to leave, Nurse gave him a new appointment. As she did this, she whispered, "I saw you steal those drugs, but I'm not going to say anything because you can help me get more out of here to sell." Convict showed no interest.

On the date of his new appointment, Nurse stated to Convict, "If you don't help me steal and sell these drugs, I'll see to it that you won't get any more; plus, I'll turn you in."

Convict reluctantly agreed to steal and help her sell the drugs. Nurse informed Convict that she would leave the rear door of the clinic open to make it easier to let himself in.

On the agreed upon evening, Convict entered the rear of the clinic, took the drugs and left. The next day, Convict and Nurse sold the drugs to Pusher. Convict was immediately arrested and charged with larceny, possession and sale of drugs, burglary, and conspiracy to commit burglary and larceny.

Nurse and Pusher were detectives assigned by the local Chief of Police to rid his town of drug pushers. You are retained as Convict's lawyer. Discuss and evaluate all issues you would raise in Convict's behalf.

18.   Paul worked as a pressman for Printa, Inc., a printing company. On January 30, 1979, while he was operating a printing press, his left hand was seized and pulled between two rollers, resulting in the loss of the hand.

In April 1979, Paul retained an attorney whose investigation disclosed the following facts:

(i) The printing press was manufactured in December 1955 by Map, Inc. and was immediately sold to Donald Duncan, a dealer.

(ii) Within one week, Duncan sold it to Printa and ordered Map to ship the press directly to Printa's plant.

(iii) Map's employees dismantled the press, crated its components and shipped everything to Printa's plant.

(iv) The press was reassembled by Formco, Inc., mechanical engineers, and was then put into service at Printa's plant.

(v) When the press was manufactured, its design was in accordance with then existing industry standards, which included a protective guard to be positioned 12 inches from the moving rollers.

(vi) During assembly there was a work stoppage and Formco did not install the guard on the press.

Paul's attorney instituted suit against Map, Printa, Duncan, and Formco. Each defendant was individually represented by an attorney who filed and served all appropriate pleadings.

At trial, items (i) through (vi), above, were stipulated. Paul's attorney also offered the following evidence:

(a) An expert's testimony that Paul's accident could have been prevented if only a protective guard had been positioned very close to the rollers.

(b) In connection with the expert's testimony, a printed regulation published in 1970 by the National Institute of Press Manufacturers indicating that printing presses should have protective guards attached at a point not more than one inch from moving rollers.

(c) A treatise in which the author stated his opinion that in addition to a guard, the safe operation of a press required an automatic electronic switch to render the press inoperable if the guard were removed.

Over the objections of all defense counsel, items (a), (b), and (c) above were admitted in evidence.

Discuss and evaluate the rights and liabilities among Paul, Printa, Map, Duncan, and Formco.

19. The diagram shows a portion of a block in T Township, New Jersey. Between 1950 and 1955, single-family residences were built on 50-foot lots on both sides of Fifth Street, except Lots 7 and 8, which were not improved until a later date. Sixth Street was a "paper street" on T's tax map until its actual construction in 1979, when it was duly accepted by T.

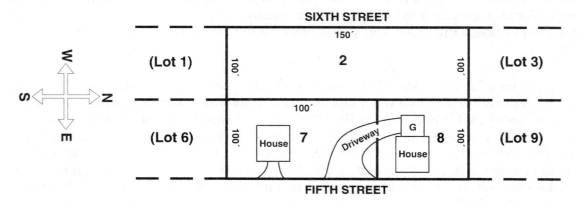

In 1955, Able, the fee simple owner of Lots 2, 7, and 8, built his home on Lot 7 and sold Lot 2 to Burt. Because Sixth Street did not exist, the deed stated, "Grantee shall have unimpeded access to Lot 2 from Fifth Street over the northerly 25 feet of Lot 7." Burt did not develop Lot 2.

In 1962, Able sold Lot 8 to David. During the negotiations, David told Able that, because of the topography of the lot, he wanted to build his house within five feet of the southerly lot line, and that most of his driveway would have to be located in the northerly 15 or 20 feet of Lot 7. Able said he did not care, but that David should check with Burt. Burt responded in writing, "As long as you don't block me from getting to Lot 2, you can do what you like with the 25-foot strip." David then closed the transaction with Able and built a house, driveway, and garage as shown on the diagram. In 1978, he installed solar heating equipment on the south side of his house at a cost of $10,000.

In 1979, after completion of Sixth Street, Burt sold Lot 2 to Charles. The language of conveyance in the deed was identical to that in the Able-Burt deed. Later in 1979, Able sold Lot 7 to Charles. Charles then submitted all necessary applications to T to divide Lot 7 in half, the northerly half to be known as Lot 7-A, and to construct a 2-family residence on Lot 7-A. The necessary variances were granted on July 15, 1980, over David's objections, and a building permit was issued to Charles the next day. Charles then notified David to remove the driveway from Lot 7-A.

David does not wish to relocate his driveway, and he is concerned that the new building will shade his solar equipment, rendering it virtually useless.

T's first and only zoning ordinance was adopted in 1965. It provides that the only permitted property use in the municipality is for single-family residences on lots 7,500 square feet or more in size.

Assume that all conveyances were by bargain and sale deeds with covenants against grantor's acts, and that all deeds were fully and properly executed, acknowledged and immediately recorded.

Discuss and evaluate David's rights and remedies.

20. The municipality of Towne, N.J., enacted a Local Land Use Ordinance which, among other things, defined and regulated "home trades and occupations" in designated zones. The ordinance further provided as follows:

> No newspaper, radio or television service shall be used to advertise any
> such home trade or occupation.

Homer conducted the practice of optometry from his residence as an approved "home occupation" in a designated zone in Towne. Contrary to the quoted provisions of the ordinance, he advertised his home occupation in a newspaper. Homer refused to discontinue the newspaper advertising and was prosecuted for violation of the ordinance.

Discuss and evaluate the issues you would raise on behalf of Homer and Towne.

21. On January 21, 1984, State Policeman Norm Trooper was on routine patrol duty on the New Jersey Turnpike. He observed a late-model automobile being driven in excess of the speed limit and noted that it had Florida license plates and was occupied by three males. Trooper pursued the car and it pulled over to the side of the road. He asked for the driver's license and registration. The operator, David Driver, handed him a valid driver's license, but was unable to produce a registration certificate for the car. However, he gave Trooper a rental agreement showing that the car had been rented to a person named I.M. Porter in Miami, Florida, on January 19, 1984.

While Driver was producing these documents, Trooper noticed what appeared to be the butt of a rifle protruding from under the front seat. He ordered all three occupants out of the car, then reached under the front seat and removed a sawed-off shotgun.

In addition to Driver, the occupants of the car were Paul Passenger and Tom Thumb. Trooper placed all of them under arrest for possession of an illegal weapon; he handcuffed and searched them and read them their *Miranda* warnings. Thumb, the rear seat passenger, protested his arrest, claiming that he was a hitchhiker who had been picked up by Driver and Passenger in North Carolina, and that he knew nothing about the sawed-off shotgun.

Trooper then conducted a search of the entire passenger compartment of the car. In the glove compartment he found a vial containing a white powdery substance which he recognized as cocaine. On the rear seat were four cartons of untaxed cigarettes and a locked briefcase bearing the initials "T.T." He broke the lock on the briefcase and found that it contained five pounds of hashish.

Trooper then removed the keys from the ignition and opened the trunk of the car, where he found two closed satchels. He opened the satchels and discovered that they contained bricks of marijuana.

On January 28, 1984, the Grand Jury returned indictments charging Driver and Passenger with possession of a sawed-off shotgun, possession of cocaine, possession of untaxed cigarettes, and possession of marijuana with intent to distribute. Thumb was indicted on charges of possession of a sawed-off shotgun, possession of untaxed cigarettes and possession of hashish with intent to distribute.

Each defendant filed a timely motion to suppress the evidence he was charged with possessing.

Discuss and evaluate the validity of Trooper's search and seizure and the merits of each defendant's motion to suppress.

22.   For purposes of this question, assume you are Leslie Lawyer, an attorney in private practice. Rusty Ferris, house counsel for Steelco, a steel company which is a client of your firm, recently sent you the following letter:

Dear Leslie:
    We need your immediate legal assistance in connection with an urgent problem.
    For the past year Steelco has stored large quantities of steel beams outdoors on its two-acre site in Industrial Port. The adjacent property is owned by Chemco. Chemco uses its property for the outdoor storage of various chemicals, including large mounds of dry sulphur.
    Several times a week, Chemco ships or receives sulphur in open dump trucks. As a result of the combined effect of Chemco's operations and wind conditions, sulphur powder is deposited over a wide area throughout the Port. We usually try to keep our steel covered with tarpaulins, but have been unsuccessful in preventing the sulphur powder from settling on our steel.
    We have experienced serious pitting and corrosion of our steel beams. Several recent shipments of steel from this site have been rejected by our customers. A chemist has advised us that sun, moisture and air have reacted chemically with the sulphur powder on our steel to form sulphuric acid, which has caused the damage to the steel. Two weeks ago, we wrote a strong letter to Chemco. We have received no response and Chemco has made no change in its operations. Steelco management is very anxious to receive advice as to its legal position. Send me a letter as soon as possible stating your preliminary opinion. Do

we have any legal rights or remedies? Under what theories? What course of action would you suggest?

I know you will need additional information if we decide to go ahead with any action you suggest. Let me know in your letter what else you need to know. I will begin gathering the information immediately. I look forward to hearing from you promptly.

Very truly yours,
(Signed) Rusty Ferris

Prepare a letter responding to Mr. Ferris.

23.   A bill has been introduced in the legislature of the State of Uphoria which would limit appointment of members of the State Police force to male citizens of the United States who are over the age of 20 years.

Senator Strate is chairman of the committee to which this bill has been referred, and he requires a carefully written summary analyzing the legal principles implicated by this bill. He retains you to prepare this summary in clear and concise language so that it may be used by members of his committee in their consideration of the merits of the bill.

Comply with the senator's request.

24.   Zuzu Corp. of Michigan manufactures and sells a small woodburning residential heater. Because of the heater's uniquely efficient design, it gained great popularity in the Midwest, and in 1980 Zuzu decided to expand its market by establishing a nationwide network of distributors. Yutz, who trades as Yutz Supply Co., a local heating and plumbing supply business in Smalltown, New Jersey, heard about the heater and wrote to Zuzu concerning a distributorship. After several telephone conversations with Zuzu's sales manager, Yutz received the following letter on Zuzu's letterhead, dated September 15, 1980:

Dear Mr. Yutz:

This is to confirm that Yutz Supply Co. is hereby designated the sole distributor for Zuzu Corp. in New Jersey. As such, you have the exclusive right to set up a dealer organization in all market areas throughout the state. We believe that New Jersey will support at least 20 dealers and perhaps as many as 30, because we have found that effective selling can be done only on a very local basis. Of course, you are also the dealer in your own trade area.

A dealer price list is enclosed, and as a distributor, you will receive a 10% commission on all units sold by your dealers. Because demonstration is the best sales tool, we require each dealer to stock at least five heaters at all times.

If you agree to the terms of this arrangement, please sign and return the enclosed copy of this letter. It will constitute our agreement, and we will immediately ship five heaters to you.

Very truly yours,
(Signed) V.W. Xavier,
Sales Manager

Yutz signed and returned the copy. About two weeks later, he received the heaters.

Yutz immediately began advertising the heater every day in a local newspaper and sold 75 units by the end of November. He added a small showroom to his building at a cost of $10,000, solely for the purpose of promoting Zuzu heaters, and his sales increased to 90 units in December 1980 and 100 in January 1981. All customers were in his local area.

Xavier phoned Yutz several times during November and December to inquire as to his progress with a New Jersey dealer organization. Each time, Yutz responded that he was about to begin looking for prospects. In fact, he never did.

On February 8, 1981, Yutz received a shipment of heaters he had ordered two weeks earlier. On February 9, Xavier called him and said, "Yutz, you're through. There should have been a thousand heaters sold in New Jersey by now, but you've done nothing to set up any dealers. We've terminated our arrangement with you as of January 15, so send back any heaters you have in stock."

Suit was instituted, and all of the foregoing facts were stipulated. At the pretrial conference, the court ordered counsel to submit written arguments on the issues of the existence of a contract and breach of contract.

As attorney for Yutz, write the arguments you would submit as directed by the court.

25.   Mr. and Mrs. Celler have agreed to sell their single-family residence in Riverbank, New Jersey, to Mr. and Mrs. Byer, for $75,000. The Cellers have retained you to represent them in this transaction.

In the course of your conference with the Cellers, Mr. Celler made the following statement:

> We bought the house new in 1975 from Ace Building Corp. For the first few years we had some occasional puddles in the basement during heavy rainstorms. However, about a year and a half ago the problem became severe. We started getting about a foot of water in the basement. There were some watermarks on the basement walls, but a few months ago we painted the entire house to get it ready for sale and now the watermarks don't show. We haven't told the Byers about the water problem and would prefer not to tell them. We might lose the sale if they found out, but we don't want any responsibility to them for this problem after we sell the house either.

Mr. Celler also told you that the Byers had gone through the house on several occasions before they decided to purchase it. The Byers had asked many questions about the house but had never inquired concerning any water problems. Mr. Celler also said that no professional home inspection has been performed.

(a)   Discuss the legal issues raised by the facts presented.

(b)   Draft the provision you would include in the contract of sale in order to meet the concerns expressed by Mr. Celler.

(c)   Explain the reasons for the provisions which you drafted.

26.   In April 1983, Babs met Allen while attending a lecture on antiques. Following the lecture, Allen asked her to drive him to the home of Mrs. Rich, a wealthy local resident. He said that Mrs. Rich might have some antiques for sale.

When they arrived at Mrs. Rich's house, Allen told Babs to wait in the car and keep the motor running. She watched him hurry around to the back of the house. Five minutes later, she saw him running back to the car carrying a bulky pillowcase, later determined to have contained valuable antique jewelry and other collectors' items. He ran to the car, jumped in and shouted, "Let's get the hell out of here quick." Babs sped away, striking and killing Mr. Nabor, who was walking his dog. She started to pull over to the curb, but Allen ordered her to keep going. "You're in this as deep as me," he said. Babs drove off.

The next day, while Babs was driving home from work, she was stopped by Officer Smart for a routine credentials check. After determining that her license and registration were in order, Officer Smart noticed a dent in the left front fender and what appeared to be dried blood on the bumper. He ordered Babs out of the car, searched the entire vehicle and discovered a piece of jewelry under the right front seat.

The piece of jewelry and the dried blood on the bumper were sent to the State Police Laboratory. The laboratory determined that a fingerprint on the jewelry was Allen's and that the dried blood was the same type as Mr. Nabor's.

In May 1983, grand jury indictments were returned, charging Allen and Babs with murder, larceny, burglary and with conspiracy to commit those crimes. No preliminary hearing was conducted prior to the indictment. Separate counsel were appointed for each defendant and their cases were severed.

For the next 11 months, prosecution requested only one adjournment for two weeks. Babs's trial was originally scheduled for April 1984, but on the eve of trial Mrs. Rich suffered a stroke. The trial was postponed at the prosecutor's request.

The trial commenced in June 1985. Because Mrs. Rich's stroke had resulted in a permanent loss of memory, the prosecution introduced a transcript of her grand jury testimony in which she identified the jewelry as having been stolen from her home. Officer Smart testified concerning his search of the car, and a State Police Laboratory technician testified as to the blood analysis and the fingerprint identification.

You are the law clerk to the appellate judge hearing the appeal of Babs's conviction on all charges. Counsel for Babs made all appropriate motions and timely objections before and during trial, but they were denied. The judge has asked you to submit to her a memorandum of law which evaluates the issues to be raised on appeal by Babs's attorney.

27.   Irma LaTouce and Lester DeJacques were employed as dancers at a Fun City, New Jersey, cocktail lounge. Both dancers received a weekly salary plus commissions on drinks purchased for them by customers between performances. Police officers observed Irma and Lester socializing with lounge patrons and brought charges against them under a local ordinance which provided:

> Entertainers in business premises where alcoholic beverages are sold are prohibited from mingling with customers.

The stated purpose of the ordinance was to prevent disorderly conduct in premises where liquor is sold, to encourage temperance, and to discourage opportunities for the solicitation of prostitution or engaging in any other immoral activity.

At the trial before the local Municipal Court, the dancers testified that the commissions were earned for socializing with the clientele, which involved conversation and casual companionship with men and women who patronized the club. They both admitted that the main purpose of this activity was to get the customers to buy more drinks. It was stipulated that there had been no disorderly conduct in the lounge and that neither defendant had solicited any act of prostitution or engaged in any other immoral activity. The court found both dancers guilty as charged and imposed a fine as provided in the ordinance.

Irma and Lester have now consulted you. They desire to appeal their convictions. Prepare a brief in support of Irma and Lester as petitioners.

28.   Medix is a manufacturer of pharmaceutical products which it sells to other companies, who market the products under their own names. One of its most successful products has been "Corona," a fully approved drug that is very effective in the treatment of advanced heart disease.

Noble, the Plant Manager of Medix, received copies of Medix's highly confidential research reports, the circulation of which was carefully restricted to key officers and employees of Medix. One such report contained strong indications of a correlation between the use of Corona and certain serious types of cancer.

Noble attempted to persuade Medix management to withdraw Corona from the market, pending completion of top priority studies on the subjects that were already under way in the Medix research department. After he was unsuccessful in this effort, Noble refused to schedule any further production runs of the drug. He was fired at once.

Noble was morally outraged with Medix for its handling of the entire situation, and, after a brief conference with his personal lawyer, Goodcause, he sent copies of the relevant Medix research report to various governmental agencies with a letter describing Medix as a "public enemy" and urging them to "throw the book at Medix." He sent Medix a copy of the letter.

Herbal, Inc., a large publicly owned company, was a major customer of Medix, whose products it sold under the Herbal label. Goodcause owns 100 shares of Herbal stock. He had also been retained by Herbal from time to time in the past to represent it in miscellaneous legal matters.

After speaking with Noble and reading the Medix report, Goodcause shared his client's views as to Medix's conduct. He arranged a meeting with the Vice President and General Counsel of Herbal, with whom he had had prior dealings, to discuss the Medix situation. As a result, he was instrumental in persuading Herbal to cease marketing all Medix products.

You are the attorney for Medix. It has advised you of all of the above facts and turned over to you a complaint filed by Noble, through his attorney, Goodcause, alleging wrongful termination of his employment. Medix has also advised you that Noble had no written employment contract. Medix has just completed its study on the side effects of Corona, the results of which are "totally inconclusive." Your research has disclosed that Medix has not violated any statute or governmental regulation in its handling of this matter.

Describe the pleadings (content) you should consider filing on Medix's behalf. Medix also requests your advice on any potential problems presented by this litigation and possible resolutions.

29.   You represent Maxco, a manufacturer of small business machines. You recently received a letter from Maxco's vice president seeking your advice. The letter reads:

> Dear Larry Lawyer:
>   In April 1981 we mailed to Able, a retailer who sells new and used office machines, an advertising circular which said:
>
> > Announcing ULTRAMAX, the compact data/word processor that can handle all your customers' office needs. Price to retailers $5,000.
>
> Able wrote to us on April 27:
>
> > I believe I could generate some interest in your Ultramax if I had one in stock to show my customers. In fact, I may have use for it myself if it can handle my typing and bookkeeping needs. Please advise.

By letter dated May 8, Maxco responded:

> One Ultramax being shipped to you on consignment per your April 27 letter. The price is $5,000.

Able received the machine on May 29. On that same day, Baker, one of Able's customers, said he had heard about Ultramax at a recent convention and wondered if Able carried it. Able told him he had one in the store, and, after a brief conversation, Baker agreed to purchase it for $6,000. He gave Able a $600 deposit and arranged to pick up the machine and pay the balance on June 10.

Able then set up the machine and tested it in his office. He was pleased to find that it completed his monthly billing procedure in about half the usual time. On the following day, one of his employees found that much of the backed-up correspondence could be quickly typed on the Ultramax.

Because of cash problems, Able could not stay current with his suppliers. One of them, Dunn, obtained a judgment for $7,000 on June 5. Upon Dunn's instructions, the sheriff went to Able's place of business on June 8. He affixed a Notice of Levy to the Ultramax, but did not physically remove the machine.

There has been an extraordinary demand for Ultramax, and Maxco's price to retailers is now $7,000. Able, Maxco, Baker and Dunn all claim ownership of the Ultramax located in Able's place of business.

Please advise us regarding our rights and remedies against Able, Baker and Dunn.

> Sincerely yours,
> Max Coco
> Vice President Maxco Company

30. Seller and Buyer executed the following instrument:

> STANDARD SALES CONTRACT of the Apex Real Estate Brokerage Agency. This is a legally binding contract. If not understood, seek competent advice.

> On this 12th day of June, 1981, Bob Burns ("Buyer") agrees to purchase from Sam Smith ("Seller") and Seller agrees to sell to Buyer through Apex Real Estate Brokerage Agency ("Broker") a one-family dwelling together with a detached garage with apartment therein on a lot approximately 100' x 150' in North Salem, New Jersey. The purchase price is $75,000, payable $7,500 as a deposit herewith and the balance on closing. This agreement is contingent upon Buyer obtaining a commitment for a mortgage loan in the amount of $50,000 at prevailing rates. Either party may void this agreement if the loan has not been arranged by August 1, 1981.

> This contract contains the entire agreement of the parties.

The instrument was prepared by Broker. Neither Seller nor Buyer consulted an attorney before signing it, because Broker indicated to both parties that the deal would be lost if either party delayed.

On June 12, 1981, the prevailing mortgage lending rate was 12%. On July 15, Buyer received a mortgage commitment at 18% interest, which was then the prevailing rate. He does not want to pay the increased mortgage interest cost.

On July 16, Buyer retained you. Your investigation of the facts and the title search reveal the following:

(a)   The property was acquired by Seller on May 8, 1975.

(b)   Seller married on January 20, 1977. His wife left him about a year later, and her present whereabouts are unknown.

(c) The property is in a one-family residential zone, but the structures and their uses predate the zoning ordinance. The apartment has been rented from time to time before and since enactment of the ordinance.

(d)   There is a provision in a prior deed which prohibits use of the property for any commercial purpose.

(e)   The next-door neighbor's driveway cuts across a corner of the subject property. Seller pointed this out to Buyer when Buyer first looked at the property.

(f)   There are recorded easements to North Salem Telephone Company and North Salem Gas and Electric Company for utilities which serve the subject premises.

A partner in your law firm has requested you to prepare a memorandum of law based upon these facts. You should include Buyer's rights and the grounds to be considered in excusing Buyer from purchasing this property.

31.   You are engaged in a trial of a personal injury case in the County District Court. Both sides have completed all proofs as to liability, but will have to come back tomorrow to present their proofs as to damages. The judge has requested both counsel to submit a short brief to him in the morning limited to the issues of liability.

The basic facts in evidence pertaining to liability are substantially uncontroverted. They are as follows:

(a)   Plaintiff, Paul Packer, is a trash collector.

(b)   Defendant, Donna Dweller, is a homeowner.

(c)   One Saturday last summer, Dweller gave permission to her 15-year-old son to have a ballgame in the backyard with a group of his friends. Because the backyard is not large, she told him they could not play with a hard ball.

(d)   While playing, one of the boys batted a baseball through the large kitchen window.

(e)   Dweller immediately sent her son to his room for disobeying her instructions not to play with a hard ball.

(f)   She then took a black plastic bag from a closet and asked the boys to carefully pick up the broken glass, put it into the bag and dispose of it in the outdoor trash can.

(g)   The boys did as she requested and went home.

(h)   The next day Paul Packer and Carl Carter, a co-employee, came to collect the trash. They both wore heavy gloves. In accordance with their usual practice, Carter took the plastic bag out of the trash can and tossed it to Packer, who threw it into the garbage truck. During this activity, Packer sustained a severe laceration to his forearm. Carter and Packer testified that they had not seen what was in the bag.

(i)   Carter testified that after getting medical attention for Packer, he opened the plastic bag and for the first time saw that it contained long, pointed pieces of glass, several of which were protruding about an inch through the plastic bag.

Choose the litigant you wish to represent—Plaintiff Packer or Defendant Dweller. Prepare the "Law and Argument" portion of the brief you would submit to the Judge in the morning on behalf of your client. Do not prepare a separate statement of facts, but incorporate into your argument any of the above facts which support your client's position.

32. Sunny, a deeply religious man who did not smoke or drink alcohol, was engaged to marry Dawn. One evening as he approached Dawn's home to meet her for a date, he saw her sitting with a man in a car parked in her driveway.

As Sunny got closer, he saw Dawn and his best friend, Walter, in a passionate embrace. He continued to watch Dawn and Walter until he could bear it no longer. He walked away, feeling angry and rejected.

Sunny noticed a tavern at the corner and decided that he wanted to drink. He ordered a shot of whiskey and gulped it down. For the next hour, he drank straight shots of whiskey. The more he drank, the more incensed he became over Dawn's unfaithfulness. After drinking about 12 shots of whiskey, he left the tavern and went to a nearby hardware store where he purchased a screwdriver. He returned to Dawn's house, and when she answered the door, he stabbed her repeatedly with the screwdriver. She died instantly.

Sunny was indicted for murder. At trial, the defendant did not dispute any of the above stated facts. A qualified expert, called by the defendant's attorney, testified that Sunny was intoxicated to a grossly excessive degree at the time of the killing. He also testified that Sunny did not know he was susceptible to such a degree of intoxication because he had never drunk alcohol before and that, by reason of his intoxication, he lacked the capacity to appreciate the wrongfulness of his act.

You are the trial judge's law clerk and he has directed you to draft the instructions to the jury on the elements and degrees of murder raised by the facts, and on the legal effect of the expert testimony offered on the defendant's behalf.

Prepare a draft of the jury instructions as requested by the Judge.

33. You recently received the following letter, dated July 25, 1982, from a client:

> Dear Counsel:
>   In June 1974, our company, Super Markets, Inc., leased from Landlord Associates a 50,000 square-foot store in the Massive Mall Shopping Center ("Shopping Center") located in Verdant Township, New Jersey. The term of the lease is 20 years with three 10-year option renewal terms. Our rental is $100,000 per year plus 2% of annual gross sales in excess of $5 million.
>   Section 10 of our lease with Landlord Associates provides as follows:
>
>> During the initial term and any extension term of this lease, Landlord shall not lease or permit to be used any other portion of the Shopping Center or any other property of Landlord within a radius of 10 miles of the Shopping Center for the conduct of food supermarket business or for the sale of any food products for off-premises consumption. Landlord agrees to include this restriction in any lease hereafter executed with a tenant within the restricted area.

In September 1981, Landlord Associates leased a 5,000 square-foot store in the Shopping Center to Fast Foodmarts, Inc., for a convenience food store. We decided not to take any action against Landlord Associates or its tenants unless it appeared that our business might become adversely affected. We recently noticed a significant drop in our sales and we are now losing money at this location.

Our lease was properly recorded in the County Recording Office. Landlord Associates' lease with Fast Foodmarts, Inc. did not contain the restriction required by our lease, and I am informed that the tenant was not advised of the restriction by Landlord Associates prior to signing its lease.

There is a health food store, a package liquor store and an ice cream store in the Shopping Center. The health food store has been in this Center for 10 years, and the other two stores opened a few years ago.

As you know, we are a major supermarket operator in the United States and all our leases contain the same provision as Section 10. We feel we must take some action in this matter because other landlords may lease space to competing supermarkets in the shopping centers where we have stores.

Please advise us regarding our rights and remedies against Landlord Associates and Fast Foodmarts, Inc. Thank you.

Sincerely yours,
Max Mogul,
Vice President of Sales

Respond to Mr. Mogul's letter.

34. The state of New Jersey Department of Energy ("DOE") has ordered Watts Electric & Power Company ("WEPCO"), a privately owned public utility, to discontinue out-of-state sales of electricity generated at its hydroelectric facility located on the Wattsis River in New Jersey. The action by DOE was taken pursuant to a New Jersey statute which permits the State to prohibit transmission of electricity generated by water power in New Jersey to points out of the state upon a finding of reasonable necessity by DOE. This finding has been made.

Several out-of-state consumers whose industrial plants are now served by WEPCO consult you for advice concerning the imminent discontinuance of supply to them as a result of the DOE order. Your clients tell you that WEPCO no longer has the capacity to continue service to both out-of-state consumers and its New Jersey consumers who require power. They confide to you that New Jersey industries will sustain substantial economic loss if there is diminished supply within the state, because power which had been expected from nuclear stations in New Jersey had not materialized. Your clients inform you that it will also be more costly to them if they have to purchase power from new sources.

You are requested to prepare a memorandum of law based upon these facts for distribution to your clients. This should include a summary of your recommendations if litigation becomes necessary.

Prepare the memorandum as requested.

35. Pat is the owner of a small delicatessen who has decided to take in Ralph as a partner. Ralph is willing to pay $30,000 to Pat for a 50% interest and is arranging for private financing.

In order to repay the loan, Ralph wants assurance from Pat that he will be able to draw at least $6,000 per year from the business. He also does not want to be responsible for prior debts of the business. The parties understand that Ralph will not be able to devote as many hours to the business as Pat.

Pat has retained you as his lawyer. He is concerned about possible future disagreements with Ralph and about what might happen if Ralph should die or want to sell his interest to another person. However, he has also told you that he does not want to lose this deal.

As Pat's lawyer, draft a short agreement addressing the objectives of both parties for submission to Ralph's lawyer.

36.   Bill and Claire wanted to go to Florida for the winter and decided to hold up a grocery store to obtain the money for the air fare. They agreed that Claire would drive the getaway car and Bill would rob the store. They also agreed that Bill would not be armed; instead, Bill would use a realistic-looking toy gun.

Claire drove Bill to the store and parked where she could observe the interior of the store. Bill entered, pulled out the toy gun, pointed it at the elderly proprietor and demanded all his money.

The proprietor suffered a heart attack, collapsed and died. Bill went behind the counter and grabbed all the cash in the register. As he was fleeing the store, he was jumped from behind by a customer, Drew, an off-duty policeman. While they struggled, Drew pulled his service revolver from his pocket. The gun discharged twice, killing Bill and another customer, Edward, who was standing nearby. On seeing the struggle and hearing gunshots, Claire drove off to her home. After staying at home for 30 minutes, she decided to return to the scene of the crime to see what happened. She parked outside the store. Upon hearing a police siren, she panicked. In her confusion, she shifted the car into forward gear and drove through the storefront, striking and killing Drew, who was still there giving a report of what happened.

Claire was apprehended at the scene. After receiving proper *Miranda* warnings and consulting with her attorney, she gave a full statement to the police, which recited all the above facts. Claire was duly indicted by the grand jury on four separate counts of murder for the deaths of the proprietor, Bill, Drew, and Edward, respectively. Her statement was introduced at trial and the jury convicted her on all four counts of murder.

You have been appointed to represent Claire on appeal and you have filed timely notice of appeal from each of the four convictions.

Prepare the "Law and Argument" portion of the brief you would submit to the Appellate Court on behalf of Claire. Do not prepare a statement of facts, but incorporate into your argument any of the above facts which support your client's position.

37.   You have received the following memorandum from your client, a title insurance company:

MEMORANDUM

TO: Counsel

FROM: Mark Meyers, V.P., Jerseyana Title Co.

DATE: February 24, 1983

Following is a title abstract with respect to a one-family residential dwelling located on a five-acre tract at 117 Hartacre Road, Ourton, N.J.

ABSTRACT OF TITLE

(a)   Deed dated February 16, 1921 from Apex Land Corp. to Arnold Able and Jane Able, his wife. Recites: Grantee agrees that (i) the premises will be used only for residential purposes, (ii) there shall be no transfer of the premises to any person who is not a United States citizen, and (iii) no structure shall be built within 100 feet of the front property line. Note: Survey of property shows house on premises is located 50 feet from the front property line.

(b)   Agreement dated November 23, 1921, between Arnold Able and Jane Able, his wife, and Ourton Utility Co. Recites: Party of the second part shall have the right to install, maintain, repair and replace electric and gas transmission lines over the premises to the dwelling erected thereon.

(c)   Deed dated July 6, 1927, from Arnold Able to Jane Able. Recites: Subject to mortgage held by Ourton S. & L. Assn. in the sum of $15,000. Note: Said mortgage duly cancelled of record on September 25, 1937.

(d)   Deed dated September 18, 1937, from Jane Airy, formerly Jane Able, to Barry Baker and Ann Baker, his wife.

(e)   Agreement dated March 19, 1942, from Barry Baker and Ann Baker, his wife, to Carl Charles and Deborah Charles, his wife. Recites: Party of second part shall have right to install, maintain, repair and replace a two-inch water line under a strip of land 10 feet wide along the westerly boundary line of the premises from Hartacre Road to the premises of the party of the second part adjoining to the south.

(f)   Mortgage dated October 20, 1948, from Barry Baker and Ann Baker, his wife, to Jersey Trust Company, given to secure sum of $35,000 due on November 1, 1953.

(g)   Will dated May 8, 1972, of Barry Baker, probated on November 15, 1980, devises premises in equal shares to decedent's children, Edward Baker and Carol Baker Parks; appoints Carol Baker Parks as executrix.

(h)   Deed dated May 13, 1981, from Carol Baker Parks, individually and as executrix under the will of Barry Baker, to Daniel Dephoe and Patricia Dephoe, his wife. Recites: Ann Baker died on January 17, 1971. Barry Baker died on November 4, 1980. Edward Baker died on January 26, 1981.

Please comment briefly on the effect that each of the above items may have on the marketability of Mr. and Mrs. Dephoe's title to the premises in question. Please advise what additional information, if any, you would require to make this determination.

Respond to Mr. Meyer's memorandum.

38. You represent Delta Company, the defendant in a products liability suit pending in the Superior Court of New Jersey. The Complaint reads as follows:

Plaintiff Jack Jones, residing at 12 Center Street, Mills Grove, Durham County, New Jersey, by way of Complaint against defendant Delta Company ("Delta") says:

1. Defendant Delta is a corporation of the State of Delaware which manufactures and sells products which are used by persons within the State of New Jersey.

2. Plaintiff was employed by Emplo Company ("Emplo") as a production line worker from 1953 until December 31, 1981, when physical disabilities forced his retirement.

3. Emplo manufactures, among other things, components for use in television sets. While plaintiff was employed at Emplo, he worked with and was otherwise exposed to DUST, a chemical manufactured by Delta and used in the production of components for television sets.

4. DUST is and was defective in that it caused persons who repeatedly use, or are otherwise exposed to it, to develop permanent and severe physical ailments, including acute respiratory diseases. Laboratory tests have confirmed these dangers, but Delta failed to provide adequate warnings.

5. As a proximate result of these defects in DUST, plaintiff was injured and rendered totally and permanently disabled, and caused great pain, suffering and emotional distress which he will continue to experience in the future. Plaintiff has been hospitalized and has undergone medical treatment for these injuries.

6. Delta is strictly liable in tort to plaintiff for these injuries.

WHEREFORE, plaintiff demands judgment against Delta for compensatory and punitive damages, together with interest and costs of suit.

You recently filed an Answer on behalf of defendant Delta. You have admitted the allegations of Paragraph 1. You have admitted that Delta manufactures DUST, a chemical that it sells to Emplo and others, but stated that Delta has insufficient knowledge or information to form a belief as to the truth of the remaining allegations of Paragraphs 2 and 3. You have denied the allegations of Paragraphs 4, 5 and 6. You have asserted appropriate affirmative defenses. You are now ready to commence discovery proceedings.

(a) Draft 15 interrogatories to be included in your initial set of interrogatories to be served upon the plaintiff. The interrogatories should be addressed to significant facts relevant to issues raised by the complaint. Your interrogatories may, within reason, contain subparts.

(b) Prepare a list of five documents or categories of documents that you would demand the plaintiff to produce for inspection and copying.

39. A New Jersey statute ("Statute No. 1") withholds from local public school districts any state funds for the education of children who were not "legally admitted" into the United States. This statute also authorized local school districts to deny enrollment to such children. A companion statute ("Statute No. 2") provides that no employer, under penalty of a $500 fine, shall knowingly employ an alien who is not entitled to lawful residence in this country.

A proper class action is pending challenging the legality of Statute No. 1. This action has been brought on behalf of certain school age children who had been denied admission to public school, because of the provisions of Statute No. 1. It is stipulated (i) that the children were not legally admitted into the United States and (ii) that they were brought to this state by their parents who were "undocumented aliens," not "legally admitted."

A proper class action is also pending challenging the legality of Statute No. 2. This action has been brought by parents of children in the above action who were refused employment because of the provisions of Statute No. 2. It is stipulated (i) that the parents were not entitled to a lawful residence in this country and were, in fact, "undocumented aliens," not "legally admitted" and (ii) that their illegal alien status was known to their prospective employers.

The above actions have been consolidated for trial.

Discuss and evaluate the legal issue involved in the challenges to these statutes.

40. Stella Starr, an aspiring model with no prior modeling experience, agreed to pose for Flash, a freelance photographer. The following document was duly signed by both parties:

> Stella Starr (herein referred to as "Model") agrees to pose for Flash (herein referred to as "Photographer") under the following terms and conditions:
>
> 1. Photographer shall pay to Model the sum of $500, the receipt of which is hereby acknowledged.
> 2. Model shall sit to be photographed in two sessions of one hour each. Photographer shall photograph Model in not less than 10 different poses for each session.
> 3. Photographer shall be the owner of all the photographs and entitled to reproduce them or license their reproduction.
> 4. Model shall receive without further charge two copies of each pose with the right to purchase additional copies at 10% above Photographer's cost.
>
> /s/ Flash
PHOTOGRAPHER
/s/ Stella Starr
MODEL

At Flash's direction, Stella appeared for the first session wearing a string bikini. She was photographed in 10 separate poses. A week later, she received two prints of each pose, pursuant to the agreement. To her horror, she discovered that the photographs had been retouched and distorted so as to give the illusion of total nudity. Some of the photographs were not very flattering in Stella's opinion. Several others were blurred and of extremely poor quality. Stella also learned that Centerfold Magazine has offered Flash $5,000 each for five of the most alluring shots of Stella. Stella refused to appear for the second session, whereupon Flash commenced an action in Small Claims Court for return of the $500. Stella has retained you as her counsel.

(a) Discuss and evaluate the defenses you would raise on Stella's behalf.

(b) Draft additional provisions to the existing agreement for Stella's use in future modeling engagements.

41. A state statute provides:

> Premises located within a radius of 500 feet of a house of worship or school shall not be licensed for the sale of alcoholic beverages if the governing body of such house of worship or school files written objection thereto.

John Schnapps was the operator of a restaurant located 15 feet from the Holy Tabernacle Church. He applied to the local Alcoholic Beverage Commission ("ABC") for approval of an alcoholic beverage license for the restaurant. The governing body of the Church filed a written objection to his application, citing the provisions of the statute quoted above. ABC denied the application on the basis of this objection.

Mr. Schnapps has retained you to appeal the denial of his application by ABC. The above facts have been stipulated for the purpose of the appeal.

Write the "legal argument" portion of your appellate brief.

42. Art Tiest, an old high school friend, has heard that you are now a lawyer and has consulted you concerning a business problem. He has explained to you that his hobby of printing decorative designs and novelty sayings on tee shirts has developed into a successful business, which he has incorporated in New Jersey under the name Phancy Phashuns Corp.

Art has advised you that he is in a very competitive business, but his big break came a couple of years ago when Chain Stores of New Jersey started buying from him. Since then, several other large stores have been stocking his products.

Very recently, Chain Stores stopped placing orders and gave Art a copy of a letter it received from one of his competitors, Hardsell Corp., another New Jersey company. The letter says that "for the benefit of the public, you ought to know that the ink used to print the Phancy tee shirts you are selling in your stores contains antimony, a poison like arsenic. . . . These products are extremely dangerous to your customers." A brief laboratory report from Jersey Labs, enclosed with the letter, states that tests have revealed the presence of antimony in the product and quotes statements from various scientific treatises comparing antimony to arsenic.

Art immediately consulted Print, Inc., his local ink supplier, which assured him that the ink is perfectly safe. Print, Inc. said that the antimony is used in its ink in very small quantities as a fire retardant. Print, Inc.'s head chemist said that antimony presents dangers only in much larger quantities and when used in a different chemical form.

A reputable independent expert retained by Art has confirmed Print's statements. The expert also says that the Jersey Labs report is accurate as far as it goes, but Hardsell has misinterpreted it and drawn unjustified conclusions from it.

Art has asked you to take immediate legal action to protect his company's interests.

(a) Carefully prepare a draft complaint you would file in the superior court on behalf of Phancy Phashuns Corp.

(b) Identify and briefly describe (but do not draft) any other papers you would file with your complaint.

43. On February 1, 1983, the Prosperity Bank was robbed by four unidentified men. In an emotional statement made at the scene, Hy Finance, the bank president, declared that the bank would pay the sum of $10,000 to the person or persons furnishing information leading to the arrest and conviction of the robbers. His words were carried live by radio and television stations in the area.

On February 15, 1983, Able, an off-duty police officer, was in a neighborhood tavern with a friend, Jack Daniels, when he overheard an incriminating statement made by one of the robbery participants. Both Able and Daniels knew about the robbery but not about the reward. While Daniels kept the suspect occupied, Able telephoned police headquarters and requested immediate assistance. Two detectives arrived within minutes and promptly placed the suspect under arrest.

On March 1, 1983, Teller, an employee of Prosperity Bank, recognized a robbery participant at the local bus terminal. His prompt call to the police resulted in the arrest of the suspect.

Upon learning that two of his cohorts were apprehended, Fink, another participant in the robbery, surrendered to the authorities and eventually pleaded guilty to a charge of armed robbery. He told the police where they could find the fourth participant, who was arrested shortly thereafter. Without requesting or receiving any promise of leniency, Fink cooperated fully with the Prosecutor's office. His testimony at trial was instrumental in the conviction of the other three participants.

Able, Daniels, Teller, and Fink all have demanded the sum of $10,000 from Prosperity Bank. Mr. Finance has retained you as the bank's attorney to resolve the confusion which has resulted from the multiple claimants.

Prepare your opinion letter to Mr. Finance, advising him of the nature and extent of the bank's obligations.

44. On May 1, 1984, Defendant Noah Fence was arrested and charged with the felony of possession of stolen property having a value in excess of $500. The stolen property consisted of color TVs and stereos which had been taken in burglaries of two local residences during April 1984.

The statute under which Fence is charged reads as follows:

    (a)   A person is guilty of possessing or receiving stolen property if he knowingly possesses, receives, or brings into this State property of another knowing that it is probably stolen.

    (b)   The requisite knowledge or belief is presumed in the case of a person who has been convicted of possessing or receiving stolen property within a two-year period preceding the transaction charged.

Previously, in January 1983, Fence had been indicted for violation of the same statute. In March 1983, he pleaded guilty to that charge and was sentenced to probation for one year and fined $1,000. There was no appeal from that conviction.

You represent Fence and are now defending him at trial on the pending charge. The prosecution has presented the testimony of the two homeowners who have identified the TVs and stereos found in Fence's possession as items taken from their homes during the burglaries. The prosecution now offers into evidence a certified copy of the March 1983 Judgment of Conviction of Defendant Fence.

State the objections you would make to the prosecution's offer and present the arguments you would make in support of each objection.

45. Mr. and Mrs. Hunter read the following advertisement in the Real Estate Section of the Jersey Gazette:

> Hillside heaven on 5 wooded acres in West Elysium, New Jersey, 4 bedrms, 4 baths, den with sliding glass doors leading to deck overlooking babbling brook. Only . . . $199,000. Call Country Realtors for appointment, 555-1234.

The Hunters called Country Realtors and visited the property that morning with Mrs. Ardsel, a real estate salesperson from that office. They all toured the house and grounds with the owner of the residence, Mr. Dweller. During the course of the tour, Mr. Hunter inquired about the brook and Mr. Dweller pointed it out to him.

A written agreement for sale of the property by Mr. Dweller to Mr. and Mrs. Hunter was thereafter signed by the parties. No mention of the brook was made in the agreement. The agreement contained the following provision:

This contract is an integrated document and contains the entire agreement between the parties. No representations, express or implied, have been made by any of the parties, the Realtor or salesperson, except as set forth herein.

In preparing for the closing of the transaction, the Hunters obtained from Mr. Dweller a copy of the survey made when he acquired the property. From the survey, the Hunters discovered that the brook was not on the land they were to purchase but was located on the neighboring parcel.

The Hunters have written to you as their attorney. Their letter recited the above facts and concluded: "We are very upset to find out that we will not own the brook. What are our rights? Do we have any liability if we call the whole thing off?"

Prepare a letter to Mr. and Mrs. Hunter explaining their potential rights and liabilities.

46.   On January 5, 1984, the Stereo Shoppe was burglarized and stereo equipment was stolen. Entry was gained through a rear window. In the red clay soil below the window, police found footprints made by high-heeled boots with a distinctive sole design.

Two days later, police received an anonymous telephone tip, which said only that "Lucy Lane was involved in the Stereo Shoppe job." Investigation disclosed that there was a former employee of the Stereo Shoppe named Lucy Lane who lived nearby. She had no criminal record, but there was an outstanding arrest warrant issued by the local municipal court for her failure to appear in court in response to a traffic summons.

At about 10:00 on a Tuesday, Detectives Tim Mack and Mary Wilson obtained a copy of the arrest warrant. According to the detectives, they went to Lucy Lane's house "to arrest her and to see what, if anything, we could find out about the Stereo Shoppe job."

Lucy answered the door clad in a bathrobe and slippers. The detectives showed her the warrant and informed her that she was under arrest. They told her to get dressed and come with them to the police station.

Lucy went to her bedroom to dress, accompanied by Detective Wilson. When Lucy opened the closet to get her coat, Wilson noticed a pair of high-heeled boots on the closet floor. Wilson picked up the boots and saw that they had a distinctive sole design similar to that found in the footprints near the Stereo Shoppe window. The boots were also caked with red clay. Detective Wilson seized the boots and then conducted a search of the living room, which revealed three stereo receivers hidden under the couch. These were also seized.

Further investigation disclosed that Lucy Lane's boots exactly matched the footprints at the Stereo Shoppe, and confirmed that the stereo receivers found under Lucy's couch were taken in the burglary of the Stereo Shoppe.

Lucy Lane has been indicted for burglary of the Stereo Shoppe. Her attorney has filed a motion to suppress the use of the boots and the stereo receivers as evidence. All of the facts stated above have been stipulated by both the prosecution and the defense.

You are the law clerk to Judge Justice, who is to decide the motion to suppress. Judge Justice has asked you to write a memorandum analyzing the issues raised by the motion and setting forth your conclusions as to how the motion should be decided.

Write the memorandum requested by Judge Justice.

47.   The Visceral Act, a federal law duly enacted in response to a public opinion survey, prohibits the mailing of unsolicited advertisements for contraceptives. Control Co., a manufacturer of contraceptives, has undertaken a direct mail marketing campaign to the general public

consisting of unsolicited pamphlets promoting its products and literature discussing venereal disease and family planning.

Control Co. wants to bring an action to enjoin the enforcement of the Visceral Act against its proposed mail campaign.

You are requested to prepare a memorandum for Control Co.'s corporate counsel:
(a)   Analyzing pertinent legal principles applicable to the facts related above;
(b)   Stating your opinion as to the outcome of the litigation; and
(c)   Giving reasons for your opinion.
Write the memorandum.

48.   Paula Price and Donna Dean are college seniors who have been roommates since they started college. They are in your law office this morning consulting with you about an automobile accident that occurred during Spring recess of their sophomore year. They both sustained serious personal injuries.

They have explained that the accident occurred after a wedding reception they had attended at the Hotel Bergen. Donna was driving and Paula was a passenger. They had just left the hotel and were traveling the main road out of Bergen Township, New Jersey, when a local taxicab driven by Tom Tyler came out of a small side street and collided with their car. Paula and Donna agreed that both vehicles were traveling at moderate rates of speed, although Donna volunteered that she may have been going about five miles per hour over the posted speed limit. The police report of the accident states that there was a stop sign on the side street at the intersection, but it was knocked down a few weeks prior to this accident and was not yet replaced by the Township.

When Paula called you a few days ago to set up this appointment, she mentioned that she had suggested to Donna that they stay overnight at the hotel. She said that she and Donna had danced all night and they were both tired. She confided that they may have had a little too much champagne punch.

Paula and Donna have explained to you that they had retained Lester Lawyer to represent them about a month after the accident, but they have not heard from him since. He has not returned their phone calls or answered their letters. They did not sign an agreement to retain Lawyer, but they gave him the $500 he requested to cover preliminary investigation expenses and filing fees.

Paula and Donna have now asked you to represent them in these matters.
(a)   Identify the causes of action Paula and Donna may have and against whom.
(b)   State the advice you would give them at this time.

49.   In April 1983, National Motors Corp. announced the production of a new automobile, the Belchfire 84, which was scheduled for distribution in the fall. National planned to manufacture a limited edition of the Belchfire and distribute one to each of its 3,000 dealers across the country.

Ann Teek, an automobile enthusiast, read the announcement in Auto Track Magazine and called Manuel Shift, the sales manager at Modern Motors, to inquire about the availability of the Belchfire. Shift replied that the car could be purchased at the manufacturer's suggested retail price, approximately $15,000, but that a deposit of $500 would be required. Teek immediately delivered a personal check to Shift payable to Modern Motors in the amount of $500. She wrote a notation upon the front of the check which read: "Deposit for car." Shift stamped the back of the check:

For deposit only
Modern Motors

The check was duly deposited to Modern Motors' account and honored by Teek's bank.

In October 1983, Teek was notified that the car had arrived, but Shift told her that due to the great demand it could not be purchased at the manufacturer's suggested retail price. He said he had already received offers from as far away as Hawaii to buy the car for $22,000 or more. Teek was invited to submit a bid. She refused and immediately filed suit against Modern Motors for specific performance.

You represent the defendant Modern Motors and are moving for summary judgment based upon the above facts which have been stipulated.

(a) List the defenses you would assert on defendant's behalf.

(b) Write the legal argument portion of the brief in support of your motion for summary judgment.

50. Good Eats Corp. and John Gray owned adjoining lands. In 1960, the manager of Good Eats spoke to Gray and asked permission to landscape a 10-foot strip of Gray's land which bordered Good Eats' property in order to make the setting of its restaurant more attractive. Gray said "sure" and Good Eats proceeded with the project.

In 1961, Gray sold his property to Bill Brown. Title was transferred by warranty deed. Gray advised Brown of the arrangement with Good Eats at the time of the sale.

Good Eats never discussed the 10-foot strip with Brown, but through the years continued to mow the grass and prune the bushes and the strip. In 1976, Good Eats sold the restaurant business and property to Fast Foods Corp. which continued to maintain the strip.

Last week, Brown came to your office. He told you that he wants to build a fence on the property line between his land and that of Fast Foods so that Fast Foods' patrons will not litter his property with food wrappers and drinking cups. He has requested your advice concerning his right to build the fence and any other rights, remedies, and responsibilities he may have pertaining to the 10-foot strip.

(a) Respond to Brown's requests.

(b) Draft the document you would have prepared in 1960 to protect the interests of Gray and his successors in title if you had represented Gray at that time.

51. In July 1982, Vicki Smith was murdered in her home in Marbel, New Jersey. The only witness was Vicki's seven-year-old daughter, Wanda. Wanda telephoned the police immediately after the murder and excitedly told them that a neighbor, Juan, "shot my mommy."

Juan was arrested and charged with the homicide of Vicki. At a preliminary hearing held in August 1982, the judge ruled that Wanda was incompetent to testify because of her age and immaturity. The charges were dismissed.

In July of 1986, Juan was re-arrested and charged with the homicide of Vicki. Wanda testified before the grand jury, and Juan was indicted for homicide.

Prior to trial, Juan's attorney made all appropriate and necessary pretrial motions. These motions were denied by the court.

During jury selection at trial, the prosecutor exhausted his peremptory challenges by removing all potential jurors with Spanish-sounding surnames. The trial court questioned Wanda and found that she was now of sufficient age and maturity to qualify as a witness, and permitted her testimony. Over objection, the court also permitted the prosecutor to introduce into evidence the tape recording of Wanda's telephone call to the police. The jury found Juan guilty of Vicki's murder.

Juan has filed a Notice of Appeal of his conviction. A senior attorney with whom you are associated has been appointed to represent Juan on appeal. She has requested that you prepare a memorandum to her which would evaluate the likelihood of success Juan would have on each issue.

Prepare the memorandum requested.

52.   Sue Asponte has been named as a defendant in a breach of contract action and has requested that you represent her. The suit asks for damages in the amount of $20,000, but Ms. Asponte has reason to believe that she only owes about $5,000. She has indicated a willingness to pay slightly more in settlement, especially if it would eliminate expert witness fees and avoid a time-consuming and costly trial. She has furnished you with a copy of the Summons and Complaint from which you have preliminarily noted the possibility of filing a counterclaim.

Ms. Asponte is opposed to an hourly rate for your services, but is willing to pay a nominal retainer plus an amount contingent upon successful defense of the action. However, she wants everything to be in writing. You have agreed to represent her on this basis.

Prepare an agreement for your client's consideration employing you as her attorney.

53.   Center Developers, Inc. ("CDI") owns a shopping center in Parboil, New Jersey. In January 1980, CDI leased a store in the center to Video View, Inc. ("VVI"), a local concern. The lease was for a term of 10 years at a minimum rental of $12,000 per year. As additional rent, the tenant was also required to pay 5% of its annual gross receipts in excess of $240,000. The lease included the following provisions:

1.   Tenant shall not assign this lease or sublet the demised premises
     without Landlord's consent.
2.   The demised premises shall be used exclusively for the sale or rental
     of video equipment, video cassettes and other related items.

In January 1983, the stock of VVI was sold to Artiste Movies, Inc. ("AMI"), a publicly traded company. VVI was then dissolved and all of its assets were transferred to Video Viewing, Inc. ("Vinc"), a newly formed subsidiary of AMI. Vinc then installed booths in the demised premises for the viewing of movies by customers. It continued to sell some video cassettes in the store as well. Vinc timely paid the monthly rent by its corporate check after January 1, 1983.

The consent of CDI to the above transaction was not sought. CDI first became aware of the changes in the tenancy in March, 1984, when Vinc reported its 1983 gross receipts, which were 25% lower than those by VVI for 1982. Vinc believes its sales were hurt by a fast food restaurant in the center which showed free videos to its patrons while they ate in the restaurant.

CDI has sent a notice of termination of the lease by Vinc. Pursuant to the lease, the parties have agreed to submit the dispute to an arbitrator for resolution. The arbitrator has ordered each party to submit a written memorandum containing the arguments in support of its position and rebutting the arguments that could be advanced by the other party.

Draft the memorandum on behalf of CDI.

54.   Blue Skies Aviation Co. ("Blue Skies") is the owner of an airplane which it stored at Hometown Airport, New Jersey. Without the owner's permission, Hy Fliar took the airplane from the hangar. Shortly after take-off he ran out of gas and crashed into the residence of Mr. and Mrs. Ground, located in Hometown, causing damage to the house and injury to the Grounds.

A New Jersey statute imposes absolute liability on airplane owners for damages caused by their aircraft to persons and property on the ground even when the aircraft is used without the owner's permission. Blue Skies claims this statute is unenforceable.

Write a memorandum discussing the enforceability of the statute.

55.   You are a new associate in the law firm of Pat Partner. Gluko, a regular client of the firm, called this morning on an urgent matter. This afternoon you and Partner have been in the office of Gluko's President, Paul Prez, and you have taken notes of the events he has described to you.

Partner and Prez agree that a lawsuit must be started at once and that immediate injunctive relief must be obtained. Partner has instructed you to go back to the office at once and prepare a draft of affidavit for Prez from your notes while he obtains more information and documents. Partner has cautioned you that Prez's affidavit should contain only facts that would be admissible in evidence. He has told you not to be concerned with legal arguments which can be placed in the brief.

Your notes of conversation are as follows:

Al Able was Gluko Dir. Mktg.
2 weeks ago he gave written notice of resign.
Prez asked why (fuzzy response about starting own biz.)
Hy Tech (major new cust. of Gluko) called Prez yesterday.
Hy Tech just visited by Stikum (Gluko chief competitor).
Told Hy Tech that Able joining Stikum on Monday as V.P. Mktg.
Stikum offered to supply prod. needs at "25% off whatever Gluko is charging you."
Prez immediately confronted Able (Able laughed, said "No comment.").
Prez fired him on the spot.
This a.m. Prez inspects Able's office (can't find Able's copy of Gluko confidential manual of cust. names and prod. formulas—these important trade secrets—Prez has looked everywhere for it—Prez thinks maybe other stuff missing too).
Over last 10 years, Gluko spent much $ on Research & Development—about $600,000—(developing specialty items—custom glues for new kinds of customers—novel and unique applications—very high profit margins for Gluko).
Prez calls Stikum "poacher," Stikum's published annual reports (copy in file) show almost zero spent on R&D.
Prez claims Stikum strategy is cheaper to steal from Gluko.
Hired away Gluko employees (Smith in '79, Taylor in '81 and Jones in '82 —Smith a chemist—Taylor and Jones were salesmen).
Stikum learned from them: identity of new Gluko customers, their special needs and Gluko's formulas for each.
Since Stikum has no R&D costs they can sell way below Gluko prices.
Stole many Gluko customers right after each employee pirated—now Hy Tech wants to know why we charge so much—Gluko has lost a bundle in profits, but very difficult to measure.
Able knows details of new product lines (B.S. in Chem. Eng.—1972)—also has close customer contacts and knows special needs.
In March '82 Gluko made all employees (including Able) sign a 2-year restrictive covenant against working with a competitor after they leave—the agreement (copy in file) also says won't ever use or disclose confidential info.
Prez thinks Able put Stikum on to Hy Tech—Prez really mad at Able (called him "traitor") because he took him straight from college and "taught him everything he knows."

Draft Prez's affidavit in support of an application for an immediate injunction.

56.   In an effort to deal with the growing problem of the failure of fathers to support their children, a state enacted the following statute:

> Any resident of this state having minor issue not in his custody which he is under any court order to support, may not marry in this state or elsewhere, unless:
> (a)   He first obtains a court's permission to marry;
> (b)   He submits proof of compliance with the support order; and
> (c)   He makes satisfactory showing that the children covered by the support order are not then and are not likely to become public charges.

Paul Pater, a resident of the state, was under court order to support his illegitimate child. He was financially unable to satisfy the prerequisites of the statute and did not attempt to obtain court permission to marry. He applied for a marriage license but was denied because he had not satisfied the statutory requirements. Pater instituted a lawsuit in an appropriate court to compel the issuance of a marriage license to him.

Discuss the issues and decide the merits of the case.

57.   At 9 p.m. on December 15, 1984, the Goldfield police received a call from a resident reporting that his home was being burglarized. Patrolman Palmer was dispatched to the scene and encountered Dan Denton walking in the direction of a car parked in front of the residence. He conducted a pat-down search of Denton, which disclosed a glass-cutting tool and car keys in his jacket pocket. Palmer used these keys to unlock the car and discovered jewelry and silver-ware hidden under the front seat. The resident identified these items as having been taken from his home.

Palmer told Denton he was under arrest for burglary. He fully advised Denton of his *Miranda* rights and asked Denton if he wished to make a statement. Denton replied, "I'm not saying anything until I talk to a lawyer."

Denton was immediately brought before the municipal court judge, who advised Denton again of his *Miranda* rights. The judge accepted Denton's application for a Public Defender to represent him. Reasonable bail was set and Denton was placed in the county jail because he was unable to post bail.

The next morning two county detectives visited Denton at the jail. They told Denton they were investigating a homicide which had occurred in September of 1984 during the burglary of a Silvertown residence. The detectives fully advised Denton of his *Miranda* rights, which Denton stated he understood. They asked Denton if he would answer some questions regarding the Silvertown murder. Denton replied:

> I'll tell you all I know about that job because I only drove the getaway car. I didn't have anything to do with killing the old lady. But I'm not talking about the Goldfield job until I get to see my lawyer.

The grand jury indicted Denton for burglary of the Goldfield residence and for felony murder of the Silvertown woman. His attorney has filed a motion to suppress (a) the glasscutter, the jewelry and the silverware seized at the time of arrest, and (b) the statement Denton gave to the county detectives regarding the Silvertown murder.

Discuss and evaluate the admissibility of this evidence.

58. Kingston University, a private institution, sponsors a "Little Sibling" program in which students are encouraged to "adopt" an underprivileged child from the surrounding community. Perri is a straight "A" scholarship student at the University. At the beginning of her freshman year, Perri "adopted" Linda as her little sister. Since then, Perri has visited or taken Linda out approximately once each week. Perri had attended Linda's family get-togethers, and Linda has visited Perri's home during school vacations. Perri has often described Linda as "the little sister I never had."

The University owns and maintains dormitories in which undergraduate students are assigned to live. Now a senior, Perri lives in the newest dormitory, which was opened two years ago. Linda is now seven years old. At the entrance to the dorm, there is a concrete stairway that leads to a wide landing.

The landing is five feet above the ground and has no side railings. The University's campus patrol shows that last year a student who had been at a "beer blast" in the dorm fell off this landing. He was not seriously injured.

On October 20, 1984, as Perri and Linda were leaving the dorm, Linda danced around the edge of the landing instead of walking down the stairs. Perri called out to Linda, "How many times have I told you not to play on the landing!" As Perri was speaking, Linda lost her balance and fell from the landing.

Linda was rendered unconscious by the fall and was taken to Kingston University Medical Center where she was treated for a head injury. Linda has lingering symptoms, including seizures, and is being evaluated for permanent brain damage.

Perri has been in a severe depression since Linda got hurt, and has undergone psychotherapy at the University Medical Center. She has dropped two of her five courses, and will have to take an extra semester in residence in order to complete her major and graduate.

Discuss and evaluate the University's liability to Linda and to Perri and the defenses and third-party claims available to the University.

59. On March 1, 1983, Slo-poke Builders entered into a written contract with Burgerama, a popular fast-food chain with numerous franchises throughout the state, to erect a restaurant facility. The contract provided that construction must be completed in time for a July 1, 1983 opening, with time being of the essence. Due to unjustified actions by Slo-poke, the building was not completed until October 1, 1983, when the restaurant opened for business.

Approximately one year later, Burgerama filed suit for breach of contract against Slo-poke, demanding damages for the three-month delay. Partial summary judgment has been granted in favor of plaintiff on the issue of liability, with the question of damages remaining for trial. Burgerama has engaged Harry Heartburn as an expert in the operation of fast-food restaurants. He had performed a market study of the area before the site was selected.

You are the attorney for Burgerama and are scheduled to meet with Mr. Heartburn tomorrow to develop the damage claims for trial.

(a) Write a short memorandum of law analyzing the items of damages that might be recoverable.

(b) Write out the questions you will ask Mr. Heartburn in order to determine which items of damages you will pursue at the trial.

60. John Lee, President of Leisure, Inc., wanted to expand the sales of his company's most successful new game, "Frivia." Lee decided to engage an independent sales agent, Export Co., to distribute and sell the game abroad.

In February 1984, Lee and Export's President, Amanda X. Porter, agreed in a conversation that Export would become the exclusive export agent for Frivia upon the following terms:

(a) The duration of Export's exclusive agency shall be five years, beginning May 1, 1984, with both parties reserving the right to cancel on 30 days' prior written notice if sales do not reach anticipated levels;

(b) Leisure shall pay Export commissions of a minimum of 10% of net sales (less shipping, insurance, custom duties, and returns), the exact rate to be mutually agreed upon no later than Leisure's acceptance of Export's first order;

(c) Export shall bear all expenses of international promotion, travel, entertainment, and any "under the table" payments that might be necessary to induce purchasing agents of overseas customers to place orders; and

(d) Leisure shall have the right, in its absolute discretion, to reject any particular orders. Export shall have the right to demand arbitration if it considers Leisure's rejection to be unreasonable.

Lee confirmed the above terms in a letter which he signed and personally delivered to Porter. During their brief discussion at this time, Lee explained that Leisure would reject only those orders which might involve serious credit or collection problems. As to the sales potential, Lee stated that each could expect net profits of "at least a million dollars."

Over the next three months, Export arranged to have samples of Frivia translated into several languages. Export also incurred substantial promotional expenses. Porter traveled to several countries and returned with initial orders of $100,000. In the meantime, Lee determined that the domestic market for Frivia was virtually exhausted. Lee told Porter that Leisure was discontinuing manufacture of Frivia and, therefore, would not fill the orders.

Prepare an opinion letter to Porter discussing Export's claims and remedies, and Leisure's defenses. Do not restate the facts, but integrate your discussion of the facts with your legal analysis.

61. Smith and Jones owned abutting properties in a low-lying area of the Borough of Suburbia.

In 1960, Smith raised the level of his home approximately two feet in order to avoid future flood damage. In the process, he removed an outdoor stairway which was entirely within his property lines at the side entrance to his house. He replaced it with a new wooden stairway that was longer and higher. The new stairway extended 15 inches onto Jones's property, but neither Smith nor Jones was aware of this fact.

In 1965, Smith completely removed the wooden stairway and replaced it with concrete steps of the same dimensions.

In 1966, for unrelated reasons, Jones had his property surveyed. The survey showed that Smith's steps extended onto Jones's property. Jones immediately demanded that Smith remove the stairway. Smith replied that he could not do so since the local fire code required an entrance in addition to the front entrance. The only other place where Smith had room for a second entrance was through a bathroom at the rear of the house.

Without resolving the problem, Jones sold his home in 1970 to Dally. A property search disclosed that title was marketable, but Dally did not have the land surveyed. Jones never told Dally of any problem with the steps.

In 1984, Dally began constructing a fence along his common boundary with Smith. In the process, he discovered that the steps extended onto his property, and demanded that Smith remove them. Smith refused for the same reasons that he had previously given to Jones. Dally immediately started a lawsuit seeking removal of the steps.

Smith has retained you as his attorney. You have decided to file an answer admitting the basic facts in the complaint, but denying the legal conclusions alleged therein and opposing the remedy sought. You have further decided to file a counterclaim against Dally.

(a) Draft the separate defenses that you would raise in response to the complaint.

(b) Draft a counterclaim which sets forth Smith's contentions and relief sought.

62. Betty and Claude are members of a radical action group. They reside with their three small children in a row house in Gotham City, New Jersey. The house is located across the street from Gotham Station, which is a stop on the main rail line running between New York and Washington, D.C.

Following the arrest of three members of their radical group, Betty and Claude made renovations in their house to fix it up as a fortress. They built a secure area in the house where they quartered their three children and then began sniping with rifles and automatic weapons at persons and trains passing in the area of the Gotham station. Within an hour, they seriously wounded six people and all activity at the busy train station had to be shut down.

Betty and Claude announced that they would hold out until the following demands were met:

(1) Release from jail of the three group members;

(2) Payment of $10 million; and

(3) Safe passage out of the country.

Their demands were refused.

The Gotham police surrounded the house but were unable to get very close to it. Sporadic gunfire was exchanged for a full day between Betty and Claude and the police. In the meantime, all train traffic on the main line remained at a standstill.

After studying the situation, the Mayor and Chief of Police of Gotham ordered Lurch, a member of the Gotham Police helicopter squad, to drop a small explosive device on the roof of the house in hopes of providing a means to gain entry. This action caused a fire that spread among the row houses. By the time the fire was brought under control, Betty and Claude had been captured and arrested. Five people died in the fire, including Betty's and Claude's three children, and two other people in neighboring houses.

You are the Prosecutor for Gotham County.

(a) List the major indictments you would consider seeking.

(b) Briefly describe the areas of investigation you would pursue prior to presenting the matter to a grand jury.

(c) Discuss and evaluate the merits of the proposed indictments and the anticipated defenses.

63. Paul Plaintive had been employed as corporate counsel to the Widget Corporation for 12 years when he was terminated on August 15, 1984. Barry Businessman was the president of Widget. Vanessa Veep was Widget's vice president for personnel.

Prior to Plaintive's termination, he had been assisting Widget's outside counsel in a lawsuit brought against Widget by a third party. During that litigation, Plaintive learned that Businessman had altered several relevant documents. Upon receipt of a proper discovery request from the opposing party, Plaintive informed Businessman that Widget had to produce the unaltered documents. On August 14, 1984, Plaintive refused to comply with Businessman's instructions to produce only the altered documents.

Veep suggested to Businessman that Plaintive be fired. They called Plaintive to a meeting on August 15 and told him he was terminated. Plaintive asked if it was because he refused to produce the altered documents. They told him that he could draw his own conclusions. Veep then told Plaintive he had 10 minutes to pack his personal belongings and leave. The entire office staff watched as a security guard escorted Plaintive to his car. That night, Plaintive suffered a massive heart attack. He is unable to return to full-time employment and his wife has been forced to leave her job to take care of him. Plaintive has learned that Veep's husband replaced him as corporate counsel on August 16, 1984.

Write a memo analyzing each legal theory or cause of action that may be available to Paul Plaintive or to Mrs. Plaintive. As to each cause of action, discuss:

(a) The elements necessary to prove a claim;
(b) The facts which tend to establish or defeat those elements;
(c) The party or parties you would name as plaintiff(s) and as defendant(s);
(d) The likelihood of proving liability; and
(e) The nature of the damages or other relief available.

64. **Article XX of the State Constitution provides:**

> No judge of any court of this State shall be eligible for election to the State Legislature. Such ineligibility shall apply during the entire term for which the judge has been appointed, even if he resigns his office prior to the end of his term.

John Johnson, a nationally known spokesman for a clean environment, was appointed Judge of the State Superior Court for a term of five years on January 1, 1984. He has recently been solicited by the Clean Air and Resources Party ("CARP") to run as its candidate for State Senator in the general election of May, 1986. Although Judge Johnson has offered to resign from the Judiciary in order to run for the Senate, the State Attorney General has issued an advisory opinion that Article XX prohibits Judge Johnson from seeking election to the State Senate until January 1, 1989.

In anticipation of litigation, Judge Johnson has requested your advice on the validity of Article XX.

Discuss and evaluate the validity of Article XX.

65.
Memorandum to: ASSISTANT PROSECUTOR
From: COUNTY PROSECUTOR
Re: STATE v. DAVE DICKSON

Investigative File #1234-8

FACTS

On July 1, 1985, Dave Dickson robbed the First Federal Bank. Speeding out of the bank parking lot, Dickson lost control of his car, jumped the curb and struck a tree. Dickson narrowly missed striking a pedestrian, Viola Victors, age 77. Dickson was apprehended at the scene.

Victors collapsed on the sidewalk outside the bank after Dickson's car struck the tree. She was taken by ambulance to the hospital, where she was diagnosed as having suffered a heart attack. The local police issued Dickson a summons for reckless driving. He pled guilty in Municipal Court to this charge on July 10, 1985 and was fined $100.

38.

Dickson was indicted by a federal grand jury for violation of the Federal Bank Robbery Act, 18 U.S.C. section 2113. He pled guilty to this charge on September 30, 1985 and was sentenced to 10 years in a federal penitentiary. Victors was hospitalized for two months for treatment of her heart attack.

She was then released to a nursing home, where she remained until her death on July 15, 1986. The medical examiner's autopsy report stated the cause of her death to be "congestive heart failure."

ACTION REQUESTED

Prepare a memorandum that analyzes and evaluates the specific homicide charges that the State might bring against Dickson. In addition, analyze and evaluate the possible defenses Dickson may raise to each charge, and discuss any evidence problems you foresee. Do not restate the facts except as necessary in your analysis.

66. Microchip Corporation developed the Mother Nature computer ("MN") designed for use by large educational institutions. MN was programmed to bring individual rooms to a desired temperature by automatically turning on and off the heating or air conditioning, thereby effecting large savings in fuel and electricity costs.

Microchip's advertising brochure described MN's technical and performance specifications. The brochure stated that MN's useful life would be five years and in several places referred to the MN as an "experimental model." The purchase price for one MN, including installation, was $750,000.

When the brochure was received at Scientific University, its computer science department evaluated the data in the brochure and calculated that over a five-year period Scientific could save $8 million in fuel and electricity costs. On the recommendation of its computer science department, Scientific sent a purchase order to Microchip for one MN "as described in the advertising brochure." Microchip acknowledged the order in a personal letter to the president of Scientific, which stated:

> We are happy to accept your order. Since the MN is on the very cutting edge of new technology, we are unable to make any express or implied warranties, whether of merchantability or otherwise. Your claim for damages of any kind for nonperformance of the MN is limited to repair and replacement of defective parts within one year of purchase.

Microchip delivered and installed the MN in September 1982. Scientific paid the full purchase price of $750,000. Because of a basic design flaw, however, MN was unable to meet its performance specifications. When MN caused the heating to fail in the Scientific greenhouse during a December snowstorm, nine years and $3 million of research by the Scientific Botany Department to develop a rare orchid, whose petals have significant medical properties, were lost.

After repeated efforts by its technicians failed to remedy the problems, Microchip agreed that further repairs or design modifications were not feasible. Scientific itself spent $100,000 trying to get the MN to function properly, but finally gave up and sold the MN to a used computer dealer for $50,000 in April 1983.

You are the attorney for Scientific and have been asked to prepare a memorandum to its general counsel discussing and evaluating: (a) Scientific's claims and damages; and (b) Microchip's defenses.

Write the memorandum.

67.   Whipple was the owner of a building in which he operated a retail convenience food store. On July 1, 1984, he entered into a written agreement with Volt, a distributor of "Puff-Man," a coin-operated electronic video game. In return for 50% of the income derived, Whipple gave Volt the exclusive right for a period of 10 years to install and maintain a "Puff-Man" in space not to exceed 15 square feet in the entryway of the building. The agreement was made binding on "the parties, their heirs, successors, and assigns," but was not recorded.

Volt installed the machine in the designated location and affixed a brass plate to the front of the machine identifying it as Volt's property. Two years after the agreement was made, Whipple conveyed the land and premises to Bravo, who continued to operate the convenience store. Bravo promptly notified Volt to remove his machine from the premises. Volt replied in writing that he had a right to keep the machine in the entryway for the full 10-year term and that Bravo had notice of this right.

Volt has commenced an action against Bravo alleging, alternatively, the existence of a lease, an easement in gross, a license, and a real covenant.

He seeks specific performance. You are defending the action on behalf of Bravo and have filed a motion to dismiss Volt's complaint.

Prepare the legal argument portion of the brief in support of Bravo's motion.

68.   The senior class of Rural High School planned a party at Paul's Pizza Parlor. The principal chose Mr. Oxide, the chemistry teacher, to make all the arrangements and chaperone the seniors. Old Miss Tilly, a long-time tenant of the apartment over the pizza parlor, learned that the party was to take place downstairs. She decided to spend the night at her sister's house.

On the day of the party, Mr. Oxide conducted an experiment for the seniors. He demonstrated how metallic sodium, a highly combustible material, when mixed with even small quantities of water, generates sufficient heat to create a fireworks effect. The school had purchased the metallic sodium from Flamco in small, tightly sealed vials.

After class, two seniors, Bunny, age 16, and Clyde, age 18, returned to the unlocked lab. They removed one of the vials of metallic sodium which Mr. Oxide had left on his worktable.

That evening, Bunny's mother noticed the vial and screamed that Bunny was a degenerate "druggie." Bunny explained that the vial contained an explosive chemical she was going to use in a fireworks demonstration that night. Her mother retreated without another word. Bunny was a "hard-to-handle" teenager who had been in trouble with the law and school authorities on several occasions.

During the party, Bunny and Clyde met behind the pizza parlor to set off the metallic sodium. As soon as Mr. Oxide spotted them he yelled: "Don't open that vial!" Clyde ran into the pizza parlor bathroom, opened the vial, and flushed the sodium down the toilet. An explosion occurred and flames shot into the air. Clyde and everyone else in the pizza parlor fled unharmed into the street.

Although a Rural ordinance required all restaurants to have fire-retardant insulation in the ceilings and walls, Paul had not made such improvements. A sprinkler system recently purchased by Paul from Early Alertco did not work because Rural Water Company failed to supply adequate water volume and pressure. Rural's volunteer fire department, despite its timely arrival, could not contain the fire because of the lack of water volume and pressure in the nearby hydrants.

Miss Tilly arrived just in time to watch with horror as the roof fell in on a lifetime of memories and her few worldly possessions. Miss Tilly has consulted you concerning her right to recover damages.

(a)   Evaluate the factual and legal bases of each potential defendant's liability to Miss Tilly; and

(b)   Discuss the nature and extent of the damages Miss Tilly could recover and indicate whether you would recommend instituting a lawsuit.

69.   Sierra Toxics, Inc. ("Sierra"), is a privately owned company engaged in the business of disposing of toxic waste generated by chemical and pharmaceutical plants. Sierra operates pursuant to a license issued by the Commissioner of Ecological Preservation of the State of Alpha. This license authorizes Sierra to contract with such plants to provide the following services: (i) collection of toxic waste at the plant site; and (ii) transporting that waste to Sierra's disposal station, which is located in Alpha, three miles from the border with the State of Beta.

Pursuant to the authority granted by its license, for the past 10 years Sierra has contracted to provide services to plants in Alpha, and a few years ago, expanded its business to serve plants just over the border in Beta. The Beta plants that contract with Sierra dispose of approximately one-half their toxic waste output through that company and the remainder of their waste through disposal companies located in Beta.

Shortly after Sierra extended its services to the Beta plants, the residents of the town in which Sierra's disposal station is situated became alarmed at the amount of toxic waste stored there. These residents were concerned about the proximity of such toxic waste both to their homes and to the reservoir located in their town which supplies water to households in the immediate surrounding area.

The residents petitioned the Commissioner of Ecological Preservation to close Sierra's disposal station. Sierra objected. The Commissioner held an open hearing on the matter at which numerous witnesses testified. After that hearing, the Commissioner resolved the dispute by issuing an order that, effective immediately, use of Sierra's disposal station would be limited to toxic waste removed from chemical and pharmaceutical plants in Alpha only. The Beta plants were barred from disposing of their toxic waste through Sierra.

Both Sierra and the state of Beta have filed suit against the Alpha Commissioner of Ecological Preservation, seeking to rescind that order. The two lawsuits have been consolidated for trial before the judge to whom you serve as law clerk. The judge has asked you to prepare a memorandum identifying the claims raised and the defenses asserted, and analyzing the legal bases for all such claims and defenses.

Prepare the memorandum.

70.   The Sacred Bible Church operated an elementary school in the State of Eden. The school receives no aid from any governmental source, but its students receive free busing from the local school district. According to its charter, the school's avowed purpose is to "morally and spiritually train and educate our children to lead a Christian lifestyle in conformity with the teachings of the Sacred Bible Church." All pupils, parents and teachers are required to subscribe to the teachings of the Sacred Bible Church. Esther, a member of the Sacred Bible Church, has taught first grade at the school for five years.

The school administrator recently learned that Esther and her husband are expecting their first child in April 1986. After consulting with the Church Directors, the administrator informed Esther that her employment as a teacher would be terminated in April because one of the Church teachings is "a mother's place is in the home."

Esther's attorney has written to the Church Directors asserting that their proposed action violates an Eden statute which states: "No employer shall discriminate on the basis of race, religion, sex, marital status, or national origin." If Esther is terminated in April, the attorney intends to file a complaint with the Eden Civil Rights Commission seeking her reinstatement.

The Church Directors have requested that you provide them with an opinion letter analyzing the validity of this statute as it applies to the termination of Esther's employment and the possible consequences of taking such action.

Prepare the requested opinion letter.

71.   Karl Gaze, noted astronomer, decided to capitalize on the popular interest in Halley's Comet. Gaze telephoned Sally Starbuck, owner of Celestial Products, for a price quotation of telescopes specially imprinted with Gaze's name. In their telephone conversation, Gaze stated: "My mail-order sales alone will exceed 100,000 units."

Starbuck quoted Gaze a price of $10 each for the first 5,000 units and $7 each for all the rest he would need. Gaze said that the price was reasonable and stressed the importance of prompt deliveries.

Thereafter, Gaze sent a purchase order to Celestial for 20,000 units at $7 each, with delivery at the rate of 5,000 units per month, beginning August 1. On the reverse side of Gaze's purchase order form were the following printed terms:

> Buyer reserves the right to cancel this order or part thereof before delivery of goods. Buyer reserves all rights to exclusive use of the "Gaze" name on all products and promotions.

Celestial issued its standard order acknowledgement form confirming only the delivery schedule which Gaze had specified in his order. The acknowledgement form provided:

> Buyer shall be liable for the full purchase price of all finished goods manufactured for buyer's account. If buyer cancels for any reason, buyer agrees to pay as liquidated damages 50% of the total contract price.

During the months of August, September, and October, Celestial delivered a total of 15,000 units. By early October, it became apparent, however, that Halley's Comet would not produce a spectacular display. Gaze's sales drastically declined.

On October 15, Gaze sent the following telegram to Starbuck: "Regretfully must cancel—perhaps we'll do better next time Halley's Comet comes around!" At the same time, Gaze sent a check to Celestial for $105,000 (representing 15,000 units at $7 each), on which was noted: "Payment in full."

As of October 15, Celestial had 10,000 finished telescopes imprinted with Gaze's name ready for shipment and parts in inventory for 25,000 more.

Discuss and evaluate:
(a)   Celestial's claims and damages;
(b)   Gaze's defenses; and
(c)   Whether Celestial should deposit the check.

72.   Mr. and Mrs. Homeowner and their two children reside in the rural Borough of Meadow View. Their home is located in a zone which permits only one-family dwellings. About a year ago they decided to build an addition to their home so that Mrs. Homeowner's widowed mother could live with them. They submitted plans to the Meadow View Building Inspector which showed an additional bedroom on the ground floor with a small efficiency kitchen and a bathroom. The addition contained no separate entrance of its own; it was connected to the remainder of the house by a hallway off the living room.

The zoning ordinance of the Borough of Meadow View prohibited multi-family dwellings in all zones. A multi-family dwelling was defined in the ordinance as "a building designed for or occupied by more than one family." The term "family" was defined as "one or more persons living and cooking together as a single housekeeping unit, exclusive of household servants."

Mrs. Homeowner told the Building Inspector that the addition was intended to create a mother-daughter type facility, but this was not stated in the application. The Building Inspector issued a building permit and construction was commenced shortly thereafter. The work was nearly completed when Watchful, a neighboring property owner, became aware of the proposed use and complained that it would violate the zoning provisions restricting all dwellings to one-family use. He immediately commenced an action against Homeowner and the Borough of Meadow View seeking to enjoin further construction and to revoke the building permit.

While litigation was pending, Meadow View amended its zoning ordinance to provide: "Mother-daughter dwelling units shall be prohibited in all residential zones." No other changes were made to the zoning ordinance, which previously made no reference to mother-daughter type uses.

Both Homeowner and Watchful have filed cross-motions for summary judgment contending that the above facts, which are not in dispute, entitle them to judgment as a matter of law.

You are the law clerk assigned to research the matter and to prepare a memorandum for the court's guidance in deciding the motions.

Write the memorandum.

73. Walt Witker is a long-time government attorney employed by the United States Department of Defense. About a year ago he was suspected of being a homosexual. A Department of Defense investigator was assigned to monitor his activities. The investigator bugged Witker's apartment and his private government office, tapped his telephone, and set up remote television cameras to observe him through peep holes placed throughout his apartment and offices. These efforts confirmed Witker's homosexual activities and disclosed curious contacts with suspicious persons.

On a recent evening at 10 p.m., the investigator made an unannounced visit to Witker's apartment. For several hours he badgered, taunted and humiliated Witker about his homosexual activities, repeatedly playing excerpts of the audio and video tapes acquired over the past year. The investigator chastised him for these activities and emphasized how vulnerable they made him to espionage efforts of foreign governments.

Finally, Witker broke down. He confided that he already had been blackmailed and had revealed defense secrets to a foreign agent. Upon the investigator's suggestion, he voluntarily wrote out a detailed statement of these events.

Witker was promptly indicted for espionage. He is making a motion to suppress each and all of the tapes, as well as the oral and written statements to the investigator.

Take your choice. Write the argument portion of a brief:

(a) On behalf of Witker in support of the motion to suppress; *or*

(b) On behalf of the Government, in opposition to the motion to suppress.

In either case, anticipate and meet the principal arguments of the other side.

74. Lawfirm leased a third-floor suite in a new office building designed for lawyers. The building was well known for its state of the art centralized electronic support facilities. Those centralized facilities included word processing, computerized research terminals, and electronic mail and telephone systems. Soon after Lawfirm moved in, a defective water pipe burst and caused flooding in the basement. Pipeco had manufactured and installed the defective pipe. The

pipe was replaced the next day, but the water damage rendered the central facilities inoperable for several weeks. Lawfirm's suite was undamaged.

As a result of this incident, Lawfirm's employees were unable to perform and bill for some of their usual work; several contracts could not be drafted and produced for Lawfirm's clients, who lost valuable deals as a result; and one major client discharged Lawfirm as retained counsel.

There is no factual dispute as to the cause of the interrupted service or its effect on Lawfirm's operations. Lawfirm has filed suit against Pipeco to recover for its economic loss.

The complaint contains three separate counts: (a) negligence; (b) strict liability; and (c) breach of implied warranties. Pipeco has moved for judgment on the pleadings, or in the alternative for summary judgment, on all three counts. You are the judge's law clerk. Write a draft opinion deciding the motion.

75.   Harry, a compulsive gambler, had a streak of bad luck and suffered heavy losses, some of which he satisfied by withdrawing the entire $900 balance in the joint checking account he maintained with his wife, Wilma. He then wrote a check for $5,000 and cashed it at the Ace Check Cashing Agency. He turned over the money to his bookie.

Unaware there were no funds left in the checking account, Wilma wrote a $200 check to the Local Supermarket for groceries.

The bank refused payment of both checks and notified Harry and Wilma of its refusal. Harry then told Wilma what he had done. Because they had no money, Harry and Wilma were unable to make good on the checks.

Harry and Wilma were arrested and indicted for having fraudulently issued bad checks. After receiving complete *Miranda* warnings, Wilma gave the police a full written statement, including what Harry had told her. Harry refused to give a statement.

At trial, the court permitted the prosecutor to introduce Wilma's entire statement into evidence, despite the objection of Harry's and Wilma's attorney, Barry Starr.

In his closing argument, the prosecutor told the jury that "Harry and Wilma must be guilty because they refused to testify at trial."

The court instructed the jury, under the criminal code, that:

An issuer of a check is presumed to have fraudulently issued it if he fails to make good the check within 10 days after receiving notice that the bank has refused payment.

After they were convicted, Harry and Wilma retained separate counsel to file appeals.

Discuss and evaluate all issues which Harry and Wilma can raise on appeal.

76.   On June 1, 1986, Owens contracted to sell his residence to Byer for $100,000 cash with a deposit of $10,000. The contract provided that the seller would convey "good and marketable title, free and clear of all liens and encumbrances." A closing of title was to take place "on or before September 1, 1986," at the office of Byer's attorney.

On August 20, 1986, Byer told Owens that he would need about two weeks additional time to raise the necessary funds. Owens replied that he had to close title on September 1, 1986, in accordance with the contract, because he needed the proceeds to purchase another home that same day. To make sure the closing was not delayed, Owens sent a certified letter to Byer on August 25, 1986, setting the closing date for September 1, 1986, at 10 a.m. at the office of Owen's attorney. Time was specifically made "of the essence."

The next day Owens realized that September 1 was a legal holiday (Labor Day). He immediately sent a telegram to Byer stating: "Disregard letter of 8/25/86. Change closing date to 9/2/86. Time still OF THE ESSENCE." Byer received both the certified letter and the telegram on

August 27, 1986. He then called Owens and requested an extension of seven days. By letter dated August 29, 1986, Owens replied: "Without waiving any of my rights, I will close title on September 5, 1986, but no later."

On August 30, 1986, Byer for the first time examined a copy of Owens's recorded deed. Title was derived from Sam Sellalot on February 1, 1952. Byer noted that the third course of the metes and bounds description recited: "From the edge of Main Street North 30° West 200 feet to Babbling Brook." Byer's survey showed it was 220 feet from Main Street to Babbling Brook. At the end of the deed descriptions were the following clauses:

A.   Reserving unto the Grantor herein a right of way from Main Street to the rear of the property for public access to Babbling Brook for fishing and other recreational purposes.

B.   Subject to rights of Powerful Electric Company to install, maintain, repair and replace electric lines over the premises to any dwelling erected thereon.

Sellalot's signature on the deed was witnessed by and acknowledged before Owens, who happened to be a Notary Public. A notary's stamp and raised seal were duly affixed to the deed.

Byer promptly notified Owens on September 2, 1986, that the deed raised certain questions in his mind. Owens replied by merely renewing his demand that Byer close title no later than September 5, 1986 or risk forfeiture of his deposit.

Because the house has increased greatly in value, Byer wants to consummate the purchase. However, he cannot raise the necessary funds until September 8, 1986, at the earliest. Byer has consulted you to represent his interests.

Draft a letter to Owens's attorney fully setting forth Byer's legal position.

77.   Yielding to pressure from religious groups, the State Legislature enacted the Anti-Pornography Tax Act. The Act imposes on local retailers a sales tax of $.05 per copy on all magazines published out of state which contain "pornographic, lewd, or obscene" material.

The Act also imposes a tax of 10% on the gross annual revenues of all domestic and foreign publishers which distribute within the State magazines displaying photographs of children under 16 engaged in "sexual activity of any kind."

The Act requires that the tax revenue be used to fund a program to feed, clothe and house teenager runaways in facilities operated by religious organizations.

You are counsel to Pent-Up Magazine, an out-of-state publisher which distributes its magazine nationally. What arguments would you make in challenging this legislation? Assume Congress has not legislated in this area.

78.   Jones and his wife, reformed alcoholics, were returning one morning from a weekend retreat held by Alcoholics Anonymous. Although aware that his automobile was very low on gasoline, Jones drove onto the New Jersey Turnpike without stopping to buy gas.

Shortly after entering the Turnpike, the automobile ran out of gas and stopped in the high-speed lane. Mrs. Jones, five months pregnant, was asleep in the car. Jones left the car with its rear lights blinking and obtained a ride to a nearby gas station.

Trooper Smith spotted the disabled vehicle and stopped his police utility truck directly behind the car. Smith did not activate the flashing warning lights atop his truck. Jones returned and began pouring gasoline into his automobile while Trooper Smith stood by and watched.

Moments later an automobile driven by Brown collided with the rear of the police utility truck which, in turn, plowed into Jones's vehicle.

Trooper Smith sustained serious head and back injuries. Neither Mr. nor Mrs. Jones suffered apparent injuries, but one month later Mrs. Jones had a miscarriage.

Jones's license had been suspended for drunk driving and had not been reinstated at the time of the accident.

The motor vehicle statute provides:

> The stopping, standing or parking of a motor vehicle on any highway
> caused by lack of fuel shall constitute a violation of this section.

Mrs. Jones has commenced an action against her husband seeking damages on her own behalf for (a) injuries arising out of her miscarriage; and (b) negligent infliction of emotional distress. Trooper Smith has also sued Mr. Jones for damages for his injuries.

You represent Mr. Jones. Discuss and evaluate the defenses Mr. Jones can raise to the claims asserted by Mrs. Jones and Trooper Smith.

79. Defendant, a nursery school teacher, was accused by the parents of three-year-old Pureheart of engaging in improper sexual contact with their child. The parents filed a municipal court complaint charging defendant with the disorderly persons offense of "simple assault," which is statutorily defined as "attempting to cause or knowingly causing bodily injury to another." Defendant pleaded guilty and was given the maximum sentence of six months in jail.

Following the tremendous publicity generated by the case, the county prosecutor obtained defendant's indictment for the second degree crime of "sexual assault," which is statutorily defined as "committing an act of sexual contact with a victim who is less than 13 years old." Defendant pleaded not guilty.

Prior to trial, Pureheart was permitted to testify in chambers with only the judge, prosecutor, and defense counsel present. Cross-examination was limited to written questions prepared by defense counsel and then asked by the judge. This procedure was allowed over defendant's objection because of unrebutted testimony by a psychiatrist at a pretrial hearing that Pureheart would suffer irreparable psychological damage if compelled to testify in open court with defendant present.

At trial the court admitted into evidence the videotape of Pureheart's testimony in chambers and proof of defendant's plea of guilty to the simple assault charge. The court rejected the proffer of expert testimony by defendant's long-time psychiatrist that defendant was psychologically incapable of committing a sexual assault on Pureheart. The judge ruled that such testimony would be inadmissible because "it embraced the ultimate issue to be decided by the jury." Defendant did not take the stand and rested without offering any evidence.

During closing argument the prosecutor told the jury: "I believe every word of Pureheart's testimony and find defendant to be a depraved and vicious beast whose conduct is more vile than the lowest form of animal life." Defendant was found guilty by the jury and sentenced to 15 years in jail to commence immediately after the simple assault sentence is served.

Discuss and evaluate the issues which defendant should raise on appeal. Assume defendant's trial counsel made all proper objections in a timely manner.

80. In November 1983, Seller, a manufacturer of Plexiglas display cases for jewelry stores, agreed in writing to sell Starco substantially all of its assets, including all finished goods. Paragraphs 10(a) and (b) of the agreement of sale contained indemnifications by Seller to Starco pertaining to accounts receivable and patents. Paragraph 10(c) stated:

Seller agrees to indemnify and hold harmless Starco with respect to any and all liabilities arising out of the manufacture by Seller of Plexiglas display cases, including any liability incurred by Starco from the sale by Starco of finished goods it purchases from Seller pursuant to this agreement. This indemnification shall exclude any liability resulting from Starco's gross negligence or willful misconduct.

Paragraph 10(d) stated:

The indemnifications contained in Paragraphs 10(a) and 10(b) shall apply only to claims arising within 180 days of the closing of the sale of assets pursuant to this agreement.

Paragraph 13 of the agreement permitted Starco to direct Seller to deliver the bill of sale for the assets to any Starco subsidiary designated by Starco. Prior to closing, Starco designated Clearvu, one of its wholly owned subsidiaries, as the proper recipient of the bill of sale. The closing was held on December 15, 1983, and a bill of sale for the assets was delivered by Seller to and in the name of Clearvu.

In August 1985, Clearvu was sued by VIP Jewelers, which had purchased from Clearvu 30 display cases manufactured by Seller and packaged and shipped by Clearvu. VIP alleged that Clearvu packed the display cases in a negligent manner, causing them to arrive on March 20, 1984, badly cracked and scratched. VIP claimed that it had to delay opening two new stores because of the condition of the display cases, thereby suffering substantial damages from loss of business and costs incurred to replace the display cases quickly.

Clearvu immediately notified Seller of its obligations under Paragraph 10(c). Seller denied all liability.

Clearvu settled its suit with VIP for $250,000 after incurring defense costs of $15,000. Starco and Clearvu then sued Seller for indemnification under Paragraph 10(c).

You are the attorney for Seller and have been asked by your client for an opinion letter evaluating the strengths and weaknesses of Seller's position.

Prepare the opinion letter.

81. On July 1, 1987, Mr. Spender borrowed $10,000 from Bullion Bank and signed a promissory note payable in 30 days. The loan application stated that the loan was for a down payment on Greenacre, a parcel of vacant land. Mr. Spender defaulted, and the bank immediately commenced suit on the note.

On September 15, 1987, Mr. Spender signed a contract to purchase Greenacre for $50,000, paying a deposit of $5,000. The contract provided for the balance to be paid at the time of closing.

Since Mr. Spender did not defend the suit by Bullion Bank, a default judgment for $10,000 was entered and docketed against him on October 1, 1987. Concerned about acquiring any assets which could be reached by the judgment creditor, Mr. Spender consulted Laurie View, a local attorney. Ms. View suggested that the lien of the judgment could be avoided if his wife took title to Greenacre in her name. The contract of sale was amended to substitute Mrs. Spender as the contract purchaser.

The closing of title was held on November 1, 1987, at which time the balance of $45,000 was paid by Mr. Spender. The deed to Mrs. Spender as grantee was recorded in due course.

On November 15, 1987, Mrs. Spender mortgaged the property to Prosperity Mortgage Company for $50,000 and used the proceeds to satisfy Mr. Spender's other pre-existing debts.

You have conducted a creditor's discovery proceeding as attorney for Bullion Bank and have ascertained all of the above facts.

Discuss the course of action, if any, the bank should pursue against Mr. Spender, Mrs. Spender, Ms. View, or Prosperity in an effort to collect its judgment. Include in your analysis the factual and legal defenses that might be raised.

82.   Al Kaholl, a student at Private University, attended an intercollegiate football game at the school's stadium with several friends. He brought a cooler containing beer and wine. University policy prohibited the consumption of alcoholic beverages in this stadium, which was enforced by inspecting containers at the gates and escorting visibly intoxicated people from the stadium. However, the security personnel made no effort to examine Al's cooler.

Al consumed a six-pack of beer and half a bottle of wine during the first half of the game. He became extremely rowdy and had an encounter with a security officer, who observed that Al was drunk.

During the half-time festivities, Al began dancing in the aisles and then ran to the walkway at the top of the stands. He leaped over the wall at the far end of the walkway, landing on the concrete steps 20 feet below. He sustained serious injuries and was rushed to the hospital.

The emergency room physician injected Al with an antibiotic. Because of the alcohol in his system, Al had an adverse reaction to this drug which left him permanently paralyzed.

Investigation has revealed that at the time of the incident, three manufacturers marketed this specific drug. The hospital has invoices showing the purchase of the drug from all three manufacturers, but has no record of which manufacturer supplied the batch that was administered to Al.

Discuss and evaluate the potential parties, claims, and defenses in a lawsuit to be instituted by Al.

83.   The state of Eden requires in-state and out-of-state distillers of alcoholic beverages who sell to Eden wholesalers to be licensed by the Eden Alcoholic Beverage Commission ("ABC"). The Eden statute regulating the distillers' sale of alcoholic beverages to Eden wholesalers provides:

    (a)   Each licensed distiller shall file with the Eden ABC, on or before the third day of each month, a schedule of the prices it will charge for alcoholic beverages sold to Eden wholesalers during that month.

    (b)   No prices other than those listed in the schedule filed pursuant to paragraph (a) shall be charged to Eden wholesalers.

    (c)   The prices listed in the schedule filed pursuant to paragraph (a) shall be no higher than the lowest prices to be charged by the licensed distiller during that month to any wholesaler located in any of the three states bordering the State of Eden.

    (d)   No distiller shall sell its alcoholic beverages to an Eden wholesaler at a price higher than the lowest price at which it sells its alcoholic beverages during the same month to any wholesaler located in any of the three states bordering the State of Eden.

The statute further provides that any violation is punishable by a fine or by suspension or revocation of the distiller's license.

On December 2, 1987, Boozinc, a licensed distiller of sloe gin, filed a price of $9 per liter with the Eden ABC. Later in December, in response to a competitor's lower price, Boozinc sold sloe gin for $7.50 per liter to wholesalers located in states bordering Eden. Boozinc continued to charge Eden wholesalers $9 per liter through the end of December.

After due notice and a hearing, the Eden ABC found that Boozinc had violated the statute, and it suspended Boozinc's license for 30 days. In accordance with the Eden Rules of Civil Procedure, Boozinc appealed the ABC's decision to the Eden appellate court.

Discuss and evaluate the legal arguments Boozinc should raise on appeal.

84.   Paul, Tony, and Eddie are each 18-year-old students at Hanover High School. The three boys, being lifelong friends, did most everything together, even though Paul had been diagnosed as being slightly retarded and is having to attend special programs in school for those who are retarded.

Last Saturday night Tony suggested to Paul and Eddie that they go and raise some extra cash that they might need for the school dance and banquet which is to be held in two weeks. Eddie, who had a part-time job in a gas station, told Tony that he was "OK with money" and needed no more. Tony then explained what he meant to Paul, and the two boys then walked to the most wealthy area of town, consisting of new homes situated on one-acre parcels of land. The boys went to the side, laundry room, door of a house where Tony removed a small pocket screwdriver from his jacket. Tony used the screwdriver to "pop" the lock on the door. The combination of the lock opening and the vibrations activated the silent alarm, notifying the police of the entry into the house.

After walking through the laundry room and kitchen, Paul decided that he was doing a "real dumb thing" and he began to leave. As he did so, he noticed a state police car approaching the driveway. Paul yelled out "it's the cops, let's go." As they ran to the rear of the house, Tony noticed a woman's pocketbook lying on a table. He opened it and removed all of the cash, $175, and several credit cards. Tony then ran to the door with Paul and left the house. Paul ran out of the house so fast that he did not realize that he dropped his school identification card on the floor in the laundry room. This card was found by the police.

The following Monday, two Hanover, NJ, police detectives went to the school named on Paul's card. The principal identified the card as being issued by his school, and also identified Paul as being a student registered in the school. The police informed the principal as to what they believed had occurred. The police went to Paul's locker with the principal and searched it. Contained therein was a small duffle bag containing dirty gym clothing, $175 in cash, and one bottle of beer.

Paul was met outside of his classroom at the end of the period by the principal. Paul was brought into a small conference room adjoining the principal's office and arrested. Paul was told his rights, and advised to call his mother, who turned out not to be at home. Paul, now shaking and crying, began to scream obscenities at the police and the principal before he gained his composure and blurted out: "OK Copper, you got me and Tony and the stuff."

Your employer, Bar Examiners, P.C., the most prestigious law firm in the state, has been hired to represent Paul in this matter. It is your job to write a memo describing possible charges against Paul, possible defenses, and whatever motions need to be filed. Please complete this assignment prior to lunch today.

85.   On March 2, 1989, Karen Client hired Contractor to build her a house at an agreed price of $1 million. It was also agreed that the construction on the house would be completed by, and ready for occupancy, no later than May 30, 1989. In conjunction with this agreement,

Contractor hired Mr. Taper to install sheetrock and frame the house. Karen approved of the contract between Taper and Contractor, with Taper being paid the sum of $200,000. In writing Karen stated "that by putting forth her approval of Taper, she agrees to no liability in favor of either Taper or Contractor with respect to each other or anyone else."

Taper completed his portion of the project on April 1. On April 2, Contractor notified Karen that the construction project could not be properly completed on time due to the eighth heart attack, and death, of the job superintendent. The following morning, April 3, Karen terminated the employ of Contractor and hired the Expensive Construction Company to complete the job at a price of $1.1 million.

As of this date, Taper has not been paid any money from any source with respect to his bill for $200,000. In Karen's mail today she received a bill for construction services by Contractor in the amount of $600,000; this to include the fees which Taper has billed Contractor.

Karen Client asks your advice on what to do before she makes any payment or puts forth an action. As an associate attorney on your firm's legal staff, write Karen a client letter advising her what she should do.

86.   Write a memo based on the issues presented in the case that follows for your employer, a judge for whom you clerk.

Brenda's fifth birthday party was an event which her father, Hank, could hardly wait to see. He planned many lavish festivities to help commemorate the event in addition to the party. Jody, John's daughter, who lived next door, who was also five, arrived at the party with a big box containing a "fun toy which daddy thinks is just right for us all to play with."

When Brenda opened the box she found "Barbie's and Freddie's Real Life Hawaiian Volcano Kit." The gift was ready for assembly and contained two test tubes of fluid which, when activated, would cause smoke and lava to come from the volcano. The label on the box stated that the gift was to be used by those over the age of five. Also, the enclosed instruction sheet warned against any movement of the fluids prior to using "as it may cause a minor explosion on mixing."

Soon the phone rang and Hank answered. It was the captain of his police bowling league team asking Hank to pick up doughnuts and coffee before the night's events. While Hank was on the phone, Brenda and Jody started to play with the volcano. Wishing they were now in Hawaii, the two girls went into the living room and put on some Don Ho music videos. While Brenda and Jody listened to the golden voice of Don Ho, and Hank retrieved doughnuts, Brenda's 17-month-old brother began to play with the volcano kit, tossing the kit all over the room and agitating the test tubes. Little brother became bored and left the room so that he too could listen to Don Ho. After watching Don Ho, Brenda and Jody went back to the volcano kit and tried to make it erupt. When the fluids were poured from the test tubes they ignited, causing an explosion which resulted in permanent disfigurement of both Brenda and Jody.

As of this morning, all of the parties who could possibly be involved in the suit have settled their actions, except for those involving Hank and John. Your memo should discuss possible liability questions with respect to Hank and John.

87.   On January 1, 1981, Lestor the lessor leased to Leslie Lost a one-family home for a period of five years at a rent of $900 per month; all utilities included. Rent was due and owing on the first day of the month; a provision in the agreement stated that if the rent was not made timely, by the seventh day of the month, the tenant, Leslie Lost, would be in violation of her agreement and in default.

The parties agreed that Ms. Lost would be provided with the option to renew her lease for another five-year period with the rent to remain at $900 per month. It was also stated that during the tenure of the lease Ms. Lost, at her option, could purchase the house at 5% less than fair market value, as determined by the New Jersey division of property taxation.

Ms. Lost paid her rent on time for the entire five-year period. On January 1, 1986, Ms. Lost paid to Lestor $900, but made no comment about renewing the lease or picking up her option. Four months later, on April 30, Ms. Lost gave Lestor $900 as April's rent and also sent to Lestor a registered letter stating that she wanted to pick up the option to renew the lease for only one year.

Lestor rejected this proposal and notified Leslie Lost that she had 30 days to vacate the home. At this time Ms. Lost tried to pick up her option to purchase the home; Lestor refused to sell.

Lestor desires to rid himself of anything and everything concerning Leslie Lost with respect to the contractual lease and option to sell/purchase the property.

Draft a memo to Lestor advising him of his possible rights and liabilities.

88. On February 1, Olivia Seezun contracted to sell her one-family home to Dee Feezence for the sum of $100,000. The contract called for an initial deposit of $20,000 followed by two payments of $40,000 each on March 1 and April 1. Because Seezun was planning an extensive trip abroad, she deposited a duly executed deed with a local attorney, Barry Sterr, who agreed to act as an escrow agent. Seezun specifically instructed Sterr to release the deed to Feezence only after the remaining two installments were paid. Notwithstanding these instructions, Sterr gave the deed to Feezence two weeks later and before any further payments had been made. Feezence promptly recorded the deed at approximately the same time that Seezun returned from her trip and resumed occupancy of the home. Shortly thereafter, Feezence sold the property to Bonnie Fyde for $130,000. The deed was recorded at once. Fyde knew nothing of the escrow transaction, but was surprised to find the home occupied by Seezun. Fyde has demanded that Seezun vacate the premises.

Miffed at the turn of events, on February 26, Seezun has retained you as her attorney and has requested your analysis of her rights and liabilities.

Prepare a written reply to your client.

89. John and David are employees of the Totally Magnificent Diamond Conglomerate, of Great Rock, New Jersey, which engages in mass distribution of uncut diamonds throughout the United States.

Because the company had been experiencing substantial losses due to pilferage, it requested all employees to submit to a polygraph test. All complied except John, who refused because he was not allowed to have his attorney present during the examination.

Upon John's refusal, the company's security officer placed an electronic eavesdropping device on John's telephone line outside his apartment building. The security officers monitored a telephone call wherein John stated to David: "They are on to us: let's move the merchandise to Florida now! Meet me at the summer house."

The security officers immediately located John's car, attached an electronic tracking device underneath, and notified the local police. The security officers, along with the police, followed John to a secluded house owned by John's estranged wife, Mary. John was stopped as he approached the front door. The police reached in his pocket and found the house keys. Both the police and the security officers entered the house and started looking for the diamonds.

In the basement, a security officer discovered several tin cans, each containing uncut diamonds inside false bottoms. Each can contained a shipping label: "Seaside Foods, Pebble Beach, Florida."

You are the assistant prosecutor assigned to handle this matter. Your supervisor has requested a memorandum setting forth the potential charges, available defenses, and anticipated pretrial motions.

Write the memorandum.

90. State legislature has recently legalized casino gambling. A Casino Watchdog Commission ("CWC") has been statutorily created and authorized to regulate every aspect of the gambling industry, including the screening, hiring, and licensing of casino employees. The enabling statute expressly prohibits all persons from obtaining casino employment unless they have first obtained a valid casino employee license from the CWC.

Pursuant to its statutory authority, the CWC has promulgated regulations governing procedures for licensing casino employees. These procedures require an applicant to complete a 24-page form which includes the following:

    a.   A detailed questionnaire about the individual's background, including areas such as marital and family status, professional and personal associates, sexual preference, and physical and mental history;

    b.   A release to be signed by the applicant authorizing direct disclosure of information to the CWC from such sources as employers, financial institutions, governmental agencies, and private clubs; and

    c.   A consent (also to be signed by the applicant) to warrantless searches whenever an employee is present in a licensed casino facility.

Anna Applicante applied for casino employment but refused to answer a number of questions on the form or to sign the required release form and consent form.

Applicante has consulted your law firm for advice, seeking to challenge the licensing procedure.

Prepare a memorandum setting forth Applicante's causes of action, the legal basis for each, and the defenses to be anticipated.

91. Crash and Gash attended a Super Bowl party at Gimpy's home. During the game, Gimpy served his friends four beers each. Gleeful that their team had won the game, Crash, Gash, and Gimpy decided to drive to Town Tavern to celebrate. Since Crash could hold his liquor and appeared to be sober, everyone agreed that Crash should drive.

The three friends arrived at Town Tavern at 11 p.m., where they celebrated until 3 a.m. During that time, the bartender served eight rounds of drinks to each of them. Since Gimpy had hosted the Super Bowl party, Crash bought four rounds of drinks and Gash bought four rounds of drinks.

At 3:05 a.m. Crash, while driving his friends home, swerved off the road and hit a telephone pole. None of them had fastened their seat belts. Gimpy, who was sitting in the front seat, broke his leg while attempting to avoid being thrown into the windshield. Gash suffered a small wound to his arm as a result of the accident. If Gash had been wearing his seat belt, he probably would have suffered a significant spinal cord injury.

Gash and Gimpy have asked your law firm to represent them. Senior Partner has asked you to write a memorandum analyzing the causes of action of Gash and Gimpy against any potential party, the defenses which may be asserted, and whether your firm should handle both cases.

Write the memorandum.

92. Mr. and Mrs. Jones decided in 1985 to add a patio to the rear of their home. They entered into a contract with Contractor to design and build the patio for $10,000. The patio was completed that year. In 1986, the Joneses sold their home to Mr. and Mrs. Smith. The purchase contract provided that the sale was subject to a "satisfactory engineering inspection" and made "upon the knowledge of the parties as to the value of whatever buildings are upon the land and not on any representations made as to character or quality." It further provides that "no representations have been made by any of the parties except as set forth herein."

In 1988, the Smiths discovered that the patio was beginning to separate from the wall of the home and that the patio floor was beginning to buckle. They hired a consultant who advised them that the problem was the result of improper design and installation of the patio.

Mr. and Mrs. Smith have consulted your senior partner regarding any claims they may have. She has asked you to prepare a memorandum setting out any causes of action available to the Smiths, including the possibility of success of each.

Prepare the memorandum.

93. Able Contracting Co., a general contractor, was asked by Developer to bid on construction of a retail store. Able sent a copy of Developer's plans and specifications for the store to Electro, an electrical contractor, requesting that Electro submit to Able a bid on the electrical work for the store on or before February 1, 1989.

On February 1, 1989, Able received a telegram from Electro which read:

> Can do electrical work on Developer's store for $22,500. Breakdown of costs are:
>
> | Materials | $15,200 |
> |---|---|
> | Labor | 13,100 |
> | Overhead & Profit | 4,200 |
> | TOTAL | $22,500 |

Able used Electro's bid of $22,500 in computing its overall bid of $230,000. Developer accepted Able's bid and entered into a written contract with Able on February 10, 1989.

On February 11, 1989, before Able had notified Electro that Developer had accepted Able's bid, Able received another telegram from Electro:

> Made mistake in adding up bid in previous telegram. Bid should be $32,500, not $22,500. Can't possibly do the job for $22,500!

Developer has refused to negotiate its contract with Able and has demanded that Able construct the store for the bid price of $230,000. Able, in turn, has demanded that Electro complete the electrical work for its bid price of $22,500. Electro has refused.

Discuss and evaluate the rights, liabilities, and remedies of Able, Electro, and Developer.

94. Al liked to gamble, particularly at cards. He often played cards at Ben's house. One night while playing at Ben's, he lost a great amount of money. When he discussed his losses with Chuck, Chuck told Al that he had also lost large sums of money playing cards with Ben, and he believed that Ben used marked cards.

Al and Chuck decided that they would go to Ben's house and retrieve their money. Upon arriving at Ben's place, they found Ben and three other men in a card game. Al and Chuck demanded that Ben return all the money they had lost. When he refused, they grabbed all the money on the table and ran out of the door. One of the players chased them. Chuck drew a pistol from his pocket, fired at the person, and wounded him in the leg.

Al is a client of the firm in which you are an associate. The senior partner has asked you to provide him with a memorandum setting out the charges that may be brought against Al and the defenses that may be available to him.

95. On July 1, 1987, Bea Holden found herself in financial difficulty and arranged to borrow the sum of $50,000 from Sol Vent. As security for the loan, Holden mortgaged her home to Vent. Among other things, the mortgage provided for annual interest of 8% and equal monthly payments to amortize the loan in 30 years. The mortgage also contained the following clause:

> ACCELERATION: If there be any change in the ownership of the mortgaged premises, the unpaid balance secured by this mortgage shall, at the option of the mortgagee, become immediately due and payable.

The mortgage was properly recorded.

On April 1, 1988, Holden listed her property for sale with Phil D. Coffers, a local realtor. Prevailing interest rates for home mortgages had increased sharply, and buyers were scarce. However, Coffers found a prospective purchaser, Hugo Broke, whose credit rating prevented him from obtaining a mortgage from an institutional lender, but who was willing to assume the Vent mortgage. Accordingly, a contract was signed by the parties which provided for a purchase price of $100,000 payable as follows:

$20,000	deposit
50,000	assumption of existing mortgage
25,000	loan from Seller
5,000	balance due at closing

Since the amount due on the Vent mortgage would be slightly less than $50,000 at time of settlement, the balance due at closing was to be adjusted as necessary to equal the total purchase price of $100,000.

To avoid the effect of the acceleration clause in the Vent mortgage, Coffers suggested that Broke not take title, but rather become a contract purchaser in possession. A deed would be signed by Holden and held in escrow by Coffers until the Vent mortgage was paid in full. At that time the deed would be delivered to Broke, subject to the balance due on the loan to Holden. The parties agreed, and suitable language was inserted in the contract which was duly recorded. Vent was not consulted.

Broke took possession of the premises on August 1, 1988, and began making monthly payments directly to Vent. After three months, he ceased making payments. As a result of a title search preliminary to a mortgage foreclosure action, Vent discovered the recorded contract between Holden and Broke. He became incensed by the fact that he was not notified of the Holden-Broke transaction. The fact that the prevailing interest rate for home mortgages had risen to 13% made him even angrier.

Vent wishes to retain you to take legal action on his behalf. He has requested a letter from you analyzing his possible remedies and chances of success.

Write the letter.

96.   Active Radio Corp. ("ARC") is the owner of a factory and surrounding property formerly owned by Glowco. Fifty years ago, Glowco manufactured illuminated watch dials and other fluorescent products. Glowco extracted radium from ore that was brought to the plant from an out-of-state location. The solid waste byproducts of the radium operation were deposited by Glowco on vacant portions of its property.

Over the years, the radium waste underwent a natural decaying process resulting in the gradual release of the radioactive gas known as radon. Inhalation of radon particles has been found to cause cancer.

Glowco ceased operations in 1945, and the property was vacant for several years. Glowco sold the property in 1948, and the property was resold twice thereafter before ARC purchased it in 1980. ARC had no knowledge of Glowco's radium operation and its dumping of waste onto the property.

Two years after its acquisition of the property, the environmental authorities informed ARC that elevated levels of radon particles existed on the site and demanded immediate remedial action. ARC was required to restrict access to the affected area and reduce employee working hours. ARC retained an engineering firm to perform testing and instituted a costly ventilation system. Simultaneously, ARC constructed an addition to the rear portion of the building to enclose the area where the radium waste had been dumped. To the surprise and dismay of ARC, this created a dangerous concentration of radon gas. ARC was eventually required to vacate the property and relocate its plant to a new site.

ARC has learned that employees of Glowco wore protective aprons, that certain of Glowco's employees had developed cancer, and that Glowco's chief engineer had become sterile while working at Glowco. It has been determined that the radon contamination is confined solely to the premises purchased by ARC.

You have been consulted for a legal opinion as to whether ARC has any common law cause of action against Glowco.

Write a memorandum of law detailing the rights and remedies available to ARC. Limit your discussion to the prevailing common law rather than any legislative enactments.

97.   Eyeway Cinema, located in Flick City, operates a drive-in-movie theater. The screen of the movie theater is visible from the adjacent highway. Concerned with increasing traffic problems in front of the theater as well as teenagers viewing the movies from a nearby parking lot, Flick City enacted the following ordinance, effective July, 1, 1988, which provides:

> It shall be unlawful for any drive-in theater in Flick City to exhibit any motion picture in which the human bare buttocks, human female bare breast, or human genitalia are shown, if such motion picture is visible from any public street or public place.

To further control traffic in the area of the theater, Flick City constructed a concrete center median along the highway adjacent to Eyeway, which prevents motor vehicles from crossing the highway. Since July 1988, Eyeway's ticket sales have declined by 25%. Concerned about its economic losses, Eyeway has consulted you to commence a suit on its behalf.

Prepare a memorandum discussing and evaluating the arguments which may be raised by Eyeway and Flick City.

98. State University has had a nationally prominent football program for many years. A recent investigation by the American Athletic Association, consisting of public and private educational institutions nationwide, including State University, uncovered serious violations of the rules and regulations of the Association. These included recruiting infractions which implicated the head football coach. After a hearing conducted by the Association in which State University participated and in which Coach was a witness, the Association placed State University on probation for two years. It ordered that further sanctions will be imposed unless Coach is suspended for the probationary period. The president of State University has notified Coach of his intent to impose the required suspension.

As part of his fight against the suspension, Coach granted an interview to the sports editor of the student newspaper in which he disputed the Association's charges. President has directed the paper not to publish the resulting article, and the editorial staff has complied.

Frustrated by his inability to tell his side of the story and threatened by loss of his job, Coach has retained your law firm to institute appropriate action.

Prepare a legal memorandum setting forth Coach's causes of action, the legal basis for each, and the defenses to be anticipated.

99. Pretendo Corp. is in the business of manufacturing video games for the retail market. Media Race, an advertising and public relations firm, has performed promotional services for numerous product lines of Pretendo. Pretendo's corporate officers were so pleased with Media's work that they issued an interoffice memorandum stating that Media was to be awarded all advertising jobs "which it was capable of handling," unless "substantial economic considerations" dictated otherwise.

Two employees of Pretendo, Creep and Crawl, heard that the company was about to release a new game to be known as "Super Maria Sisters." They communicated this fact to a friend, Conniver, a competitor of Media, who submitted an unusually low bid for the advertising contract. In addition, Creep, Crawl, and Conniver sent an anonymous letter to Pretendo claiming that the advertising community regarded Media's work as "juvenile," and that its last campaign was a "costly flop."

Media, which was asked by Pretendo to bid and was capable of doing the promotional work for "Super Maria Sisters," submitted an estimate substantially higher than Conniver's. The job was awarded to Conniver.

You have been consulted by Media and have been asked to provide a legal opinion as to the possible causes of action available against any of the parties involved.

100. On May 1, 1989, Buyer purchased a new car from Dealer for $17,000. A $2,000 down payment was made by Buyer. Dealer provided Buyer with financing for the balance of the purchase price consisting of 60 equal monthly installments of $350. Dealer offered all new car buyers the following warranty:

> Dealer warrants each new car. This Warranty covers any repairs and
> needed adjustments to correct defects in materials and workmanship.
> Dealer will make any repairs and adjustments (parts and/or labor) for

12 months at no charge. No other Warranties, express or implied, will cover this vehicle.

On May 10, 1989, the car's cruise control failed to operate properly and a warning light flashed "STOP ENGINE." The car was returned to Dealer the next day, and redelivered to Buyer three weeks later. At that time, Dealer explained that the problem was caused by a malfunction of the car's electrical system. From mid-June to mid-August of 1989, the car was returned to Dealer on three separate occasions for the same problem. After the last such instance, Buyer drove the car for two weeks without difficulty, but in constant fear that the warning light would again flash.

On August 30, 1989, Buyer called Dealer stating that he no longer wanted the car, and that he would make no further monthly installment payments. The next day, Buyer left the car in Dealer's lot with the keys in the vehicle and told Dealer: "You will hear from my lawyer."

Dealer notified Buyer on October 1, 1989, that the car would be resold in a week if Buyer did not bring the payments current and pick up the car. Dealer sold the car on October 15, 1989, for $12,000.

Dealer has sought your legal advice. He would prefer to settle the matter to avoid the potential expense of litigation. Dealer has asked you to prepare a letter containing your legal analysis of the claims he could assert against Buyer, the claims Buyer could assert against him, and the probability of success of each claim.

101. On July 1, 1986, Ty and Wy Knott purchased a one-family home in Suburbia for $100,000. To finance the purchase, they borrowed $40,000 from their daughter, Blanche, for whom they signed a note and mortgage. The mortgage provided for payment of principal and interest in a lump sum at the end of two years.

Soon after taking occupancy, there was considerable marital discord between the spouses, although they continued to reside together in the home. However, each expressly disinherited the other in their respective wills.

In June of 1987, Blanche transferred the mortgage by written assignment to "my father Ty individually" for a consideration of $4,000. Ty never disclosed the assignment to Wy and the assignment was not recorded. Upon the death of Ty one year later, Wy succeeded to sole ownership of the home as surviving tenant by the entireties. The home's value had appreciated greatly since its purchase by the Knotts.

When the note and mortgage became due on July 1, 1988, Ty's estate commenced suit against Wy for payment of $40,000 plus accrued interest on the ground that the estate was now the holder of the mortgage, which remained as a lien on the property. Wy counterclaimed, seeking either a complete discharge of the mortgage obligation or partial reimbursement from the estate of her late husband.

Your law firm has been retained by Wy Knott.

Prepare an office memorandum to the senior partner setting forth the merits for your client's position.

102. Al is the proprietor of a liquor store located in Peach Tree County, New Jersey. At approximately 10 p.m. one evening, Al was counting the day's receipts while Ed, his employee, was in the rear storeroom recording the inventory. Suddenly, two men wearing masks entered the store, brandishing hand guns. One of the men yelled, "Give me all the cash from the register!" As Ed walked out of the storeroom, he startled the gunmen and was shot and killed instantly.

The gunmen grabbed the money from the register along with a small green felt bag containing a diamond bracelet inscribed "Happy 25th Anniversary—Al" and fled the store.

Approximately two weeks later, William and Robert, based upon the description provided by Al, were arrested and advised of their rights.

Two days later, Detective David from Stanford County, New Jersey, unaware of the pending charges, interviewed Robert regarding various crimes that had occurred in his county. During the course of the questioning, Robert was asked if he owned a hand gun, wherein he blurted out, "William shot him; not me!" He then provided the details of the events at the liquor store and told Detective David where the bracelet could be found. Detective David reported this information to the Peach Tree County Detectives. The detectives proceeded to an apartment leased to William's fiancee, where the bracelet was hidden.

They knocked on the door, whereupon Philip, age 11, let them in. The detectives proceeded to the bedroom and discovered the gun and the diamond bracelet in the lower cabinet drawer underneath some clothing.

William and Robert have come to your law firm seeking representation.

The senior partner, a corporate attorney, has requested that you prepare a memorandum of law setting forth the probable charges, defenses, any pretrial motions to be raised, the likelihood of the success of such motions, and any difficulties anticipated in representing their interests.

Write the memorandum.

103. Dick is brought to trial on an indictment charging him with larceny of a dangerous drug, a statutory offense. The prosecution's theory of the case, as revealed by its opening statement, is that Phil saw Dick enter Phil's Pharmacy, loiter about the prescription counter, reach behind the counter, grab two bottles, and flee by car. Phil called police officers, who arrested Dick after a lengthy high-speed chase.

At the trial before a jury, the following events occur:

(a)   The prosecution offers in evidence a properly authenticated transcript by Officer Oats, given during a previous trial of Dick for reckless driving, based on the high-speed chase from Phil's Pharmacy. Oats's testimony was that during that chase and while Dick's car was passing over a bridge, two objects were ejected from Dick's car window and into the river below. It is stipulated that Dick was represented by counsel at the earlier trial and that Oats is now deceased.

(b)   The prosecution offers the testimony of Phil that the bottles seized by Dick were labeled "DLD," that the bottles were the original labeled containers received from the supplier, and that the bottles had not been opened.

(c)   The prosecution requests the court to take judicial notice that "DLD" is a derivative of opium. The statute under which Dick is prosecuted does not list "DLD" as a "dangerous drug," but does define dangerous drugs to include "any derivative of opium." In support of its request, the prosecution offers for the court's inspection a standard pharmacological dictionary, which defines "DLD" as an opium derivative.

(d)   The prosecution offers the testimony of Dick's divorced wife, Win, that during her marriage to Dick, the latter frequently used narcotics but attempted to conceal that fact from Win.

Assume all appropriate objections are made by Dick.

How should the court rule on each of the prosecution's offers and requests? Discuss.

104. Dave, a waiter at Bill's Cafe ("Cafe"), is on trial by jury for the crime of arson, defined by statute as setting a building afire either intentionally or with gross and reckless disregard for human life.

(a)   The prosecution's first witness was Sam, a cook at Cafe, who testified, over objection, that just prior to the time Cafe burst into flames, Bart, another waiter, ran into the kitchen shouting that Dave was spilling gasoline all over the lobby, and that someone should call the police because what Dave was doing would kill them all. Bart cannot be located by either party.

(b)   Ellen, assistant manager of Grill Restaurant ("Grill"), was called as a witness by the prosecution and testified, over objection, that Dave had been a busboy at Grill before he became employed at Cafe, and that she had fired him after she found Dave showing other employees how to construct a gasoline bomb.

(c)   After the prosecution rested, Dave took the witness stand and testified that he had been ordered to clean the lobby doors and ornamental brasswork at Cafe, and that he was using gasoline as a cleaning solution in that work when a patron entered and flipped a lit cigarette butt on the lobby floor, igniting the gasoline. On cross-examination, over objection, the prosecution elicited the fact from Dave that, two years earlier, he had been expelled from college for cheating on a final exam.

(d)   The defense next called Dr. Hix, a chemist, who testified, over objection, that based on his pretrial review of standard scientific treatises, as well as his own experimentation, it was his expert opinion that although use of gasoline as a cleaning fluid cannot be recommended, its use for that purpose in normal circumstances is reasonably safe, if the gasoline vapor is kept from contact with hot filaments or burning objects.

(e)   In rebuttal, the prosecution, over objection, asked the judge to take judicial notice that gasoline vapor is so combustible that use of gasoline as a cleaning fluid in space occupied by other persons constituted gross and reckless disregard for human life, as a matter of law. The court stated that it took such notice.

Assuming that all objections were properly made, should the evidence objected to in items (a) through (e) have been admitted? Discuss.

105. In 1979, Dale confessed to car theft, but the confession was inadmissible in a prosecution for that theft because of a lack of a *Miranda* warning. Dale was acquitted of that charge.

In 1988, Dale was brought to trial on a charge of grand larceny. The indictment charged that Dale wrongfully obtained possession of a 1985 Buick Skylark, the lawful property of Acme, a corporation engaged in the auto rental business, and converted it to his own use. The car was discovered wrecked and abandoned. At the trial by jury, the following occurred:

(a)   The prosecution's first witness was Mang, who testified that he is a supervisory employee of Acme and is thoroughly familiar with the computerized system by which the company keeps track of the status and location of cars owned by the company. Mang further testified that whenever a car is leased or returned, the details of the transaction are entered into the Acme computer by the employee handling the transaction and that the corporation relies on the computer records exclusively for information on its cars. Finally, Mang testified that he has by proper means consulted the company's data bank and that the car that Dale is charged with stealing is shown by the computer as within company possession and not out on rental.

(b)   The prosecution then called Gum, the officer who discovered the car, who testified that at the time of recovery, the car contained several shirts bearing a laundry mark DAL.

(c)   The prosecution introduced evidence that the car in question was a 1985 Buick Skylark. The prosecution then rested. The defense then moved for a directed verdict of acquittal on the ground of an absence of proof that the value of the stolen property exceeded $100, the minimum amount necessary to support a charge of grand larceny. The court denied the motion.

(d)   After Dale testified in his own behalf on direct examination that "I have never stolen a car in my life," the prosecution introduced evidence of Dale's 1979 confession.

Assume that in each instance all appropriate objections were made.

Were items of evidence (a), (b), and (d) properly admitted, and was defendant's motion for a directed verdict (c) properly denied? Discuss.

106. An automobile, owned and operated by Paul, collided with a taxicab driven by Don and owned by Cabco. Paul and Don were injured. Vicky, a passenger in Paul's automobile, suffered a broken leg. While she was undergoing necessary surgery to repair the fracture, she suffered a cardiac arrest and died. Action was brought in the state court by Paul against Cabco for personal injuries. The parties stipulated to the above facts.

At the trial by jury, the following occurred:

(a) Paul testified: "After the accident, I went over to the cab. Don was hurting real bad, and Don said, 'This wouldn't have happened if I hadn't been in such a hurry to pick up a fare.'"

(b) Cabco's counsel asked Paul on cross-examination if he had ever had a traffic accident. Paul answered: "No." Cabco's counsel then introduced a properly authenticated copy of a three-year-old unrelated conviction of Paul for vehicular manslaughter, a felony.

(c) Vicky's physician, Doc, testified as a witness for Cabco that, while Vicky was being prepared for surgery, he asked her how the accident happened, and she responded: "Don't tell anybody, Doc, but Paul and I were smoking marijuana. I dropped a lighted joint, and Paul had his head down looking for it when we hit the cab."

Assume that in each instance all appropriate objections were made. Were the items of evidence properly admitted? Discuss.

107. Parks, a patron of Delta Theatre, after watching the motion picture, started to descend a carpeted stairway to the men's room. He fell when halfway down the stairs and broke his leg. Two months later he sued Delta for his injuries, alleging that his foot had caught in a tear in the carpet which he could not see in the dim light, and that Delta had negligently permitted the carpet to remain in its dangerous condition. Delta denied there was any defect in the carpet and alleged that Parks had fallen because he was intoxicated.

The following evidence was admitted at trial:

(a) Parks introduced the testimony of Ward that Ward was at the bottom of the stairway when Parks fell, and that an unknown person rushed down the stairway to Parks and said, "I saw you trip on that tear in the carpet. Are you hurt?"

(b) Parks introduced the testimony of Carter that a week after the accident Carter was called to lay a new carpet and that the old carpet had been removed before his arrival.

(c) Delta introduced the testimony of Adams that he had sat next to Parks; that Parks had spoken to him just before Parks left his seat; that Adams followed Parks as he was going down the stairway and saw Parks fall; that in his opinion Parks was intoxicated and that his impression was that Parks fell because of his intoxication.

(d) Delta introduced the testimony of Martin, manager of the theater, that prior to Parks's fall, thousands of persons had used the stairway, that there had been no complaints and no reports of any person falling.

(e) Delta introduced testimony of Attorney Nate that at Parks's request he visited Parks a month after the accident and that during the visit Parks said to him: "I fell on the stairway in Delta Theatre. I had too many drinks and I think that is why I fell. But I hear Delta has put a new carpet on the stairway and I want you to sue for me and say the old carpet had a tear in it and that is why I fell, although as far as I know, the carpet was O.K." Nate further testified that he then refused to represent Parks.

Assuming that in each instance all appropriate objections were made, did the court err in admitting items of evidence (a) through (e)? Discuss.

108. In a rape conviction against Roe, the following events occurred at the trial by jury:

(a) Adam, a neighbor of the victim, Tess, testified that within five minutes after the rape was alleged to have occurred, Tess ran to his house sobbing and said that she had just been raped by a man with a large brown blemish on his left arm.

(b) Detective Cable testified that, on receiving Tess's report, he examined the file of known sex offenders, that Roe was listed as a previously convicted rapist, and that Roe was described as having a blemish on his left arm.

(c) Tess testified that she saw Roe on the sidewalk, recognized the blemish on Roe's left arm, and told a police officer that Roe was the man who had raped her.

(d) Roe's wife voluntarily testified for the prosecution that Roe returned home on the night in question in an agitated state with scratches on his arm.

(e) Roe testified in his defense and denied the act, saying that he had never been near Tess's house. In rebuttal, the prosecution offered one of Roe's shoes, seized in an illegal search of Roe's house. The shoe was introduced together with expert testimony that a shoe print identical to the shoe print made by Roe's shoe had been located outside the window the rapist had used to enter Tess's house.

(f) At the prosecution's request, the judge ordered Roe to bare his left arm for the jury's inspection. Roe refused. The judge allowed the prosecutor to argue in closing argument that Roe's refusal was an attempt to hide evidence, from which the jury might infer guilt.

Assume all proper motions and objections were timely made. Did the court err in admitting the testimony in items (a) through (d), in admitting the shoe and testimony in item (e), or in permitting the prosecutor's argument in item (f)? Discuss.

109. Frankie discovered that his wife, Lolita, was having an affair with her music teacher, Chad. Distraught, Frankie confided in his business partner, Johnnie, and said, "You know how to handle this problem." Johnnie nodded his head in the affirmative and took off in the company van, after Frankie gave him the keys.

At approximately 11:00 p.m., Johnnie and two friends waited in the parking lot at the rear of the music school. Lolita's lover, Chad, exited the music school. Johnnie confronted him, threw a burlap sack over his head and struck him several times. Johnnie and his companions tied Chad's hands and dumped him in the rear of the van.

As they were driving along Interstate 295, they continually beat Chad, ultimately breaking his arm. After driving approximately 10 miles, the vehicle stopped and one of the assailants said, "Let's get rid of him for good." Chad, still bound and hooded, was left standing in the highway as the van drove off. Moments later, a motorist struck Chad, killing him instantly.

Upon reading a newspaper account of Chad's death, Lolita panicked, suspecting that Frankie had discovered the affair. She contacted the police and was interviewed by Detective Casanova to whom she revealed her affair and suspicions.

Detective Casanova convinced Lolita to wear an electronic transmitter. Later that evening, while at home, Lolita confronted Frankie with her suspicions. He replied, "If you don't want the same thing, you'd better keep your mouth shut." After Detective Casanova heard this statement through the transmission device, he interviewed Frankie and Johnnie at their office.

Frankie and Johnnie have retained your law firm in anticipation of being charged. The senior partner has assigned the matter to you requesting a memorandum setting forth the potential charges, available defenses and any anticipated pretrial motions.

Write the memorandum.

110. At approximately 7:00 a.m., John, who had borrowed his fiancee's car to get a newspaper, stopped at a corner newsstand. Suddenly, Al and Steve, both age 17 and armed with handguns, entered his vehicle through the rear doors. John was told, "Don't look back, or I'll put a bullet in your head. Just drive." John panicked and as he sped off with the assailants, struck and killed Tommy, who was chasing a basketball in the street.

After approximately two miles, John was ordered to stop the motor vehicle. He was blindfolded, bound, and left on the side of the roadway.

Al and Steve drove the vehicle to "Discount Auto Parts," a front for an illegal "strip shop." Frank, the owner of "Discount," paid Al and Steve $500 each for their "services." The vehicle was immediately dismantled and the parts were shipped to affiliated "strip shops" throughout the state.

At approximately 1:00 p.m., Al and Steve attempted to sneak into their third period gym class at Sunset High School and were observed by Officer Ruthless, an off-duty patrolman who had been hired by the board of education to maintain order. While outside the boys' locker room, Officer Ruthless saw Al place a brown paper bag into his locker and heard him say, "I hope that kid with the basketball is OK."

Officer Ruthless then instructed Al and Steve to accompany him to the principal's office, where he told the principal of his observations. The principal instructed Steve to enter his office while Al remained in the adjacent office. Officer Ruthless stationed himself in front of the principal's office door to observe Al and to prevent Steve from leaving.

The principal began to question Steve, who replied, "Why should I answer any questions from you without a lawyer?" The principal became enraged at Steve's remark and threatened him with disciplinary action. The principal continued questioning Steve for approximately two hours, when Steve finally confessed to the principal and implicated Al and Frank, the strip shop owner.

The principal and Officer Ruthless than proceeded to Al's locker, opened it, and discovered $1,000 in cash in the paper bag.

You have been assigned by the county prosecutor to prosecute Al, Steve, and Frank. The prosecutor has requested a memorandum analyzing the factual and legal bases for all charges, anticipated defenses, and anticipated prosecutorial and defense motions.

Prepare the memorandum.

111. Adam was the fee owner of a parcel of land bordering the Atlantic Ocean which he named "Windswept." Adam also was the grantee of a riparian grant from the State of New Jersey contiguous to the aforesaid parcel. The riparian grant extended along the entire shoreline of Windswept and seaward a distance of 500 feet to the exterior line.

In 1985 Adam conveyed all of his interest in his seaside property to Brown by warranty deed which contained the following recital:

> Under and subject to an easement to be given by the party of the first
> part to the State of New Jersey for the area from the mean high water
> line to 150 feet westerly thereof, the purpose of said easement being to
> reserve said area as a public bathing beach.

There has been no other instrument purporting to convey an easement on the subject property to the State.

Windswept is in an area of the shore where there is significant natural movement of sand resulting in dramatic shoreline changes. Additionally, approximately one-half mile north of Windswept the State has constructed a jetty to assist in the preservation of the shoreline. These factors have resulted in accretion to such a degree that the original grant is now dry land and the mean high water line along Windswept's shore is approximately 50 feet seaward of the location of the exterior line of the riparian grant.

Last year the State for the first time fenced in an area along the shoreline of Windswept extending upland 150 feet from the current mean high water line and established a free public bathing beach. Brown, however, wishes to use his property as a private beach club in which he will sell memberships. The State has refused to close down its beach operation.

Brown has come to the firm in which you are a new associate seeking to find a way to compel the state to terminate the public beach. You have been asked by a firm partner to prepare a memorandum analyzing all arguments available to Brown in a potential lawsuit and the likelihood of success as to each.

Write the memorandum.

112. At 2:30 a.m., Ted, while masked, entered the home of John and Mary seeking money and jewelry. He confronted them and held them at bay by simulating possession of a gun. He shouted, "If I don't get some money quick, you're both dead."

He forced Mary to bind and gag John. Then he searched for money and jewelry. Unable to find anything, he became angry, physically assaulted her, causing her to fall. As she fell, she struck her head against a cabinet, knocking her unconscious. At approximately 3:15 a.m., Ted escaped through a bedroom window. An hour later John was able to free himself, call the police and rush Mary to the hospital, where she died from head injuries. He reported to Officer Smith that he was outraged by watching the assault on Mary.

Six months later, Ted was arrested for a parole violation. Upon his arrest, Officer Smith noticed that Ted had numerous convictions for physically assaulting women. Officer Smith became suspicious and arranged to have Ted submit to a lineup.

John was initially unable to identify Ted as the assailant. Officer Smith then ordered Ted to say "If I don't get some money quick, you're both dead." At first, Ted refused. When he was about to be returned to his cell, he decided to cooperate. As Ted finished speaking, John exclaimed, "That's him! That's him! I will never forget that voice."

You are the public defender assigned to represent Ted on this case. Draft a memorandum analyzing the potential charges, available defenses and any pretrial motions.

Write the memorandum.

113. John suffered a fractured wrist on January 15, 1988, which he alleges Doctor negligently failed to diagnose. John sent his x-rays to Expert for evaluation as to whether Doctor committed malpractice. Expert concluded that the x-rays showed a fractured wrist. However, he lost the x-rays.

Expert prepared a report stating that it was his personal opinion that Doctor committed malpractice. In arriving at his opinion, Expert relied upon his examination of the x-rays. He also relied upon his interview with Adam, the emergency room nurse, in which Adam told Expert that he did not see Doctor examine John's wrist.

In his report, Expert indicated that he was a medical doctor, licensed since 1990. Since that time, he was employed by Hospital in its obstetrics clinic. He further indicated that because of his employment in Hospital, he was able to observe emergency room care by other physicians from time to time.

In preparation for his malpractice trial against Doctor, John asked Faithful, his office manager, to total his medical bills. In December of 1991, Faithful called each of the doctors and hospitals from whom John received medical services to find out the amount of their bills. Faithful prepared a written summary of the medical bills which John intends to use to establish the amount of his medical bills at the time of trial.

Your law firm has been retained to represent Doctor at trial. Senior Partner has asked you to prepare a memorandum outlining the areas in which the expected testimony of John's witnesses can be attacked, the legal basis for each challenge, and the likelihood that the challenge will succeed.

Write the memorandum.

114. Robert Jones, an employee of Z Corp., sustained a serious hand injury in July of 1992, while operating a punch press. When hired as a punch press operator in May of 1992, he had no experience and received no training from Z Corp. on the use of the punch press. There were no instructions as to use of the punch press on either the press itself or in any operator manuals. The accident occurred when his foot inadvertently hit the foot pedal which activated the punch press and crushed his hand. The area where the punch press came down was always accessible and unprotected.

Press Corp. manufactured the punch press in 1949. The foot pedals which activated the punch press had no component part to prevent accidental contact. There were no components around the punch press which kept the operator's hands away from the machine.

In 1952, Johnson Corp. purchased Press Corp.'s assets including all equipment, goodwill, customer lists, and manufacturing plant. Johnson Corp. changed its name to AB Press Corp. and continued to manufacture punch presses at the same plant. Press Corp. was dissolved as a corporate entity.

In 1988, Z Corp. purchased the punch press which was in a used condition. In that same year, a change in the law required that foot pedals be replaced by hand-activating buttons.

AB Press Corp. was aware of the 1988 change in the law requiring hand-activated buttons, but took no steps to notify owners of the punch press, even though it had current owner's lists, including Z Corp.

In 1991, Z Corp. hired Brown Manufacturing Company to rebuild the punch press in the least expensive way. Brown Manufacturing Company made substantial modifications but did not change the foot-activating pedals or add any protective components to the punch press. Brown Manufacturing Company made no express recommendations to Z Corp. as to additional modifications necessary to make sure that the punch press was in conformance with all statutory and safety requirements.

Robert Jones has retained your law firm to represent his interests. Senior Partner has requested that you prepare a legal memorandum identifying which defendants Robert Jones should sue, the causes of actions against each defendant specified, an analysis of the factual and legal basis for each cause of action, an analysis of the factual and legal basis of all available defenses to each defendant, and potential crossclaims.

Write the memorandum.

115. Fred and Joan were married for 30 years when Fred was diagnosed as having cancer. During the last of his many hospital stays, Fred lapsed into unconsciousness and was unable to eat. Joan agreed to the insertion of a nasogastric tube which was used to feed and medicate Fred. She also authorized efforts to resuscitate Fred when he went into cardiac arrest. Unfortunately, these efforts failed.

Grieving at her husband's loss, Joan told the treating physician that she regretted prolonging Fred's suffering. She also told Marie, her only child, that she hoped to go peacefully when her time came.

Shortly after Fred's death, Joan spoke to her minister concerning the use of extraordinary means to prolong life. Joan was assured that such efforts were not required by her faith. Joan also discussed the concept of a "living will" with her attorney, Mr. Jones.

Several years later, Joan suffered extensive brain damage in a car accident. Hoping for some improvement, Joan's daughter Marie, authorized various efforts to stabilize her mother's condition. However, when Joan failed to improve, Marie asked that all extraordinary means to prolong her mother's life be terminated. Dr. Peters, who cared for Joan on a daily basis, declined. It was his opinion that Joan reacted to certain stimuli and, therefore, could not be characterized as being in a persistent, vegetative state.

Upset that her mother's wishes were not being honored, Marie secured the services of Dr. Morgan, a neurologist renowned for his study of comatose patients. Although Dr. Morgan had no written record of Joan's reactions during his three-hour examination, he concluded that she was in a persistent and irreversible vegetative state based upon his recollection of her responses to stimuli.

Marie has also discovered among her mother's papers, an undated, unsigned handwritten note stating:

> Must finalize living will—
> it is important to die with dignity
> not to continue life by artificial means

Your law firm has been retained by Marie to commence legal action seeking to remove her mother from all artificial means of life support. The senior partner has asked you to prepare a memorandum analyzing all available evidence, addressing particularly its reliability and trustworthiness and considering whether the available evidence meets the requisite standard of proof that Joan, if competent, would decline continued medical treatment.

Prepare the memorandum.

116. On April 30, 1993 at 9:30 p.m., Tom Jones, 17 years old, and his brother, Ed, 15 years old, were walking on Green Street in Alpha, New Jersey. Green Street is in a residential area and the rear of the residences abut railroad tracks owned by Toot Train Company, a privately owned company. The entire length of the railroad tracks is fenced in on Toot's property and Toot maintains exclusive control over its fences.

Joseph Brown resides on Green Street. Toot's fence, which abuts Brown's property, had a hole in it. Brown was aware that children walked across his property and entered the railroad tracks through this hole. Brown took no steps to repair the fence or post warnings. He never complained to Toot about the hole in the fence.

Tom and Ed Jones crossed Brown's property intending to climb through the hole in the fence onto the railroad tracks. At this point, the fence is one foot from the railroad tracks. Tom climbed through first and was walking on the railroad tracks away from the hole. While Ed climbed through the hole, his leg became entangled in the fence. His upper body was over the railroad tracks.

Tom's back was to Ed and he did not notice that his brother was stuck, nor did he observe one of Toot's trains approaching from his rear. Ed saw the train and tried to yell to his brother. Ed tried to break free. He could not break free from the fence or twist off of the railroad tracks.

Fred Martin, the engineer employed by Toot, was operating the train, proceeding at 40 mph. He saw the boys 500 feet away, applied his brakes and sounded his horn, but the boys did not move. As the train was almost on Ed, he was able to twist off the railroad tracks, and break free from the fence. He avoided being struck, but he observed the train strike Tom. Tom turned around right before he was struck, but it was too late to avoid contact. Ed ran over to Tom and held him as Tom tried to speak to him. After a few minutes, Tom died in Ed's arms. Ed suffered serious emotional harm requiring psychiatric treatment.

Ed and Tom's parents instituted suit as guardian on behalf of Ed and as administrator of Tom's estate. The matter has proceeded to trial. As the Law Clerk for the Judge, you have been asked to prepare the legal memorandum, discussing the potential causes of action against each party, identifying the party, the factual and legal bases for each cause of action, and all legal defenses of each party. Discuss each potential cross-claim.

Write the memorandum.

117. Larry Loveless is a well-known community activist, owner of a computer software company, and professor of social ethics at Carnal College in Valhalla, where he resides with his wife of 10 years. Larry often provides news commentary on Morality TV regarding family values and moral behavior in Valhalla.

An issue of the 1996 campus newspaper for Carnal contained a section entitled "The Lighter Side," which consisted of pictures of faculty members accompanied by humorous captions. One of the newspaper photos contained a picture of Larry Loveless and Linda Lawsuit, a mathematics professor at Carnal, engaged in intense conversation. The caption stated: "Your place or mine?" Other photos of faculty members in this section of the newspaper contained similar captions.

Rudy Rude, a local reporter for Moon Magazine, obtained a copy of the photo and caption of Larry and Linda. The next day, without attempting to verify the caption's accuracy, Moon Magazine ran a cover story with the headline: "Prominent Activist Nabbed in Classroom Hanky Panky."

Linda Lawsuit suffers from hypersensitivity to stressful situations. Upon seeing the cover photo and headline in Moon Magazine, Linda became hysterical and fainted. Thereafter, she suffered episodes of deep depression requiring extensive psychiatric treatment.

Rudy Rude also owns a software company. He and Larry have been longtime competitors for a lucrative supply contract. As a result of the adverse publicity about Larry from the Moon Magazine article, the contract was awarded to Rudy's business.

Under Valhalla's public morals statute, marital infidelity is punishable by six months in prison and/or a $1,500 fine. Rudy filed a citizen's complaint accusing Larry and Linda of violating the infidelity statute. This, too, was immediately reported by Moon Magazine. A finding of no probable cause was subsequently issued. Larry and Linda were exonerated much to their relief; they had secretly dated each other two years ago.

Larry and Linda have contacted your law firm for advice as to their civil remedies. The senior partner has asked you to prepare a memorandum outlining the causes of action, the parties to be sued and their defenses, and the factual and legal bases for each.

Write the memorandum.

118. While a law student, Bob became involved with an animal rights group: People Against Animal Cruelty ("PAAC"). PAAC often picketed stores that sold fur garments and laboratories that used animals for research purposes. After admission to the bar of his home state in 1995, Bob continued his PAAC activities and also provided legal advice to the group.

In October 1996, PAAC began picketing the K & G Fur Salon. Carrying placards graphically detailing the horror of animals caught in traps, the picketers tried to block the store's entrance. PAAC members, led by Bob using a bullhorn, shouted "Murderers, you have blood on your hands!" to all customers. During a particularly heated exchange, a vial of red liquid was thrown toward the store's entrance where it shattered, showering glass and red liquid over an exiting customer. The responsible PAAC member was arrested and charged criminally.

Following this incident, counsel for K & G applied to the State Chancery Court for an injunction. This application, heard by Judge Gunne, was vigorously opposed by Bob on behalf of PAAC. Despite Bob's best efforts, Judge Gunne entered an order restraining PAAC (i) from demonstrating on the sidewalk immediately in front of the fur salon; (ii) from waving their placards in the faces of passers-by; and (iii) from using the bullhorn to amplify their "disturbing comments."

A local television reporter asked Bob about the ruling as he left court. Although Bob knew nothing of Judge Gunne's background, he angrily replied that the Judge was "biased" against animal rights groups since he was an avid hunter and procured fur coats for various family members. According to Bob, Judge Gunne intentionally misapplied the law to harm PAAC and to aid furriers.

This interview, broadcast on the evening news, was seen by members of the County Ethics Committee. After reviewing the matter, the Committee charged Bob with violating the court rule which prohibits attorneys from making "reckless statements concerning the qualifications of a judge." A copy of this complaint was served on Bob, who has 20 days to respond.

Overwhelmed by his legal problems, Bob has contacted your law firm. He seeks advice as to any and all legal remedies, whether federal or state, available to him and to PAAC. The partner assigned to this case has directed you to prepare a legal memorandum analyzing all causes of action, the legal theories for each, all possible defenses, and the likelihood of their success.

Write the memorandum.

119. Last week, John Doe was fired from his job. He was so depressed that he went to a tavern where he consumed three bottles of beer followed by three shots of bourbon over the course of one hour. He left the tavern feeling dizzy and disoriented. He did not want to go home, so he wandered around the streets until he realized he did not know where he was. Nothing looked familiar.

It was getting late, and he wanted to find a place to sleep. He came upon a clothing factory that was closed for the day. He broke a ground-floor window in the back, crawled in, and prowled around looking for a place to get comfortable. He noticed racks of ski jackets. Since he was feeling cold, he took one of the jackets off the rack, wrapped it around its shoulders, and snuggled down in a corner where he fell asleep.

About an hour later he was awakened by a security guard who was patrolling the premises. The guard shook John's shoulder, and John kicked out his legs, causing the guard to fall and cut his head on a sharp corner. Bleeding profusely, the guard called for police assistance from a cellular phone on his person. A uniformed police officer arrived within 10 minutes; he approached John and told him he was under arrest. John dragged himself to his feet and started swinging his arms at the police officer. During the scuffle that ensued, the ski jacket John had wrapped himself in fell from his shoulders to the floor.

The police officer subdued John, handcuffed him, read him his *Miranda* rights, and charged him with burglary, simple assault on the security guard, assault on a police officer, and resisting arrest.

John has retained you to represent him on these charges. Prepare a file memorandum outlining all defenses you see presented by the facts as given, and all the responses you anticipate from the prosecutor.

Prepare the memorandum.

120. In 1971, Mr. and Mrs. Barry bought a large lot in Stillwell and immediately legally subdivided it into two lots, A and B.

They constructed a house used as their residence on Lot A. Stillwell did not have a municipal water supply, and the residents had to dig their own wells. The Barrys could not successfully dig a well on Lot A due to underground rock covering the entire lot.

They dug their well on Lot B within 15 feet of the Lot A border. The wellhead and the pipe to their house were located on Lot B.

In 1983, the Barrys sold Lot B to Mr. and Mrs. Able with the recorded deed containing the following clause:

> The Barrys, the Grantors, reserve to themselves, their heirs, assigns, and successors in title, the ownership of the well system, associated piping on Lot B, and a guaranteed right of ingress and egress necessary to repair, replace, and maintain the well system and all associated piping to guarantee the adequate flow of water.
>
> The Barrys' interest is binding on the Ables, their assigns, their heirs, and all successors in title. Neither the Ables nor their successors will disturb, destroy, or infringe on these rights. This conveyance is made subject to this reservation.

In 1985, the Ables built their residence on Lot B. They lived there until they sold their property to the Smiths in 1987. The deed from the Ables to the Smiths did not contain the quoted clause from the Barrys' deed. The Smith property had its own wellhead and well system some distance from the Barrys' wellhead.

In 1990, Mr. Barry, while repairing his well pipe located on the Smiths' property, found a container with $100,000 in cash wrapped in newspapers dated from 1960. The container was located two feet under the well pipe.

The Smiths saw Mr. Barry find and take the container, but they never inquired about the container or its contents. The Smiths were aware of the Barrys' modest lifestyle, and they were generally aware that the Barrys had no surplus cash or assets. In the next few years, the Barrys purchased a new Mercedes Benz, renovated their house, and took a worldwide cruise, with a total cost of approximately $50,000.

In 1996, the Smiths put a fence around their property and disconnected the Barrys' wellhead and the piping, thus eliminating the water supply to the Barrys' house.

The Barrys filed a complaint seeking enforcement of the deed and damages. The Smiths have come to your law firm for advice about defending them in the lawsuit and their legal interest in any cash which may have been found on their property by the Barrys, and the chances of success in suing for return of any such cash.

The senior partner has asked you to prepare a memorandum outlining: (i) the factual and legal theories for each cause of action and defense; (ii) the likelihood of success of the defenses; (iii) any potential third party actions; and (iv) the probability of success of the action against the Barrys. You are to assume there are no applicable statutes.

Prepare the memorandum.

121. Resale is in the business of purchasing goods which it then sells to wholesalers, distributors, and manufacturers. Resale learned that Bikrite, a bicycle manufacturer, wanted to obtain bicycle lights to give to customers as an inducement to purchase a "Cyclone," one of its most popular models. Resale entered into a written agreement with Lytco, a bicycle light manufacturer, for the purchase of bicycle lights which Resale intended to later sell to Bikrite. The agreement between Resale and Lytco provided:

> Resale agrees to purchase from Lytco 5,000 bicycle lights, designed for use on the Bikrite "Cyclone," at $10 per light, including cost of delivery.

Lytco's cost to manufacture and deliver each light is $5.

As soon as the agreement with Lytco was signed, Resale entered into a written agreement with Bikrite which provided for Bikrite's purchase of "5,000 bicycle lights at $15 per light." It was estimated by Bikrite's marketing analyst that the giveaway of the bicycle light would increase Bikrite's net profits in the sale of the "Cyclone" by $100,000 in the first year alone.

Upon Lytco's delivery of the bicycle lights in sealed cartons to Resale, a representative signed the receipt, which read: "Received: 5,000 bicycle lights in as is condition." Resale immediately shipped the unopened cartons of bicycle lights to Bikrite. Upon the opening of the cartons at Bikrite's premises, it was readily observable that the lights were too small to fit the "Cyclone." Bikrite refused to pay Resale, and Resale refused to pay Lytco. The bicycle lights were returned to Lytco.

The president of Resale was uncertain about the rights and liabilities of her company. She has asked her law firm for an opinion letter on the potential causes of action that could be filed against Resale, all possible defenses to each cause of action, and the scope of damages.

Prepare the opinion letter.

122. George, an accountant with XYZ Corp., was charged with embezzling $20,000 from the company's employee pension fund. He retained Joseph Esquire to represent him, and gave Mr. Esquire his personal diary which contained evidence of the embezzlement.

On June 1, 1996, George purchased a $250,000 life insurance policy from Top Notch Insurance Company; the policy was payable to George's estate. Six months later, on the eve of his criminal trial, George was killed when the automobile he was driving struck a tree.

Jennifer, the administratrix of George's estate, sought payment of the life insurance proceeds. Top Notch refused payment on the ground that George had committed suicide, the only exclusion under the policy.

Jennifer filed suit against Top Notch. At trial, over Jennifer's objection, Joseph Esquire testified that, during numerous consultations, George appeared anxious, distracted, and extremely depressed. He further testified, over Jennifer's objection, that he reviewed George's personal diary in preparation of the criminal trial and discovered an entry that stated: "I would rather die than go to trial."

Dr. Jones, the assistant medical examiner who performed George's autopsy, had died prior to trial. Over the objections of Top Notch, the court permitted Sally, Dr. Jones's secretary, to testify about the contents of Dr. Jones's autopsy report. The report revealed that George's blood alcohol content was .19. The report also contained Dr. Jones's opinion that: "George was intoxicated at the time of the accident and his intoxication possibly caused the accident."

The jury rendered a verdict in favor of Top Notch Insurance Company.

Jennifer now seeks advice on how to proceed. The senior partner has requested that you prepare a memorandum analyzing the merits of all evidence rulings at the trial.

Prepare the memorandum.

123. Wonder Drug, Inc., a well known pharmaceutical company in Toxic Town, New Jersey, but recently out of business, once designed and manufactured an innovative medical device called "Pro-Pregnancy," specifically prescribed for use by women experiencing difficulty carrying a fetus to term. As a prescription device, it was not sold over the counter but administered to consumers exclusively through their treating physicians. The device bore the following warning label in big red letters which was intended to advise prescribing doctors: "CAUTION—UNDER NO CIRCUMSTANCES TO BE USED SIMULTANEOUSLY WITH FERTILITY MEDICATIONS."

The device continues to be sold by numerous manufacturers across the country, has become an almost generic product, and is widely distributed by Middleman, Inc., a large drug wholesaler, which then sells the device directly to pharmacies and store owners.

Prior to the original sale of "Pro-Pregnancy," it was cleared by the Food and Drug Administration, which specifically regulates the language on its labeling. The Food and Drug Administration has a special federal statute, the Food, Drug and Cosmetic Act, which provides:

> No state or political subdivision of a state may establish or continue in effect with respect to a medical device any requirement—(i) which is different from, or in addition to, any requirements applicable in this law and (ii) which relates to the safety or effectiveness of the device.

Lucy Luckless was pregnant again—this most recent pregnancy occurring after three previous miscarriages in as many years. After years of taking hormonal treatments and fertility medications, Lucy had been prescribed "Pro-Pregnancy" and after years of disappointment, it appeared that a new addition to the family might be on the way.

Lucy and her husband Bruce "Lively" Luckless decided to give a party to celebrate her fifth month of pregnancy. During the party, a great deal of alcohol was consumed, and Lucy joined in the celebration. Her physician, Dr. Dan Devious, had failed to advise her not to consume alcohol during her pregnancy. Later that night, while still feeling somewhat inebriated, she took her old brand of fertility medication, having forgotten that she was also using "Pro-Pregnancy."

Within the next few days, she again miscarried and became so distraught she suffered a nervous breakdown. The preliminary medical reports have been inconclusive as to the precise cause of the miscarriage. No invoices can be found that help determine which manufacturer made the batch of the devices sold to her pharmacist/store owner.

Her husband, Lively, immediately hired Sue Quicklee, who has joined all parties—the doctor, Middleman, Inc., known manufacturers of the device, and the drugstores where the device may have been purchased—lodging claims for negligence, failure to warn, strict liability, and breach of implied warranty in a state court action. Her complaint specifically demands several million dollars of punitive damages. You have been retained to jointly defend all parties (all of whom have waived all conflicts) and you must now prepare a memorandum outlining all possible defenses.

Prepare the memorandum.

124. When David was 20 years old, he went to live with his infirm and elderly father, Sam. David spent much of the day keeping Sam company and taking care of his medical needs. It was David's intention, out of love and respect for Sam, to live with him until David turned 26, although he never told this to Sam.

Sam had disliked living alone, and he took great comfort in David's presence. So much so that, shortly after David moved in, Sam told him, "I will give you $200,000 on your 26th birthday if you continue to live with me until then." David thanked his father, and told him that he would be happy to remain with him.

A few months later, David received a job offer and a proposed employment contract from an out-of-state company. David declined the offer, however, because he would be receiving enough money from Sam on his 26th birthday to equal what he otherwise would have earned had he accepted the employment contract.

When David was 25, Sam told him that he was not going to give him $200,000 on his 26th birthday because David had recently been spending more time with David's girlfriend than with

Sam. David would frequently leave the house early in the morning to be with his girlfriend and would not return until late at night.

David went to see a neighborhood lawyer. He advised the lawyer that he wanted to sue Sam immediately. Before he did so, however, he wanted the lawyer to prepare a memorandum analyzing the factual and legal bases for the lawsuit, the scope of damages, and the factual and legal bases of all potential defenses. You are that neighborhood lawyer.

Prepare the memorandum.

125. Perry and Victor used to be friends, but a while ago they had a disagreement that ended their friendship. They started engaging in a course of playing practical jokes on each other, just to see who could annoy whom the most.

Recently, Perry saw a news story on television about the increase in thefts of air bags from automobiles. The story showed a film of the actual removal of an air bag from the steering wheel of a car.

Perry decided he would remove the air bag from Victor's car as a joke. One night he went to the parking lot of Victor's apartment building and found Victor's car unlocked. Following the steps he remembered from the television news story, Perry removed the air bag from its compartment inside the steering wheel of the car. He replaced the compartment cover and went home with Victor's air bag.

The next day, while driving his car, Victor was hit head-on by an intoxicated driver. As a result of his injuries from this collision, Victor died a few hours later in the hospital emergency room.

The police investigating the accident examined Victor's car and noticed that the air bag had been removed. The intoxicated driver was arrested and charged with death by auto, but the police continued investigating the matter of the missing air bag. They spoke to the emergency room doctor who had tended to Victor on the night of his death. The doctor told the officers that, in his opinion, an air bag would most likely have saved Victor's life.

Through a series of leads in their investigation, the police learned about Perry's and Victor's ongoing feud. Two uniformed officers went to Perry's apartment and rang his bell. When Perry opened the door, one of the officers asked if they could come in. When Perry asked, "What for?" the officer told him they just wanted to talk to him about Victor. Perry became agitated and tried to close the door. The officer stuck his foot in the opening and pushed in on the door.

Perry ran to his bedroom at the back of the apartment, with the two officers in pursuit. In his bedroom, Perry grabbed a bulging shopping bag and tried to throw it out an open window. An officer grabbed his arm, retrieved the shopping bag, and found an air bag inside.

"Where did this come from?" the officer asked. "I found it on the street," Perry answered. "Then why were you trying to get rid of it?" the officer asked. Perry shrugged and refused to say anything further. The officers then told Perry he was under arrest for Victor's death and advised him of his *Miranda r*ights. On the way out of the apartment with Perry, an officer noticed on the living room sofa articles which had been cut out from the newspaper about Victor's fatal accident. On one of the articles were handwritten the words: "It wasn't supposed to go this far." The officer took the news articles, air bag, and Perry to the police station.

Perry has been indicted for murder, which this jurisdiction defines as:

(i) Purposely causing death or serious bodily injury resulting in death;
(ii) Knowingly causing death or serious bodily injury resulting in death; or
(iii) Causing death or serious bodily injury resulting in death during the commission of robbery, sexual assault, burglary, kidnapping or criminal escape.

He has come to you to represent him. **Prepare a memorandum outlining the defense(s) you determine should be raised in his behalf, including any pretrial motion(s), and the prosecutor's likely response(s) to these defense(s) and motion(s).**

Prepare the memorandum.

126. In an effort to revitalize its downtown commercial district, Olde City adopted an ordinance last year prohibiting peddling in an area designated a "pedestrian mall."

This measure was opposed by Mike, a highly vocal political opponent of the president of the Olde City Council. Mike has received a license to operate a pushcart pursuant to a state statute which granted armed services veterans a right to peddle. Since receiving his license 19 years ago, Mike stationed his vending cart in front of the Olde City Municipal Building and from there sold hot dogs, sandwiches, and various soft drinks. His customers were also offered political commentary on the happenings in City Hall, much of it critical of the current administration. This location, which has proved quite successful for Mike, is sited within the Olde City "pedestrian mall."

Mike has obtained the support of various veterans' groups who have pressured Olde City to exempt pushcarts operated by veterans. In an effort to placate these interest groups, the council has amended its ordinance to exempt those military veterans who have held state peddler licenses for more than 20 years. Although several veterans come within this exemption, Mike does not.

Your law firm has been retained by Mike to pursue any legal remedies available to him. The partner assigned to this case has determined to file the action in federal court and has directed you to prepare a legal memorandum analyzing all potential causes of action, the legal theories for each, all possible defenses, and the likelihood of their success.

Write the memorandum.

127. In 1988, Mr. Smith was the owner of a retail business located on the east side of Route 2 in Sand Hill, New Jersey. Mr. Smith also owned two abutting properties on the west side of Route 2; one was a parking lot and the other was a one-family dwelling in which he lived.

Due to the noise, congestion, and pollution created by the parking lot, he could not comfortably live in the house without an easement. In order to create a buffer between his house and the abutting parking lot, he created an easement on a 12' x 60' portion of the parking lot. He planted grass in that area and put up a fence between the parking lot and the grassy area.

In 1989, Mr. Smith sold the one-family dwelling to Ms. Jones. In the deed there was a reference to the easement. Ms. Jones maintained the fence and mowed the grassy area during her period of ownership.

In 1990, Mr. and Mrs. Frank purchased from Mr. Smith the retail business on the east side of Route 2 and the parking lot on the west side of Route 2.

In 1992, Mrs. Frank, individually, purchased the one-family dwelling from Ms. Jones. The deed from Ms. Jones to Mrs. Frank did not reference the easement. Mrs. Frank maintained the fence and mowed the grassy area during her period of ownership. The parking lot remained very busy during this time and the house could not be used comfortably without the easement.

In 1993, Mr. Paul purchased the retail business and the parking lot on the west side of Route 2. The survey which Mr. Paul obtained when he purchased the property did show the fence on the parking lot on the west side of Route 2.

Mr. Paul's deed contained language that the purchase was subject to restrictions of record and a survey.

Mr. Paul wants to quiet the title and to extinguish the easement. He has come to your law firm for advice as to his legal rights and obligations and the potential success of the quiet title action.

The senior partner has asked you to prepare a legal memorandum outlining the factual and legal bases for the lawsuit and the factual and legal bases for potential defenses and the probability of success of the lawsuit.

Prepare the memorandum.

128. Mary, age 11, lived with her parents, George and Susan Goodness, in Happytimes, New Jersey. On June 1, 1990, Susan left home for a two week business trip out of state.

On June 5, Mary went to the school nurse complaining of abdominal pain. After examining her, the nurse alerted the Bureau of Children's Services (hereinafter "BCS") to the possibility of sexual abuse. Nancy Smith, a representative from BCS, was assigned to investigate the matter.

Nancy began her investigation by taking Mary to Hopewell Medical Center, where she was examined by Dr. Paula Johnson, a gynecologist in the Rape Crisis Unit. The examination revealed physical evidence of possible sexual abuse.

Nancy interrogated Mary for approximately three hours. Mary finally admitted that, after her mother left on her business trip, her father sexually abused her.

At the trial of George's sexual abuse charge, the state called Nancy Smith as a witness. Over defense counsel's objection, she testified that, when she confronted George with Mary's accusation, he became "pale" and "visibly upset." She further testified, over objection, as to Mary's detailed description of the sexual assault.

The state also called Dr. Johnson, who testified as to the physical evidence. Over objection, she also testified that Mary's emotional response to the gynecological examination was consistent with that of a child who had been sexually abused.

Due to Mary's shyness and embarrassment, and over the objection of counsel, Mary testified through closed circuit television.

For the defense, the local pastor of George's church testified that George had a reputation of good character in the community. On cross-examination, over defense counsel's objection, the pastor was asked whether he knew that George had been convicted of burglary 15 years earlier and whether that would change his testimony.

George did not testify at trial. He was convicted, and on appeal he has raised erroneous evidentiary rulings as a basis for reversal.

You are the Appellate Division Judge's law clerk and must prepare a memorandum analyzing the merits of George's claims of error.

Prepare the memorandum.

129. Up-State University, a private institution, recently renovated its science building. The architectural plans provided for the installation of a new elevator unit.

Descend, Inc. manufactured the unit, which has a safety interlock device to control the door opening. Due to the complicated design of the science building, Descend, Inc. contractually delegated installation to Astute Elevator Service.

One evening, Thomas, a student, returned to the third floor laboratory to perform some experiments after the building had closed. He took the elevator to the third floor and locked it. Unbeknownst to Thomas, Professor Forgetful, a tenured faculty member, had returned to retrieve a notebook that was located in his second floor office. While reading a manuscript, Professor Forgetful pressed the exterior elevator door button, the elevator doors opened, Professor Forgetful stepped forward and fell down the elevator shaft. He was knocked unconscious and sustained a fractured spine, resulting in permanent paralysis.

The family of Professor Forgetful has contacted your law firm. The senior partner has requested that you prepare a memorandum identifying and analyzing the liabilities of all the parties, potential counterclaims, and cross-claims.

Write the memorandum.

130. On October 1, 1988, Disco World ("Disco") entered into a written five year lease with Shopping Center ("Center"), the owner of a strip shopping center, "for the retail sale of records, tapes, compact discs and allied products." The lease was renewed in writing on October 1, 1993, for a five year term "under the same terms and conditions." From October 5, 1989, to the present, Disco has continuously sold lottery tickets in its store.

On January 15, 1996, Center entered into a written lease with News Store ("News") for the store adjacent to Disco. The lease provides that News has the "exclusive right to sell newspapers, magazines, greeting cards, and lottery tickets in the shopping center." On January 16, 1996, upon taking possession of its store, News wrote to Center and Disco demanding that they immediately control the loud and obnoxious music generated by Disco. On February 20, 1996, News wrote to Center and Disco stating that Disco's loud and obnoxious music was ruining its business and objecting to Disco's sale of lottery tickets.

Center has hired your senior partner and expressed concern about what action it may take against its tenants as well as any claim that may be made against it and between its tenants. The senior partner has asked you to prepare a memorandum setting forth your legal analysis of all potential causes of action and remedies Center may have against News and Disco and all potential defenses, counterclaims, and cross-claims.

Write the memorandum.

131. Al and Burt have been good friends for years. Al had a long standing feud with Chet over some money he claimed Chet borrowed from him and never repaid. Al asked Burt to accompany him to Chet's house to help him "scare" Chet into paying his debt. Without asking any questions, Burt immediately said, "Sure" and climbed into the passenger seat of Al's car.

As Al drove to Chet's house, he told Burt, "I am so fed up with Chet for not paying me, I really want to hurt him." Al then showed Burt a gun he had pulled out from under the driver's seat. Burt admired the gun and asked Al if he was going to use it to scare Chet. Al said, "Probably," and stuffed the gun inside his jacket.

Upon arrival at Chet's house, Al got out of the car and told Burt to slide over to the driver's seat, "in case we need to leave in a hurry." Burt nodded, said nothing, and moved into the driver's seat. He saw Al knock on the door, saw the door open slightly, and then saw Al enter the house and close the door behind him. Through an open window Burt could hear Al's and Chet's voices raised in argument. Suddenly Burt heard a gunshot. Al rushed out the door, jumped into the car and yelled at Burt, "Drive away from here as fast as possible!"

As he sped away, Burt asked Al what happened. Al showed Burt a wallet and a gold chain, and told him he had taken all that from Chet "as payment on my debt." Al added, "Well, Chet didn't exactly want to pay me. I had to show him I meant business; so I pulled out my gun. He freaked out and tried to grab it from me. That's when it went off and shot him in the leg. I grabbed his wallet, pulled the chain off his neck and ran out of there." Al then pulled his gun out of his pocket, and shoved it into Burt's jacket, saying, "Here, get rid of this for me."

Burt drove Al home, gave him his car keys, and started walking home. On the way, he passed a wooded lot, and he threw Al's gun into the underbrush. He then went home and went to sleep.

The next day two police officers who were investigating Chet's shooting came to Burt's house. They informed Burt that they had already arrested Al, based on what Chet had told them. They also told him that, at the police station, Al had admitted shooting Chet but said the gun had been supplied by Burt. The police officers placed Burt under arrest and advised him of his rights to remain silent and to consult an attorney if he wished. Burt nodded and the officers handcuffed him and put him in the back seat of the patrol car.

During the ride to the police station, one of the officers said to Burt, "Al is the one we really want, but we need some evidence to corroborate his confession. You could really help us, and yourself, if you could tell us where the gun is." Burt then replied that the gun was in a wooded lot near Al's house. He directed the police officers there, and after a brief search the officers found the gun.

Both Al and Burt have been charged with armed robbery, possession of a handgun with intent to use it unlawfully, and illegal possession of a handgun. Burt has asked you to represent him, and has told you the facts as stated above. In preparation for representing Burt, you have decided it would be helpful to do a file memorandum discussing the nature of his charges, what defenses are available to him, what pretrial motions you should bring and what the prosecutor's likely response will be.

Prepare the memorandum.

132. Bill Jones sued for personal injuries he sustained in an automobile accident which occurred on August 17, 1994, when his vehicle was struck by a vehicle driven by Carol Adams.

Jones was driving north on Rose Avenue in Smithville when Carol Adams made a left turn from a side street, Ash Road, which was controlled by a stop sign. She pulled directly into the path of Jones.

Adams entered Ash Road by making a left turn from Fourth Avenue, even though at the intersection there was a sign on Ash Road which prohibited through traffic. Adams made this turn to avoid a traffic light at Fourth Avenue and Rose Avenue.

At the scene after the accident, a police officer recommended to Jones that he sign a careless driving summons against Adams, which he did. No stop sign violation summons was issued to Adams.

At the scene, Adams stated to the police officer that she did make a left turn from Fourth Avenue onto Ash road, ignoring the "no through street" sign. She also stated that she was in a rush as she was late getting home.

Adams was acquitted of the careless driving summons in a municipal court trial.

At the trial of Jones's case in July 1995, Jones, over objection, had admitted photographs of the scene of the accident taken in the spring of 1995. The intersection had been widened and repaved and the stop sign was in a different location than it had been on the date of the accident.

Over objection, Jones was cross-examined on his signing the careless driving summons against Adams and the fact that he did not sign a summons for any stop sign violation.

The police officer, over objection, testified that Adams stated that she was in a rush. The court sustained an objection as to her statement regarding ignoring the "no through street" sign.

Jones alleged that he sustained a convulsive disorder as a result of the accident. On direct examination, Dr. Neurologist diagnosed the convulsive disorder and related it to the accident. On cross-examination, Dr. Neurologist retracted his statement as to causal connection. Adams's attorney moved to strike Dr. Neurologist's opinion on the convulsive disorder, but the motion was denied.

Jones utilized an accident reconstruction expert, Mr. Ace, who was a professional engineer, but never certified as an accident reconstruction expert by any university. Over objection, Mr.

Ace qualified as an expert. He offered an opinion as to the reasonableness of Jones's speed, based on a mathematical formula which was not recognized by a majority of engineers in the accident reconstruction field. Adams's attorney moved to strike this testimony, but the motion was denied.

At the trial level, Adams was found free of negligence. Jones filed a motion for a new trial, challenging the court's evidence rulings.

You are the trial judge's law clerk and you are assigned to write a memorandum outlining the correctness of all the trial court's evidentiary rulings, citing the factual bases and all applicable rules of law in support of your memorandum.

Write the memorandum.

133. Ajax Enterprises, Inc., an international producer and marketer of farm equipment, entered a contract with Smallco, Inc., a small machine shop, for Smallco to manufacture a part for a new line of tractors Ajax was planning to market. In order for Smallco to manufacture the part, it was necessary that Smallco install new, specialized equipment at great cost. Smallco obtained a loan at its local bank to finance the new machinery, and in connection with that application, submitted to the bank a letter from Ajax's vice president of engineering confirming the agreement between Ajax and Smallco. Additionally the loan was personally guaranteed by Bumbler, Smallco's operator and sole shareholder.

The written agreement between Ajax and Smallco, which was prepared by Ajax's legal department, had the following provisions:

1) Smallco will produce the parts exclusively for Ajax;
2) Ajax will purchase a minimum number of parts per month at a price established by Ajax's accounting department as being sufficient to cover all of Smallco's costs, debt service and a reasonable profit;
3) Smallco will be prohibited from producing similar parts for any other farm equipment manufacturer for two years after the termination of the agreement; and
4) The agreement may be terminated by either party, on 30 days' written notice.

Smallco installed the new machinery and successfully commenced production, and Ajax began the required monthly purchases.

After six months, Ajax underwent an extensive corporate reorganization. New management decided to curtail production so that Smallco's products were no longer needed. The contract was terminated in accordance with the 30 day notice provision.

Six months later Smallco, not being able to profitably utilize the new machinery, defaulted on the bank note and was forced to liquidate its business.

Bumbler has come to your firm for help with any claims he may have against Ajax. Your senior partner has asked you for a memorandum setting out each possible claim which may be asserted against Ajax, the basis for each claim, and the relative merits of each claim, including the nature and measure of damages which may be sought.

Prepare the memorandum.

134. Following training, Helen and Joe were hired by the Center City Police Department on April 1, 1986. Helen was assigned to Special Investigations, while Joe worked in the Criminal Investigations Unit. Both have promising careers and have been promoted to supervisory positions within their respective units.

Recently, Helen and Joe became engaged, setting April 6, 1996, as their wedding date. When the chief of police learned of their plans, he informed Helen and Joe that if they marry, they will be in violation of the city's anti-nepotism policy which prohibits "relatives of city employees in supervisory positions from working in the same department." This policy, which does not apply to nonsupervisory employees or to relatives working in different departments, was adopted by Center City, as an ordinance, in 1987.

The ordinance requires the relative with less seniority to resign or be transferred from the department. Historically, women have had less seniority.

Noting that the two have identical years of service, the chief informed Helen and Joe that should they marry, it would be their decision who should resign. Later the chief called Helen into his office and told her, "I trust you will do the right thing."

Neither Helen nor Joe wish to give up their career in law enforcement. They have, therefore, postponed their wedding plans. However, they remain engaged and have retained your law firm to challenge the Center City ordinance. You have been asked to prepare a memorandum outlining the possible causes of action, the legal theories for each, possible defenses, and the likelihood of their success.

Write the memorandum.

BAR REVIEW

Essay Answers

1.   TORTS

On behalf of Arthur and Elderly, I would bring a cause of action against Dr. Beard for negligence, a cause of action against Restlawn for negligence through the doctrine of respondeat superior, causes of action against Rack and Pinion for the intentional torts of battery, false imprisonment, and intentional infliction of emotional distress, and a cause of action against Fairshake for being vicariously liable for the acts of Rack and Pinion under the doctrine of respondeat superior. Furthermore, on behalf of Arthur, as representative of Lucy's estate, I would bring survival actions against each of the parties mentioned above for the torts alleged. Additionally, I would bring wrongful death actions on behalf of Arthur and Elderly against the same parties for the same torts as alleged in the survival actions.

Dr. Beard: I would commence a cause of action against Dr. Beard for negligence resulting from his permitting Lucy to leave Restlawn. The issue here is whether a prima facie case for negligence exists. A prima facie case for negligence exists where (i) the defendant has a duty to conform to a specific standard of conduct for protection of the plaintiff against an unreasonable risk of injury; (ii) there is a breach of such duty by the defendant; (iii) the breach is the actual and proximate cause of plaintiff's injury; and (iv) there are damages.

Here, Dr. Beard is a psychiatrist who diagnosed Lucy as being "SUICIDAL." As a result, Dr. Beard had a duty to Lucy to keep her committed at Restlawn to ensure that she would not harm herself. Dr. Beard breached this duty by allowing Lucy to leave Restlawn. By allowing Lucy to leave, Lucy was able to go to Fairshake, where it was foreseeable that Lucy, a diagnosed schizophrenic, could get herself involved in a situation that could lead her to commit suicide. As a result, I would commence a cause of action against Dr. Beard for negligence.

(It should be noted that Dr. Beard may claim that the suicide was a result of an unforeseeable intervening cause (the actions of Rack and Pinion). This defense usually fails. Here, however, it may succeed, resulting in Dr. Beard being relieved of any liability, if the intentional torts committed by Rack and Pinion are determined to be unforeseeable intervening causes, constituting superseding forces.)

Restlawn: I would commence an action against Restlawn alleging it is vicariously liable for the torts committed by Dr. Beard under the theory of respondeat superior. At issue here is whether Dr. Beard's actions were within the scope of his employment relationship with Restlawn. Vicarious liability is liability that rests upon a special relationship between the tortfeasor and the person to whom the tortious conduct is imputed. Respondeat superior is a doctrine that will hold an employer vicariously liable for the tortious acts committed by its employees if the acts occur within the scope of the employment relationship. Here, Dr. Beard committed the tortious act of negligence while working as a staff psychiatrist for Restlawn. As a result, Restlawn will be held vicariously liable for the tortious acts committed by Dr. Beard within the scope of his employment relationship with Restlawn.

(It should be noted that if Dr. Beard is relieved of liability due to superseding forces, as discussed above, so, too, will Restlawn be relieved.)

Rack and Pinion: The causes of action I would bring against Rack and Pinion are for the intentional torts of battery, false imprisonment, and intentional infliction of emotional distress, all of which arise out of their actions inside Fairshake supermarket.

Battery: At issue here is whether the acts of Rack and Pinion were of a magnitude sufficient to qualify as battery. Battery consists of an act of the defendant that brings about harmful or offensive contact to the victim, intent of the defendant to bring about such contact, and the defendant's act being a substantial factor in causing the victim's injury. Here, Rack and Pinion told Lucy that they were going to find out "the hard way" whether Lucy was shoplifting, then they escorted her to a room where they seated her, slammed the door shut, and told her she was "not going anywhere." This conduct of Rack and Pinion led to the ultimate injuries suffered by Lucy. Furthermore, the acts of Rack and Pinion to Lucy would be considered offensive to a reasonable person. As a result, the elements of battery are met.

False imprisonment: At issue here is whether the confinement of Lucy by Rack and Pinion is sufficient to constitute false imprisonment, and, if it is, whether an exception exists to permit Rack and Pinion to confine Lucy in the manner that they did. The intentional tort of false imprisonment consists of an act of the defendant that, as intended, causes the victim to be confined or restrained to a bounded area. Furthermore, the victim must be either aware of or harmed by the confinement, and there must be no reasonable means of escape known to the victim. Here, Rack and Pinion confined Lucy to a detention room, where they ensured, by "slamming the door shut," that she would not be able to escape. Lucy was aware of the confinement, as she begged to be let go but was not. It should be noted that shopkeepers have a privilege to detain suspected shoplifters if there is a reasonable belief that the victim is shoplifting, the detention is reasonable (and only nondeadly force is used), and the detention only lasts a reasonable length of time sufficient to make an investigation. Here, neither is it apparent that Rack and Pinion had a reason to believe that Lucy was shoplifting, nor is it established that the investigation and detention was conducted in a reasonable manner. Therefore, there is a sufficient basis for commencing actions asserting false imprisonment.

Intentional infliction of emotional distress: At issue here is whether the acts of Rack and Pinion were outrageous enough to be considered intentional infliction of emotional distress. The intentional tort of intentional infliction of emotional distress occurs when a defendant commits an extreme and outrageous act intended to cause, and actually does cause, the victim to suffer severe emotional distress. Here, without any privilege to do so, Rack and Pinion intentionally detained and intimidated Lucy, inflicting in her extreme emotional distress. As a result of her suffering extreme emotional distress, Lucy ran head-first into the door, resulting in her death. It should be noted that under the "eggshell skull" theory, a tortfeasor takes his victim as he finds her. Therefore, Lucy's suicidal tendency is not a supervening factor that relieves Rack and Pinion from liability, and the elements of intentional infliction of emotional distress are met.

Fairshake Supermarket: I would commence an action against Fairshake for each tort that I commenced an action for against Rack and Pinion. At issue here is whether Fairshake is liable for torts committed by its employees. Causes of action exist against Fairshake for each intentional tort that Rack and Pinion are liable for, because Fairshake is vicariously liable for the intentional torts of its employees that are committed within the scope of their employment. One way liability is imposed vicariously is through the doctrine of respondeat superior.

The doctrine of respondeat superior holds an employer vicariously liable for tortious acts committed by its employee if the tortious acts occur within the scope of the employment relationship. Generally, intentional torts of an employee do not fall within the tortious acts that an employer can be held vicariously liable for. However, an employer will be held vicariously liable for intentional torts of its employee if force is authorized in the employment, friction is generated on the job, and the employee was in the process of furthering the business of the employer. Here, Rack and Pinion were authorized to detain suspected shoplifters, which caused friction between the suspect and Rack and Pinion, and, if the suspect was in fact shoplifting, Rack and Pinion were in the process of furthering Fairshake's business. As a result, I would allege a cause of action against Fairshake under the theory of respondeat superior for each intentional tort action alleged against Rack and Pinion.

Survival and wrongful death causes of action: Since Lucy is deceased, in order to bring the causes of action against the defendants discussed above, the causes of action must survive her death. Survival statutes allow a plaintiff's causes of action for property or personal damage to survive her death. At issue here is who can bring the causes of action and what they can recover if there is a recovery. The facts establish that Arthur is the representative of Lucy's estate. As a result, Arthur may bring survival actions against Restlawn and Dr. Beard for negligence and against Fairshake, Rack, and Pinion for the intentional torts set forth above. Recovery under a survival statute is limited to the recovery of all damages from the time of injury to the time of death. As a result, Arthur, on behalf of Lucy's estate, will be able to recover damages awarded for all of the torts alleged above.

In many states, wrongful death statutes exist to permit recovery by certain family members for economic damages suffered by the family members as a result of the decedent's death. Depending on the jurisdiction, it is either the next of kin or the personal representative that is authorized to bring the cause of action. The recovery is limited to the pecuniary injury suffered and does not permit recovery for the decedent's pain and suffering. As a result, recovery should be permitted for the loss of support suffered by Arthur and Elderly as a result of Lucy's death.

2. REAL PROPERTY

(a) Uzer's rights and liabilities: Uzer will be forced to honor the easement reserved by Oaner, he will be able to select where the easement is located, and he will likely be able to limit the width of the easement to 20 feet. At issue here is whether a purchaser of a parcel of land must honor an express reservation in a prior deed, and, if so, how will any ambiguities in the easement be interpreted.

Uzer must honor the easement held by Oaner. The holder of an affirmative easement has the right to use a tract of land for a specified purpose. An easement is an interest in land, presumed to be of perpetual duration, and subject to the Statute of Frauds, thus requiring it to be in writing and signed by the grantor. Here, when Oaner conveyed the parcel of land to Byer in 1997, the deed expressly provided that Oaner reserved "a right of way over the lands conveyed" to Byer "for vehicular and pedestrian traffic between Forest Avenue and the remaining lands of" Oaner. As a result of this express affirmative easement, the Statute of Frauds is satisfied, and Oaner has an easement appurtenant on the servient tenement, the parcel sold to Byer, that runs with the land and grants Oaner the right to enter and use the land as a passageway to the lands still owned by him. Since an easement is presumed to be perpetual in duration, when Uzer purchased the land from Byer in 2001, Byer was not able to convey any greater interest in the property than he had acquired from the prior grantor, Oaner, therefore Oaner may now enforce the easement against Uzer.

Uzer will be able to designate the size and placement of the passageway from Forest Avenue to Oaner's other land, the dominant land. At issue here is how will any omissions or ambiguities in the easement be interpreted. When an easement is created, if its location is not specifically identified on the servient tenement, an easement of sufficient width and height to make the intended use reasonably convenient is implied. Courts, when interpreting easements, generally look to the intent of the original parties and resolve any ambiguities in favor of the grantee. Here, the easement states only that Oaner reserves "a right of way over the lands . . . for vehicular and pedestrian traffic." There is no mention in the easement of either the width of the right-of-way or for what purposes the dominant land, the land held by Oaner, was to be used. Prior to Byer conveying the land to Uzer in 2001, Oaner had an opportunity to designate the size and place of the passageway, but Oaner opted not to. As a result, since a court will find in favor of Uzer, the grantee of the easement, with respect to any ambiguities in the written easement, Uzer will be able to designate the location and dimensions of the right-of-way.

It should be noted that Oaner will argue that the width of the easement should be 60 feet since the zoning law recently changed to require a 60-foot right-of-way for construction of an office building, and that such a 60-foot passageway would be reasonable since, Oaner will argue, the easement agreement was for a passageway 50 feet wide. The court will likely disagree with Oaner. First, the easement is subject to the Statute of Frauds, and the width of the easement was not stated in the written agreement. Second, Oaner had the opportunity to designate the size and location of the easement prior to Byer conveying the land to Uzer, but he elected not to. Third, the court will not create an unreasonable burden on, or interfere with, the use and enjoyment of the servient tenement solely because the zoning law has changed, especially in a situation where it is not clear that the use affected by the change in the zoning law was ever considered when the parties that created the easement did so.

(b) Easement I would have requested on behalf of Oaner (Grantor): Grantor hereby reserves to himself, and his heirs, successors, and assigns, a right-of-way over the lands herein conveyed to Grantee, for purposes of ingress and egress between Forest Avenue and the remaining lands of Grantor.

Grantor further reserves the right to locate the easement, and to subsequently change its location, in accordance with his own needs, provided that such location shall not unreasonably burden the use and enjoyment of the servient tenement.

Grantor shall be entitled to the use of a right-of-way with a width of up to 50 feet, or the maximum width required for any access road required as a condition of site development under the applicable zoning laws at the time of site development, whichever shall be greater.

Grantor further reserves the right to construct a passageway as is needed to facilitate travel between the servient and dominant tenements.

Grantee shall contribute to the repair and maintenance expenses of the passageway in proportion to his common use thereof. Grantee shall not park vehicles, make improvements, plant trees or shrubs, or in any way obstruct the right-of-way or access to or from the right-of-way.

No development or improvements on the premises of the servient tenement shall be undertaken, without prior notice to Grantor, affording Grantor an opportunity to assess whether such undertakings would possibly restrict or impair Grantor's right-of-way.

This reservation of easement shall run with the land and be of perpetual duration, unless expressly revoked by Grantor.

This agreement shall be binding on and inure to the benefit of the parties hereto, their heirs, successors, and assigns.

3. CRIMINAL PROCEDURE

Fourth Amendment arguments: The Fourth Amendment to the United States Constitution, binding on the states under the due process provisions of the Fourteenth Amendment, provides that citizens shall not be subject to unreasonable searches and seizures. For a search to be reasonable under the Fourth Amendment, it generally must be pursuant to a warrant. A search conducted without a warrant is unlawful and considered invalid and evidence discovered during the search should be excluded from evidence, unless the search is within one of the six categories of permissible warrantless searches. At issue here is whether the search was within the automobile exception, thus permitting a warrantless search.

The seizure of the automobile and the search that followed were violations of Frank's Fourth Amendment rights. The stopping of a vehicle and detention of its occupants constitutes a seizure within the meaning of the Fourth Amendment. The automobile exception is one circumstance where a warrantless search is permissible. Under the automobile exception, a police officer is permitted to stop a car for "inspection" if the officer has a reason to believe that a traffic violation has occurred based on the officer's own observation. If the officer has no reason to fear the occupant of the car, the officer may not conduct a full search of the vehicle without a warrant, unless the officer has probable cause to believe that the vehicle contains contraband or fruits, instrumentalities, or evidence of a crime. In the instant case, the police officers' search of the car was not pursuant to a search warrant, the officers did not have probable cause to believe that a crime was committed, justifying an arrest and search, and the officers did not have reason to fear any occupant of the vehicle—the police officer only observed Frank driving with one of the car's headlights not operating, for which Frank was lawfully stopped. Since an arrest is not generally made for an inoperable headlight, and since there was nothing to indicate that Frank or the passengers were dangerous, the police officers had no right to remove and search behind the rear seat of the car—all that is justified is an inspection, which allows the officers to check the automobile's exterior, check the driver's license and registration, and have the vehicle's occupants step outside of the car, allowing the officers a plain view of the interior.

The search of the car was invalid under the Fourth Amendment, even after the police officers received consent from one of the passengers in the vehicle. The police may conduct a valid warrantless search if they have a voluntary and intelligent consent to do so. In order for the consent to be valid, the person consenting must be a person with an apparent equal right to use or occupy the property to be searched. The person consenting to the search does not have to have actual authority to consent, but the police officers must reasonably believe that the person has actual authority to consent. Here, although the consent appears voluntary, the consenting person was a juvenile passenger in the car with Frank, the 50-year old driver. It was unreasonable for the police officers to believe that the passenger had actual authority to consent to the search. Furthermore, the scope of the search is to be limited by the scope of the consent, which extends only to all areas to which a reasonable person under the circumstances would believe it extends. Even if the consent was voluntarily given by someone with apparent or actual authority to do so, the consent would have extended to a search of the car's interior, but certainly not to the removal of the rear seat, as no reasonable person would expect the consent to extend to such a search. As a result of the consent being invalid, as well as the search extending beyond that consented to, the evidence seized from behind the rear seats is inadmissible.

The arrest of Frank was illegal as it resulted from an illegal search and seizure. An arrest occurs when the police take a person into custody against his will for purposes of criminal prosecution or interrogation. A police officer may arrest a person without a warrant if the officer has reasonable grounds to believe that a felony has been committed and that the person being arrested committed the felony. Here, at the time the police officers were ticketing Frank for an inoperable headlight, there was no reason to believe that Frank had committed a crime. As a result, the arrest was unlawful.

The Fifth Amendment argument: Frank's confession is inadmissible as it was obtained in violation of his Fifth Amendment rights. The Fifth Amendment, applicable to the states through the Fourteenth Amendment, provides that no person shall be compelled to be a witness against himself, meaning that a person shall not be compelled to give self-incriminating testimony. Judicial doctrine dictates that a person in custody must, prior to interrogation, be clearly informed that (i) he has the right to remain silent; (ii) anything he says can be used against him in court; (iii) he has the right to the presence of an attorney; and (iv) if he cannot afford an attorney, one will be appointed for him if he so desires. [Miranda v. Arizona, 384 U.S. 436 (1966)] The police must give anyone in police custody and accused of a crime *Miranda* warnings prior to interrogation. A suspect, however, may waive his *Miranda* rights, so long as he does so knowingly, voluntarily, and intelligently. Here, there is no indication that Frank was ever read his *Miranda* rights by any police officer at any time, thus Frank never did knowingly, voluntarily, and intelligently waive these rights. As a result, Frank's confession was obtained in violation of his Fifth Amendment rights, and it must be excluded from the State's case as evidence of guilt.

The unconstitutionality of the lineup: The lineup in which Frank was identified as the armed robber was unconstitutional. An identification denies due process when it is unnecessarily suggestive and there is a substantial likelihood of misidentification. Here, the armed robber was a middle-aged male, and the only people in the lineup were Frank and three juveniles. Such a lineup is unnecessarily suggestive and has a substantial likelihood of resulting in a misidentification, as there is only one middle-aged male to choose from. Therefore, the identification should be excluded from the State's case as it denies Frank due process.

The fruit of the poisonous tree argument: The money found in Frank's car cannot be used as evidence by the State as it was obtained in violation of Frank's rights. The fruit of the poisonous tree doctrine provides that all evidence obtained or derived from exploitation of illegally obtained evidence must be excluded from admission in evidence, unless it can be proved that (i) the evidence was obtained from a source independent of the original illegality, (ii) there was an intervening act of free will by the defendant that breaks the causal chain between the evidence and the original illegality, or (iii) the discovery of the evidence was inevitable. Here, the search of the car violated Frank's Fourth Amendment rights. As a result, any evidence derived from the search of the car must be excluded from evidence. Therefore, in addition to the money being excluded under the fruit of the poisonous tree doctrine, the confession and the identification also should be excluded under this doctrine.

The Sixth Amendment argument: The jury verdict violates Frank's rights under the Sixth and Fourteenth Amendments to the United States Constitution. The right to a jury trial guaranteed by the Sixth and Fourteenth Amendments is a fundamental right, essential for preventing miscarriages of justice and for assuring that fair trials are provided for all defendants. At issue is whether a right to a unanimous verdict is also guaranteed. The Supreme Court has held that although a jury that is comprised of only five people is not a sufficient size to promote adequate group deliberation, insulate members from outside intimidation, and provide a representative cross-section of the community [Ballew v. Georgia, 435 U.S. 223 (1978)], a jury comprised of six people is a sufficient size [Williams v. Florida, 399 U.S. 78 (1970)]. However, the Supreme Court later determined that although the Constitution does not provide a right to a unanimous verdict, a six-person jury must convict by unanimous vote. [Brown v. Louisiana, 447 U.S. 323 (1980)] As a result, the 5-1 vote for conviction is not sufficient to convict Frank.

(EDITOR'S NOTE: The constitutional defects in Frank's arrest and interrogation are the focus of this answer. But for these defects, Frank would have been liable for the felony murder of Customer. The felony murder doctrine provides that a killing committed during the commission of, or in attempt to commit, an enumerated felony is murder. Malice aforethought is implied from the intent to commit the underlying enumerated felony, in this case armed robbery. For the doctrine of felony murder to apply, (i) the defendant must be guilty of the underlying felony; (ii) the felony must be distinct from the killing itself; (iii) the death must have been a foreseeable result of the commission of the felony; and (iv) the death must have been caused before the defendant's immediate flight from the felony to a place of temporary safety. The majority rule holds the felon responsible for the death of another, even if the killing is at the hands of a police officer pursuing the felon. Here, while Frank was fleeing from the crime, and before he reached a place of temporary safety, Customer was shot and killed by a police officer. As a result, if Frank is found guilty of the crime of robbery, Frank will be rightfully found guilty of felony murder.)

4. CONSTITUTIONAL LAW
PART A

Dad may challenge the court's order terminating his parental rights as a violation of his fundamental rights protected by the United States Constitution. At issue here is whether State's statute removing Suzy from Dad's custody infringes on a fundamental right, and, if so, whether such infringement is narrowly tailored to serve a compelling state interest.

The Fourteenth Amendment provides that no State shall "deprive any person of life, liberty, or property, without due process of law." The Supreme Court has long recognized that the Fourteenth Amendment's Due Process Clause guarantees at least fair process and includes a substantive component that "provides heightened protection against government interference with certain fundamental rights and liberty interests." [Washington v. Glucksberg, 521 U.S. 702 (1997)] In addition to the specific freedoms protected by the Bill of Rights, the "liberty" specially protected by the Due Process Clause includes the right to direct the upbringing of one's children. [Pierce v. Society of Sisters, 268 U.S. 510 (1925); Meyer v. Nebraska, 262 U.S. 390 (1923)] Here, State interferes with Dad's fundamental right to raise his daughter, Suzy, as State removed Suzy from Dad's custody upon the death of Mom.

Laws that infringe or intrude upon fundamental liberties must survive strict scrutiny. The Fourteenth Amendment prohibits states from infringing on fundamental liberty interests, no matter what process is provided, unless the infringement is narrowly tailored to serve a compelling state interest. Here, the interest of State that is served by requiring minor children of unwed fathers to become wards of the state upon the death of the mother of the children is the expeditious placement of the children for adoption while using minimal court time and facilities. Whereas questions regarding the safety of a child are compelling interests of the state justifying state interference with the fundamental right to care for one's child, judicial economy and ease of administration cannot reasonably be described as compelling state interests justifying the state's removing a child from the custody of her parent.

As a result, State's statute unconstitutionally infringes upon the fundamental parental right to direct the upbringing of one's child, and the statute must be declared unconstitutional. Accordingly, barring proof of Dad's inability and unfitness to care for Suzy, State will be prohibited from injecting itself into the private realm of the family to remove Suzy from Dad's custody.

The statute is also a violation of the Equal Protection Clause of the Fourteenth Amendment. At issue here is whether distinguishing unwed fathers from other parents is a constitutionally permissible classification. The Equal Protection Clause prohibits state action that creates classifications using arbitrary criteria. At issue here is whether it is rational to distinguish fitness as a parent on the basis of whether a father was married. Therefore, in order for State's statute to be valid under the Equal Protection Clause, it must be rationally related to a legitimate state interest, and the statute must not be arbitrary or irrational. Here, there does not appear to be a rational basis for affording a divorced or widowed father a fitness hearing before determining whether to remove a child from his custody and automatically removing a child from an unwed father's custody.

State provides that the children of parents, other than unwed fathers, can be taken from them only after a hearing that provides proof of unfitness as a parent. An unwed father, however, is uniquely subject to the more simplistic statutory provision that establishes his unfitness as a parent. By use of this statute, State need not prove unfitness in fact, because it is presumed at law.

State's interest in separating children from unwed fathers without a hearing designed to determine whether the unwed father is unfit to be a parent is purely one of judicial economy and ease of administration. State spites its own goals, however, when it needlessly separates a child from the custody of a fit unwed father.

The question here is not the legitimacy of the state ends, however, rather it is whether the means used to achieve these ends are constitutionally defensible. Here, they are not, as the automatic removal of Suzy from Dad's custody, without an opportunity for a hearing as is provided to other parents, is arbitrary and irrational. [Stanley v. Illinois, 405 U.S. 645 (1972)] As a result, the statute is a violation of the Equal Protection Clause of the Fourteenth Amendment and is unconstitutional.

(It should be noted that if the statute provided for a hearing to determine Dad's fitness to be a parent, before State could sever completely and irrevocably Dad's rights as a parent to his natural child, Suzy, due process requires that State establish Dad's unfitness by at least clear and convincing evidence. [Santosky v. Kramer, 455 U.S. 745 (1982)])

PART B

The Supreme Court has held that an inheritance statute absolutely excluding illegitimate children from inheriting from their intestate fathers is a violation of the Equal Protection Clause. [Trimble v. Gordon, 430 U.S. 762 (1977)] Therefore, State's statute will not be enforceable and must be redrafted. At issue here is why is a statute mandating the statutory disinheritance of illegitimate children whose fathers die intestate a violation of the Fourteenth Amendment's Equal Protection Clause and how may the statute be redrafted to avoid violating the Equal Protection Clause.

The Equal Protection Clause prohibits state action that creates classifications using arbitrary criteria. Here, the law discriminates against illegitimate children of fathers who die intestate. Distinctions drawn between legitimate and illegitimate children are reviewed under the intermediate scrutiny standard, and the classification must be substantially related to an important governmental objective. [Clark v. Jeter, 486 U.S. 456 (1988)] Regardless of whether State's purpose is to orderly dispose of decedents' estates or to promote traditional family relationships, State's classification does not meet this standard and is unconstitutional. [Trimble v. Gordon, 430 U.S. 462 (1977)]

The orderly disposition of property at death requires an appropriate legal framework, and each state is entitled to enact laws that govern such disposition, so long as the laws do not infringe on constitutional rights. Inheritance rights can be restricted without jeopardizing the orderly settlement of estates or the dependability of titles to property passing under intestacy laws. For example, State may draft an inheritance statute that places reasonable burdens on illegitimate children of intestate men to require them to establish proof of paternity either during the father's lifetime or within a reasonable time after the father's death. [Lalli v. Lalli, 439 U.S. 259 (1978)] Here, State's statute is overbroad as it extends well beyond any reasonable purpose and excludes categories of illegitimate children unnecessarily from inheritance.

5.   CONTRACTS

To: Senior Partner
From: Attorney
Re: BP v. Norvis; Claims for injunctive relief

Norvis ("N") will most likely be unable to obtain any equitable relief against Tenzer ("T") and Loman ("L"), though it may be possible to get a judgment for damages.

An express agreement not to compete, if made in exchange for good and valuable consideration, will be enforceable as long as it meets a "reasonable standards" test. The agreement, to be valid and enforceable, must be (i) necessary for the protection of the purchaser, and (ii) reasonable in scope as to subject matter, time, and geographic ambit.

The public policy behind this test is to prevent the illegal restraint of trade. Courts have held that such a covenant is not unreasonable and may be enforced against the seller of a company if it is for a period not greater than 10 years. The issue of geographic ambit is more difficult to determine and must be based on facts of each individual case.

In this case, there are two covenants not to compete at issue. The first restricts T from engaging in or working for a similar company for a period of 20 years anywhere in the United States. This covenant was part of the sales contract for BP. There was mutual consideration passed for the contract and thus, the contract is valid and enforceable. The noncompete covenant will be enforceable unless it is overly broad. In some jurisdictions, if the covenant does not pass the reasonableness test it would simply not apply. However, New Jersey is a "blue-pencil" jurisdiction, which means that the court will conform the agreement to make it acceptable.

The subject matter is reasonably limited to the specific business of BP and will stand. Twenty years would be regarded as excessive. The court will take into consideration the fact that five years have already passed and would either make that the duration of the covenant or extend it a bit further.

The geographic scope involved is also a problem. Taken as a whole, T is precluded from doing any business whatsoever in the field of home blood pressure devices even though BP's business extends only to four states. Though it may have been N's intention to expand to a national market, it appears that N may have been overreaching in trying to prevent T from working in the same line throughout the whole country. This is evident both in fact (in five years, the company expanded its sales to only two additional states though it had the opportunity to expand further) and by implication (N fired L though L could have expanded BP into the national market).

Therefore, it appears that the covenant not to compete is unenforceable on its face because it is an illegal restraint on trade. However, the court will "blue-pencil" the agreement to make it conform to a reasonable standard.

The second covenant not to compete was made by L in an employment at will contract with N. L's employment contract with BP appears to lack the new consideration required to make the agreement enforceable, since L was already employed at BP. On this basis, the agreement should not be valid.

However, if valid, the agreement would not likely stand up to the reasonableness test. In balancing the time, scope, and geographic ambit of the covenant against L's ability to pursue his occupation, the court is likely to hold that the covenant is too broad.

It is the policy of this state that noncompete agreements in employment contracts should not exceed five years. In light of the fact that five years have already passed, the court will most likely find the agreement unenforceable even if it becomes subject to "blue-pencilling."

However, N may be entitled to recover damages against L for his three-year breach if the non-compete agreement is held valid.

Based on the facts presented, N will not be successful in obtaining injunctive relief against T and L. Injunctive relief is granted by the court when a party can show that (i) without such relief during the course of litigation they will suffer irreparable harm, and (ii) they have a substantial likelihood of succeeding on the merits. The purpose of the relief is to maintain the status quo between the parties until a full trial can be had.

Here, N waited three years before deciding to bring an action against T and L. Injunctive relief at this point would be ineffective to vindicate any claimed right of BP.

Therefore, injunctive relief, temporary or permanent, will not be granted because BP could not make a showing of immediate irreparable harm in light of the three-year lapse from the time of the breach to the date of BP's action.

T and L also have the defense of laches. Laches is available as a defense when the plaintiff unreasonably delays in bringing an action and that delay is prejudicial to the defendant. It is generally held that laches begins at the time the plaintiff first has knowledge that his rights are being infringed.

N's failure to bring this action three years ago when he first learned of T and L's activities is prejudicial because of the large investment in time, money, and effort by T and L in promoting their product. Thus, T and L have the defense of laches because the three-year delay by N in bringing this action is prejudicial to T and L.

Therefore, except for the possibility of money damages from T and L and because of their breach of the noncompete agreement within the reasonable time set forth by the court, N will not be entitled to relief against T and L because (i) both agreements not to compete violate the policies of restraint of trade; (ii) N cannot show that failure to grant BP injunctive relief will cause immediate and irreparable harm; and (iii) N's failure to bring a timely action makes the defense of laches available to T and L.

6. TORTS

Peter v. Dave: Peter will be able to establish a prima facie case for trespass to land. Peter will have to prove: (i) the physical invasion of his land by Dave; (ii) intent on Dave's part to bring about the physical invasion of Peter's property; and (iii) causation.

Physical invasion of plaintiff's land occurs although Dave did not personally go onto Peter's land. Dave "set the force in motion" which he knew, or should have known, would result in trespass to Peter's property. There need be no intent to trespass; intent to do the act which constitutes trespass will satisfy the intent requirement. The crowd was under Dave's "control" and he caused them to invade Peter's land. Since trespass is an intentional tort, damage is presumed; Peter is entitled to nominal and actual damages. Punitive damages are recoverable if Peter proves that Dave desired or intended the destruction caused by the crowd.

Peter might argue that even though Dave did not intend to trespass, the act of climbing on the car, given the likely response of the crowd, evidenced a lack of due care with regard to persons and property in the area and Dave is therefore negligent. If Peter proves negligence, but not intentional trespass, he may not be awarded punitive damages. There are no apparent defenses available to Dave; there was no necessity that he stand on the car nor that he bring people onto Peter's property for any purpose.

Mayor v. Dave: To make out a prima facie case for defamation, the Mayor will have to plead and prove that defamatory language was "published" of or concerning him which caused damage to his reputation, by the fault of Dave. The Mayor's claim arises from two specific episodes. First, the accusation that the Mayor is "immoral and unfit to hold political office" may be slander; when a slander relates to a person's ability in his profession he need not plead special damages because damages are presumed. This statement of unfitness was shouted at a sizeable crowd, attacks the

Mayor's professional capacity, and completes the prima facie case. However, a public official may not recover for damages for "defamatory falsehood relating to his official conduct unless he proves that the statement was made with actual malice, that is, with knowledge that it was false" or with reckless disregard for the truth. [New York Times, Inc. v. Sullivan, 376 U.S. 254 (1964)] The *Times* rule will probably protect Dave since there is no suggestion that he knew the transcript was false when he read it, and his slander was based on what the transcript said. Though the episode dealt with a private aspect of the Mayor's life, it was arguably relevant to the question of whether he was fit to be an elected official.

The second defamation involves reading the divorce transcript. Reading from a written document is libel. Since the defamation is clear from the face of the transcript, there is no requirement that special damages be proved. However, once again the *Times* fault standard will probably protect Dave. In addition, there is a privilege of record libel, *i.e.,* the privilege to make fair and accurate quotations from a judicial transcript without being liable for its inaccuracies. Truth, of course, is a complete defense. Furthermore, even if some parts of the transcript were false, those parts may have been minor enough that the gist of the transcript was true.

Wilma v. Dave: Although Wilma is clearly a private figure for purposes of a defamation action, the divorce action of the mayor might be considered a matter of public concern, which would shift the burden of proof on the truth or falsity issue from Dave to Wilma. In any case, however, the fact that the statements were true will preclude Wilma from succeeding on a defamation complaint.

Should Wilma allege intrusion upon plaintiff's affairs or seclusion (invasion of privacy), she will have to prove an act of intrusion by Dave about something private which would be objectionable to a reasonable person. Or, she could bring the action in the name of "Public disclosure of private facts against plaintiff." Nonetheless, the publication is privileged where the matter is of legitimate public interest, and where the matters published are taken from an official proceeding there is an absolute privilege. Generally, a person once in the public eye remains so for privilege purposes although time has elapsed.

Should Wilma allege a case of intentional infliction of emotional distress, she must show that Dave's conduct went beyond all bounds of decency, that it caused severe emotional distress to her, and that she has suffered damages. This allegation will likely be met by a privilege defense. (*See* above.) Wilma's greatest chance for recovery is to allege that Dave acted with malice, which goes to a reckless disregard for the truth. [Time v. Hill, 385 U.S. 374 (1967)] As indicated in the decision on defamation, however, Wilma will have difficulty establishing malice.

Dave v. Police: Dave will be unsuccessful in asserting a case for false imprisonment because there was no intent on the police's behalf to confine Dave; Dave voluntarily subjected himself to an area that he knew, or should have known, would soon be barricaded. Also, Dave was not held for any more time than was necessary to discover the mistake. There can be no action for false arrest because there was no arrest.

Any allegation by Dave for these intentional torts will be rebutted by defenses to intentional torts including consent, defense of property, and defense of others. The police officers also acted out of (what they believed to be) necessity to avoid potential injury or danger. The act here (refusing to let Dave out of the van) was for the public good and is an absolute defense. Although Dave may have consented by mistake, the police did not take advantage of this mistake; apparent consent may be inferred from Dave's conduct.

7.   REAL PROPERTY

The fact there was a private restrictive covenant on the lot at the time Husband bought it raises the question of whether the seller can deliver a marketable title to buyer.

All contracts for the sale of land contain (unless otherwise expressly provided) an implied warranty by the seller that he will deliver to the buyer a marketable title at the date of closing. The seller's basic obligation under this warranty is to deliver title free from reasonable doubt either in fact or law.

Title is deemed marketable if a reasonably prudent buyer, ready and able to purchase, will accept it in the exercise of ordinary prudence.

Among the types of defects that render a title unmarketable are problems occasioned by private restrictions such as that found in this case. The restriction here certainly reduces the uses to which the property can be put.

Because of this potential problem, more information is needed to determine whether the private restriction here is reasonable and enforceable. If it is not enforceable, then it would not prevent the seller from rendering marketable title to buyer. The validity of this private restriction may also affect seller's ability to give the required covenants for title.

The attorney would also need to obtain information on the shared driveway. This is important in determining exactly what interests in the driveway seller can convey.

The next question posed is what are the laws concerning premises leased to tenants and what effect these laws will have on the desired conveyance. This information is necessary to determine when the seller will be able to actually complete the conveyance.

It is also important to know whether there is any law in the state that would validate an existing nonconforming structure or use, although in violation of a present zoning ordinance, after a certain period of time. This is important because the house is, and always has been, in violation of the zoning ordinance. If there is such a statute, then no change need be made to the house before the sale.

If there is no such law, the buyer ought to be informed that the house is in nonconformance with the current zoning restrictions, and that plans to enlarge the house would be substantially thwarted.

Finally, one would need to know whether there is any possibility of obtaining a variance to allow a residential use should the proposed commercial zoning of the area be effectuated. If such a variance is not possible, then buyer should not buy the house since, with his advance knowledge of the rezoning possibility, he may not be able to maintain his residency there for long once the area is rezoned.

There should be contingencies in the contract that seller convey marketable title and all required covenants of title, that title shall not pass until the present tenants have been given adequate notice and have to quit the premises, and that seller will perform whatever acts are necessary to perfect buyer's title.

A possible problem (assuming that the lawyer handling the closing is as unaware of the termite problem as the buyer) would be the buyer's option to declare the sale void because of seller's fraudulent concealment of what appears to be a material factor (not just termites, but a "large" and "active" colony).

Another possible problem is that it must be ascertained how seller obtained title to the property. Here, seller's late husband obtained the property *before* they married.

8.   CRIMINAL LAW/PROCEDURE

(a)(1)   Brown would be guilty of felony murder. A killing of a nonparticipant during the commission, flight after the commission, or attempted commission of a felony is murder. Here, the underlying felony is robbery. Robbery is the taking of personal property of another from the other's person or presence by force or intimidation with the intent to permanently deprive her of it.

A defendant can be found guilty of felony murder when resistance by the victim results in death to a third-party bystander. Defendant is not liable for the death of a co-felon resulting from resistance of the victim.

The malice aforethought required for murder is implied from the intent to commit the underlying felony. It is also necessary to determine if death was a foreseeable result of the commission of the felony.

The death penalty may not be imposed for felony murder where defendant did not take or attempt or intend to take a life, or intend that lethal force be employed.

12.

If the pretrial identifications were unconstitutional, Naomi's in-court identification of Brown must be excluded from evidence unless it can be shown that Naomi had an independent source for her in-court identification.

There are two possible sources for unconstitutionality: the Sixth Amendment right to counsel and the Due Process Clause. There was no Sixth Amendment violation here because the right to counsel does not attach until a defendant has been charged, and both identifications here occurred pre-charge. The Due Process Clause is violated where a defendant can show that an identification is unnecessarily suggestive and there is a reasonable likelihood of misidentification. This standard might have been violated here: Detective Rite's pointing to Brown and suggesting that Brown was Naomi's attacker was unnecessarily suggestive since Brown was the only person to choose from, but it is unclear whether there was a reasonable likelihood of misidentification—Naomi indicated only that Brown looked something like her attacker. The subsequent lineup probably was not unnecessarily suggestive (no facts on suggestiveness were presented), but it might be considered tainted because of the prior identification.

If the initial identifications were unconstitutional, Naomi's in-court identification must be excluded unless the prosecution can show that Naomi has an independent source for the in-court identification. The court should consider Naomi's opportunity to observe Brown at the time of the crime, her ease in identifying Brown, and the presence or absence of misidentification.

(2) If the court finds that the jury's view of Brown in the elevator was damaging and prejudicial, a mistrial will be justified. Upon making the motion, trial court could have conducted voir dire to determine the effect on the jury.

Inasmuch as the viewing was brief and accidental, and the nature of the possible prejudice was not related to any of the traditional due process concerns subject to abuse by governmental authorities, it would appear that the court's denial of defense counsel's motion constituted nothing more than mere error rather than prejudical error.

(b) There is no constitutional right to a preliminary hearing, nor does the federal Constitution require such a hearing prior to an indictment.

With respect to the formation of the grand jury, there is no right to have the jury selected on a **proportional** basis, even where the question is the right to a selection of a grand jury from a **representative cross-section** of the relevant community. Absent some particularly compelling evidence of bias, such as systematic exclusion of all members of a racial group, it is unlikely that the make-up of the grand jury will suffice as a basis for challenging the indictment or conviction.

It is clear, at least, that the rules restricting the make-up of petit juries can differ from those governing the make-up of grand juries because the functions of each jury differ; the former is a trier of fact and the slightest prejudice has an impact, while the latter is an investigator and accuser.

9. CONTRACTS

Dear Mr. Dealer:

Your sale of a tractor to Mr. Growe is a sale of goods, and therefore your rights and liabilities will be determined by the Uniform Commercial Code ("U.C.C."). According to section 2-201 of the U.C.C., a contract for the sale of goods worth $500 or more will be unenforceable, unless there is some writing which evidences the essential terms of the agreement, which is signed by the party to be charged with enforcement of the agreement. But this rule does not apply to contracts for the sale of goods where the goods are actually received by the purchaser and accepted by him, or where he pays for them. Thus, you and Mr. Growe have a valid contract for the sale and purchase of one tractor, and your rights will be determined by referring to the U.C.C.

Although Growe had a right to damages for breach of warranty, any right that he might have had to reject the tractor or revoke acceptance certainly had expired by July 1974.

Under the U.C.C., a buyer has a right to reject goods that do not conform to the contract at any time prior to acceptance. Acceptance occurs (i) when the buyer, after a reasonable opportunity to inspect them indicates to the seller that they conform to the contract, (ii) when the buyer fails to reject within a reasonable time, or (iii) when the buyer does any act inconsistent with the seller's ownership. After acceptance, the buyer has no right to reject goods unless the buyer can revoke acceptance. A buyer has a right to revoke acceptance when the buyer discovers a defect in the goods that substantially impair their value and (i) he accepted them on a reasonable belief that the defect would be cured or (ii) he accepted them because of the difficulty in discovering the defect or because of the seller's assurance that the goods would be conforming. If the buyer has accepted nonconforming goods and can no longer revoke acceptance, the buyer's only remedy for the nonconformity is damages, but to recover damages, the buyer must notify the seller within a reasonable time after discovering the defect.

Applying the law to the facts here, Mr. Growe has no contractual remedy.

It is unclear when acceptance occurred under the facts here. Since the contract was "C.O.D.," Mr. Growe had no right to inspect the tractor prior to delivery and so had a reasonable time after delivery to inspect the tractor. He informed you of the defect in the tractor the same day that he picked it up, which is certainly within a reasonable time. However, the facts indicate that he did not choose to reject the tractor but instead requested that it be repaired. Nevertheless, it could be argued that this did not amount to an acceptance, or that if it did, Mr. Growe would have a reasonable time after you returned the tractor to him in which to reject. You returned the tractor to Mr. Growe in February, and he indicated that the tractor was fine. This probably was sufficient for acceptance. Even if it was not sufficient, Mr. Growe's keeping the tractor until July certainly would constitute an act inconsistent with your ownership and the passage of more than a reasonable time within which to reject.

Mr. Growe might argue that he still could revoke his acceptance after harvest-time because the defect was difficult to discover, but this argument should fail because Mr. Growe did not seem to have any difficulty discovering the defect initially. It seems unreasonable for him now to claim that the defect was not easily discoverable.

You probably have no liability for any defect in the tractor. An express warranty would have arisen from any affirmation of fact that you made or model that you showed Mr. Growe, but nothing here tells me that any express warranties were made. No implied warranty of fitness for particular purpose would have arisen, since the facts do not indicate that Mr. Growe relied on you to choose a tractor for him (a prerequisite of this warranty). The only other possible warranty claim would arise from the implied warranty of merchantability—when goods are sold by a merchant, the merchant impliedly warrants that the goods, among other things, will be fit for ordinary purposes. Assuming that the poorly performing engine makes the tractor unfit for ordinary purposes, there would be a breach. However, as indicated above, a prerequisite to recovering damages for breach of warranty is timely notice. Here, Mr. Growe received the tractor in February, said it was fine, but noted that he wanted to wait until harvest, several months later, before giving final approval. The U.C.C. provides no such test period. Notice of a defect must be received within a reasonable time after a defect is discovered or should be discovered, and Mr. Growe surely should have been able to discover the poor performance before July. Thus, you will not be liable for breach of warranty damages.

Note that Mr. Growe himself has been in breach of contract from the start. The C.O.D. term of your contract expressly made payment and delivery conditions concurrent. Mr. Growe gave you a check on delivery, which is sufficient to suspend his duty of performance, but payment by check is not final until the check is paid, and the check here was never paid. While Mr. Growe might argue that he had a right to stop payment on discovering the defect, since we determined above that he has since accepted the tractor, he is now in default. (Note that Mr. Growe might even be liable in tort for fraud, since he wrote a $10,000 check when he had only $200 in his account, but it would have to be proved that Mr. Growe had no intention of paying the check when he wrote it.)

Even though Mr. Growe was in default, you had no right to repossess the tractor. The U.C.C. allows the seller of undelivered goods to withhold them when payment is not duly made, and allows the seller of delivered goods to recover them within 10 days of delivery if the goods are sold on credit and the seller discovers the buyer's insolvency. Otherwise, the only right to repossess goods arises where a security interest is taken. Nothing in the facts indicates that you took a security interest in the tractor, and neither of the other two rules is applicable. Thus, your repossession was wrongful.

Since your repossession was wrongful, Mr. Growe may now maintain a conversion action. An action for conversion will lie where a person wrongfully interferes with another's possessory rights in goods and as a result the other is substantially or permanently deprived of the goods. Damages are the value of the goods at the time of the taking. (Alternatively, Mr. Growe could bring an action for trespass to chattels, entitling him to diminution in value and return of the tractor, but since the tractor was badly damaged and he did not like it anyway, this seems unlikely.) In any case, you would be allowed to set off the money that Mr. Growe owes you for the purchase of the tractor.

Finally, you will probably not be found liable for the injuries to Innocent caused by Phuzz's negligent driving of the tractor. Under the legal doctrine of "respondeat superior," an employer will be held liable for the acts of an employee where the acts were committed in the scope of the employment of the employee, and in furtherance of the interest of the employer. On the other hand, an employer is not liable for the acts of an independent contractor unless inherently dangerous activities were involved or the employer was negligent in the selection of the contractor, neither of which is present here. In this case, Phuzz is clearly an independent contractor rather than an employee. He was hired just to do a particular job for a set amount, and was not directed or supervised in how the job was to be carried out. Thus, you will not be liable to Innocent for Phuzz's negligence.

Yours truly,

10. CONSTITUTIONAL LAW

The municipality is faced with the following issues: (i) defiance of an ordinance prohibiting rentals to two or more unrelated persons; (ii) amendment of a zoning ordinance to permit occupancy by the elderly of mobile homes; (iii) nonresident user charges at public beaches to benefit the elderly financially; (iv) amendment to the zoning ordinance to prohibit conversion of rental apartment houses into condominiums; and (v) exemption from the ordinance in (i) for the elderly.

The issues involve questions of constitutional law. Taken in sequence:

Ordinance prohibiting group rentals: It is constitutional and not violative of equal protection for a community to determine its residential character by zoning to limit the inhabitants of family homes to persons related by blood. This was the issue in *Village of Belle Terre v. Boraas*, 416 U.S. 1 (1974). New Jersey, however, as a matter of state constitutional law, has taken a more restrictive view of the powers of its municipalities to control local demographic trends through zoning. Although not characterized as a zoning ordinance, the prohibition of group rentals acts as a zoning or land control regulation, and comes under the principles established for zoning. The ordinance itself is probably unconstitutional in that it is too restrictive of the types of residents who may live in the community.

It is, after all, a nine-room house. And, presumably, a "fair share" approach (using the New Jersey rule) for this region of the state requires that some housing be available for groups of "two or more unrelated persons." Tough enforcement of the ordinance may be impracticable because of its dubious constitutionality; however, the municipality is not precluded from enforcing its health and safety code and related penal provisions against disorderly conduct and traffic infractions.

Amendment for mobile homes: The town is entitled to accede to the demands of the senior citizens by amending its zoning ordinance to allow persons 62 years of age to reside in mobile homes. This was held to be constitutional by the New Jersey Supreme Court in *Taxpayers Association of Weymouth TP. v. Weymouth TP.*, 71 N.J. 249 (1976). The ordinance as changed is permissible as a method of helping the elderly in a crowded housing market and does not unduly affect other classes of residents. Hence, the town is able to modify its zoning in this respect.

Nonresident user charges: The town probably can place a user charge on nonresidents with the proceeds earmarked for senior citizens. While the Privileges and Immunities Clause of Article IV prohibits states from discriminating against nonresidents when fundamental rights are involved (such as where nonresidents are charged more for commercial licenses than residents are charged and the increased charge is not due to increased costs arising from the fact that the licensee is out-of-state), the Clause will not prevent the difference in charges for recreational licenses because no fundamental right is involved—there is no fundamental right of citizenship to swim for recreational purposes. Thus, the town is free to charge nonresidents more to enter its beaches.

Amendment prohibiting condominium conversion: The town could agree to an ordinance, given state authority to do so, that would prohibit conversion of rental apartments into condominiums. The constitutional difficulty would be the authority of the town to enact such an ordinance, which is not a restriction on use (zoning) so much as on nature of ownership, and whether the degree of restriction on alienation of property was such that it violated due process in its procedure, or constituted a "taking" of private property for "public" use. Assuming that the town had the authority to create such a restriction on private property, there would probably be no problem constitutionally. The degree of restraint on the property is not so great as to amount to a deprivation of private property. The analogy here is to a zoning ordinance that prohibited additions or alterations to rental apartment buildings—there is a restraint on private property, but not so much that it renders the real property virtually worthless. Given proper procedures, it is likely that such an ordinance would be constitutional. Since the question turns on the degree of restraint, it is not clear whether an ordinance could prohibit all or only some conversion of rental apartments into condominiums.

Exemption for elderly: With respect to an exemption to the group rental ordinance, it is clear under the *Weymouth* principle that senior citizens are a class that, upon a showing of lack of housing, may be favored constitutionally by the state's zoning power as exercised by a municipality.

It is clear that the town must consider the balancing of interests and equality of treatment involved in enforcing its ordinances or in amending them. Other alternatives outside the scope of the question include the raising of income subsidies to the elderly, public housing projects, and the like.

11. CONSTITUTIONAL LAW

Transporting goods without a permit: Dave could rely on the notion that he was carrying out the duties under the contract that were carefully planned and controlled by the federal government. This defense has been described as "shar(ing) in the government's immunity" [Green v. ICI America, 362 F. Supp. 1263 (E.D. Tenn. 1973)] or asserting the "government's contract defense" [Merritt, Chapman & Scott Corp. v. Guy F. Atkinson, 295 F.2d 14 (9th Cir. 1961)].

The Supremacy Clause has been held impliedly to require that activities of the federal government be free from burdensome state regulations. This means that the state may neither unduly interfere with the functioning of federal agencies nor directly control work that a contractor is performing for the United States. The states may, however, regulate government contractors so long as the regulations do not prescribe the manner in which they are to perform their contracts.

In the present case, Dave is a contractor performing services solely for the federal government. If he must comply with the State X requirement that commercial carriers obtain permits from the Public Utility Commission, granted only to financially responsible carriers that use safe equipment, the federal government's operations could be severely hindered. Not only might the processing procedure delay construction, but the state standards restrict the federal government's initial choice of carriers. In a very similar case, the Supreme Court held that one who contracted with the federal government to construct facilities at an Air Force base need not obtain a license to do business from the state. [Miller v. Arkansas, 421 U.S. 1002 (1975)] Since Dave is therefore immune from the permit requirement, he cannot constitutionally be prosecuted for failure to satisfy it.

Driving while license suspended: Since Dave is a carrier, a state requirement that all persons driving motor vehicles have a valid operator's license would clearly interfere with his work for the federal government. As noted earlier, such a requirement could unduly limit the government's choice of contractors and interfere with operations after the contract is entered into. In a case involving a federal employee rather than a contractor, it was held that the state could not require the employee to obtain a driver's license in order to operate a mail truck. [Johnson v. Maryland, 254 U.S. 51 (1920)] This same immunity would presumably extend to federal contractors while they are operating vehicles pursuant to their contract.

In the present case, however, Dave did not simply refuse to obtain a driver's license. He had a license when he began performing his contract, and lost it only after ignoring a number of speeding citations. The state would take the position that if Dave is not immune from the speeding charges, as discussed below, he cannot be immune from charges arising from his failure to honor the license suspension—which is the penalty for ignoring the citations. The argument is not persuasive, however, and is inconsistent with the principle of governmental immunity. If the speeding charges are valid, the state does indeed have an interest in punishing Dave; but where there is a conflict, this interest must yield to the federal interest in carrying on its operations free from undue state interference.

Speeding: Dave probably exceeded his authority under the contract when he violated the speed laws. Dave's immunity should not extend to speeding violations, since the federal interest is not unduly interfered with or impaired by enforcing the speed law against Dave. When the federal government entered into the contract with Dave, it presumably did not contemplate that Dave would exceed the speed limit when delivering supplies. The facts do not indicate any interest of the federal government that would be served by allowing Dave to freely violate the speed law. And since the governmental immunity should only arise when a conflict exists between the state interest (in protecting against the harm of speeding) and federal interests, immunity should not be given to Dave on the speeding charges.

Vagueness: Dave may avoid conviction on the speeding charges on the ground that the state speeding law is vague. The speeding statute requires that drivers not drive at speeds "greater than what is reasonable under the circumstances." Persons of common intelligence would probably differ on the application of the statute so that there could be significant disparities in enforcement; *i.e.*, on any given stretch of road, at any given time, one law enforcement officer might believe 40 mph to be a reasonable speed, while another officer might consider 70 mph to be reasonable. A motorist, in turn, might feel that 50 mph is reasonable. Whether the motorist is cited therefore depends on which officer observes him.

Because of this vagueness and probable discrepancies in application of the statute, Dave should be able to avoid prosecution under the statute unless, perhaps, he was driving at a speed that no person of common intelligence would believe reasonable (*e.g.*, 90 mph in a school zone). Unless Dave were such a "hardcore" violator, however, the state should not be allowed to prosecute him on the speeding charge.

12. TORTS
BRIEF IN SUPPORT OF PLAINTIFF POTTER

(a)   As against Mistkill, two theories of recovery are available to Potter: negligence and strict liability.

Recovery is permitted on negligence principles under the common law rule that a manufacturer owes a duty of care to all persons who may foreseeably be damaged or injured by negligence in manufacturing the product. A majority of states extend that duty to claims for property damage.

Potter's claim against Mistkill has been proven as a matter of law and has been established by the doctrine of res ipsa loquitur. The prerequisites to the doctrine's application have been met: (i) The inference of negligence has been established because Potter has demonstrated that the accident causing his injury is the type that would not normally occur unless someone was negligent; (ii) Potter has established that the instrumentality which caused the injury was in the sole control of the defendant; and (iii) Potter in no way contributed to the property damage or injury. Since Potter has proven the res ipsa element, a prima facie case has been made out for him. No directed verdict may be given to defendants.

There has been raised a presumption of negligence that should result in a judgment for Potter in the absence of facts that would rebut the presumption.

Mistkill's negligence is a cause in fact of the death of Potter's horse; but for the adulteration of the spray, the horse would not have died.

Potter's horse's susceptibility to strychnine presents no bar to Potter's recovery because of the "eggshell skull theory." It is well recognized that a defendant "takes his victim as he finds him." The horse's susceptibility may have been one cause of his death; Mistkill's negligence is a proximate cause of the horse's death and Mistkill should be liable to any one who may foreseeably be damaged by negligence in manufacturing the product; and farm animals are foreseeably present where crops are sprayed. Mistkill is therefore liable to Potter on a negligence theory.

Strict liability principles eliminate the necessity of proving Mistkill's negligence directly or inferentially. Many statutes impose upon a manufacturer strict liability in tort to a bystander for damages to person, property, or chattels. Injury which proximately results from a defect in a product which was being used in the manner for which it was intended can be redressed on a strict liability theory. Under these facts, Potter is entitled to recover from Mistkill.

Product-oriented theories of strict liability emphasize that the unreasonably dangerous nature of the product, not the conduct of the defendant, is crucial. Although there was no evidence of negligence in manufacture, a poison which causes a fatality is unreasonably dangerous if the defect existed when the product left Mistkill, and the product was being subjected to normal use.

Furthermore, since the privity defense has eroded, protection is afforded to non-user bystanders so long as injury to such persons is foreseeable. An animal on farmland is highly foreseeable.

(b) Upwind's conduct renders it liable to Potter for injuries sustained. Although Upwind's activity took place on its own land, Upwind had a landowner's duty to exercise due care and prevent exposure of adjoining landowner's property to unreasonable risk of harm. The Agricultural Department recommendations are evidence of compliance with a standard required by law and a state of the art in crop spraying, but such does not conclusively establish due care. Wind is one of the factors that Upwind was, or should have been, aware could alter the effectiveness of aerial spraying.

Where an activity involves substantial risk of damage to the person or property of others despite the actor's exercise of due care, and the activity cannot be performed with complete safety, and it is not an activity commonly engaged in in the community, then the activity is considered abnormally dangerous. Liability for abnormally dangerous activity exists in the absence of negligence, if there is injury proximately caused by such activity. Aerial spraying is often recognized as an abnormally dangerous activity; the risk of a crash, debris, and poison clearly exist. If the trier of fact here determines that aerial spraying is not commonly engaged in in this community, then liability will and should be imposed upon Upwind.

Upwind should be found strictly liable for Potter's damage; poisoned animals are well within the scope of the risk created and the horse's death was the result of the abnormally dangerous propensity of aerial spraying.

13. CONTRACTS

TO: Senior Partner

FROM: A. A. Associate

Bill's rights against Cliff depend on whether a bilateral contract for the purchase and sale of land was formed. As stated further on, it would appear that there was no contract, *i.e.*, that the offer to sell was effectively withdrawn before Bill's acceptance was effectively communicated.

On August 9, Cliff communicated to Bill a present offer to sell his farmland, sufficiently describing the essential terms of the proposed transaction. The effect thereof was to create in Bill (as offeree) the power to form an executory contract by a timely acceptance. At this point, however, only a simple offer was outstanding, meaning that it could be revoked by Cliff at any time prior to an effective acceptance.

On August 10, the parties engaged in further negotiations, but no acceptance was forthcoming: Cliff merely repeated the written offer and added a pledge not to revoke the offer for 30 days. Cliff further requested Bill to "think about it seriously." Arguably, a valid option contract was formed by Bill's promise to "think about the offer seriously." But while he may contend that he promised to do something he was not previously bound to do (*i.e.,* he was not obligated to give serious consideration to the offer but for this promise), it is doubtful that a court would interpret these communications as forming an option agreement, on the theory that no serious bargained-for exchange of promises occurred so that the alleged option was lacking legally sufficient consideration. An "option" is a promise to keep an offer open for a stated period of time which is supported by consideration; something of value is bargained for and given in exchange for the promise. Without such consideration, the promise is not legally binding and can be revoked at any time.

On August 14, Bill sent Cliff a notice of his unequivocal acceptance. But an acceptance will not form a contract unless it takes effect prior to termination of the offer. These facts state that before dispatch of the acceptance, Bill had learned from Cliff's brother that the farm had been conveyed to a third person. Under the generally accepted rule, where the offeree acquires reliable information that the offeror has entered into a wholly inconsistent contract, the offer is thereby revoked; this is the case notwithstanding that notification did not come from the offeror himself. Since the facts give no indication that Cliff's brother is not a reliable source, prima facie it appears that the offer was effectively revoked and that Bill's subsequent acceptance was late. This would preclude a finding of the formation of any contract between Bill and Cliff.

Having failed to establish an option, Bill might try to recover on a theory of detrimental reliance by alleging his costs in traveling to inspect the property and his successful efforts in obtaining financing. A number of courts following the Restatement 2d position hold that where the offeror could reasonably foresee that the offeree would rely on the offer, and the offeree does so rely on the offer to his detriment, the offeror is thereby precluded from withdrawing his offer for a reasonable period of time. In this case, however, it is doubtful that Bill will succeed. Since a unilateral contract was not contemplated, such acts do not constitute "part performance," and the steps taken do not appear sufficiently detrimental to establish an estoppel. Thus, the better argument is that no conduct on Bill's part altered the inherent revocability of Cliff's offer.

However, should a court find that the offer was in fact irrevocable, either because an effective option contract was formed, or because of a detrimental reliance theory, then it would follow that Bill's acceptance gave rise to a valid contract. He then could pursue either an action at law for damages, or seek a decree in equity for specific performance. The fact that the innocent third party, Smith, has reconveyed the land to Cliff removes a substantial impediment to Bill's right to equitable relief. Had Smith kept the land, his equity being last in time would have cut off Bill's remedy of specific performance. Damages in an at-law action would be the difference between the contract price and actual purchase price.

14. CRIMINAL LAW/PROCEDURE
LIABILITY FOR ATTEMPT

The substantive elements of an attempted crime consist of an intent to perform an act which, if achieved, would constitute a crime, and an overt act beyond mere preparation for the offense. Bob's acts were adequate to accomplish his criminal purpose. Attempt is a specific intent crime; the intent is to complete the crime. Bob has produced no evidence of a defense. It is no defense to an attempted crime that it would have been impossible for the defendant to complete his plan because Art disarmed the bomb. Evidence that Bob had the requisite mens rea to commit the crime charged proved beyond a reasonable doubt that Bob was guilty of the offense charged.

SEARCH AND SEIZURE

Admissibility of bomb: To invoke the exclusionary rule, Bob must have "standing." Bob has standing if he establishes that (i) he had a property or possessory interest in property searched or seized and (ii) has a legitimate expectation of privacy in the area searched. Bob can assert a possessory interest in the bomb but it is unlikely that he had a legitimate expectation of privacy in Carl's car. Due to Bob's lack of standing, the bomb is admissible against him.

Even if Bob did have standing, the bomb would still be admissible because the search was incidental to a lawful arrest. The legality of Bob's arrest will depend upon whether the police had probable cause to arrest. Art's hearsay information was from a reasonably reliable informant and was corroborated by the officer's personal observations that a felony was being committed. Since the officers had reasonable grounds to believe that a felony had been committed and Bob committed it, the officers had probable cause to make a warrantless arrest. After arresting Defendant, police may search the person and areas into which he might reach to obtain weapons or destroy evidence.

The search would also fall under the "automobile" exception since the police had probable cause to believe that the vehicle contained evidence of a crime; the emergency exception, given the nature of the evidence (a bomb) and its location (a residential area); and the plain view exception if it was in or on the car where it could be seen.

Admissibility of sales receipt: Bob has standing to invoke the exclusionary rule. He is the owner of the car and has a reasonable expectation of privacy in his own car. However, the sales receipt will be admissible. An inventory search of the car that police lawfully took into possession is reasonable. The inventory was limited to those items in plain view. The inventory was done pursuant to departmental practice for the purpose of caretaking and not investigation.

Also, the sales receipt is the result of a valid warrantless search under the plain view exception. The police officer inadvertently discovered the evidence when he was lawfully present. Police Officer had a legal right to write the ticket when he inadvertently viewed the sales receipt on the dashboard.

ADMISSIBILITY OF ADMISSIONS

Pre-indictment admissions: Although the Fourth Amendment protects a person's conversations from warrantless government intrusion where uttered in expectation of privacy, it does not protect a person's "misplaced confidences." The accused takes the risk that those to whom he voluntarily chooses to reveal incriminating information will turn out to be "false friends"—supposed cohorts in crime who are actually police agents.

Moreover, since Art could properly testify concerning his conversations with Bob, properly authenticated recordings of such conversations are also admissible as corroboration thereof. Realistically, the recordings are even more reliable than Art's testimony alone.

Post-indictment admissions: The result is different, however, as to Bob's incriminating admissions to Art after his indictment. Here, there are both Fifth and Sixth Amendment violations.

Under the Sixth Amendment, once an accused has been formally charged with a crime (here, by indictment), he has a constitutional right to assistance of counsel at all critical stages of the proceedings, and interrogation by the police or anyone working on their behalf is such a critical stage. Since Bob was not afforded the right to counsel when the conversations at the jail occurred, Art's testimony—and the recordings—should have been held legally inadmissible.

The jailhouse conversations can be challenged as a violation of Bob's Fifth Amendment privilege against self-incrimination. The "interrogation" is considered custodial because Bob was not free to leave and it was likely to elicit incriminating responses. No *Miranda* warnings were given and so the conversations were inadmissible. Whether the use of these statements at trial requires automatic reversal is unclear. However, there will be a heavy burden on the government to prove that this was harmless error.

The "harmless error" test is invoked where evidence was received at trial in violation of the Fourth Amendment. The prosecution bears the burden to establish beyond reasonable doubt that the evidence did not contribute to Bob's conviction (*i.e.,* there is so much other evidence of guilt that there was no reasonable possibility that the jury verdict turned on this admission).

15. REAL PROPERTY

The Spaceburger lease of Blackacre: The Spaceburger lease of Blackacre is void with respect to W.

A tenancy by the entirety is an estate held by husband and wife as a fictitious unit with right of survivorship. Neither tenant can obtain partition nor can he act so as to defeat the right of survivorship of his co-tenant. Under common law, a grant to the husband and wife during the marriage necessarily creates a tenancy by the entirety. It is immaterial whether the entire consideration for the property is given by one spouse or both.

Here, the deed given to H for Blackacre created a tenancy by the entirety for H and W, notwithstanding the fact that H paid all the consideration. With respect to H's right to lease Blackacre to Spaceburger, although the reported cases have taken divergent views on this subject, the emerging trend is that a lease by one of the spouses without the consent of the other is void. Here, there is no indication that W consented to the lease of Blackacre to Spaceburger. Accordingly, since W became sole owner of Blackacre after H's death, she may refuse to honor the Spaceburger lease and instead may honor the Colonial Furniture lease.

Spaceburger's right to use Whiteacre as a parking lot: Assuming, arguendo, that Spaceburger's lease of Blackacre was valid with respect to W, Spaceburger could not have prevented the sale of Whiteacre to Department Store.

Under the facts given, H's statement to Spaceburger's president that ". . . your patrons can park (at Whiteacre) free when the on-site lot is full," at best creates an oral license to use Whiteacre.

A license is a personal privilege held by the licensee. Its informal nature is described by saying that the Statute of Frauds is inapplicable to its creation. The essential characteristic of a license is that it is revocable by nature. It may be revoked at any time by a manifestation of the licensor's intent to end it. This manifestation may be by a formal notice of revocation or it may consist of conduct which obstructs the licensee's continued use. Here, clearly, the sale of Whiteacre constitutes conduct which terminates the license.

The unrecorded mortgage: In general, an unrecorded mortgage does not constitute a valid encumbrance on land, unless and until it is properly recorded. Additionally, an unrecorded mortgage will be inoperative with respect to any liens or claims attaching after its execution and before it is recorded.

Here, Whiteacre was sold to the Department Store before any mortgage was recorded. Under the doctrine of equitable conversion, after a contract for the sale of realty is executed, the interest of the seller of the property (H) is deemed personal property and the interest of the buyer of the property (Department Store) is deemed real property. Thus, under rules of equity, Bank cannot record a mortgage given by it on realty which has been "converted" to personal property. Accordingly, Bank will become a creditor of H's estate to the extent of the $20,000 due on H's mortgage note.

F's rights: The doctrine of equitable conversion will cause the proceeds from the sale of Whiteacre to pass to the estate as personal property. Hence the Bank will not be able to obtain the $10,000 proceeds of the land sale to satisfy its mortgage. F will receive the estate assets, $25,000 ($10,000 proceeds from Whiteacre plus $15,000 savings account) minus Bank's claim for $20,000 and other claims and expenses. (Note that W will not claim an elective share of the estate because she receives more through her survivorship right in the tenancy by the entirety.)

The zoning problem: The state and its subdivisions may enact zoning statutes to reasonably control the use of land for the protection of the health, safety, morals, and welfare of its citizens. In general, most jurisdictions hold that aesthetic considerations by themselves do not justify the enactment of zoning ordinances and that a zoning regulation, insofar as it is solely designed to maintain the appearance of a neighborhood, is invalid. However, aesthetic considerations can be a valid factor in determining whether a zoning ordinance is valid.

Here, it appears that the sole purpose of Jersey Town's ordinance is to preserve the character of the neighborhood. Thus, Spaceburger, assuming arguendo that it obtained valid title to Blackacre, would be able to challenge it as being unconstitutional. In the alternative, Spaceburger could seek a conditional use permit or possibly a variance.

Actions Spaceburger could have taken to avoid its predicament: As outlined above, with respect to the zoning ordinance, Spaceburger would have challenged its enactment on constitutional grounds or sought a conditional use permit or variance. With respect to Blackacre itself, had Spaceburger undertaken a thorough title search, it could have attempted to obtain W's signature for the lease.

16. CONTRACTS

Validity of assignments: Ace's assignment to Factor Co. and, in turn, Factor Co.'s assignment to Bank were effective. In order for an assignment relating to the sale of goods of $500 or more to be effective, the assignment: (i) must be in writing; (ii) the right which is assigned must be adequately described; (iii) the assignor must manifest an intent to transfer his rights under the contract completely and immediately to the assignee; and (iv) consideration, although not required, creates an irrevocable assignment.

Both Ace's assignment to Factor and Factor's to Bank were in writing; the rights being assigned, the accounts receivable, were adequately described; the assignments were effective immediately; and the assignments were supported by consideration (cancellation of indebtedness and for value). Thus, irrevocable assignments of the rights to the accounts receivable vested first in Factor and then in Bank.

The reassignment to Bank from Factor of the accounts receivable served to establish privity of contract between Distor, as obligor, and Bank, as obligee. Further, privity of contract was extinguished between Distor and Ace. Thus, Bank alone was entitled to performance on the accounts receivable and Distor's defenses relating to those accounts could be raised only against Bank.

Defenses available to Distor: Distor may raise any defenses against Bank which it could have raised against Ace which were inherent in the assigned contracts. Accordingly, the guarantee in the Ace-Distor contract was still in effect when Factor's distress sale caused Distor to suffer a loss. Furthermore, Distor reasonably relied, to his detriment, on the Ace guarantee by making similar guarantees to retailers, knowing that he had a right of recourse against Ace. Distor can thus raise the guarantees expressed in the contract as defenses against Bank. As a set-off against the amount Distor owes, a court should determine the loss Distor incurred on the unsold Boomers as well as any liability Distor may have to any retailers arising out of its representations in reliance upon Ace's guarantee.

Distor would not be entitled to a set-off against Bank with respect to the $50,000 in damages arising out of Ace's breach of contract with Distor in August 1979. The general rule of law is that if an obligor (Distor) acquires for value any defense good against the assignor (Ace) before the obligor has notice of the assignment, the assignee (Bank) takes subject to that defense. Distor received notice of the assignment in July 1979, and Ace's breach of contract occurred in August 1979. Accordingly, this defense of Distor's did *not* come into existence before he had notice or knowledge of the assignment. Thus, the Bank will take free from such defense. Distor will have to sue Ace directly to collect damages.

17. CRIMINAL LAW

Conspiracy: A conspiracy must involve a "meeting of the minds" between at least two independent persons. Moreover, there must be a meeting of at least two "guilty" minds, *i.e.,* between two persons who are actually committing themselves to the scheme. As the detective Nurse did not have a "guilty" mind, Convict cannot be convicted of conspiracy.

Intoxication as a defense to larceny: The intoxication defense relates to intoxication caused by any substance, including drugs. Its availability is limited to specific intent crimes, and it is used to show that defendant did not have the requisite intent. Since larceny is a specific intent crime (*i.e.,* defendant must have an intent to permanently deprive the clinic of its interest in the property), I would argue that at the time of Convict's taking of the drugs, he was suffering from one of his frequent delusions relating to his recent intake of narcotics in the prison.

Coercion as a defense: The fact that Nurse threatened to turn Convict in if he did not comply with her request to steal and sell the drugs does not constitute coercion. Coercion is a defense only where the defendant (i) is compelled to act by a threat of imminent infliction of death or great bodily harm and (ii) reasonably believes that the threat will be carried out. A threat to turn someone in to the police for illegal conduct is not a threat of death or imminent bodily harm, even where imprisonment for life may result. Thus, Convict's actions are not excusable under a coercion defense.

Entrapment as a defense: Entrapment occurs if the intent to commit the crime originated not with the defendant but rather with the creative activities of law enforcement officers. If this is the case, it is presumed that the legislative intent was not to cover the conduct and so it is not criminal. If a person is "predisposed" to commit crimes of the sort at issue, however, he already has the intent to commit it. A predisposed person cannot be entrapped, so the prosecution's response to claims of entrapment is often to attempt to prove predisposition. Thus, the issue here is whether Convict was predisposed to commit the crimes of which he is charged.

The facts indicate that while he had a history of narcotics convictions, Convict was not predisposed after his release to sell narcotics. Furthermore, there is no evidence against Convict that he engaged in the distribution of narcotics during his 10 years of imprisonment. Thus, I would argue that Convict was not a predisposed person and therefore was entrapped into obtaining possession of the drugs and selling them to one who was in fact an instrument of the police department. Note that since Nurse and Pusher were working under the control of the local police department, their inducements were not private inducements to which the defense of entrapment would not apply. Furthermore, the entrapment defense would clearly be effective if the jurisdiction wherein Convict was tried adopted the minority rule. Under this rule, a defendant would be entitled to acquittal if the police activity was such as was reasonably likely to cause an innocent, *i.e.,* unpredisposed, person to commit the crime. The defendant's own innocence or predisposition would be irrelevant.

Finally, note that while the Supreme Court has held that under federal law an entrapment defense cannot be based upon the fact that a government agent provided an ingredient for the commission of the crime, even if the material was contraband, a few states have made the provision of essential material, such as drugs, entrapment. Thus, if Convict is tried in one of these states, the entrapment defense would be effective for this reason as well.

Burglary: One of the elements of burglary is a "breaking," which may be actual or constructive. Actual breaking requires some use of force, no matter how minimal, to gain entry. Note that as Nurse left the door open, there appears to have been no use of force. Constructive breaking, which consists of gaining entry by means of fraud, threat, intimidation, or by use of the chimney, is not applicable to these facts. Furthermore, since Convict had the consent of an employee of the clinic to enter, any use of minimal force to gain entry is not a breaking. Since there was no breaking here, there was no burglary.

Rule against multiple convictions: It should be noted that many jurisdictions are developing prohibitions against convicting a defendant for more than one offense where the multiple offenses were all part of the same "criminal transaction." In some states, this is prohibited by statute. In others, courts adopt a rule of merger or of double jeopardy to prohibit it. Thus, I would argue as a last resort that Convict cannot be convicted for all the offenses of which he is charged under the "criminal transaction" rule.

18. TORTS

Printa: A prima facie case for negligence could be established against Printa. In the business of printing, Printa had a duty to conform to a specific standard of conduct for the protection of its printing press operators against unreasonable risk of injury. Printa breached that duty by not complying with 1970 regulations published by the National Institute of Press Manufacturers indicating printing presses should have protection guards attached at a point not more than one inch from moving rollers. As the accident occurred in 1979, Printa had a number of years to effectuate this safety measure, and in view of Printa's day-to-day operations with printing presses, it should have been aware of these standards. On the basis of the expert's testimony, it appears that Printa's breach of duty was the proximate cause of Paul's injury. There is no evidence that Paul was contributorily negligent or had the last clear chance to prevent the accident. It should be noted that the treatise is not conclusive as to the standard of conduct reasonably expected of Printa unless the information contained therein was such that the average printing press operator would have knowledge of said information. Consequently, the fact that the printing press did not have an automatic electronic switch which could have prevented the accident in the absence of a guard is not necessarily evidence of negligent conduct on the part of Printa.

Map: Map's liability may be determined by examining (i) common law negligence principles and (ii) products liability theories. It appears that Map was not negligent in the manufacture and design of the press. As stipulated at trial, Map's design of the press at time of sale was in accordance with then existing industry standards. It thus was not in breach of a duty to conform to a specific standard of conduct. As a general rule of law, no duty is imposed upon a person to take precautions against events which cannot reasonably be foreseen. Furthermore, Map did not have a continuing duty more than 20 years later to keep ultimate buyers of its products informed of significant developments in the safe operation of the machines. Such an obligation would be totally impractical, particularly when it sold its products through dealers and therefore in many cases would have no knowledge of the identity of the users of its machines.

On the basis of the foregoing, Map would not be liable on a products liability theory based on negligence. A strict liability theory would be inapplicable since, at the time of sale, the product was not unreasonably dangerous so long as a protective guard was positioned 12 inches from the rollers. Finally, an action based on implied warranty of merchantability would fail since (i) the press was fit at time of sale for the ordinary purposes for which it was used, and (ii) the buyer (Printa) was under an obligation to notify Map within a reasonable time after he discovered or should have discovered a breach in warranty (*i.e.,* lack of protective guard), and no such notice was given. Moreover, such a warranty action would be time barred under U.C.C. section 2-725, since more than four years had elapsed since the sale.

Duncan: Duncan would not be liable on the basis of negligent manufacture or design of the press since he was a mere distributor. His liability, if any, would be based on an implied warranty or strict liability theory. Under these theories, Paul need not prove that Duncan was at fault in producing or selling an unreasonably dangerous product—only that the product in fact was unreasonably dangerous. A protective guard was shipped to Printa, and therefore it is unlikely that Duncan would have any continuing liability.

Formco: Any liability on the part of Formco would be grounded in negligence. By failing to install the guard on the press, Formco clearly breached its duty to conform to a specific standard of conduct. Formco was a mechanical engineering concern; thus it was required to exercise a high degree of knowledge and skill in the assembly of the press.

The next issue is whether Formco's breach of duty was the proximate cause of Paul's injury. At the time of assembly, Formco would have conformed to its duty of care by positioning the guard 12 inches from the rollers. The expert's testimony, however, states that the accident could have been prevented only by a guard positioned close to the rollers. Furthermore, as indicated in the treatise, an electronic switch could have prevented the accident if the guard were removed. Formco thus would have to show that its negligence was not the actual cause of the accident. Under the "but for" test, Formco may be able to prove that even in the absence of a failure to install the guard, the accident would still have occurred and therefore the injury is not the direct result of its act.

Paul: A problem of causation exists where two or more persons have been negligent (*i.e.,* Printa and Formco), but uncertainty exists as to which one caused Paul's injury. Paul must only prove that harm has been caused him by one of them (with uncertainty as to which one). The burden of proof then shifts to Printa and Formco and each must show that its negligence is not the actual cause. As noted above, it is unlikely that Paul would have an effective cause of action against Map and Duncan.

19. REAL PROPERTY

Under the facts, Able's statement that he did not care if David located his driveway on Lot 7 at best creates an oral license from Able to use Lot 7 for such purpose. A license is a personal privilege held by the licensee. Its informal nature is described by saying that the Statute of Frauds is inapplicable to its creation. The essential characteristic of a license is that it is revocable by nature. It may be revoked at any time by a manifestation of the licensor's intent to end it. This manifestation may be by a formal notice of revocation or it may consist of conduct which obstructs the licensee's continued use. Ordinarily, the sale of the lot to a third party (*i.e.,* Charles) constitutes conduct which terminates the license. However, once an oral license has been "executed" to the extent that it would be inequitable to permit its revocation (*e.g.,* David has expended substantial funds in the location of his home in reliance on the license), the licensor may be estopped from revoking the license. Thus, David could argue that Able's conveyance of Lot 7 to Charles did not result in a revocation of the license.

Note that it cannot be said that an easement was created by prescription, *i.e.,* long, continued use. As David has only used the driveway for 17 years, such use does not meet the requisite 20-year statute of limitations period.

Burt had an easement over Lot 7 which was expressly granted in his deed from Able. Moreover, Burt apparently conveyed a valid easement to David. The description was sufficient (the 25-foot strip could be referenced to Burt's deed) and the easement would be good against later takers of Lot 7 if they knew or were charged with notice of it. Charles did have actual notice of Burt's easement since the language of conveyance in the deed to Charles was identical to that in the Able-Burt deed. While the easement to David was not recorded, one might argue that Charles had constructive notice through David's use of the driveway. Of course, Charles may argue that the easement terminated at the time Burt sold Lot 2 to him. At this point, Sixth Street was completed and the circumstances giving rise to the creation of the easement (*i.e.,* right of access to Lot 2) were no longer present. Thus, if Burt's easement expired when the necessity ended, Burt's easement to David would have also terminated since David's easement was contingent on the existence of Burt's easement.

Note that if David's easement did not expire at the time of conveyance of Lot 2 from Burt to Charles, it would not be a persuasive argument by Charles that the easement to David expired upon Charles's purchase of Lot 7. Generally, an easement is extinguished if the owner of the servient tenement and the owner of the easement came together in one person. Thus, while the easement in Burt's deed to Charles was extinguished at the time Charles acquired Lot 7, if David's easement is deemed to be in existence after Charles's purchase of Lot 2, David's easement will survive Charles's purchase of Lot 7 because Charles will be purchasing said lot with constructive, if not actual, notice of David's easement.

David may argue that he built the solar heating equipment at considerable cost subsequent to and in reliance upon the zoning ordinance which permitted only single-family residences. Charles's zoning permit not only violates the single-family requirement, but also the requirement that a housing structure be on at least a 7,500 square foot lot. By dividing Lot 7 in half, the structure would be placed on a 5,000 square foot lot. While David's home is situated on a 5,000 square foot lot, lot and home existed at the time of passage of the zoning act and therefore his lot size is consistent with those 50-foot lots on which single-family residences were built in the 1950s. Thus, a defense based on "unclean hands" is unlikely to prevail. Nevertheless, Charles may argue that so dividing his lot would not be incongruous with existing lots on Fifth Avenue and therefore the variance granted was appropriate. Note that Charles would have difficulty in justifying the zoning variance on the basis of "unnecessary hardship" since it is not due to unique circumstances, and the variance would result in substantial detriment to another citizen of the community. David should seek a restraining order or injunction to prohibit Charles from building a two-family residence in violation of the zoning ordinance and on grounds of equity.

20. CONSTITUTIONAL LAW

Homer could argue that the zoning ordinance infringes on his First Amendment right to freedom of commercial speech or advertising. Homer's advertising of his home occupation in the newspaper falls within the ambit of First Amendment protection and should not be restricted since the advertising is neither false nor deceptive nor involves the solicitation of illegal goods or services. Thus, arguably the ordinance is not a valid regulation of Homer's speech activity.

Homer may also argue that restraints on "home trades and occupations" violate the Equal Protection Clause of the Fourteenth Amendment since other trades and occupations are not subject to advertising restrictions. When socioeconomic legislation is challenged on this basis, the courts will generally sustain the legislation if there exists any conceivable rational basis for the distinction. One rational basis may be that mass advertising may result in too much commercial activity in a residential area and therefore disrupt traffic safety and the neighbors' rights to quiet enjoyment of their homes. This argument which Towne might employ is lacking in substance, however, since word-of-mouth advertising may have the same impact, and if one is permitted the right to practice a trade in his house, that right should not be limited in a way that restricts communication of the availability of one's services.

Note that land use is not a fundamental right for equal protection purposes. However, Homer may show that the ordinance deprives him and others of a fundamental right, *i.e.*, freedom of speech. In this case, the courts would use a "strict scrutiny" test. The state must show that the ordinance fulfills a compelling state interest in order for it to be upheld.

Homer might argue that his Fourteenth Amendment substantive due process right (*i.e.*, property right to earn a livelihood without undue interference) is being violated. Since a fundamental right (freedom of speech) has been limited, this ordinance must be necessary to promote a compelling or overriding government interest (rather than rationally relate to any possible legitimate end of government). As the ordinance is presumed valid, the burden is on Homer to prove its invalidity. This should not be a difficult burden to satisfy since there appears to be no compelling interest in upholding the statute and Homer's commercial free speech activity is restricted. It should be noted, however, that the United States Supreme Court has largely abandoned substantive due process review of economic regulation. The trend appears to be that an ordinance does not violate substantive due process if it bears some rational relationship to a permissible state or local government objective. Consequently, substantive due process violation may not be an effective argument in favor of Homer.

Homer may still challenge the reasonableness of the ordinance under state constitutional due process standards. One test used by the state courts is that the ordinance is arbitrary if there is no rational relation between it and the objective sought *or* the detriment to the landowner outweighs any public good realized from the regulation. Homer should therefore argue that the hardship to him and others in being effectively deprived of a livelihood clearly outweighs any public good realized from the regulation. Towne, however, may be able to show that the ordinance is designed to protect a large group of homeowners at the expense of the few subject to the ordinance.

Finally, Homer might argue that the ordinance constitutes a "taking" of property. The Fifth Amendment prohibits the government from taking private property without just compensation, but the government generally is allowed to regulate land use. To determine whether land use regulation constitutes a taking, the United States Supreme Court has employed two tests: (i) If the regulation denies the land owner **all** economic value of the regulated land, there generally is a taking. (ii) Where the regulation merely decreases the economic value of the regulated property, the Court employs a balancing test, considering the social goals sought to be promoted, the diminution in value to the owner, and the owner's reasonable expectations regarding use. Here, the regulation merely decreases the value of Homer's land; thus, the balancing test is appropriate. The social goal sought to be promoted appears to be to keep residential streets primarily residential. The diminution in value to Homer is small, and his expectation of running a full-fledged business out of his home probably is unreasonable, since through zoning the town would have the power to prohibit home businesses altogether. Thus, a taking probably would not be found.

21. CRIMINAL PROCEDURE

Driver's and Passenger's motions to suppress the sawed-off shotgun, cocaine, and untaxed cigarettes will be denied because the search for and seizure of these items did not violate any of Driver's or Passenger's constitutional rights. Furthermore, Driver's and Passenger's motions to suppress the marijuana found in the trunk will not be granted because the search for and seizure of the marijuana did not violate their Fourth Amendment right, as applied to the states through the Fourteenth Amendment.

Thumb's motion to suppress the sawed-off shotgun, untaxed cigarettes, and hashish will be denied, because the search for and seizure of these items did not violate any of Thumb's constitutional rights.

An evaluation of the totality of the circumstances will be made to determine whether an individual had a reasonable expectation of privacy, considering factors such as ownership of property seized and location of property at time of search.

Tom Thumb had no standing as to the gun or untaxed cigarettes. The car was not his and the items were in plain view. It is arguable that he has standing regarding the attache case since he owns it, and it was near him and locked; but the expectation of privacy in an automobile is less than that of a residence.

Driver has no standing because he did not establish that he had permission to be driving the vehicle.

Passenger has no standing. He failed to assert a property or possessory interest in property searched or seized and has no expectation of privacy.

Under the Fourth Amendment, through the Fourteenth Amendment, a valid stop of an automobile by a police officer requires an "articulable and reasonable suspicion" that either the automobile is not registered, the motorist is unlicensed, or the automobile's occupants are subject to seizure for violation of the law. [Delaware v. Prouse, 440 U.S. 648 (1979)]

In this situation, Trooper, while on routine patrol duty, saw the subject vehicle "being driven in excess of the speed limit." Therefore, he actually witnessed the automobile's driver violating the law. Based on this fact, when Trooper pulled the vehicle over, he was acting properly.

Trooper was not violating the Fourth Amendment rights of the occupants of the automobile at the time he seized the shotgun. This is so under *Harris v. United States,* 390 U.S. 234 (1968), which held that objects falling in the plain view of an officer who has a legal right to be where he is are subject to seizure without a warrant and may be introduced into evidence.

Here, at the time that Trooper saw the shotgun, he was waiting for Driver to produce the license and registration based on the fact that the car was speeding. Accordingly, the gun was in the plain view of Trooper while he had a legal right to be where he was, and his seizure of same did not violate the constitutional rights of any of the occupants of the car.

Trooper was acting properly when he arrested Driver, Passenger, and Thumb. First, the fact that the registration that Driver produced was a car rental form in the name of a third individual not then present was sufficient probable cause to arrest Driver and those acting in concert with him (Passenger and Thumb), assuming that there was no satisfactory explanation given as to how the vehicle was acquired.

Second, Trooper was acting properly when he arrested Driver, Passenger, and Thumb for possession of an illegal weapon. A police officer can arrest without a warrant if he has a reasonable basis or probable cause to believe that a crime has been committed by those whom he is arresting.

In this situation, Trooper saw the butt of a rifle protruding from under the front seat. It was certainly reasonable for Trooper to conclude that all three occupants of the car had knowledge of the rifle. Accordingly, Trooper had probable cause to arrest Driver, Passenger, and Thumb without a warrant. The fact that Thumb claimed to be a hitchhiker did not negate the validity of the arrest, for Trooper could certainly have not made a complete investigation of Thumb's claim while situated on the New Jersey Turnpike.

Trooper did not violate Driver's, Passenger's, or Thumb's Fourth Amendment rights when he searched the passenger compartment of the car without a warrant, thereby discovering the cocaine, untaxed cigarettes, and the hashish which was contained in the briefcase. This is so because Trooper discovered these items through a search he conducted incident to a lawful arrest.

A search incident to lawful arrest is one of the exceptions to the warrant requirement. In such a situation, the police may search those arrested and all areas into which they might reach to obtain a weapon or destroy evidence. For this purpose, the entire passenger compartment of a car, including its glove compartment and articles contained in the car (locked or unlocked) are considered to be within the arrestee's reach.

Trooper did not violate Driver's and Passenger's Fourth Amendment rights when he opened the trunk of the car and further opened the two satchels containing the bricks of marijuana.

In this situation, the luggage in the trunk was subject to search. When the police have probable cause to search a vehicle, they can search the entire vehicle including the trunk and *all containers* that may contain the object for which they are searching. Since Trooper had probable cause to believe the car contained drugs, there was no violation of the defendants' rights.

22. TORTS

Dear Mr. Ferris:

Steelco has the following causes of action under the theories set forth below:

Negligence: Negligence is a breach of duty of care which is the actual and proximate cause of damage to a plaintiff's person or property.

It is well known that loose sulphur is a highly corrosive material which when combined with moisture in open air can produce sulphuric acid. Thus, the loose sulphur is an unreasonably dangerous condition on Chemco's land, and Chemco owes Steelco a duty of care to store its loose sulphur so that it does not contaminate the atmosphere nor affect adjoining lands; in this case, Steelco's property. For Chemco not to do so is to pose an unreasonable risk of harm to Steelco's property. Here, it appears that Chemco breached that duty of care by storing large open mounds of the sulphur and by transporting it in open trucks.

Whether or not the sulphur is the actual and proximate cause of damage to your company's steel depends on information which you should provide me. As you know, for negligence liability to accrue, Chemco's careless storage of its sulphur must be the cause-in-fact of the damage occurring to the steel. Under the "but for" test, if Chemco is the only possible discharger of corrosive chemicals in your area, then "but for" Chemco's careless storage of the sulphur, Steelco would have suffered no damage. However, you have advised me that the damage is taking place at the property in Industrial Port. Accordingly, I would appreciate it if you would advise me if there are any other factories or plants in the vicinity which may be sources of corrosive materials. If there are other sources of corrosive materials besides Chemco, then Chemco's sulphur operations will not suffice for causation-in-fact unless we can determine that those operations constitute a substantial factor in causing the damage.

With respect to the proximate cause issue, it is certainly clear that the resulting damage to the steel is within the risk of harm posed by Chemco's activities. Moreover, it is foreseeable that air and moisture will combine with loose sulphur to cause the deposit of sulphuric acid on adjoining properties. Thus, Chemco cannot reasonably argue that the air and moisture are superseding intervening forces.

Thus, subject to the information you will provide me regarding neighboring sources of corrosive materials, Steelco has a strong negligence case against Chemco.

Strict liability for ultrahazardous activity: In order to establish a strict liability case against Chemco for conducting an ultrahazardous activity, we must show: (i) an absolute duty on the part of Chemco to make the materials safe; (ii) a breach of that duty; (iii) breach of that duty was the proximate cause of the damage to the steel; and (iv) damage to the steel.

As far as elements (iii) and (iv) are concerned, my comments above regarding causation are applicable here, and of course, we can prove damage to the steel.

However, whether a court will find that Chemco's sulphur operations constitute an ultrahazardous activity is an open question. As you know, an activity may be characterized as ultrahazardous if it involves a substantial risk of serious harm to person or property, no matter how much care is exercised. The courts generally impose three requirements in finding an activity to be ultrahazardous: (a) the activity must involve a risk of serious harm to persons or property; (b) the activity must be one that cannot be performed with complete safety no matter how much care is taken; and (c) the activity is not commonly engaged in the particular community.

Here, there is no doubt that Chemco's sulphur operations involve a serious risk of harm to Steelco's property. However, more information is needed from you to determine whether sulphur can be handled in complete safety. If such is the case, then there can be no ultrahazardous activity cause of action against Chemco. Similarly, more information is needed as to whether other companies in and around Industrial Port are conducting corrosive materials operations. By the nature of the Industrial Port, this may be likely, and if such is the case, again, this particular cause of action cannot be asserted against Chemco.

Private nuisance: Private nuisance is a substantial, unreasonable interference with another private person's use or enjoyment of property which he actually possesses or to which he has a right of immediate possession. For an interference to be substantial, it must be offensive, inconvenient, or annoying to an average person in the community. It will not be characterized as substantial if it is merely the result of plaintiff's hypersensitivity or specialized use of his own property. Here, the sulphuric acid contamination will corrode anything made of metal, assuredly a material which is on every piece of property in Industrial Port. Thus, it cannot be argued that the damage to Steelco's steel is merely the result of a specialized use of its property.

For an interference to be considered unreasonable, the severity of the inflicted injury must outweigh the utility of defendant's conduct. In balancing these respective interests, courts take into account that every person is entitled to use his own land in a reasonable way, considering the neighborhood, land values, and the existence of any alternative courses of conduct open to defendant.

Here, it certainly can be argued that the severity of injury inflicted upon Steelco outweighs the utility of Chemco's conduct. However, again, the nature of the other companies operating in Industrial Port is crucial to determining whether Chemco's activities are unreasonable. If other nearby companies routinely discharge corrosive materials, then Chemco's activities could be considered "reasonable" in this particular area. Thus, it is necessary for you to provide me with information on the other industries in Industrial Port.

It should be noted that Chemco's sulphur operations probably do not constitute a public nuisance since the latter is an act which unreasonably interferes with the health, safety, or property rights of the community at large, *e.g.,* blocking a highway or using a building to commit criminal activities such as prostitution, bookmaking, etc.

Finally, although a nuisance cause of action may exist against Chemco, a trespass to land action probably does not. In the latter, there is an interference with the landowner's exclusive possession; in the former, there is an interference with use or enjoyment. Here, you have given no indication that Steelco's exclusive possession of its land has been interfered with.

Please provide me with the requested information as soon as possible.

Very truly yours,
Leslie Lawyer

23. CONSTITUTIONAL LAW

The state of Uphoria's bill would be valid as to its age and citizenship requirements, but would be unconstitutional due to its gender classification.

Under the Equal Protection Clause of the Fourteenth Amendment, it is arbitrary and unconstitutional for a government to treat similar people in a dissimilar manner.

There are three tests for determining whether a classification violates the equal protection guarantee of the Fourteenth Amendment.

The first test is the strict scrutiny-compelling state interest test. This test is used if the classification is based on a suspect classification, which includes race, national origin, or alienage. Under this test, the law is considered to be invalid unless found demonstrably necessary to a compelling objective.

The second test involves intermediate scrutiny. Under this test, the court will strike down a law unless it bears a substantial relation to an important government interest. This is the test used in situations such as that here, where there is a classification based on gender. Gender classifications will be struck down if they rest on "unduly tenuous fit" [Craig v. Boren, 429 U.S. 190 (1976)], or serve no actual objective beyond efficiency or ease of administration [Reed v. Reed, 404 U.S. 71 (1971)], or can be rationalized, but not in terms of the legitimate interests expressly articulated in the law's defense.

The third test is the rational basis test (minimum scrutiny). Under this test, the classification is valid if there is any conceivable basis upon which the classification might relate to a legitimate governmental interest. This is a very "loose" test and it is very difficult for a law to fail it. This test is used for all classifications relating to matters of economics or social welfare.

The gender designation of Uphoria's bill limiting the appointment of state police officers to males would fall under the intermediate scrutiny test due to its inherent gender classification. Therefore, this component will only be upheld if it is substantially related to an important governmental interest.

This gender classification is not related to an important governmental interest. This classification is an arbitrary and capricious discrimination against women. If Uphoria claims that its bill is based on ability to do the work, it can design a test which will test each individual's (male or female) ability to perform the work required of a state police officer, and not unfairly discriminate against women. Accordingly, under the mere rationality plus test, this bill would be found invalid due to the fact that it discriminates against women without having a fair and substantial relationship to an important governmental objective.

The bill also limits appointment of police officers to citizens of the United States. Since this component of the bill is based on alienage, it ordinarily falls under the strict scrutiny-compelling interest test. However, there is an exception to this rule which provides that if, as here, the law discriminates against alien participation in state government, then the mere rationality test is applied. Under the mere rationality test, a state can validly refuse to hire aliens as police officers, or for other positions which have direct effect on the function of government. [Ambach v. Norwick, 441 U.S. 68 (1979)] Accordingly, the bill would be valid as far as its requirement is concerned that only citizens be appointed to the state police force.

The bill sets the age for appointment of a police officer to be over that of 20 years. The Court has held that age is not a suspect classification so a rational basis analysis can be applied. The test for determining the constitutionality of age restriction statutes has been codified in 29 U.S.C. section 622, which allows restriction on age where "age is a bona fide occupational qualification ("BFOQ") reasonably necessary to the normal operation of the particular business."

Age restrictions (both minimum/maximum hiring age and maximum retirement age) have been upheld as BFOQ's for airline pilots, police officers, and bus drivers, among others. The 20-year-old minimum age requirement in this statute is constitutional as being BFOQ. It is in the state's interest to have police officers who are physically and emotionally mature enough to handle the stress of police work.

24. CONTRACTS
ARGUMENT REGARDING EXISTENCE OF A CONTRACT

A contract for a sole distributorship of Zuzu Corp. products in New Jersey exists between Zuzu and Yutz Corp.

For a contract to be created, the following must be shown:

(i) mutual assent, *i.e.,* an offer and acceptance;

(ii) consideration or some substitute therefor; and

(iii) no defense to the creation of the contract.

Mutual assent: Zuzu's September 15, 1980, letter constitutes an offer to provide a sole distributorship for products in New Jersey, which offer was accepted by Yutz.

For an offer to be created, there must be (i) an expression of a promise, undertaking, or commitment to enter into a contract; (ii) certainty and definiteness in the essential terms; and (iii) communication of the above to the offeree.

Here, Zuzu clearly promised to grant Yutz a sole distributorship and that promise was communicated to Yutz. As discussed below, Zuzu's letter clearly defined the essential terms of this distributorship contract.

It is axiomatic that an offer must be definite and certain in its terms; *i.e.,* enough of the essential terms have been provided so that a contract including them is capable of being enforced. What is essential for the requisite certainty is an offer which will, of course, depend upon the kind of contract contemplated.

Here, the essential terms of enforcement of this sole distributorship contract are present:

(a) Identity of offeree and subject matter: Here, Yutz is identified as the offeree and the subject matter is set forth as the distributorship agreement.

(b) Nature of work to be performed: Here, the nature of work to be performed is Yutz's distribution within New Jersey of Zuzu's products.

(c) Price to be paid: Here, the letter incorporates by reference a dealer price list and specifies that Yutz will receive a 10% commission.

Accordingly, it is clear from the foregoing that Zuzu made a valid enforceable offer, which was accepted by Yutz by the signing and returning of the letter.

Consideration: For a contract to be enforced, it must contain a bargained-for change in legal position between the parties, *i.e.,* valuable consideration. Basically, two elements are necessary to constitute consideration. First, there must be a bargained-for exchange between the parties. Second, that which is bargained for must be considered of legal value, or as it is traditionally stated, some benefit to the promisor or detriment to the promisee.

Here, there is mutuality of consideration. As far as Zuzu is concerned, it has incurred a legal detriment by agreeing to give a sole distributorship of its products to Yutz. Yutz has given consideration by impliedly promising to use its best efforts to sell as many Zuzu products as possible within New Jersey.

In the event Zuzu argues that the consideration given by Yutz was illusory, at the very least a substitute for consideration—promissory estoppel (detrimental reliance)—can be found on behalf of Yutz.

Under the doctrine of promissory estoppel, a promise is enforceable to the extent necessary to prevent injustice if (i) the promisor should reasonably expect to induce action or forbearance; (ii) the promise is of a definite and substantial character; and (iii) such action or forbearance is in fact induced. Here, Zuzu should reasonably have expected to induce Yutz to make substantial expenditures for the sale of Zuzu's products. The promise made by Zuzu, a sole distributorship, was of a definite and substantial character; and Yutz's forbearance was in fact induced by his daily advertising in a local newspaper and by his building the showroom solely for the purpose of promoting Zuzu heaters.

Thus, based on the foregoing, there is consideration on both sides of this contract and assuming, arguendo, that there is not, there is certainly detrimental reliance on behalf of Yutz which mandates enforcement of this contract.

There are no defenses to this contract: Here, there is no evidence showing that the parties to the above agreement never formed a contract, nor is there evidence of illegality in the contract. Moreover, there is no evidence that the parties lacked capacity to contract. Finally, the contract satisfies the Statute of Frauds since it is in writing.

Thus, there is no doubt that a contract exists between Zuzu and Yutz.

ARGUMENT REGARDING BREACH OF CONTRACT
Yutz did not breach the contract.

To establish a breach, one must be able to prove that a party under a present duty to perform has not done so. The two basic issues are: (i) whether a present duty to perform has arisen, and (ii) whether the duty to perform has been discharged. Before the latter issue can be reached, the former issue must be found in the affirmative.

Here, Zuzu alleges that Yutz had a duty to set up a dealer organization in New Jersey, and that by failing to do so, Yutz breached the distributorship agreement. However, that is not the case since by the express terms of the contract, Yutz was under no *duty* to set up a dealer network. Rather, Yutz was merely granted the *right* to set up such a network. The fact that Yutz elected not to exercise that right does not mean he breached any duty. Because the duty alleged by Zuzu was nonexistent, its breach could not have occurred.

Similarly, there was no specification in the contract that Yutz was under a duty to sell a certain number of heaters by a certain time, although Zuzu alleges the contrary by claiming that 1,000 heaters should have been sold in New Jersey by February 1981. Since no such duty arose, Zuzu cannot now claim its breach.

Accordingly, by virtue of the foregoing, Yutz did not breach the contract.

25. CONTRACTS/REAL PROPERTY
(a) Legal issues raised by the facts: The legal issue raised herein is whether or not the Cellers have an affirmative duty to disclose the water leak to the buyers. The Cellers' duty depends on whether or not their painting over the water marks created by the leak was a concealment of the defective condition, for only if the painting was in fact a concealment would the Cellers have an affirmative duty to disclose the leaks.

Although it is a close question, the painting over the water marks was not a concealment based on the facts presented herein; therefore, the Cellers have no affirmative duty to disclose same.

In New Jersey, the rule is that contracts for the sale of real property carry no implied warranties of quality or fitness for the purpose intended. However, if the seller has knowingly made any false statements to the buyer, or if he has actually concealed conditions on the property, then he is liable in damages for the concealment of the condition.

If Celler had not painted over the water marks, there would be no question that he has no duty to disclose the leak because Byer could easily discover same during a reasonable inspection of the property. However, in this situation Celler, while painting the entire house, covered over the water marks. Based on the facts presented, it does not appear that Celler painted the house for the purpose of covering up the water marks. Instead, he painted the house so as "to get it ready for sale." Often when painting walls and ceilings various defects are covered over. In this situation, it could not be expected that Celler would deliberately leave the water marks showing.

Accordingly, the painting over of the water marks does not constitute a concealment of the leaks, and therefore the Cellers do not have a duty to inform the Byers of them.

The belief of the Cellers as to the cause for the leak is relevant only so far as they may sue the builder of the house (Ace Building Corp.), for there is an implied warranty of fitness in a sale of a new house by a builder.

(b)   I would include the following provisions in the contract of sale:

The seller has not made and does not make any representations as to the physical condition of the subject premises, and the buyer hereby expressly acknowledges that no such representations have been made. Seller shall conduct a complete physical inspection of the premises within three days of the signing of this contract. If any substantial defects are found, the seller shall have the option to remove the same and repair any damage caused thereby within 30 days of being notified in writing of the condition or to declare this contract null and void. The buyer agrees to take the premises "As is."

(c)   The above provision would be placed into the contract as to expressly limit any potential liability that Celler might have for the water leaks.

The provision states that the seller made no representations whatsoever. Accordingly, this protects Celler from liability for any of his statements. The provision allows Byer to conduct a complete physical inspection within three days. This time limit is necessary so that Celler knows as quickly as possible if Byer will contend that there are defects in the premises.

The provision also gives Celler the option to either void the contract if defects are found or to repair them. This clause gives Celler the option to void the contract if he feels that the required repairs will be too costly to him.

The "as is" wording indicates that Byer will take the property in the actual condition that it is at the time of closing. Once the property is transferred, Celler will no longer have any duty toward the property.

26. CRIMINAL LAW/PROCEDURE
SUBSTANTIVE CRIMINAL ISSUES

Larceny: Under the facts, Babs is not guilty of larceny.

Larceny is the trespassory taking and carrying away of the personal property of another with the intent to permanently deprive the owner of his or her interest. Here, Babs did not trespass on Mrs. Rich's land and did not "take" the antiques from the house. Nor did she carry away the antiques physically from the house, although the prosecutor may argue that her car transported the antiques away. Babs had no specific intent to permanently deprive Mrs. Rich of her property. Accordingly, the essential elements of larceny with respect to Babs are lacking.

As discussed below, there was no conspiracy between Babs and Allen. Accordingly, Babs cannot be vicariously liable for any larceny committed by Allen.

Burglary: Babs was improperly convicted of burglary.

At common law, burglary is the trespassory breaking and entering of a dwelling place of another in the nighttime with the specific intent to commit a felony therein. Modern statutes have expanded the "time" concept to include daytime and nighttime.

Here, Babs did not possess the requisite specific intent. Moreover, she did not break and enter the dwelling of Mrs. Rich to commit the larceny of stealing her antiques. Therefore, the elements of burglary have not been proved against Babs.

Finally, since there was no conspiracy involved (as discussed in the following answer on the murder issue), Allen's act of burglary cannot be attributed to Babs as a co-conspirator.

Murder

Felony murder: Babs could only be found guilty of Mr. Nabor's murder under the felony murder rule. Under that doctrine, a defendant is guilty of murder for a killing—even an accidental one—committed during the course of a felony. To be guilty of felony murder, defendant must be guilty of the underlying felony. Babs lacked the necessary intent for larceny or burglary and therefore cannot be convicted of felony murder.

Conspiracy: A conspiracy is a combination or agreement between two or more persons to accomplish some criminal or unlawful purpose, or to accomplish a lawful purpose by unlawful means. It is necessary to have a specific intent to enter into an agreement and a specific intent to achieve the objective of the agreement. When the felony murder rule is combined with conspiracy law, the scope of liability becomes very broad. If in the course of a conspiracy to commit a felony a death is caused, all members of the conspiracy are liable for murder, if the death was caused in furtherance of the conspiracy and was a foreseeable consequence of the conspiracy. If Babs was involved in a conspiracy to commit a felony, she could be convicted of felony murder. Here there was no conspiracy between Babs and Allen to commit larceny or burglary because there was no agreement to do so and the requisite specific intents are missing from the facts. Accordingly, felony murder liability cannot be vicariously attributed to Babs under a conspiracy theory, and accordingly Babs cannot be guilty of murder.

(Editor's note on accomplice liability and lesser charges of homicide, *e.g.,* involuntary manslaughter and criminally negligent homicide: At this point in the essay answer, the student may be tempted to discuss other lesser crimes of which Babs may be guilty. Certainly, under the facts, the issues of Babs's possible accomplice liability, *i.e.,* aiding, abetting, or assisting the principal in the commission of a crime, or possible guilt of involuntary manslaughter, could be discussed if the question merely asked the student to discuss all possible issues in the case. However, here the question directs the student to discuss the issues that would have been raised by an *advocate* representing Babs in relation to the conviction. For example, an advocate would seek acquittal of Babs's convictions for the crimes of murder, larceny, and burglary by seeking to prove that the prosecution did not meet its proof beyond a reasonable doubt for those crimes. Note that the question does *not* state that Babs was convicted of being an accomplice or of having committed involuntary manslaughter. Thus, Babs's lawyer, on appeal, would not be appealing convictions of the latter crimes. Moreover, Babs's lawyer would not seek to obtain acquittal by showing that Babs did not in fact commit lesser crimes.)

Duress defense: Babs's lawyer would probably raise and address the defense that Babs was acting under duress when she hit Nabor. However, assuming the court permitted Babs's felony murder guilt to stand, the duress defense probably should not lie. Under the legal excuse of duress, a person is not guilty of an offense, other than homicide, if he performs an otherwise criminal act under the threat of imminent infliction of death or great bodily harm, provided that he reasonably believes death or great bodily harm will be inflicted on himself or on a member of his immediate family if he does not perform such conduct. Here, Babs is being charged with homicide, so the duress defense would not apply. Moreover, there are no facts indicating threats of imminent harm or death. Allen's statement "You're in this as deep as me," was not threatening enough to constitute duress.

PROCEDURAL ISSUES

The stop of the car: The Fourth Amendment prohibits unreasonable searches and seizures and is applicable to the states through the Fourteenth Amendment. Under those amendments, the police may not stop a single automobile simply to check license and registration. They must reasonably believe the stopped car violated a traffic law. If they have no such belief, they may stop automobiles at roadblocks to check license and registration so long as they stop every car that passes the checkpoint or have some articulable neutral principle (*e.g.*, every ninth car) to justify the stopping.

Here, the facts seem to indicate that Officer Smart did not stop the car for a traffic law violation, but merely to check credentials. Since there is no indication that Babs was stopped at a lawful roadblock checkpoint, it seems clear that the stop was improper and in violation of the Fourth and Fourteenth Amendments.

The dried blood evidence: In order for Babs to raise an objection under the Fourth and Fourteenth Amendments, she must show that she had a reasonable expectation of privacy; *i.e.,* she must have had standing to object and the item seized must not have been held out to the public.

Here, it is clear that Babs was driving her own car because Officer Smart had found her registration in order. Thus, it can be argued that she had standing with respect to things seized from the car. However, a person does not have a reasonable expectation of privacy in objects held out to the public, such as paint on the outside of a car. In this case, the dried blood on the bumper (which was in plain view of Officer Smart) is analogous to paint on a car, and accordingly, Babs had no valid objection to its admission in evidence. So, although the dried blood was obtained incident to an illegal stop, it is admissible evidence because there was no expectation of privacy.

The search of the car and the seizure of the jewelry: A warrant is necessary to conduct a search unless one of the exceptions to the warrant requirement applies. Under the "automobile exception" to the warrant requirement, the police must have probable cause to believe that the vehicle contains evidence of a crime. Here, it can be strongly argued that the "dent" in the bumper and "dried blood" did not give Officer Smart probable cause to search the car. Thus, the jewelry and Allen's fingerprint found therein must be excluded from evidence under the fruit of the poisonous tree doctrine. Here, unlike the dried blood, the jewelry was not found in an area open to the public and accordingly, having a reasonable expectation of privacy with respect to the jewelry, Babs may assert her Fourth and Fourteenth Amendment rights. Assuming, arguendo, that the dried blood and bumper "dent" did give Officer Smart the requisite probable cause, it must be remembered that the stop of Babs's car was illegal. Therefore, evidence obtained pursuant to the illegal stop for which Babs had a reasonable expectation of privacy (in this case the jewelry and fingerprints), is not admissible at trial.

Mrs. Rich's grand jury testimony: Under the Sixth and Fourteenth Amendments, a defendant in a criminal prosecution has the right to confront adverse witnesses. Here, Mrs. Rich's grand jury testimony is hearsay—evidence of a person's statements other than those made at trial.

Hearsay admitted in evidence denies a defendant the right to confront the hearsay declarant unless (i) the prosecution has made a good faith effort to obtain the in-court testimony of the witness and has failed; and (ii) the defendant has had an opportunity to cross-examine the person or has otherwise had an opportunity to test its accuracy. Here, the prosecution could not obtain Mrs. Rich's testimony because of her stroke. However, the facts indicate that Babs's lawyer had no previous opportunity to cross-examine Mrs. Rich. Certainly, a defense lawyer cannot do so during a grand jury hearing. Accordingly, admission of Mrs. Rich's testimony in evidence is in violation of Babs's right to confrontation under the Sixth and Fourteenth Amendments.

Right to a speedy trial: The Sixth and Fourteenth Amendments provide that a defendant has a right to a speedy trial. Whether such a right has been violated depends on (i) the length of the delay; (ii) the reason for the delay; (iii) whether the defendant has asserted his right; and (iv) the prejudice to the defendant. Here, the trial occurred more than one year after it was scheduled. The facts state that all motions were timely made, thereby establishing that Babs asserted her rights. There is no evidence that Babs suffered prejudice from this delay. The length and reason for the delay seem to be reasonable due to Mrs. Rich's illness.

27. CONSTITUTIONAL LAW
FIRST AMENDMENT ISSUES

Under the First Amendment, "Congress shall make no law . . . abridging the freedom of speech, or of the press. . . ." This guarantee has been held applicable to the states by reason of the "liberty" protected by the Due Process Clause of the Fourteenth Amendment.

Freedom of association and belief: The First Amendment protects freedom of association. Here, it appears that the ordinance impinges on the rights of the entertainers to talk and mingle with the customers. As such, the ordinance has the effect of chilling this vital First Amendment right. Thus, on this ground, the ordinance is unconstitutional.

The ordinance is overbroad: No law can withstand First Amendment scrutiny if it could be revised so as to exert less restraint on communication while still achieving its basic purpose; if a less restrictive alternative is available, the law is overbroad. Here, the stated purposes of the ordinance are to (i) prevent disorderly conduct; (ii) encourage temperance; (iii) discourage prostitution; and (iv) prevent any other immoral activity. While the latter purposes are legitimate interests of the state of New Jersey, the ordinance, as written, restricts expression and conduct which are in no way connected with prostitution, immoral activity, etc. Accordingly, the ordinance chills speech and conduct which are protected under the First Amendment. Certainly, the ordinance could be worded to only restrict the activities which are the focus of its basic purposes, *i.e.,* prevent prostitution and drunkenness. Prohibiting mingling of customers and entertainers goes beyond these legitimate purposes. Therefore, the ordinance is unconstitutionally overbroad.

The ordinance is vague: Laws regulating speech-related activities are unconstitutional if too vague to make absolutely clear what they forbid. To the extent their vagueness suggests that they prohibit constitutionally protected speech, they have a "chilling effect" on speech. Here, the ordinance prohibits the entertainers from "mingling" with customers. The word "mingling" is too vague to define what conduct is proscribed by the ordinance. Thus, it appears that the entertainers may be forced to refrain from conduct and expression protected by the First Amendment in order not to be considered "mingling" with the customers. Because this ordinance has, in this manner, the effect of "chilling" activity and expression which is protected by the First Amendment, it is unconstitutional.

Effect of Twenty-First Amendment on First Amendment rights: The Twenty-First Amendment gives the states much control over the sale and use of intoxicating liquor within its borders. Thus, Fun City's attorneys could argue that the ordinance is a valid exercise of the state's constitutionally granted powers with respect to intoxicating liquors. However, this argument fails because, as a general rule, individual rights guaranteed by the Bill of Rights and the Fourteenth Amendment outweigh state liquor control laws. Here, the ordinance which constitutes a liquor control regulation chills First Amendment rights made applicable to New Jersey under the Fourteenth Amendment. Accordingly, the ordinance is unconstitutional.

SUBSTANTIVE DUE PROCESS ISSUES

Substantive due process protects certain fundamental rights not articulated within the text of the Constitution. It is a test of the "reasonableness" of a statute in relation to the government's power to enact such legislation. It prohibits arbitrary government action. The Due Process Clause of the Fourteenth Amendment applies to state and local governments.

Under substantive due process principles, where a fundamental right is limited, the law (or other government action) must be necessary to promote a compelling or overriding state interest. Fundamental rights include interstate travel, privacy, voting, and all rights implied under the First Amendment.

Here the ordinance, as discussed above, chills the entertainers' First Amendment rights of association and speech. From the facts, Fun City has shown no compelling or overriding interest to do so. Accordingly, on this ground, the ordinance violates substantive due process.

EQUAL PROTECTION ISSUES

Under the Equal Protection Clause of the Fourteenth Amendment (applicable to the states), and as an implicit guarantee of the Due Process Clause of the Fifth Amendment (applicable to the federal government), governmental acts that classify people improperly may be invalid. It is arbitrary and unconstitutional for the government to treat similar people in a dissimilar manner. Under the "strict scrutiny" test, the classification must be necessary to promote a compelling interest. This test is employed when the classification relates to anyone who may exercise a fundamental right or when it is based on a "suspect" trait.

Here, the ordinance seeks to classify the entertainers as a class of individuals who cannot exercise certain fundamental rights—those granted by the First Amendment. Thus, to sustain the classification, Fun City must show that it has a "compelling interest" to do so. Clearly, Fun City does not have a compelling interest to make such a classification and, therefore, the ordinance violates equal protection.

CONCLUSION

For the foregoing reasons, Irma's and Lester's convictions should be reversed. Irma and Lester have been charged with violation of an ordinance which is overbroad and infringes upon their guaranteed constitutional rights.

28. TORTS
NOBLE V. MEDIX LAWSUIT

Affirmative defenses to wrongful termination of employment claim: An answer to Noble's lawsuit should be prepared. For a first affirmative defense, Medix should allege that since Noble did not have a written employment contract, his employment was terminable at will for any reason. For a second affirmative defense, Medix should assert that Noble was fired for justifiable cause, *i.e.,* insubordination in refusing to schedule any further production runs of "Corona."

Counterclaim for defamation to Medix: The answer should contain a counterclaim for defamation against Noble for libeling Medix by describing it in writing as a "public enemy" and by stating that the government should "throw the book at Medix."

A cause of action for defamation exists where defamatory language of and concerning the person defamed is published to third persons, causing damage to the reputation of the party defamed.

Here, Medix can assert a defamation counterclaim against Noble for the following reasons:

Defamatory language: Defamatory language is language which tends to adversely affect one's reputation. In a limited sense, a corporation, unincorporated association, or partnership may also be defamed, *e.g.,* by remarks as to its financial condition, honesty, integrity, etc. Here, the letters written by Noble certainly contain defamatory remarks with respect to Medix in that they describe Medix as a "public enemy," etc.

Of and concerning the person defamed: The person defamed must establish that a reasonable reader would understand that the defamatory statement referred to the person defamed. Here, there is no doubt that the letters written by Noble identify and pertain to Medix.

Publication to third persons: A statement is not actionable until there has been a "publication." The publication requirement is satisfied when there is a communication to a third person who understood it. Here, it is clear that Noble's defamatory statements were communicated and understood by the various government agencies which received letters.

Damage to the reputation of the person defamed: The defamation which occurred here was libel. Libel is a defamatory statement recorded in writing or some other permanent form. In most jurisdictions, if defamation is in the form of libel, general damages are presumed, *i.e.,* special damages need not be established. Most of the other jurisdictions hold that if the defamation is libel per se, *i.e.,* the statement is libelous and defamatory on its face, the defamation is actionable without pleading or proving special damages. Here, it is clear that the defamation was libelous on its face by referring to Medix as a "public enemy."

Additional requirements if statement was on matter of public concern: Noble's statement about the cancer-causing effect of a popular drug is arguably on a matter of public concern, requiring Medix to prove falsity and fault on Noble's part. Medix must show that Noble's assertions were false and that Noble was at least negligent in making them. Given the final outcome of the studies, Medix has a good chance of proving these elements.

Defenses to defamation counterclaim: Even if these elements are established, Noble has some strong defenses to any defamation counterclaim asserted by Medix.

Qualified privilege of making statement to one acting in the public interest: Statements made to those who are to take official action of some kind are qualifiedly privileged. Here, Noble's letters to the various government agencies were sent with the ostensible purpose of protecting the public from a cancer-causing drug. Thus it appears that Noble has this qualified privilege. To defeat this qualified privilege, Medix would have to allege that Noble acted with malice. Malice means that the statement was made with knowledge that it was untrue or with reckless disregard as to its truth or falsity. Here, it is unlikely that Medix can show that Noble acted with malice, because the basis of his letters was the research report showing possible cancer-causing links. While he may have been negligent in making statements based on preliminary reports, it does not appear that he acted with reckless disregard of truth or falsity.

Qualified privilege of making a statement in the interest of the publisher: Where the publisher of a defamatory statement makes the statement to defend his own actions, property, or reputation, it may be privileged. Here, Noble could argue that he wrote those letters to rehabilitate his reputation damaged by his allegedly wrongful firing. Although Medix may again argue that Noble acted with malice, this argument is unlikely to succeed for the reasons stated above.

Motion to remove Goodcause as Noble's attorney: A motion should be brought before the court for removal of Goodcause as Noble's attorney in this case for various ethical considerations.

A lawyer is compelled to avoid professional relationships where there is a potential conflict of interest which is likely to adversely affect his ability to exercise independent and professional judgment. In general, employment must be refused where such judgment will or reasonably may be affected by the lawyer's own financial, business, or property interests. Here, Goodcause should be asked to withdraw from representation of Noble in *Noble v. Medix* because it appears that he "represents" both sides of this controversy. Goodcause has been retained by Noble, yet Goodcause has been retained for legal representation by one of Medix's largest customers, Herbal. Moreover, Goodcause owns stock in Herbal. Since Goodcause has a financial interest in the outcome of Noble's lawsuit and also has a financial interest in one of Medix's largest customers, it appears that Goodcause has a conflict of interest.

Even assuming, arguendo, that Goodcause has no conflict of interest, an attorney is under the ethical duty of avoiding even the appearance of impropriety. By virtue of the arguments stated above, if Goodcause continues to represent Noble in the *Noble v. Medix* litigation, such an appearance of impropriety will exist. Accordingly, Goodcause should be removed from representation of Noble in this litigation.

MEDIX V. GOODCAUSE

Medix should commence a lawsuit against Goodcause for tortious interference of contract. Goodcause used his position to gain access to the management of Herbal and convinced Herbal to cease marketing all Medix products. This caused damage to Medix in terms of lost sales. Goodcause would probably argue that he was only acting in Herbal's best interest by advising it of potential lawsuits that could arise as a result of distributing Medix's products.

Medix could also assert a cause of action for defamation against Goodcause for reasons similar to the defamation counterclaim against Noble.

29. CONTRACTS

Dear Mr. Coco:

To resolve this issue, it is necessary to discuss all aspects of the contract formation, breach, and events which transpired during the transactions you detailed in your letter.

Offer and acceptance between Able and Maxco: The initial issue here is whether a contract for the sale of the Ultramax from Maxco to Able was formed. Maxco circulated an advertising circular for the Ultramax. As a general rule, advertisements, catalogues, circular letters, and the like containing price quotations are usually construed to be mere invitations for offers. They are announcements of prices at which the seller is willing to receive offers. These "invitations for offers" not only lack present contractual intent, but also lack the certainty of terms essential to an operative offer.

Able's inquiry to Maxco in response to the advertising circular regarding the Ultramax constituted an offer by Able. The requisite essential terms of performance—(i) identification of the offeree, (ii) identity of the subject matter, and (iii) quantity—were provided with a sufficient degree of certainty so as to be capable of enforcement. Able wrote to Maxco as offeree and stated that he wanted one Ultramax. This was sufficient to be considered an offer even though other terms were not spelled out completely. The courts have applied the standard of "reasonableness" consistent with the parties' intent with respect to terms which are uncertain.

Maxco's letter of May 8 was an acceptance of Able's offer and formed an enforceable contract between the parties. As no specific manner of acceptance was prescribed in the offer, Maxco's ***promise*** to ship the Ultramax created a bilateral contract.

Although the Ultramax did not arrive at Able's until May 29, the offer did not expressly limit acceptance to an act, and under case law and the U.C.C., which generally regulates the sale of goods, a timely promise to perform the act constitutes valid and binding consideration sufficient to support enforcement of the contract.

The additional terms included in Maxco's letter of May 8 (price and delivery on consignment) did not violate the acceptance. The U.C.C. provides that between merchants, additional terms become part of the contract unless: (i) expressly limited by the offer; (ii) they materially alter the offer; or (iii) notification of objection is given within a reasonable time. None of these exceptions exists in this case. Therefore, a valid contract was created between Able and Maxco, and Able does not have to pay Maxco until he sells the Ultramax as per the condition of delivery on consignment.

Baker's rights to the Ultramax: Baker entered into a contract to purchase an Ultramax from Able on May 29. Under U.C.C. section 2-502, a buyer may replevy identified goods from the seller if the seller becomes insolvent within 10 days after the buyer has paid the first installment on their price. Here, Baker made partial payment on the Ultramax and it can be argued that Able became insolvent by June 8, the date Dunn levied upon the Ultramax (10 days after May 29). Thus, whether Baker has a right to take the Ultramax in Able's possession as a bona fide purchaser for value depends on whether the Ultramax was identified as being Baker's.

Under the U.C.C., identification is a designation of specific goods as ones to be delivered under the contract of sale. Identification takes place at the time the contract is made if it calls for the sale of specific and ascertained goods already existing. In other cases, identification takes place when the goods are shipped, marked, or otherwise designated by the seller as the goods to pass under the contract.

Here, it is not likely that the Ultramax in the store was specifically identified by Able as belonging to Baker. The mere reference to the "one in the store" cannot be considered as sufficient identification. Certainly the Ultramax was not marked as belonging to Baker. Indeed, Able's use of the machine for his own office work would indicate that Able intended the Ultramax for himself rather than Baker. Accordingly, it can be concluded that the Ultramax was not identified as belonging to Baker, thereby precluding Baker from replevying it.

Although Baker cannot replevy the goods, he may nevertheless allege that by making partial payment he obtained title paramount over the rights of others. However, under the U.C.C., the general rule is that title passes when the seller completes his performance with respect to physical delivery of the goods. Here, Able did not complete physical delivery of the Ultramax before the levy served by Dunn. Thus, title did not pass to Baker and, accordingly, he has no rights to the Ultramax.

Maxco's rights to the Ultramax: U.C.C. section 2-702 provides that when a seller learns that a buyer has received delivery of goods on credit while insolvent, he may reclaim the goods upon demand within 10 days after the buyer's receipt of goods. However, the seller's right to reclaim is subject to the rights of a buyer in the ordinary course of business or other good faith purchaser. Moreover, under Article 9 of the U.C.C., a levying lien creditor may cut off the seller's rights if the seller has not perfected his security interest by filing a financial statement.

Here, Maxco shipped the Ultramax to Able on consignment. In such a case, U.C.C. section 2-236 provides that where goods are delivered to a person for sale and that person maintains a place of business at which he sells goods of that kind under a name other than that of the person who has entrusted the goods to him, his creditors may attach the goods in his possession unless the entruster files a financing statement under Article 9 of the U.C.C. or proves that the person who has the goods is generally known by his creditors to be substantially engaged in selling goods on consignment.

Unfortunately, Maxco loses the Ultramax to Dunn (the lien creditor) because Maxco failed to perfect its security interest in the machine. Moreover, assuming arguendo that Dunn had not levied, Maxco could have lost the Ultramax to Baker had Baker been able to prove that the Ultramax was identified as belonging to him.

Dunn's right to the Ultramax: By virtue of the above discussion, Dunn's rights to the Ultramax supersede the rights of the other parties. He has an interest in the Ultramax to the extent of his judgment. To the extent the Sheriff's sale of the machine produced proceeds exceeding the amount of the judgment plus the Sheriff's costs, Dunn will have to turn over the excess to Able.

Contractual recoveries by the parties:

Maxco: Maxco's recovery should probably be limited to the $5,000 stated in the offering circular. However, since the final price term was left silent, Maxco could argue that since the Ultramax was to be sold on consignment, Able is liable for the increase of the price of the machine at the time of its "forced sale," *i.e.,* the levy by Dunn. Under the latter argument, Able could be held liable for $7,000, the market price at the time of levy.

Baker: Able has breached the contract of sale with Baker by virtue of the former's inability to deliver the Ultramax. As discussed above, Baker is unable to replevy the Ultramax. Therefore, he is entitled to recover his down payment of $600, and recover the difference between the contract price ($6,000) and the market price at the time he learned of the breach ($7,000) or $1,000. In the alternative, if Baker chooses to use his cover remedy, he may recover (in addition to the $600 deposit) the difference between the contract price and the amount he would actually have to pay for replacement goods.

Very truly yours,
Larry Lawyer

30. CONTRACTS/REAL PROPERTY
DEFECTS OF CONTRACT

Contract of adhesion: In order to have an enforceable contract, a bargain must be struck between the parties after meaningful negotiations. In a case where one party is in such a superior bargaining position so as to put the other party in a "take it or leave it" position with respect to the terms of the contract, the courts have held such a contract an unenforceable contract of adhesion. Here, the contract was prepared by the seller's agent, the broker, and thus may be imputed to the seller. Since the buyer signed this contract under undue pressure, it can be argued that equity will relieve him from its obligations. There is evidence of undue influence from Broker's representation to Buyer (and to Seller) that delay would forfeit the deal. Often, a broker cannot effectively represent the interests of both a buyer and seller of real estate. Full disclosure is essential and if there is any evidence that Broker was acting in Seller's interest by urging Buyer to sign without legal consultation, then Buyer has, in effect, signed an unenforceable contract. Bargaining power between two parties must be the result of noncoercive negotiation.

Statute of Frauds: Any contract for the sale of land or any interest in, or concerning, land for longer than one year must be in writing signed by the party to be charged therewith (or his agent). To satisfy the Statute of Frauds, the writing must (i) identify the parties; (ii) describe the land; (iii) state the purchase price; and (iv) contain mutual promises to buy and sell the land. Here, the Statute of Frauds is not satisfied because there is an inadequate description of the land. The description "on a lot approximately 100' by 150' in North Salem, New Jersey" is too vague to identify the property. The deed and contract must identify the land precisely enough to be readily identifiable by anyone. The contract should contain the lot and bloc number of the lot on the North Salem tax assessor's map as well as the street address or a surveyor's description in metes and bounds. Here, the latter provisions are lacking, and accordingly, the contract is unenforceable under the Statute of Frauds.

Mortgage financing clause: The contract contains a patent ambiguity in that it provides that it is contingent upon the buyer obtaining a mortgage commitment at "prevailing rates" but that each party may void the agreement if the loan has not been "arranged" by August 1, 1981.

First, with respect to "prevailing rates," the contract does not adequately define this term. Prevailing rates at one time can be radically different from prevailing rates at another time. Thus, the parties may have committed a mutual mistake of fact by "agreeing" to this term because this mutual mistake goes to "the heart of the bargain."

Second, the contract does not adequately define "arranged." It is possible that the buyer could obtain a mortgage commitment but prior to the closing the lender could refuse to fund the mortgage loan for failure to meet conditions of the commitment. In residential house closings, one of these conditions is always that the buyer must obtain "marketable title." Thus, the buyer could find himself with a mortgage commitment and yet find that the loan cannot be "arranged" because of defects in marketable title. This ambiguity shows a mutual mistake of fact which should render the contract unenforceable.

DEFECTS IN MARKETABLE TITLE

All contracts for the sale of land contain, unless the contract expressly provides otherwise, an implied warranty by the seller that he will deliver to the buyer a marketable title at the date of closing. The seller's basic obligation under the warranty is to deliver a title that is free from reasonable doubt either in fact or law. This does not require a perfect title, but rather, one which is free from questions that might result in litigation. Title is marketable if a reasonably prudent buyer, ready and able to purchase, will accept it in the exercise of ordinary prudence. Here, the following problems indicate that the seller cannot deliver marketable title.

Status of Seller's marriage: The status of Seller's marriage could cast a cloud over the conveyance of marketable title. Although Seller purchased the property before marriage, he may have since conveyed the property to himself and his wife as tenants by the entirety. Tenants by the entirety own by the whole and by the part. Each tenant has equal rights to possession and control; the estate is held only by a husband and wife and there is a valuable right of survivorship in this estate. If the property is presently held by such an estate, Seller's wife would have to sign both the contract and deed, or by mutual agreement with Seller, sign a release of her rights. A tenancy by the entirety can only be terminated by (i) death of either spouse or (ii) divorce (which renders parties tenants in common) or (iii) mutual agreement. Nevertheless, abandonment by one spouse is an insufficient ground on which to terminate the tenancy. However, if a conveyance was at any time made to Seller's wife, which would render the property held by tenants by the entirety, it would be easily discovered by the routine title search if the conveyance had been duly recorded. Therefore, this problem does not necessarily affect marketability of title.

Zoning problems: In general, public restrictions (zoning regulations) do not render title unmarketable, although an existing violation will render title unmarketable if no variance is obtained. There, the problem focuses on a "use" made of the property prior to and after enactment of the ordinance. A use existing at the time of passage of a zoning act which does not conform to the statute cannot be eliminated at once. Some statutes provide for the gradual elimination of such conforming uses within a certain period of time. Here, it is not clear whether the one-family zoning ordinance had a nonconforming use phase-out period and if it did, whether said period lapsed. It is unclear whether the apartment use was continuous since enactment of the ordinance. If in fact the apartment was rented only "from time to time," Boarder's tenancy is likely in violation of the ordinance and title is unmarketable because it is not free from questions which might result in litigation.

Restrictive covenant in the prior deed: Arguably, renting an apartment is using the property for a commercial purpose. If so, the existing use of the property violates this covenant. A purchaser of land must read restrictive covenants in prior deeds of his chain of title. This restrictive covenant is an equitable servitude because it is a restriction on the use to which an owner may put his land. One who takes the property with notice of a restriction is bound by the restriction and there is no need for privity of estate for enforceability. Although a bona fide purchaser who takes without notice of an unrecorded restriction cannot be bound, it appears that Seller had record notice (prior deeds in grantee's chain of title) of this covenant. Seller's breach poses a cloud on title.

The clause "conveyance shall be made subject to easements and restrictions of record" is a standard clause. The test of which easements and restrictions render title unmarketable depends upon whether property use or market value is substantially reduced.

Driveway: This might pose no problem that would affect marketability of title. If the neighbor's driveway utilizes a tiny corner of Seller's land and Buyer was on actual notice of this easement, Buyer has a weak argument. If the neighbor obtained an easement by either express grant (formalities of a deed), implication (necessity), or by prescription, this condition will not affect marketability. Seller concealed nothing; there is evidence that Buyer was fully aware of the condition.

Easements: The recorded easements to the two utility companies are easements in gross. These easements are for a commercial purpose and are both necessary and ordinary. They generally pose no problems as to marketability of title because duly recorded easements are easily discovered in the routine title search.

Conclusion: The contradiction contained within the body of the contract that the property will be conveyed free of encumbrances, in light of the fact that there are existing encumbrances, renders this contract quite ambiguous and contradictory in its terms. There are strengths to Buyer's argument that this contract is unenforceable.

31. TORTS
PRIMA FACIE CASE GENERALLY
For Packer to establish a prima facie case in negligence against Dweller, he must prove:
(i)   The existence of Dweller's duty to conform to a specific standard of conduct;
(ii) That this duty has been breached;
(iii) That the breach of his duty was the actual and proximate cause of the injury sustained;
(iv) Damages.
Packer's brief must contain legal and factual support for each item noted. Dweller's defense must prove that no duty has been breached because the necessary standard of care has been exercised.

The briefs which follow illustrate the legal issues and facts on which each party would rely.
BRIEF IN SUPPORT OF PLAINTIFF PACKER
Standard of care: While working on Dweller's property, Packer is considered an invitee: Packer is present under an implied invitation and performs a service for the benefit of Dweller. As an invitee, Packer is owed a standard of care higher than that owed to a licensee. A licensee is generally on another's property for his own benefit. Since Packer is an invitee, Dweller has a duty to warn of concealed, dangerous conditions known to Dweller (the duty owed to licensees), *plus* a duty to inspect the premises to discover such conditions, and then to make them safe. The duty of the land possessor to "make safe" a dangerous condition can generally be satisfied by a simple warning. Although facts (f) and (g) reveal that Dweller attempted to make safe the dangerous condition, Dweller simply created a second dangerous condition whereby Packer has sustained severe injury.

That Packer is on Dweller's property as an invitee is clear; the service is entirely for Dweller's benefit and in response to Dweller's implied invitation. Thus, there is a duty owed to Packer. Dweller's conduct falls short of that level demanded by law and is therefore a breach of that duty. Entrusting and instructing the boys to clean up the glass in a particular fashion reflects that Dweller was on actual notice of the extent of the potential danger posed by the broken window while it was on the ground. That her instructions were followed emphasizes that Dweller had full knowledge of the condition and the attempt to assuage foreseeable injury. It should be noted that even if Dweller did not have actual notice, she would have the duty to inspect the premises, including the garbage bag.

Dweller's attempt falls below the standard required as a matter of law because she did not in fact make safe the condition which caused Packer's injury. The duty owed has been further breached because it is neither reasonable nor safe to leave window glass protruding through a black plastic bag which Dweller knows will be handled by sanitation workers. It is foreseeable that Packer, in his capacity as sanitation engineer, would come in close contact with the bag which contained the broken glass.

Causation: Packer's injury is not a direct result of the baseball-shattered window, but rather the direct result of Dweller's conduct in disposing of the broken window. It is foreseeable that Packer would naturally dispose of Dweller's trash in his usual manner. Tossing the trash bag is a foreseeable intervening act and cannot serve to absolve Dweller from liability for injuries sustained as a result of her negligence. Although certain superseding forces will relieve a defendant from liability for negligence, the foreseeable act of trash collection does not fall into any of the exceptions which serve to break the causal connection.

The usual and accepted practice for sanitation collectors on the job is for one partner to toss the trash to the other who stands closer to the sanitation truck. This partnership effort is efficient and widely utilized. To Dweller, as homeowner, it should have been foreseeable that razor sharp glass protruding through a black opaque plastic bag would cause injury to almost any party who should come in contact with the bag. At the very least, it is foreseeable that injury would be sustained by the very party who would ultimately dispose of the glass, *i.e.,* Packer.

Therefore, since the practice engaged in by Packer and Carter was widely accepted and clearly within the popular state of the art of their livelihood, there can be no contributory negligence.

Although it is true that a person assumes the risks inherent to any line of work, these risks must be known if the law is to recognize them as assumed risks. Granted, there are risks inherent to the job of sanitation engineer (*i.e.,* disease, poison, etc.). However, for Packer to know that a homeowner will be so careless as to leave glass protruding through an opaque bag is to render Packer a psychic.

BRIEF IN SUPPORT OF DEFENDANT DWELLER

Standard of care: Whether Dweller, as land possessor, owes a duty to Packer depends upon Packer's status while present on Dweller's property. The applicable standard of care also depends upon this classification.

Packer is an invitee while on Dweller's property. Packer is a privileged entrant; he is performing a service of legitimate purpose for Dweller, and Dweller derives the major benefits of Packer's activity. Arguably Packer is a public servant and thus a licensee serving the general public by preventing pollution and disease, but where the entrant provides a direct service for the possessor, he is an invitee. Invitees enjoy a higher standard of care than do licensees.

Generally, a trash collector (Packer) enters the possessor's premises in response to an express or implied invitation. The duty owed to the invitee is a general duty to use reasonable ordinary care in keeping the property reasonably safe. The land possessor (Dweller) has a duty to warn of concealed dangerous conditions and thereafter make them safe. Inherent in this definition is the duty to make reasonable inspections to discover dangerous conditions and to warn of or neutralize these conditions in a reasonable manner and within a reasonable time. The invitee enters the possessor's premises with the expectation that the premises will be reasonably safe from dangerous concealed conditions.

Dweller exercised reasonable care by immediately supervising the disposal of the broken window. The pickup and disposal into a large bag designed for trash, and the final disposal into an ordinary outdoor garbage receptacle is a standard and usual means by which to clean up a broken window.

To Packer it may appear that glass windows are found less frequently in trash than are other items. However, it is not unforeseeable that outdoor trash cans lined with trash bags will contain glass or other sharp instrumentalities. Dweller disposed of the glass in a prudent fashion; it would be unreasonable to require a property owner to label contents of trash bags.

Although there was a dangerous condition on Dweller's property while the broken glass lay on the ground, Dweller rectified that potential danger and therefore breached no duty to Packer as an invitee. Furthermore, it appears that the glass actually protruded from the garbage bag, so that the dangerous condition was not concealed. A landowner has no duty to warn of or make safe obvious dangerous conditions. Thus, Dweller breached no duty to Packer.

Defenses: Although the usual practice for garbage collection may have been for Carter to toss the trash bag to Packer, it is not unforeseeable to Packer that injury might result depending on the contents of any trash bag.

The nature of Packer's work demands that he assume certain risks inherent to the job. Packer voluntarily assumes known risks which are reasonably foreseeable. It is an implied assumption of risk (to Packer) that there will be sharp-edged items in many trash containers. Packer voluntarily encounters and assumes a known risk by continuing to catch tossed trash bags. It is foreseeable that such practice will result in injury because it is unreasonable to expect that people will not be disposing of any sharp-edged items. Therefore, Packer is deemed to have assumed the risk of the very injury he has sustained due to the manner in which he performs his services. His own usual practice does not render the practice sensible nor careful.

Distinguishable from assumption of risk is contributory negligence, whereby one who unknowingly encounters a risk is himself negligent and therefore barred from recovery. Were Packer's and Carter's usual practice negligent, Packer will be denied any recovery. Arguably, fact (h) connotes a finding that the practice was acceptable. Nevertheless, the likelihood of trash containing glass is obvious enough to warrant the very danger encountered by Packer as one inherent to the nature of his job and a negligent practice. Trash collectors wear gloves as protection against certain types of injury; that trash will contain items that could cause injury if thrown is highly foreseeable. Thus, Packer's conduct falls below the standard of a reasonable person engaged in identical activity.

The last clear chance doctrine, which is a plaintiff's response (defense) to a charge of contributory negligence can mitigate the harsh result whereby contributory negligence serves to bar recovery. Nevertheless, the facts illustrate that it was Packer (and/or Carter) who had the last opportunity to avoid the accident. If one of them had looked, he would have seen that the bag contained glass, that the glass protruded through the bag, and that the likelihood of injury was high if the bag was tossed to Packer. Packer's injury could only have been avoided if Packer and Carter had not been negligent in their routine.

32. EVIDENCE/CRIMINAL LAW
EXPERT WITNESS

The jury must be informed that expert testimony may be given legal effect. There are qualifications that must be met before the testimony may be given legal effect:

Proposed instruction #1: The jury may rely on and give legal effect to the testimony of Expert Witness if you find that the subject matter is appropriate for expert testimony. The subject matter must be so complex that the need for specialized knowledge in the field to which he has testified renders it appropriate subject matter. The purpose of the expert testimony must be to assist you, the jury, as the trier of fact. [Fed. R. Evid. 702] The testimony is to be given legal effect if you find that Expert Witness possessed specialized knowledge or expertise in the area to which he testified.

(The expert testimony may have legal effect only if the witness himself qualifies as an expert. The jury has heard Expert X's credentials and qualifications. An expert witness need only possess special knowledge on the subject to which his testimony relates. It is in the trial judge's discretion whether the expert qualifies as such and the facts here indicate the witness was qualified to testify to Sunny's condition. This decision made by the trial judge is reviewable only for abuse. Therefore, the jury need not be instructed on this qualification.)

Proposed instruction #2: For the expert testimony to be given legal effect, the expert must have possessed and demonstrated reasonable certainty or reasonable scientific possibility for his opinion. The expert must have communicated more than speculation in arriving at his opinion.

Proposed instruction #3: For expert testimony to be given legal effect, the opinion of Expert Witness must be supported by a proper factual basis. The opinion of Expert Witness may be based upon his firsthand knowledge and/or his observations, or the opinion may be based on facts that are submitted to the expert by the traditional hypothetical question. For the opinion to be given legal effect, this hypothetical question must have included all facts in evidence which would affect his opinion. The expert may have been asked to assume certain facts and then give inferences in view of these assumptions. The clearer the assumed facts have been made to you as jurors, the more credibility you may give to the expert testimony. (Federal Rule of Evidence 705 represents the modern trend that the hypothetical need not be formally set forth to the witness.)

Proposed instruction #4: As per Federal Rule of Evidence 704, the expert may testify as to his opinion on an issue which is ultimately to be decided by the trier of fact. Federal Rule of Evidence 702 demands that testimony related to an ultimate issue must indeed assist the jury to determine a fact in issue. Therefore, testimony by Expert Witness that in his opinion defendant Sunny lacked capacity to appreciate the wrongfulness of his act may be weighed by the jury as any other testimony. The standard by which to weigh the testimony is whether the testimony assisted the jury.

Although an expert may not express an opinion on an issue of law, an opinion that defendant Sunny lacked capacity to appreciate the wrongfulness of his act is a conclusion based on facts as to an issue of fact, provided the testimony is to aid the jury and does not usurp the function or province of the jury as the ultimate trier of fact.

(Although not at issue because not presented by the facts in this question, it is essential to remember that jury instructions in a criminal matter will include instructions regarding the presumption of innocence, presumption of sanity, and role of the jury as the ultimate trier of fact, and the jury will be instructed that the prosecution has the burden of proving the defendant guilty of the offense beyond a reasonable doubt.)

SPECIFIC CRIME

The specific crime that the defendant has been charged with must be set forth in an instruction explaining what elements constitute that crime.

Proposed instructions to the jury: Your deliberation as a jury will begin and it is for you to determine whether a crime has been committed and if so, what crime. Although there has been a death, it may not be a murder. For example, if the death results under circumstances in which the defendant's acts are lawfully justified, or if the defendant is not, under the circumstances, responsible in law for his acts, or if the circumstances indicate the lack of some fact or factor which the law says is necessary for guilt, or if the necessary facts are not proved beyond a reasonable doubt, we may then have death without criminal liability, or a killing without a crime.

It is therefore your duty to examine not only the fact of killing and of death, but also the circumstances surrounding it, before you can determine whether or not the defendant is guilty of the crime charged, or of some lesser crime, or of no crime at all.

Second degree murder is the unlawful killing of a human being with malice aforethought. Malice aforethought is determined by circumstantial evidence. If you find that the defendant had any of the following states of mind, then you may find him guilty of second degree murder. The applicable states of mind are:

(i)   Intent to kill (express malice), or
(ii) Intent to inflict great bodily injury.

After considering all of the evidence, before you can convict this defendant or anyone of murder, you must believe and decide that the People have established beyond a reasonable doubt that he intended to kill the victim. There can be no murder unless the killer intended to cause death. If you find no such intent to kill—if, for example, you find an intent to injure but not an intent to kill—you must consider one or more of the lesser degrees of homicide.

Second degree murder is still different from first degree murder because first degree murder requires premeditation. Premeditation and deliberation would render a crime first degree murder. But if the defendant is found incapable of premeditation by reason of intoxication and you find the defendant possessed one of the states of mind necessary for second degree murder, you may find him guilty of second degree murder.

To reduce the crime from murder to voluntary manslaughter, certain standards must be met:

(i)　There must be reasonable provocation as would arouse sudden and intense passion.

(ii)　The defendant must have been in fact provoked.

(iii)　A reasonable person so provoked would not have cooled off between the provocation and the killing.

(iv)　The defendant must not in fact have cooled off. If the jury finds that a reasonable person and the defendant would not have cooled off from the time of the killing, then the crime would be mitigated to voluntary manslaughter.

(*Note:* Most courts recognize only two instances of reasonable provocation for purposes of voluntary manslaughter: Exposure to, injury by, or threatened with violent physical force; or discovery of one's spouse in the act of adultery.)

The fact that the killing may have been done in a passion upon adequate provocation is a mitigation of the offense and not a defense to the crime.

DEFENSES

Intoxication is a defense to a crime only when it negates an element of the crime. For example, if the intoxication prohibited the defendant from forming the requisite state of mind for murder, then you may not find him guilty of murder. The defense of intoxication is an affirmative defense. This means that the defendant has the burden of proving his intoxication.

Since second degree common law murder does not require premeditation or deliberation and thus intoxication would not prevent a defendant from formulating the state of mind needed for common law murder, voluntary intoxication is no defense to second degree murder.

Voluntary intoxication must be distinguished from involuntary intoxication. For voluntary intoxication to serve as a defense as to a crime, the intoxication serves to negate the intent or knowledge which the crime requires. Therefore, you may find that the defendant, because in an intoxicated state, actually lacks the intent or knowledge necessary for the crime. Although intoxication can reduce first degree murder to second degree murder, intoxication cannot reduce second degree murder to manslaughter.

Involuntary intoxication can serve as a defense to any crime, regardless of its elements, because it robs the defendant of his ability to know right from wrong and he is not able to be guilty of a crime in terms of the law. But there are stringent standards which must be met for the defendant's intoxication to be rendered involuntary.

Involuntary intoxication can result from a person mistakenly taking a substance which impairs his/her sensibilities, or in this case pathological intoxication, which is where the defendant knew what he was taking but the amount taken was grossly excessive. [Model Penal Code §2.08 (5)(c)] The intoxication is involuntary if the defendant was unaware that he was susceptible by an atypical reaction to the substance taken.

Therefore, Sunny may be found to have been involuntarily intoxicated if you find that although he knew the substance as alcohol and as an intoxicant, he had no knowledge of its effects in excessive degree or of his own susceptibility to such quantities of whiskey. Involuntary intoxication may be treated as a mental illness, in which case a defendant is entitled to acquittal if, because of the intoxication, he meets the test for insanity, *i.e.,* if he was unable to know the nature or quality of the act he was doing, or its wrongfulness.

33.　REAL PROPERTY
Supermarket, Inc.
Massive Mall Shopping Centers
Verdant, New Jersey
Attn: Max Mogul, Vice President of Sales
Dear Mr. Mogul:

This is in reply to your letter of July 25. The operation by Fast Foodmarts in Massive Mall in competition with your store is clearly in violation of the restrictive covenant in Section 10 of your lease with Landlord Associates. In my view, this covenant is valid and enforceable, and I recommend that suit be filed immediately seeking damages for breach of the covenant against Landlord Associates, and an injunction against the operation of the Fast Foodmarts store. I am optimistic that you will prevail in your case against Landlord and recover damages based on your decrease in sales. I cannot express the same assurances about your probability of success in obtaining injunctive relief against Fast Foodmarts, Inc.

The case against Landlord Associates should not be a difficult one. The Landlord's covenant to not lease any space in the shopping center for the conduct of any other business involving the sale of food products for off-premises consumption during the term of the lease is enforceable because it is commercially reasonable and was part of the material consideration for the lease agreement. The Landlord actually committed two separate breaches: (i) entering into the lease in September 1981 with Fast Foodmarts, and (ii) failing to disclose the restriction to subsequent lessees, as required in your lease. I cannot think of any defenses available to the Landlord. Very early in the proceedings I would file a motion for partial summary judgment, arguing that the September 1981 lease violates the restriction in the June 1974 lease as a matter of law. If granted, you would only need to prove damages, which are well documented.

Once the action is filed, you might consider withholding further payment of rent pending the outcome of litigation. You could then deposit your normal monthly rent payment into an interest bearing account and, if necessary, it will be available for deposit in court. In addition to damages sustained thus far, we would also be seeking an abatement of future rents or a setoff against a claim for unpaid rent. However, this should only be done as part of litigation. You should not withhold the rent as a means of self-help. The courts have consistently held that under a commercial lease, the Landlord's covenants to perform are independent of the tenant's covenant to pay rent. You should avoid doing anything that would leave you vulnerable to a suit for eviction.

Your rights against Fast Foodmarts, Inc. are not as clear. First of all, I do not think that the purely legal remedy of damages would be available to you because of the legal relationship between the parties. Fast Foodmarts, as a co-tenant, and not a purchaser or assignee of the Landlord, is not in privity with you of estate or contract. Therefore, it cannot be held liable for a breach of the covenant. I also doubt that the restriction would meet the test of a covenant running with the land, since it was created as part of a conveyance of a leasehold interest of limited duration.

The appropriate remedy to pursue would be injunctive relief in equity. But considering all the facts and circumstances of your case, you should be aware of several potential problems which could operate to deny you relief.

It must be shown that Fast Foodmarts, Inc. was on notice of the restriction. A chancery judge will weigh the potential economic injury to the defendant that might result from a grant of the injunction against the potential injury to you that is likely to result from a denial. If the court were to find that Fast Foodmarts was an innocent purchaser for value, chances are that the injunction would not issue.

I realize that you recorded the lease, and assumed that recordation would be constructive notice of the restriction to all the world. I am concerned, though, that a court of equity, in its wide discretion, could hold that it is not commercially reasonable to impose a duty on a prospective lessee to examine a title search before entering a lease. Your position should be that you acted in good faith and with all due diligence to put subsequent lessees on notice by providing in the lease that the Landlord disclose the restriction to future tenants. If Fast Foodmarts were injured by enforcement of your rights, recourse would be available to them against the Landlord on grounds of fraud and breach of the lease.

The problem of your delay in taking action is a more serious one. I wish you had alerted me immediately when you became aware of the lease between Landlord Associates and Fast Foodmarts, instead of deciding to "wait and see" for almost 10 months. You should have acted promptly to seek injunctive relief, by order to show cause, on the grounds that performance of the lease threatened imminent and irreparable harm to your interests. Instead, you acquiesced while it made a substantial investment in the enterprise. It can be argued that your conduct did not amount to a waiver because you accepted no benefit from Fast Foodmarts' continued operation. But, you should be aware that a court could hold you estopped by your failure to earlier protect the lease, or barred by the doctrine of laches for your failure to sooner seek judicial relief.

With respect to the operation of the health food, ice cream, and liquor stores, I do not believe you have a sound cause of action. The health food store's tenancy preexisted yours and could not be affected by your lease. The liquor store and ice cream store deal in specialty items. It would be difficult to prove that it was the intent of the parties to restrict that sort of competition. Even if you did prove the requisite intent, the restriction might be held to be overly broad and therefore unreasonable.

Please advise me of your intentions in the matter.

Very truly yours,
Larry Lawyer

34. CONSTITUTIONAL LAW
MEMORANDUM OF LAW

The statute allowing the state to prohibit transmission of electricity generated by water in New Jersey to points outside New Jersey probably is unconstitutional under the Commerce Clause and possibly for other reasons as well.

Although Article I, Section 8 of the United States Constitution vests Congress with plenary power to regulate interstate commerce which includes the transmission of electricity, that power is not exclusive. States may adopt nondiscriminatory legislation that does not unduly burden interstate commerce as long as the state law does not conflict with a federal law and Congress has not preempted the field.

Here, it is unclear whether the New Jersey law conflicts with a federal law or whether the field has been preempted by Congress, because nothing in the facts indicates that there is any kind of federal legislation involved. If there is federal legislation and the New Jersey statute directly conflicts with that legislation, the New Jersey statute will be struck down under the Supremacy Clause as violating Congress's commerce power. The Supremacy Clause and Commerce Clause would also invalidate the New Jersey law if Congress has adopted a regulatory scheme so pervasive and comprehensive that, by implication, it occupies the entire field and preempts all state attempts to regulate the supply of energy. Preemption is often found where a federal agency is created to administer over the area. (Although Congress certainly regulates many aspects concerning energy production, such as whether navigable rivers may be dammed and nuclear energy safety, it is doubtful that preemption will be found here. [*See, e.g.,* Pacific Gas & Electric Co. v. State Energy Commission, 461 U.S. 190 (1983)—holding that states could regulate the economic aspects of nuclear power; federal legislation is concerned only with nuclear safety])

Even if there is no direct conflict with federal law and no preemption, the New Jersey statute still probably violates the Commerce Clause. As indicated above, even where Congress has not acted, state legislation of commerce will violate the Commerce Clause if it either discriminates against interstate commerce or unduly burdens interstate commerce. Here, the New Jersey statute on its face discriminates against interstate commerce. Thus, under the general rule it violates the Commerce Clause. However, there is a narrow exception that must be considered: a state discriminatory regulation will be upheld if it furthers an important noneconomic state interest (such as health or safety) and there are no reasonable alternatives available (*i.e.,* the state law must be necessary to an important noneconomic state interest). It is unclear whether the state law here that allows out-of-state transmission of electricity to be prohibited only on a finding of "reasonable necessity"—requires assessment of reasonable alternatives. In any case, the exception probably does not apply because no important noneconomic government interest is being served—although there clearly is a shortage of electricity in the area, the only interest that seems to be involved is protecting in-state industries from competing with out-of-state industries in purchasing electricity. [*See* Hughes v. Oklahoma, 441 U.S. 322 (1979)— striking down a state law prohibiting export of live bait fish that were in short supply] Thus, the state law violates the Commerce Clause.

The New Jersey statute might also violate the Contracts Clause, but the facts are insufficient to make a clear determination. Under the Contracts Clause, state regulation cannot substantially impair a party's rights under an existing contract unless the regulation serves an important government interest and is narrowly tailored to achieve that interest. Here, nothing indicates whether WEPCO owed a continuing contractual duty to supply the out-of-state industries with electricity. If a contractual duty exists, the other elements for a violation of the Contracts Clause probably also are present for the same reason that the exception to the Commerce Clause does not apply (*see* above).

An action should be filed immediately in the Federal District Court of New Jersey seeking to enjoin enforcement of the regulation. The State of New Jersey, DOE, and WEPCO should be named as defendants, as well as the administrative official who made the finding of reasonable necessity and promulgated the order. WEPCO is a necessary party to the case because in addition to the injunction, you will be seeking declaratory relief to determine the respective rights and obligations of the parties. You may not, however, seek an award of monetary damages. WEPCO cannot be liable for failing to supply you because they acted in accordance with law. As to New Jersey and its arm, DOE, the court has no jurisdiction to award damages. The Eleventh Amendment prohibits suits for monetary damages by citizens of one state against a state, without its consent to be a party to the suit. However, lawsuits seeking injunctive relief and determination of rights involving questions of constitutionality are excepted from the bar of the Eleventh Amendment.

35. CONTRACTS

AGREEMENT, dated February 1, 1983, by and between Pat Jones of Paramus, New Jersey (hereinafter Pat) and Ralph Smith of Fairlawn, New Jersey (hereinafter Ralph).

WHEREAS, Pat is the owner of a retail business selling food and beverages for on-and-off-premises consumption, commonly known as a delicatessen; and

WHEREAS, Pat desires to sell and Ralph desires to buy a 50% interest in said business; and WHEREAS, the parties desire to form a partnership under the laws of the state of New Jersey for the purpose of operation of said business:

NOW, THEREFORE, IT IS MUTUALLY AGREED AS FOLLOWS:

1. Pat shall sell and Ralph shall buy a 50% interest in the delicatessen business owned and operated by Pat at premises located on Main Street in Hackensack, New Jersey, including all good-will, stock and trade, equipment, fixtures, rights under leases and contracts, accounts receivable, and all other benefits and advantages derived from the operation of the business, which are more specifi-cally enumerated in Schedule 1, attached hereto.

2. And as for the purchase price, Ralph shall pay to Pat the sum of THIRTY THOUSAND DOLLARS, payable as follows:

a)	Down payment upon execution of this agreement, to be held in escrow by the attorney for Pat until the effective date of existence of the partnership	$3,000
b)	Balance payable within 30 days of the date of the execution of this agreement or upon the effective date of the existence of the partnership, whichever occurs later.	$27,000
		$30,000

3.   This agreement, and the respective obligations of the parties, is contingent upon Ralph's ability to obtain suitable financing for a term of five years at prevailing rates of interest. Ralph agrees to make a prompt and diligent effort to obtain such financing. If Ralph is unable to obtain suitable financing, he shall notify Pat in writing within the period of 30 days following the execution of the agreement, whereupon Pat shall, at his option, offer suitable financing terms to Ralph, or declare this agreement void, and return all sums paid by Ralph on account of this agreement.

4.   A partnership is hereby created under the laws of the state of New Jersey. The commencement of the existence of the partnership shall be effective upon the expiration of 30 days following execution of this agreement or upon Ralph obtaining financing, whichever is later.

5.   All profits and losses of the partnership enterprise shall be shared equally between the parties.

6.   It is agreed and understood, in view of Pat's experience and expertise and his availability to devote his full-time attention to the business, that Pat shall be considered the managing partner.

7.   It is agreed and understood that Ralph, because of other commitments, shall not be available to work in the store on a full-time basis. Ralph expressly covenants and agrees to diligently devote himself to the best interests of the business, and to not engage in any enterprise or venture which competes with or is in any way detrimental to the best interests of the partnership business. Ralph further agrees to defer to the authority of Pat as to decisions involving routine management of business operations. Ralph shall, however, be entitled to fully participate in significant decisions involving business policy, or concerning fundamental changes in the status of the business, and all such decisions will require joint approval of Pat and Ralph.

8.   Pat shall receive a salary of $200 per week for the performance of his management duties and in consideration of his greater time and effort devoted to the business. This salary shall be subject to adjustment, from time to time, as may be mutually agreed to by the parties.

9.   Pat acknowledges and agrees that Ralph has entered into this agreement in reliance on Pat's representation that the business is capable of generating sufficient annual income, based upon the past earnings history, for Ralph to earn a distributed share of net profits, after payment of costs, operating expenses, and overhead, of at least $6,000. In the event that the income of the business, at the close of the first fiscal year of operation, is insufficient to yield a net distributed share of profit to each partner in the amount of at least $6,000, Ralph shall have the right to sell his partnership share back to Pat for a price to be determined in accordance with the following formula: his full contribution of $30,000, less any profits realized, with accrued interest at 12% per annum. This option shall be exercised within the first 30 days of the second fiscal year of operation or otherwise waived.

10.   Pat agrees to indemnify and hold Ralph harmless from any and all debts incurred in the operation of the business as a sole proprietorship up to and including the effective date of the commencement of the partnership pursuant to this agreement. Ralph shall assume equally all other liabilities incurred by the partnership in the operation of the business.

11.   Neither partner shall sell, assign, pledge, or mortgage his interest in the partnership without the written consent of the other party.

12.   In the event of the death of either partner, the business shall be continued to the end of the fiscal year in which the death occurs. At the close of the fiscal year, the surviving partner shall, at his option: continue to operate the business under the terms of this agreement, paying the 50% net share of the profits (or charging a 50% share of the losses), to the estate of the deceased partner; or buy out the interest of the deceased partner at a price to be based upon 50% of the net worth of the business as valued in the annual financial statement prepared by the partnership's accountant.

13.   Disputes and controversies which cannot be settled by the parties, may, with the consent of both parties, be submitted to arbitration. In the event that both parties do not consent to arbitration of the dispute, either party may propose to buy or sell the interest of the other partner at a price based

upon 50% of the net worth of the business as reflected in the partnership's annual financial statement. In the event that the parties cannot reach an accord as to the terms of the buy-out, the partnership shall then be dissolved, the partnership assets liquidated, and the proceeds divided into two equal shares and distributed to the partners.

14. The term of this agreement shall commence immediately upon execution by the parties and shall continue for the duration of the partnership, unless terminated or modified by the parties in writing.

Dated:

_____
Pat Jones

_____
Ralph Smith

36. CRIMINAL LAW

STATE	)	
	)	SUPERIOR COURT
vs.	)	
	)	APPELLATE DIVISION
CLAIRE	)	

BRIEF FOR APPELLANT
POINT I

In order to convict Defendant of murder, the State was either required to prove that Defendant, with specific intent, deliberately killed any of the victims, or that she was liable for the murder of any of the victims, as a matter of law, under the felony murder rule. The facts are uncontradicted that she was not directly or personally responsible for the death of any of the victims except for Drew.

As to the killing of Drew, Defendant lacked the requisite intent to be guilty of murder. In a state of panic and confusion, she accidentally shifted the get-away car into forward gear, instead of reverse, thrusting the car forward, striking and killing Drew. These unintentional acts could support a conviction of manslaughter or death by auto, if shown to be reckless or negligent, but not murder.

She should not be guilty under the felony murder theory. She reached a place of "temporary safety." Therefore, the impact of the felony murder rule ceases and deaths subsequently caused are not felony murder.

POINT II

To support a conviction of murder, under the felony murder doctrine, the State would have to show that a killing occurred during the course of the commission of any one of several felonies (robbery included) to which Defendant was a party, provided that the death was a foreseeable consequence of the acts constituting the commission of the felony. If a killing is caused during the commission of a felony and it does not qualify for felony murder, the killing would be classified as involuntary manslaughter.

It is conceded that Defendant is in all probability guilty of one or more felonies. She was certainly involved in a conspiracy to commit a robbery, arguably, an armed robbery. She was an accessory to that robbery and aided and abetted its commission. Furthermore, even though Defendant planned to use a toy gun in the robbery and so clearly did not intend to kill anyone, most authorities agree that a death caused by fear from the commission of a robbery is a foreseeable consequence of the robbery, it does not matter that the victim had a heart condition of which the defendant was unaware, and it does not matter that the defendant did not even touch the victim. Thus, Defendant can be found guilty of felony murder.

POINT III

Similarly, Defendant would be guilty of the death of Edward, the innocent bystander. The courts hold that resistance by the police is a foreseeable consequence of the commission of a felony such as robbery. Therefore, if an innocent bystander is killed by police during the commission of a robbery, the robber and his accomplices can be held liable for the death of the innocent bystander even though the robber had no intention of killing anyone.

However, Defendant cannot be found guilty under the felony murder doctrine for the death of Bill. The majority rule is that a felon cannot be found guilty under the felony murder doctrine for the death of a co-felon caused by the police or a resisting victim (the Redline doctrine).

CONCLUSION

For the foregoing reasons, it is respectfully submitted that the judgment of conviction entered in the proceeding below regarding the deaths of Drew and Bill be reversed.

37. REAL PROPERTY

TO: Mark Myers, V.P., Jerseyana Title Company
FROM: Counsel
DATED: March 1, 1983

As per your request, I have reviewed the abstract of title relative to premises known as 117 Hartacke Road, Ourton, New Jersey, and I would offer the following comments as to the marketability of title:

(a)   The restrictions contained in the deed dated 2/16/21 should be noted in your Preliminary Report Title and listed as exceptions to coverage in the title insurance commitment. However, I do not consider them to be valid encumbrances significantly affecting marketability of title for the following reasons:

(1)   The restriction of the use of the premises for residential purposes is currently not violated and seems likely to remain so. You may wish to offer the insured a guaranty against damages resulting from violation or reversion. I recommend that the local zoning ordinance and master plan be examined to see if the use mandated by the restriction is compatible with the local zoning scheme.

(2)   Similarly, you should note in your preliminary title report the violation of the front setback line, as shown by the survey, but I do not believe this violation impairs marketability of title either. Investigate to determine the date of construction. If this violation has existed openly and notoriously for many years, the covenant would probably not be enforceable in equity.

(3)   The restriction against transfer of title to a noncitizen is clearly unconstitutional as a violation of equal protection, and an unenforceable restraint on alienation.

(b)   Utility easements and rights-of-way are routine, and necessary to insure availability of power and essential services. Conveyances made subject to such easements do not affect marketability.

(c)   I note from the abstract that Jane Able took title from her husband, Arnold, on 7/6/27, subject to a certain mortgage, and thereafter conveyed on 9/18/37, to Baker, et ux, under the name Jane Airy, apparently paying off the mortgage and having it canceled of record on 9/25/37. I have two questions about these items:

(1)   Your abstract of title contains a recorded mortgage in the chain, but refers to it only by deed recital. How was the mortgage canceled, if it was never recorded?

(2)   I am concerned about the change of Jane Able's name to Jane Airy. If the name was changed by remarriage, were her husband's rights of courtesy properly disposed of? Even if Miss Able were not remarried and merely changed her name, did she have a valid power of sale as Jane Airy, without executing the deed as Jane Able? Please investigate Jane Able's marital status at that time. Perhaps Jersey Trust Company, a subsequent mortgagee, will have relevant back title information.

(d)   The recorded agreement of 3/19/42 between Baker and Charles is an easement appurtenant, granted for the purpose of installing and maintaining the water supply to the Charles property, the servient tenement. Such an interest may affect marketability as a technical matter, and should be listed as an exception in your title commitment. Technically, if the contract between Parks and Dephoe did not contain the appropriate disclaimer, *i.e.,* "subject to easements of record," the Dephoes would have had a right to avoid the contract. However, as a practical matter, such easements are common, and do not raise serious questions warranting litigation as to the use and enjoyment of, or title to, the premises.

(e)   There is apparently no record of cancellation of the 1/20/48 mortgage from Baker to Jersey Trust Company. It is highly possible, considering the fact that the mortgage was due and payable over 30 years ago, that it was paid and satisfied but never canceled of record. However, this cannot be assumed and the title flaw must be resolved. Jersey Trust Company, or its successor in interest, should be contacted to ascertain whether the obligation remains open, and if not, a discharge of mortgage should be prepared and sent to them to be duly executed, and thereafter recorded.

(f)   Barry Baker's will, dated 5/8/72, devises his real property in equal shares to his children. However, your abstract contains no record of the termination of the interest of Ann Baker. Most likely, Ann Baker took title with Barry Baker from Airy on 9/18/37 as tenants by the entirety, but the deed should be examined to make certain of that fact. If she was a tenant by the entirety with her husband, then upon her death, her interest would divest, and would vest in Barry Baker in fee. If that is the case, her death certificate must be obtained.

If Ann Baker and Barry Baker took title as tenants in common, it would have to be expressly stated as such in the deed, because the law treats any marital tenancy as by the entirety, where it is not otherwise expressly stated in the deed of acquisition. In that case, the records would have to be searched for a probated will of Ann Baker, to make sure that she devised her interest to her husband, or to Edward Baker and Carol Baker Parks in equal shares. If there was no will, you should make certain that no outstanding interests in the property were created on her death by the laws of intestacy.

(g)   Several questions are raised by the 5/13/81 conveyance from Carol Baker Parks to Dephoe:

(1)   Proof of death of Ann Baker and Edward Baker must be obtained, because the deed recital is not sufficiently reliable for title purposes. (We know of the death of Barry Baker, by reason that his will was probated.)

(2)   The marital status of Carol Baker Parks must be determined. Presumably, there is a Mr. Parks, and if he is alive, his marital interest (courtesy, dower, right of joint possession, etc.) must be disposed of by an additional conveyance. If he is deceased, there is no need to determine his heirs, because such marital interests in the property are limited in duration of life estates.

(3)   We must also dispose of the one-half undivided interest in the premises of Edward Baker, specifically devised him under his father's will. Did Edward Baker leave a will, or if he died intestate, did he leave surviving issue or heirs other than his sister, Carol Baker Parks?

As you know, determinations of marketability are subjective, within certain standards of practice and custom. Titles are rarely perfect or completely free of encumbrance. The test I have applied to each of these items is whether they raise a question of title which would require a lawsuit for resolution.

38. TORTS

JACK JONES,	)
Plaintiff,	)
	)
vs.	)
	)
DELTA COMPANY,	)
Defendant.	)

A.   Defendant demands certified answers by the Plaintiff to the following Interrogatories within the time provided by law:

1.   State your full name, age, residence, address, telephone number, Social Security number, and present military status.

2.   Set forth your employment history during the five years preceding the commencement of this action, giving the names and addresses of the employers and dates of employment.

If you contend that you were unemployed at any time during the period referred to in the preceding interrogatory due to physical disability, describe in detail the nature of your physical disability.

3.　With respect to any injuries, illnesses, or physical disabilities allegedly sustained in the course of your employment related to the use of the chemical DUST, state whether any proceedings were instituted to collect any benefits under the Workers' Compensation Law of New Jersey, federal, or private disability insurance plan.

If so, set forth:

(a)　the nature and dates of the proceedings; and

(b)　the amount of temporary or permanent benefits awarded.

4.　With respect to your particular place of employment at the time you contend you worked with any product manufactured by this Defendant, state:

(a)　the name and address of your employer, the name of your immediate supervisor, your title or position, and rate of pay;

(b)　the nature of your duties and responsibilities;

(c)　your years of experience at that particular job; and

(d)　special training granted to you by your employer to perform that particular job.

5.　Describe in detail the specific manner in which this Defendant's product known as DUST was used on your job.

6.　State:

(a)　the date on which you first came in contact with the product;

(b)　the frequency with which you used it thereafter;

(c)　any specific instructions or warnings about the use of the product given to you by your employer; and

(d)　whether the product, when used by you, was in your possession in its original container.

7.　State the date that you first noted any physical reaction or illness which you contend resulted from your use of DUST; and

(a)　Describe in detail the reaction or symptoms of the reaction or illness, specifically identifying the affected part or parts of the body.

(b)　At the time you first noticed the alleged reaction referred to in the preceding interrogatory, was your employer notified? If so, to your knowledge was any report filed? State what action, if any, was taken.

8.　At the time you first noticed the alleged reaction referred to in the preceding interrogatory, did you consult a physician, either of your own choosing, or at your employer's direction? If so, state:

(a)　the name and address of each doctor consulted;

(b)　the dates of each such consultation and statement of the doctor's diagnosis of the condition; and

(c)　the description of any treatment rendered by each doctor.

9.　If you were at any time hospitalized for treatment of any illnesses allegedly related to use of products manufactured by the Defendant, state the name of the hospitals and dates of admission(s) and discharge(s).

Describe treatment rendered, surgical procedures, if any, and condition at time of discharge.

10.　Describe the progress of the alleged condition referred to in the preceding interrogatory, in terms of:

(a)　whether you continued to use DUST on your job;

(b)　whether the condition or illness deteriorated, improved, or remained stable; and

(c)　whether the progress of the condition was monitored by any physician.

11.　Set forth all serious illnesses which you have suffered during the past 10 years, with particular emphasis on respiratory ailments, describing in detail the symptoms, duration of the illness, treatment or hospitalization received, and nature of any permanent after-effects. Include in your answer a description of any chronic allergies suffered by you.

12.　Set forth with particularity the facts you will rely on in support of the allegation in Paragraph 4 of the Complaint, that use of, or exposure to the chemical DUST, causes permanent and severe physical ailments or respiratory diseases.

13. With respect to the laboratory tests referred to in Paragraph 4, state:

(a) the name of the person or firm conducting each test;

(b) the dates on which the tests were conducted;

(c) the conditions under which the tests were conducted; and

(d) the results disclosed by each test.

14. Set forth the names of all persons having knowledge of facts relevant to this matter, and include as to each person named, a concise statement of their particular knowledge.

15. State the names and addresses of all expert witnesses retained or consulted by you relative to this matter, and include a concise statement of the substance of the proposed testimony of each expert witness named.

B. The Defendant demands that the Plaintiff produce the following documents within 20 days of the service of this demand:

1. All doctors' reports prepared at the Plaintiff's request by any of the physicians named in his Answers to Interrogatories.

2. All written reports of the results of any laboratory tests conducted by the person or persons referred to in Paragraph 4 of the Complaint.

3. All personnel reports or related documents on file with the Plaintiff's employer, relevant to any physical condition or reaction allegedly caused by the product DUST.

4. Complete copies of hospital records for all hospitalization set forth in Answer to Interrogatory No. 9.

5. Copies of any and all reports submitted to you by experts, intended for use at trial.

39. CONSTITUTIONAL LAW

Statute 1 probably is unconstitutional, Statute 2 probably is constitutional. At issue is the power of the states to regulate illegal aliens.

States do have some power to regulate illegal aliens. Although Article I, Section 8 of the United States Constitution grants Congress plenary power to regulate aliens, the Supreme Court has held that the grant is exclusive only with respect to naturalization and denaturalization; states may adopt regulations concerning other aspects of alienage. Thus, since the statutes here do not involve naturalization or denaturalization, they are in an area in which states may regulate. However, the mere fact that the states have the power to regulate over an area does not make every regulation that a state may adopt valid; the regulation must not violate any other constitutional principle. Here, it may be argued that the New Jersey statutes violate equal protection.

The Equal Protection Clause prohibits government from treating similarly situated people in a dissimilar manner absent sufficient justification. What is sufficient justification depends on the classification employed or the right involved. If the classification is suspect or the right is fundamental, the discrimination will be upheld only if it is necessary to achieve a compelling interest. If gender or legitimacy are involved, the discrimination will be upheld only if it is substantially related to an important government interest. In other cases, the discrimination will be upheld as long as it is rationally related to a legitimate government purpose. The Supreme Court has held that while alienage is a suspect classification when dealing with legal aliens, illegal alienage is not a suspect classification. However, the Court has not adopted a specific approach for illegal alienage cases. Under a statute very similar to Statute 1 here, the Court held that denial of education benefits to children of illegal aliens violated equal protection under an intermediate scrutiny analysis. [Plyer v. Doe, 457 U.S. 202 (1982)] Thus, Statute 1 is unconstitutional.

It is unclear whether the Court would use the intermediate standard for Statute 2, because in *Plyer* the Court was very concerned with the long-term effects of denying an education to children who had no control over their illegal alien status (they were brought in by their parents). If intermediate scrutiny is applied, the Court might very well find that Statute 2 is substantially related to the important government interest of preserving jobs for persons legally in the country. The statute certainly would be upheld under the rational basis standard. In any case, a statute similar to Statute 2 has been upheld by the Supreme Court based on the fact that it furthered the federal policy against employing illegal aliens. [DeCanas v. Bica, 424 U.S. 351 (1976)] The Court generally reviews federal regulation of aliens under a rational basis standard, and where a state statute furthers a federal policy, the Court grants the state more deference than it otherwise would.

Accordingly, Statute 2 should be upheld, and Statute 1 should be struck down as violative of equal protection.

40. CONTRACTS

(a)   Under his contract with Stella, Flash acquired rights to two distinct types of performances in consideration of his payment of $500. In part, the contract was an employment agreement, and Flash acquired the right to Stella's services as a photographic model for two one-hour sessions. He also acquired the exclusive right to market, distribute, reproduce, and/or license the distribution or reproduction of the photos. Flash's proprietary interest in his work product was therefore absolute, entitling him exclusively to all income generated by their sale.

Stella, however, retained other noneconomic rights concerning the use of the photos. Nowhere does the contract give Flash either an express or an implied right to alter Stella's likeness in an unflattering or suggestive manner. His conduct in doing so provides a factual basis for several defenses available to Stella in the pending contract action.

The first requisite of a contract is that the parties manifest a mutual assent to the same bargain at the same time. Objective manifestation of intent controls. In this case, mutual assent turns upon whether a reasonable person, in reviewing this contract, would interpret its terms in such a way as to entitle Flash to alter Stella's photos, particularly in a lewd and suggestive manner. Further, the trier of the fact must determine whether a reasonable person would believe that Stella assented to the terms as ultimately interpreted by Flash. It is submitted that no reasonable person would believe that she was assenting to such a possible interpretation of the terms of the contract as stated, or would believe that she was relinquishing her rights to the extent that Flash asserts Stella did.

On the other hand, the plaintiff will contend that he purchased the photos for value from Stella, entitling him to do with them as he pleased. He will assert that the contract operated as a waiver and release by Stella of all rights to object or interfere. Notwithstanding his assertions, he still has not established the existence of the requisite mutual assent. There are four rules of law which would preclude Flash from recovering under the contract, depending on the proof Stella can offer regarding the apparent unforeseen alteration and use of the photos.

(1)   If Flash intended to alter the photos at the time of the making of the contract, knowing that Stella, relying on his good faith, was unaware of his intentions, the situation would constitute fraud in the factum, rendering the contract void. In other words, Stella had no knowledge of what she actually bargained for.

(2)   If Flash misrepresented or actually lied about his intentions with respect to the use of the photos, this would constitute fraud in the inducement, rendering the contract voidable at Stella's option, upon her discovery of the misrepresentation.

(3)   If Stella can prove that Flash knew or had reason to know that she would not have entered into the contract unless "proper" use was made of the photographs, the contract may be rescinded based upon the doctrine of unilateral mistake of fact. For rescission to occur, two conditions must be present: (i) enforcement of the contract against Stella would be oppressive, or at least result in an unconscionably unequal exchange of values; and (ii) rescission would impose no substantial hardship on Flash. It is clear that both requisites are met by Stella.

(4)   If Flash was able to extract an unfair and oppressive bargain from Stella (considering the detriment to Stella's interests and pecuniary benefit to Flash) by reason of his vastly greater experience

and sophistication and his consequently stronger bargaining position, then, in equity, a court could and should find the contract to be unenforceable by reason of its unconscionability.

In addition to the aforementioned defenses which are based on infirmities in the formation of the contract, Stella's lack of understanding, or Stella's inferior bargaining position, if Stella can prove the tort of intentional misrepresentation she may elect to avoid the transaction and obtain restitution, and she may also bring an affirmative action for tortious fraud.

Finally, even if the court were to find the contract valid and enforceable at the time of its formation, if the court finds that there was fraud or misrepresentation that relates to the content or legal effect of the writing, the court may impose the remedy of reformation. It should be noted that nondisclosure is treated as the equivalent of misrepresentation where one party knows that the writing does not express the intention of the other and knows the other's intention. In this case, the court could require Flash to preserve the integrity of the photos in order to prevent substantial injustice. In this way, Stella, who satisfactorily performed until she became aware of the alteration of the photos, would be entitled to damages in the event that Flash's misconduct continues.

(b) Additional provisions to the agreement:

(1) Photographer shall not retouch or alter the photograph in such a way as to substantially change the model's appearance or image, so as to be misleading about the nature or subject matter of the photograph.

(2) Model reserves the right, in order to assure compliance by photographer with the provisions of Paragraph 5, to inspect and approve "proofs" of each and every photograph proposed for distribution before such distribution shall take place.

(3) In addition to the compensation provided herein for employment of Model for modeling services, Model shall be additionally entitled to receive a royalty of 10% of all revenues earned by the photographer arising out of each and every publication and republication of her photographs.

(4) Photographer shall obtain the written permission of the model, which will not be unreasonably withheld, prior to distributing photographs in any manner for reproduction.

41. CONSTITUTIONAL LAW

The statute on which the Alcohol Beverage Commission relies in denying the application by Appellant (Schnapps) for an alcoholic beverage license on the basis of the objection by the Holy Tabernacle Church, is an unconstitutional infringement on Schnapps's right to due process of law under the Fourteenth Amendment of the Constitution.

The state of New Jersey is constitutionally authorized to regulate the manufacture, distribution, and sale of alcoholic beverages within the state. But it cannot enact a regulatory scheme which contravenes other fundamental constitutional rights. Regulatory legislation which limits the rights of producers, distributors, and consumers must affect all present or prospective producers, distributors, and consumers in a uniform way, on the basis of clear and rational standards. Such legislation may create regulatory agencies, and delegate administrative functions to such agencies. But these administrative functions must be carried out in a ministerial fashion, applying the standards enunciated by the legislation. Under the statute in question, no standards for the granting or denial of applications are provided, and there is no requirement that any basis for an objection by a church or school be set forth.

The legislation might be immune to this attack if it forbids issuance of liquor licenses to *any* premises located within 500 feet of a church or school. Such a law, while more restrictive on its face, would actually preclude the possibility of abuse of discretion.

It would not be objectionable for the law to provide for the right of a school or church to state an objection to the granting of a particular application, provided the applicant was afforded notice of the objection and an opportunity for a hearing. In this way an appropriate administrative officer, after hearing the arguments of the applicant and objectors, could then make a fair and reasonable determination, based on articulable standards administered by the state agency and not by one of the adverse parties.

However, under the present law, the effect of an objection by a church or a school is to automatically deny an application without need for explanation, and without benefit of a hearing. Therefore, the statute is unconstitutionally violative of the applicant's due process rights.

The statute also violates the Establishment Clause of the First Amendment, as applied to the states through the Fourteenth Amendment, which prohibits excessive entanglement of governmental and church functions.

Sunday closing or "blue" laws have been upheld in many jurisdictions as a valid exercise of state police powers to promote health, safety, welfare, and morals. But such laws do not grant any church decisionmaking powers.

The effect of the statute as written is an improper delegation of a legislative power to a religious body. Even a grant of administrative powers to the governing body of a church would be obviously improper. But here, where there are no guidelines or standards, but merely a thinly disguised grant of power to a church to deny license applications with unbridled discretion, there is a constant potential for arbitrary and discriminatory action.

42. TORTS

PHANCY PHASHUNS CORP., A New Jersey Corporation,	) SUPERIOR COURT OF NEW JERSEY)) CHANCERY DIVISION: ESSEX COUNTY)
Plaintiff,	))
vs.	)) CIVIL ACTION
HARDSELL CORP., A New Jersey Corporation,	))
Defendant.	)

COMPLAINT

Phancy Phashuns Corp., a New Jersey corporation, complaining against the above named defendant, alleges and says:

FIRST COUNT

1.   At all times herein mentioned, plaintiff is a New Jersey corporation, engaged in the manufacture and resale of decoratively designed T-shirts.

2.   At all times herein mentioned, defendant is a New Jersey corporation, also engaged in the manufacture and resale of T-shirts in the same market areas as plaintiff.

3.   On or about June 1, 1983, by written communication to Chain Stores of New Jersey, a major trade account doing business with plaintiff, defendant willfully and maliciously published a false statement that certain toxic and dangerous substances were used in the manufacture of products marketed by plaintiff, which rendered them extremely dangerous to the health of customers of Chain Stores of New Jersey.

4.   Defendant published the said libelous statements, in reckless disregard for the reputation and economic well-being of the plaintiff, though he well knew that said statements were false and misleading.

5.   As a direct and proximate result of defendant's libelous communication, Chain Stores of New Jersey has ceased doing business with plaintiff.

6.   By reason of the publication by defendant of defendant's libelous statements as aforesaid, the plaintiff has been and will continue to be injured in its good name and reputation, and has suffered

severe economic injury by reason of lost income and profit in the amount of $50,000, and will continue to suffer such injury in the amount of at least $5,000 per month.

WHEREFORE, plaintiff demands judgment against the defendant on this count for actual, compensatory, special and punitive damages, as well as interest and costs of suit.

SECOND COUNT

1.   The plaintiff repeats the allegations of the First Count of the Complaint as if more fully set forth herein.

2.   Defendant's written communication to Chain Stores, containing false and misleading statements that plaintiff's products contain dangerous substances, was made with the intent and purpose of interfering with the harmonious and productive commercial relationship that existed between plaintiff and Chain Stores of New Jersey.

3.   As a direct and proximate result of this tortious interference with its contractual relations, plaintiff has suffered and will continue to suffer substantial loss of profits and income, and other severe economic damage.

WHEREFORE, plaintiff demands judgment on this count against defendant for punitive and compensatory damages, interest, and costs of suit.

THIRD COUNT

1.   The allegations of the First and Second Counts are repeated as if more fully set forth herein.

2.   Defendant, in publishing and circulating false and disparaging remarks about the quality of plaintiff's products, has engaged in unfair competition, by unreasonable and unscrupulous means, contrary to the laws of this state.

3.   As a result of the tactics of unfair competition employed by defendant, as aforesaid, plaintiff has suffered, and will continue to suffer severe, irreparable, and incalculable economic damage.

WHEREFORE, plaintiff demands judgment on this count for:

a)   punitive and compensatory damages;

b)   an order permanently enjoining defendant from further publishing and distributing false and disparaging remarks about the nature of plaintiff's products;

c)   an accounting of income and profits from sales from customers diverted to defendant from plaintiff by means of defendant's tactics; and

d)   interest and costs of suit.

B.   ADDITIONAL PAPERS FILED

(1)   Affidavit of Art Tiest, or other appropriate corporate officer, verifying the allegations of the Complaint;

(2)   Form of Order directing defendant to show cause why a Preliminary Injunction should not be issued prohibiting defendant from further communicating with plaintiff's customers about the quality of its products;

(3)   Notice of Motion for Partial Summary Judgment as to liability for libel on the First Count;

(4)   Certification of Art Tiest, with independent expert's report in support of Motion.

43. CONTRACTS

Dear Mr. Finance:

Your statement of February 1, offering a reward for information leading to the arrest and conviction of the bank robbers, is considered at law to be an offer to make a unilateral contract. A unilateral contract is a contract in which a promise is given by one party to the contract in exchange for performance of some act by the other party (or parties) to the contract. By supplying information which led to the arrest and conviction of those responsible for the robbery, each of the claimants accepted your offer. Thus, unless you can raise some defense to enforcement of the contract, each of the claimants is entitled to some part of the $10,000.

While it is possible that you could raise some defense against each of the claimants, it is unlikely that you can successfully avoid having to pay the $10,000 to one or more of them. You may choose to wait until one or more claimants institutes an action to recover the reward, and then raise your defenses. But since it is likely that you will be liable to at least one of the claimants, you are advised to commence what is known as an interpleader action. In this proceeding, you would deposit the $10,000 with the court, and allow the claimants to litigate their respective rights to the money among themselves. While this course of action requires you to give up the reward money without any chance of retaining any of it, in the long run it may prove to be the cheapest and least troublesome course of action. Having made this recommendation, it is still useful to review the claims of each claimant, as well as possible defenses to each claim.

Mr. Fink, being one of the perpetrators, has the weakest case for recovery under the contract. It is a general principle of contract law and a matter of public policy of this state that the courts will not enforce a contract for the benefit of one who has engaged in illegal activity related to the subject matter of the contract.

Mr. Able's claim may be resisted on two grounds. First, as a police officer, Mr. Able had a pre-existing duty to assist in the apprehension of suspects whether he was on duty or off duty at the time. It is a rule of law that one cannot enforce a contract to be compensated for an act which that person was under a duty to perform before entering into the contract. Second, it is a rule of law that one may not accept an offer of which one has no knowledge. Although Mr. Able knew of the robbery, he did not know of your reward offer at the time that he assisted in the apprehension of the robbers. Thus, he could not accept your offer because he did not perform the acts with intent to accept your offer.

Similarly, Mr. Daniels did not know about the reward offer, and thus his acts, while otherwise sufficient to constitute acceptance, fail because of his lack of intent.

With respect to Mr. Teller, while it can be argued that his status as a bank employee required him to communicate his knowledge, so that under the preexisting duty rule mentioned above with regard to Mr. Able he could not recover, it is more likely that a court of law would find that Mr. Teller's contract of employment did not place him under such a duty. Resisting Mr. Teller's claim will almost certainly result in costly litigation.

In summary, then, it is advised that the costs of litigation are substantial enough in the face of the likelihood of eventual loss of the reward monies to warrant depositing the reward with the court and commencing an interpleader action, in which the claimants may litigate their respective claims among themselves, and in which the bank need not be represented, except perhaps to raise the aforementioned defenses in the unlikely event that all of the claims may be resisted successfully.

Very truly yours,

44. EVIDENCE

Defendant objects to the introduction into evidence of the Judgment of Conviction of defendant for a prior offense on the following grounds:

(a) The Judgment of Conviction is inadmissible because it is hearsay. By definition, hearsay is a statement or writing by an out-of-court declarant offered to prove the truth of the matter asserted. A conviction may be admissible in a civil action under the public records exception. But under the traditional view, still followed by most states, the Judgment of Conviction is not admissible in a subsequent criminal proceeding to prove an element of the offense or even to support a presumption, because to admit it would deprive the defendant of the opportunity of confrontation and cross-examination of the hostile witness. There are instances where a prior conviction can be introduced, such as for purposes of impeachment of the credibility of a witness, or where the prior conviction involves motive, opportunity, intent, preparation, plan, knowledge, identity or absence of mistake, as in cases where repeat offender status is in issue, or where the State seeks to rebut character evidence introduced by the defendant.

Note that the Federal Rules of Evidence are different, and specifically provide that judgments of felony convictions are admissible in both criminal and civil actions to prove any fact essential to the judgment. Under the Federal Rules, felony convictions are defined as crimes punishable by death or imprisonment in excess of one year. This situation, however, involves a state criminal statute and, therefore, state rules of evidence control.

(b) A presumption in a criminal case is a permissible inference. The jury is not required as a matter of law to regard the basic facts as sufficient evidence of the presumed fact. Its existence must be proved by the prosecutor beyond a reasonable doubt.

The relevancy of the evidence is important. Here, the conviction should not be admissible because it is so prejudicial against the defendant that the minds of the jury might be overwhelmingly influenced toward finding the defendant guilty of the present offense by reason of his conviction of the prior offense. Even an instruction to the contrary could not rehabilitate the defendant's tainted presumption of innocence. At the very least, the proposed introduction of a prior conviction warrants a special hearing by the judge, out of the presence of the jury, to investigate the facts and circumstances underlying the conviction, in order to determine whether its evidentiary value outweighs the risk of prejudice.

Given the plea bargaining process, defendants are induced to enter pleas of guilty for a variety of reasons.

45. CONTRACTS/REAL PROPERTY

January 1, 1984

Dear Mr. and Mrs. Hunter:

This is in reply to your inquiry regarding your right to avoid your contract with Dweller to purchase his home in West Elysium.

There is a well established doctrine of law known as caveat emptor or buyer beware. This means that a seller under contract, particularly in real estate transactions, is not bound by any implied warranties or representations as to the quality or quantity of the land being sold. It is your duty as prospective buyers to carefully examine the property before you sign a contract unless the contract provides specific warranties or representations or contains contingencies that reserve your right to cancel if certain conditions are not met, such as disclosure by a search of a clear title.

The Dweller contract contains no representations or contingencies with respect to the physical nature of the property. In fact, Mr. Dweller's survey was available for you to examine before you signed the contract.

The law does provide a remedy known as rescission, which allows the termination of a contract where it is shown that the contract was formed under questionable circumstances, and its enforcement would be unreasonable or inequitable. I could attempt to rescind this contract on your behalf, but given the facts and circumstances of this contract, I am not certain that you would prevail.

There are several grounds upon which an action for rescission can be based. Among these grounds are failure of consideration, mistake of fact, or fraud. Some explanation of these terms is in order.

Under the law of contracts, you have a right to receive what you bargained for, and if you do not, there is failure of consideration. A defense based on mistake of fact involves the fundamental principle that the formation of a valid contract requires the mutual assent of the parties. If one is mistaken as to the subject matter of the contract, particularly where the other party is aware of the mistake, mutual assent does not really exist. Similarly, if one is induced to enter a contract by fraudulent misrepresentation, there is no true assent by that person.

In order for you to succeed in an action for rescission on grounds of either failure of consideration, mistake, or fraud, you would have to convince the trial judge that at the time of the signing of the contract, it was your intent to purchase the home if and only if you could acquire title to the brook as part of the purchase. If the court were persuaded by your testimony that this were the case, then the argument could be made that the brook was a material part of the consideration and, without the brook, you were not getting what you bargained for. This premise might also support an argument that you only purchased the property in reliance on your good faith belief that the brook was on the property, whether that belief was a product of your own mistaken impression, or the misrepresentation of the seller or his agent.

There would be problems in your case. Proving fraud would be difficult since the realtor's ad only said "overlooking babbling brook," and Mr. Dweller had no duty to voluntarily advise you. The court might not accept your contention that ownership of the brook was a material part of the consideration. For your investment, you received a valuable piece of real estate, which was an adequate consideration, and you still have the view.

Please advise.

Very truly yours,

46. CRIMINAL PROCEDURE

The examination by Detective Wilson of Lucy Lane's boots is a valid warrantless search, and the ultimate seizure to hold them as evidence was proper.

The detectives, by their own admission, went to the house to arrest Lucy on the warrant issued by the Municipal Court for failure to appear and, while there, to see what they could find. Though the detectives may have started out with the improper purpose of using the warrant as a pretext for what was actually a fishing expedition, subsequent events validated the search with respect to the boots.

The police conduct in the situation was at all times reasonable. In executing the arrest warrant, the police were lawfully on the premises to take Lucy into custody. The outstanding warrant was issued for a valid purpose, independent of the burglary investigation, and not a sham device concocted by these officers to justify a warrantless search.

The anonymous and uncorroborated informant's tip was insufficient to establish the requisite probable cause in the minds of the officers to justify the issuance of a search warrant. The entire chain of events on the scene occurred inadvertently. The arresting officers had no way of knowing in advance either that the suspect would be undressed, or that the boots would be in plain view on the floor of the closet.

Since it was necessary for Lucy to dress in order to accompany the officers to headquarters, she had to leave the officers' presence and it was appropriate that an officer accompany her into the bedroom to prevent any attempted escape or other foul play. She inadvertently opened her closet door, exposing the high-heeled boots in question to plain view of Detective Wilson. The presence of caked red clay on the boots, taken into consideration with the anonymous tip about Lucy's involvement, established sufficient probable cause to warrant closer examination, and upon closer examination, the distinctive heel design was enough to conclusively justify the seizure of the evidence of a crime.

The stereo equipment under the couch, however, was not in plain view. None of the recognized exceptions to the requirement of a search warrant would apply to legitimize Detective Wilson's search beyond Lucy's person. It would not be a valid search incidental to a lawful arrest because it was not in the immediate area where she could reach for weapons or destroy evidence. There was no exigency or threat of the loss of evidence which would have prevented these police officers from proceeding immediately after the arrest to obtain the necessary warrant.

In conclusion, the motion to suppress the evidence must be granted in part and denied in part. For reasons stated above, the stereo equipment should be suppressed, but the boots are admissible evidence.

47. CONSTITUTIONAL LAW

MEMORANDUM

TO: Control Co.
        Attention: Corporate Counsel
RE: Constitutionality of Visceral Act

62.

A company's right to advertise or disseminate information about its products, whether by direct mail distribution or otherwise, is protected as commercial speech by the First Amendment to the Constitution. Commercial speech, which involves profit-oriented activities, is probably not protected to the same absolute degree as other forms of expression, such as political beliefs, but it is nevertheless protected. As long as the information is true and not misleading, then its distribution may only be restricted to protect a substantial state interest.

The distribution by mail of pamphlets promoting contraceptives or containing informative materials on venereal disease and family planning could only conflict with the interest of two classes of potential recipients, those who by virtue of their religious beliefs reject the practice of contraception, and those who might find materials dealing in such sensitive subject matter to be personally offensive or obscene. Analysis of the constitutionality of the Visceral Act requires a determination of whether the protection of the rights of these individuals to be shielded from such harm represents such a substantial state interest that, on balance, it outweighs Control Co.'s First Amendment right to distribute this information as commercial speech.

Those who choose not to engage in birth control on the basis of their religious beliefs certainly have the right, upon inspection of these materials, to discard them and not read the information or buy the products. The rights of others who elect to practice birth control, and who might benefit by these materials, are also constitutionally protected. Their right to obtain and use birth control products is protected by a constitutional zone of privacy as articulated in *Griswold v. Connecticut*, 381 U.S. 479 (1965).

Furthermore, if the Visceral Act were to be upheld as a means of preventing distribution of the birth control materials on the basis of the religious beliefs of the objecting individuals, then it would run afoul of the First Amendment's prohibition against the establishment of a religion. Receipt of third class mail is not a sufficient harassment or intrusion to warrant the insulation of the nonbelievers from exposure to these pamphlets at the expense of the rights of those who choose to receive them.

There is no compelling state interest to be found in the statute that justifies the abridgement of fundamental personal liberties contained in the "penumbra" of First Amendment rights.

In conclusion, the Visceral Act must be struck down as unconstitutionally violative of guarantees available to Control Co. under the First Amendment, and to the general public which has a fundamental right of access to such information.

48. TORTS
CAUSES OF ACTION
Paula v. Donna: As a passenger in Donna's vehicle, Paula is owed a duty of care by the host driver. Donna admitted exceeding the speed limit by five miles per hour. Though it may ultimately be proven that the speeding was not causally related to the accident, and that Donna was free of negligence, there is also the chance that a jury could find that Donna was to some degree comparatively negligent and liable for contribution. Therefore, it is good practice to include Donna as a party defendant in any action commenced on behalf of Paula. In the event of such a suit, the defense of comparative negligence would be available to Donna; *i.e.,* Paula freely and voluntarily entered the vehicle though she knew that Donna was very tired and slightly inebriated, and therefore, her comparative negligence should bar or diminish her recovery.

Donna and Paula v. John Tyler: Tyler's negligence in running a stop sign, and in entering a favored street from a side street without first making certain that the intersection was free of oncoming traffic, was allegedly the proximate cause of the accident.

Paula and Donna v. John Tyler's employer: The cab company may be vicariously liable under the doctrine of respondeat superior; *i.e.,* the accident occurred during the course of John Tyler's employment, as the agent of the cab company, operating for its commercial benefit.

Paula and Donna v. Hotel Bergen: The hotel may be liable under the Dram Shop Law; *i.e.,* it knew or should have known that a guest of the hotel had excessively consumed alcohol, but continued to serve Donna alcoholic beverages, impairing her ability to drive, which arguably contributed to the accident.

Donna and Paula v. Bergen Township: The municipality should be joined under the Tort Claims Act, alleging that the town failed to repair the stop sign after reasonable notice and opportunity to make such repair. A jury could draw a permissible inference that if the stop sign had been in place, John Tyler might have come to a full stop before entering the intersection. As a matter of law, Tyler should not have entered a T intersection anyway, until he had the right of way. But the absence of the stop sign could certainly be found to be a contributing factor.

Paula and Donna v. Lester Lawyer: A malpractice case may lie against Lester Lawyer; not in the immediate action but subsequently, if the immediate cause of action fails by reason of any of the several acts of professional negligence by Lester Lawyer. Included are his failure to diligently prosecute the action, and his failure to disclose the potential conflict of interest between driver and passenger, and to advise the women that they needed separate representation. Depending on the exact date of the accident (the facts do not state the exact date of the sophomore spring break), Lawyer may have delayed commencement of suit beyond the two-year statute of limitations for personal injury claims, and has certainly failed to put the municipality on notice of a claim within the 90-day statute of limitations which applies to tort claims cases.

ADVICE

The women must immediately be advised to seek separate representation. One may retain me and the other must consult with other counsel immediately. Lester Lawyer must be contacted immediately to release his file, in order to make use of any reports or facts disclosed by investigation. A retainer agreement must be signed and authority obtained to commence suit immediately against all defendants, as well as a notice of motion seeking to file a notice of claim out of time. Finally, the women must be advised to no longer discuss the case with each other or anyone else but an attorney.

49. CONTRACTS

(a) Defenses

(1) Lack of a valid contract (no offer or acceptance)

(2) Statute of Frauds

(b) Argument

(1) Without an offer and an acceptance, there can be no mutual assent and thus no binding contract.

Price quotations generally do not constitute offers even when addressed to a particular customer. Quotation of prices fall into the category of negotiations preliminary to offers, not only for the reason that present contractual intent does not appear, but also because the certainty essential to an operative offer is absent.

Shift's quote of an approximate price for a car not yet in stock clearly does not constitute an offer, for lack of intent. Shift merely answered Ann Teek's questions. There is no evidence of present contractual intent on his part.

The lack of discussion and agreement relating to essential terms such as delivery date and payment terms further prevents an offer from being construed from Shift's conversation, for an offer must define the essential terms of performance on both sides with a sufficient degree of certainty so as to be capable of enforcement.

Accordingly, Shift did not make an offer to which Teek could proffer a proper acceptance.

Similarly, the tender of the "deposit" check for $500, without more, lacked the essential elements of an offer.

Essential terms include identification of the subject matter, the price to be paid, and the time of performance. The check, which simply bore the memo "deposit for car," clearly lacked sufficient certainty as to its terms. If the check was intended to be a confirmation of the conversation with Shift, then a more complete memorandum of terms relating to the reason for tendering the check should have accompanied the tender. Teek's failure to specify terms caused her deposit to fail as an offer. Thus, Shift's depositing the check could not constitute an acceptance. There was no mutual assent, *i.e.,* the parties were not agreeing to the same bargain at the same time.

In light of the foregoing, a valid contract did not exist between Teek and Shift, and Teek's complaint should be dismissed.

(2) A promise for the sale of goods of $500 or more is not enforceable unless evidenced by a writing. [U.C.C. §2-201(1)]

Under the Statute of Frauds, as incorporated in the U.C.C., a contract for the sale of goods worth $500 or more is only enforceable if there is a writing, containing the following elements, sufficiently described: (i) identity of the parties; (ii) identity of the subject matter; (iii) definite statement of terms; (iv) consideration; and (v) signature by the party to be charged.

Although Teek's check did identify the parties and did bear both signatures, by virtue of the endorsement by Modern Motors, these two elements alone are not sufficient to comply with the requirements of the Statute of Frauds.

The notation on the check, "deposit for car," is not a sufficient description of the subject matter of the contract. Further, there is nothing that indicates the terms of the contract or the actual consideration between the parties.

The payment of the deposit by check was also not sufficient partial performance to remove the contract from the purview of the Statute of Frauds. If payment is made in part by the buyer and accepted by the seller, the contract is enforceable only as to "goods for which payment has been made and accepted." [U.C.C. §2-201(3)(c)] Part payment, therefore, would give rise only to partial enforcement. Thus, a deposit which is minimal in comparison to the total purchase price of the item would not lead to enforcement of the contract.

Finally, this was not a divisible contract for periodic shipment of goods, for which receipt of $500 could have been construed as payment for some part. The partial performance required to render this contract enforceable would have been delivery of the car and acceptance of partial payment, on specified terms for goods received.

For the foregoing reasons, the motion by the defendant, Modern Motors, for summary judgment, should be granted.

50. REAL PROPERTY
PART (a)

Dear Mr. Brown:

In reply to your inquiry about your rights, I am afraid that you have no right to build a fence on the boundary of your property separating it from the adjoining parcel owned by Fast Foods Corp. It is likely that such an act might violate certain vested rights of your neighbors.

You will recall that at the time you acquired the property in 1961, you were advised by John Gray, the grantor, that he had made an agreement with Good Eats Corp., your neighbor's predecessor in title, that allowed Good Eats to landscape and maintain a 10-foot-wide strip of land immediately adjoining your property. You took title to the property with prior actual notice of the agreement, and continued to allow Good Eats Corp. to perpetuate this use of the premises. For the next 15 years, they improved and maintained this piece of property and Fast Foods Corp., their successor, maintained it for eight years thereafter. During the entire time, the property was continuously used in this manner, with your consent, and you derived an incidental benefit from this use.

Under the law of real property in this state, Fast Foods Corp. has the right to further continue this use, free of interference, under either of two theories of law. It is quite likely that a court of equity would determine that Fast Foods was vested in 1981 (20 years after you acquired title) with a nonpossessory interest in this land known as a prescriptive easement. Its use of the land has all of the characteristics of an easement, lacking only formal creation by written grant. While you still retain record title to the property, which carries the right to sell it, Fast Foods Corp. has the right to use it for a specified purpose that is directly beneficial to it, in that it keeps its commercial property more attractive to the public.

Easements are ordinarily created by an express written conveyance. At the time that John Gray granted permission to Good Eats to landscape the property, he probably intended only to grant them a license which would be revocable by him at will. However, during the entire time of your ownership, there was never any discussion between adjoining owners as to the legal status of the property. Good Eats and Fast Foods originally entered on the property under claim of right. You never expressly consented, nor did you attempt to regulate or limit the use. For more than 20 years Good Eats and its successor used the property in this fashion continuously, openly, notoriously, and exclusively. This possession and use was adverse to any claim of right you had to exercise unrestricted control or dominion over the property. After the running of 20 years of such use, Fast Foods was arguably vested with the right to an easement by prescription, under the doctrine of adverse possession.

You might wish to attack these rights in a suit to quiet title, and determine the rights of the parties. You might even successfully attack Fast Foods' claim of right to a prescriptive easement by showing that possession was with your consent, and not sufficiently adverse or hostile. However, a court would be likely to hold, even in that event, that in equity, Fast Foods was possessed of an irrevocable license.

The basis for such a holding would be as follows: Your neighbor assumed the burden of the investment of expense and labor to improve the property, which ran not only to its benefit, but to yours as well. To allow you to cut off its access to a use of the property after you have enjoyed the benefits of its investment would be likely to result in unjust enrichment. Its license has become coupled with an interest in the property, which renders it irrevocable (and therefore tantamount to an easement) so long as Fast Foods continues the present use. At such time as the property is no longer put to its present use, you might succeed in terminating the interest provided that you were successful in proving the interest to be merely a license and not an easement.

PART (b)

THIS AGREEMENT, dated February 1, 1960, is between John Gray, residing at 100 Main Street, Anywhere, New Jersey (hereinafter "Grantor") and Good Eats Corp., a New Jersey corporation (hereinafter "Grantee").

WHEREAS,

1)   Grantor is the owner of certain premises at 100 Main Street, Anywhere, New Jersey;

2)   Grantee is the owner of a certain retail food business located at 98 Main Street on premises abutting Grantor's land;

3)   Grantee wishes to use, occupy, and maintain a 10-foot-wide strip of Grantor's land adjacent to its premises.

Now, in consideration of the following mutual covenants, the parties hereby agree as follows:

1.   Grantor hereby grants and conveys a temporary easement to Grantee to enter upon the 10-foot-wide strip of land, more particularly described in Schedule A, for the purpose of landscaping and maintaining said property.

2.   This grant shall be revocable at will by the Grantor, his successors, heirs and assigns, at any time, on 30 days' written notice to the Grantee.

3.   The property shall be maintained by Grantees at their own cost and expense. The Grantees agree and acknowledge that any investment made by them for the use, occupancy, maintenance, or improvement of the property will be made for their own benefit, and shall not under any circumstances be charged to the Grantor, directly or as a lien against the premises.

4.   Grantee enters upon the premises at its own risk and expressly agrees to indemnify Grantor, his successors and assigns, and hold them harmless from any and all claims, by the Grantee or third parties, of damage to person or property.

5.   Upon termination of this grant, whether by revocation by the Grantor, or abandonment by the Grantee, the premises shall be relinquished to the possession of the Grantor, in at least as good condition as it was at the time of the making of this Agreement, and all claims of right, title, or interest in the premises by Grantee shall be extinguished.

WITNESS:

JOHN GRAY
GOOD EATS, CORP.
BY:

51. CRIMINAL LAW/CRIMINAL PROCEDURE/EVIDENCE
MEMORANDUM OF LAW

I.   THE FOUR-YEAR DELAY IN PROSECUTION OF DEFENDANT, BETWEEN HIS INITIAL ARREST AND ULTIMATE CONVICTION FOR MURDER, DID NOT VIOLATE HIS CONSTITUTIONAL GUARANTEE OF A SPEEDY TRIAL.

The Sixth Amendment of the Constitution, as applied to the states through the Due Process Clause of the Fourteenth Amendment, guarantees criminal suspects the right to a speedy trial. The issue of whether or not a defendant has received a speedy trial in a particular case is to be determined according to several factors: the length of the delay, reason for the delay, prejudice to defendant, and whether or not he has asserted the right in a timely manner.

In this case there does not appear to have been significant prejudice to Juan as a result of the delay. He is in no worse position to defend the case in 1986 than he would have been in 1982, by reason of loss of evidence or unavailability of witnesses. Neither was he subject to the more subtle forms of prejudice recognized by the courts, such as loss of employment, diminished esteem in the community, or stress occasioned by the prospect of continuous or imminent criminal prosecution.

Defendant is not entitled to speedy trial relief for the period between the dismissal of the charges and later refiling. [United States v. MacDonald, 456 U.S. 1 (1982)]

II.   TRYING THE DEFENDANT FOR MURDER, AFTER THE SAME CHARGE HAD PREVIOUSLY BEEN DISMISSED BECAUSE THE STATE HAD NO CASE, DOES NOT VIOLATE THE CONSTITUTIONAL PROHIBITION AGAINST DOUBLE JEOPARDY.

The Fifth Amendment, as applied to the states through the Fourteenth Amendment, affords a suspect the right to not be subject twice to the jeopardy of conviction for the same offense. The issue is whether Juan was subject to jeopardy during the earlier proceedings.

It is well settled that jeopardy does not attach in the course of criminal proceedings until commencement of trial, which is marked by the impanelling of a jury. Juan was previously before a judge, in connection with being charged for the murder of Vicki Smith, but only at a preliminary hearing. Preliminary hearings are held for the benefit of the defendant, to determine if the state has sufficient evidence to hold the defendant for trial. In Juan's case, the preliminary hearing worked to Juan's benefit and cannot be considered as having placed him in jeopardy.

III.   THE PROSECUTION'S USE OF PEREMPTORY CHALLENGES TO REMOVE ALL JURORS WITH HISPANIC NAMES MAY VIOLATE DEFENDANT'S CONSTITUTIONAL RIGHT OF TRIAL BY JURY.

The Sixth Amendment guarantees the right to trial by jury. This means a jury of one's peers, and as a matter of due process, it must include a representative cross-section of the community. Juan had no constitutional right to insist that the composition of his jury include a member of any particular ethnic group. However, the systematic exclusion of any ethnic group is objectionable.

The defendant need only show that peremptory challenges were used by the prosecutor in a particular case as a device to intentionally eliminate from the jury all persons of any particular ethnic group. The prosecutor must then show that such challenges were not made on racial or ethnic grounds. There appears to be no evidence of any legitimate basis for the challenges in this case.

IV.   THE TAPE RECORDING OF THE CHILD'S VOICE SHOULD NOT HAVE BEEN EXCLUDED AS INADMISSIBLE HEARSAY.

Statements made by an out-of-court declarant offered to prove the truth of the matter asserted, particularly where the declarant is available for testimony in court, are usually ruled inadmissible as hearsay. This is particularly true in criminal proceedings, where the admission of hearsay evidence usually violates the defendant's right under the Sixth Amendment to confront hostile witnesses. There are recognized exceptions to the rule such as where the state cannot, despite diligent inquiry, produce the witness, or where the evidence is, for some reason, particularly credible.

In the present case, the offer into evidence of the tape recording of Wanda's call to the police is clearly hearsay. However, two factors may operate to relax the hearsay rule. First, the declarant is available to confront and cross-examine as a witness. Second, the recorded statement may qualify as a "res gestae" type of exception, in that it was an excited utterance which described a startling event, contemporaneously with the occurrence of the event; therefore it was credible. Generally, these exceptions do not require that the declarant be unavailable. On closer examination, these exceptions may not apply to the facts and circumstances of this case. The defense can cross-examine Wanda at 11, but cannot cross-examine the tape recording of the witness at the time she made the statement. Also, the excited utterance of a seven-year-old may not be entirely trustworthy. Wanda was disqualified as incompetent to testify at age seven. This may have been based in part on her suspected inability to communicate or appreciate the requirement to tell the truth. But there was also a question about the child's ability to perceive and understand an event. However, there is a well-founded argument that the admission of the declaration is not based on the competency of the infant but that it was part of the entire situation.

52.   CONTRACTS

This agreement, dated February 1985, is between Sue Asponte (hereinafter "Client") and Larry Lawyer (hereinafter "Attorney").

In consideration of their mutual promises, the parties to this Agreement hereby agree as follows:

1.   Client agrees to retain Attorney and Attorney agrees to represent Client in the defense of a certain action pending in Superior Court entitled *John Doe vs. Sue Asponte*, and in the prosecution of any counterclaim which Attorney may deem appropriate to file.

2.   Client has paid to Attorney a retainer in the sum of $500, receipt of which is acknowledged hereof. Said retainer shall be nonrefundable, and shall cover all services rendered by Attorney in the initial consultation, preliminary settlement negotiations, and filing of responsive pleadings.

3.   To save Client undue inconvenience and expense, Attorney agrees to seek a prompt amicable resolution of the matter and, toward that end, is hereby authorized to offer up to $6,000 in settlement of plaintiff's claim.

4.   In the event that this matter cannot be promptly settled, the Attorney shall be compensated for additional services rendered in the course of litigation, including but not limited to discovery, motions, trial preparation, and trial, in accordance with his success in defending the action. The exact amount of Attorney's fee, payable upon conclusion of the matter, shall be calculated in accordance with the following formula: 33-1/3% of the difference between $20,000 (plaintiff's demand, and therefore, Client's maximum exposure), and the actual amount of judgment entered or settlement paid, whichever is applicable.

5.   Client shall be responsible for payment, in advance, of all costs, including filing fees, stenographic fees, and expert witness fees.

6.   Client acknowledges having been advised by Attorney of her right to compensate Attorney for the reasonable value of his services, based upon hours of service rendered. The Client has rejected such an arrangement, in the belief that it would be fair and reasonable to pay Attorney a fee, contingent upon a successful result, using the reduction of her maximum liability as a basis for evaluation of Attorney's services.

7.   Client acknowledges having made factual representations to Attorney, upon which he has relied in evaluating the merits of her case, and estimating the difficulty in preparing a defense and the probability of success. If, in the course of discovery or investigation, Attorney finds the facts and circumstances of the matter as presented by Client substantially inaccurate, he reserves the right to revoke this agreement, bill the Client for services rendered to that point at his normal rate of $100 per hour, and withdraw from further representation (with court permission).

DATED:
Larry Lawyer
Sue Asponte

53. REAL PROPERTY

CENTER DEVELOPERS, INC.	)	AMERICAN ARBITRATION ASSN.
vs.	)	CASE NO.
VIDEO VIEWING, INC.	)	MEMORANDUM IN SUPPORT OF LANDLORD

I.   THE LEASE IS VOIDABLE AT THE OPTION OF THE LANDLORD BY REASON OF THE ASSIGNMENT, CONTRARY TO THE PROVISIONS OF THE LEASE.

The provision in the lease prohibiting assignment or sublet of the premises, without the landlord's consent, is valid and enforceable. It was a material provision of a commercial lease, freely bargained for between the parties. It serves a valid business purpose of the landlord/developer and its enforceability has been upheld by the courts.

If after the acquisition of the stock of VVI by AMI, the corporate identity of VVI as a subsidiary was maintained, it might have been arguable that there was no assignment of the lease. But upon the dissolution of VVI and transfer of its assets to Vinc, the nonassignment clause was clearly breached. Neither VVI nor AMI sought the consent of the landlord, but rather they attempted to accomplish the assignment in a deceptive and surreptitious manner.

CDI has served Vinc with proper termination notices and has the absolute right to recover possession of the premises. The tenancy is at an end and Vinc has the status of a holdover.

It is respectfully submitted that, unfortunately, the arbitration panel lacks the jurisdiction to provide the landlord with the most appropriate remedy, *i.e.,* a judgment for possession.

II.   THE LANDLORD IS ENTITLED TO DAMAGES SUSTAINED AS A RESULT OF THE TENANT'S BREACH OF THE COVENANT RESTRICTING TENANT'S USE OF THE PREMISES.

Covenants in commercial leases, restricting or limiting the use of the premises to certain business activities, are valid and enforceable. This is particularly true in the context of a shopping center, where such covenants are made to protect the interest of co-tenants as well as the landlord.

A covenant of this type, concerning use of the property, runs with the land and is binding on Vinc as a successor, though it was never in privity with the landlord, whether or not the assignment is held valid.

Several remedies are afforded to landlords as relief for breach of a lease covenant by a tenant. Termination of the lease is an option which the landlord already seeks in this matter on other grounds. Injunctive relief might be available, but probably not entirely sufficient on the facts of this case. The tenant has already operated in breach of the covenant for more than a year, and an injunction would therefore amount to "too little, too late." Moreover, courts will often decline to do equity where an adequate remedy at law is available.

The landlord is clearly entitled to an award of damages resulting from the breach of the covenant. The damages are provable and calculable.

The change in the nature of the business by Vinc resulted in 25% decrease in revenue from sales. Whether or not this occurred because another business showed free videos has no bearing on the issues of this case. The landlord consequently suffered a loss of rental income which, by the terms of the lease, is functionally related to gross receipts.

III.   THE LANDLORD DOES NOT WAIVE HIS RIGHT TO ENFORCE THE LEASE BY ACCEPTING RENT AFTER A BREACH OF WHICH HE HAS NO KNOWLEDGE.

Waiver is not available to the tenant as a meritorious defense. The use of the deceptively similar name, Video Viewing, Inc., was an obvious attempt by AMI to conceal from the landlord the fact of the assignment and the change in the nature of the business. In accepting rent payments by checks bearing a name so similar to that of the original tenant, the landlord understandably failed to notice the change. Once the gross receipts were reported and the landlord had reason to be aware of the change, he acted reasonably and promptly to assert his rights.

Courts will not consider conduct as constituting a waiver unless it is done knowingly and purposefully.

IN CONCLUSION, it is respectfully submitted that the landlord can only be made whole by a termination of the tenancy and appropriate award of damages.

54. CONSTITUTIONAL LAW

The New Jersey statute imposing absolute liability on airplane owners for accidental damage caused to persons and/or property on the ground is constitutionally valid and enforceable, even in cases where the aircraft involved was stolen or borrowed without permission.

The law is a valid exercise of the police powers of the state of New Jersey to pass legislation in areas affecting the health, safety, welfare, and morals of its people. The statute does not create an unreasonable burden on interstate commerce; nor does it shift any benefits to or from anyone in the stream of commerce.

It is not an attempt to regulate aviation or air traffic, because it exerts no power or influence over airplanes while in flight, but merely affects the rights and liabilities of parties involved in or affected by aviation accidents. Therefore, the fact that the federal government may have preempted the field of aviation regulation has no bearing on the validity of this statute.

The aviation industry condemns this legislation as a deprivation of property rights without due process of law as required by the Fourteenth Amendment, because it dispenses with the need for victims to prove a case of negligence as a basis for liability. This raises a question of substantive due process and the appropriate test of a law's validity, whether the law is reasonable rather than arbitrary or capricious, and whether it bears a real and substantial relationship to the objective sought.

The purpose of the law is to shift the risk of damage or loss due to aviation mishaps from the innocent victims to the owners of the aircraft. It is within the proper police powers of the states to shift risks of injury, regardless of fault, as has been done with workers' compensation legislation, to those who economically benefit from the activity which creates the risk. The owners still retain the right to pursue recovery against the responsible party, but that difficult burden is assumed by those who can best afford it.

For similar reasons, the law does not violate the Fourteenth Amendment's Equal Protection Clause either. The law has an effect on the rights and liabilities of aircraft owners as a class. But aircraft owners are not a suspect or sensitive classification. The ownership of aircraft is not a constitutionally protected fundamental right, so no compelling state interest need be demonstrated to uphold the law's validity. It is only necessary to show a rational basis for the classification. The balancing of the state's interest in protecting those innocent members of the unsuspecting public who may be killed, hurt, or financially ruined by a craft, against the possible detriment to the interest of the aviation industry in the form of increased financial burden (which encourages safety measures) weighs heavily in favor of the law's validity.

55. EVIDENCE

STATE OF NEW JERSEY   )
COUNTY OF ESSEX   )   ss:

SUPERIOR COURT OF NEW JERSEY
CHANCERY DIVISION

GLUKO, a New Jersey Corporation,)
              vs.)   DOCKET NO.
STIKUM, a Corporation, and)   CIVIL ACTION
AL ABLE)

AFFIDAVIT IN SUPPORT OF ORDER TO SHOW CAUSE

PAUL PREZ, being of full age and duly sworn, on his oath, alleges and says:

1)   I am the president of Gluko, a New Jersey corporation, engaged in the manufacture and sale of adhesives, with offices in Newark, New Jersey.

2)   On or about February 1, 1985, I terminated from the company's employ, defendant Al Able, our former Director of Marketing, who had been a trusted employee of the company for several years, since he was recruited out of college.

3)   My reason for firing Mr. Able was that I believed that I had good reason to suspect him of disloyalty in favor of our competitor and in breach of his contract of employment. I base this belief upon certain facts and circumstances as set forth below.

4)   I was recently advised by Hy Tech, a major new customer, that he had been recently solicited by Stikum, our chief competitor, with offers to supply similar products at substantially lower prices.

5)   I had no reason to disbelieve Mr. Tech, because Stikum has been soliciting Gluko's customers for years. Unfortunately, by their unscrupulous marketing methods, they gain an unfair advantage.

6)   Stikum achieves their superior marketing position by raiding Gluko for its employees, thereby obtaining access to confidential information, including product information, customer lists, and other trade secrets. Since 1979, they have hired a chemist and two salesmen that were formerly in our employ.

7)   In this way, Stikum not only can identify our customers and their needs, but they can duplicate our products. They can, in fact, produce these products at lower cost because by using our product information, they can save on the cost of research and product development. Copies of their last three annual reports, showing negligible investment in R & D, are annexed hereto as Exhibits "A-C."

8)   In order to protect ourselves against these practices, the company adopted corporate policy, effective March 1982, requiring all employees to sign employment agreements, containing restrictive covenants prohibiting them from working for a competitor for a period of two years after they leave the employ of Gluko. A copy of Al Able's employment agreement is annexed hereto as Exhibit "D."

9)   I have good reason to believe Al Able may be planning to go to work for Stikum and is soliciting my customers on its behalf in violation of his covenant. I base this belief on the following facts:

a.   About two weeks before he was fired, he submitted his resignation on two weeks' notice. In response to my inquiry as to the reason for his leaving, he offered a vague and unconvincing explanation.

b.   On the morning of his firing, I inspected his office, looking for the return of important company property which he had failed to return, including customer lists and product formulas. None of these items have been located as of this date.

c.   Able has established valuable customer contacts while in our employ, including the Hy Tech account.

d.   Considering Stikum's previous record of enticing our employees and soliciting our customers, it seems very unlikely that the solicitation of Hy Tech, shortly after the resignation of Able and disappearance of customer lists, would be merely coincidental.

10) This affidavit is made in support of plaintiff's application for an Order, enjoining Al Able from working for Stikum and soliciting Gluko's customers, pending a final adjudication in this matter.

11) I have no actual knowledge that Able is working for Stikum. However, I submit that the facts set forth herein establish a high probability that this is about to occur. If this is not his intention, then he will not be prejudiced by the injunctive order. However, if he is free to go to work for Stikum, the result will be imminent and irreparable harm to my company's interest.

Sworn and Subscribed to on February 2, 1985.

PAUL PREZ

56. CONSTITUTIONAL LAW

Paul Pater should ultimately prevail in having the child support enforcement statute struck down as unconstitutional on several grounds, at the appellate level, if not in the mandamus action.

The statute violates the Due Process Clause of the Fourteenth Amendment because it operates to deny certain individuals a fundamental right, *i.e.,* the right to marry, without due process of law. The right to marry is a fundamental right, inherent in the rights to liberty and privacy of all persons. Regulations affecting these rights are reviewed under the strict scrutiny standard and will be upheld only if they are necessary to protect a compelling interest.

States are authorized to regulate marriage as a valid exercise of their police power to promote the public health, safety, morals, and general welfare. Valid regulations of marriage such as age restrictions and blood test requirements deal with the quality of the marital relationship itself. The statute in question, on the other hand, attempts to deny the right to marry as a punishment for other conduct. A statute that metes out punishment without first affording a defendant reasonable notice and a hearing is constitutionally invalid. This is particularly true where, as here, the statute may deprive an indigent father of his rights by reason of his poverty.

This law is substantively, as well as procedurally, violative of the due process guarantees. In the first instance, its requirement that one must obtain court permission as a condition of marriage grants overly broad discretion to the court without well-defined standards, thereby creating a dangerous potential for abuse. It further places a requirement on the applicant for a marriage license to show not only that his children are not presently public charges, but also are not likely to become public charges. This requirement that he make representations or promises about the future is unreasonable on its face. Finally, the law creates an irrebuttable presumption that fathers who fail to comply with support orders have done so willfully and intentionally. If, as in the present case, the reason for his failure to support his children is the father's financial ability, then the statute would have no deterrent effect anyway and, therefore, would fail in its legislative purpose.

A related attack on the statute would be the argument that the statute is an unconstitutional bill of attainder. A bill of attainder is legislation that designates a class of individuals in terms of their past conduct, and punishes that class of individuals without benefit of judicial process. The offensive statute in this case designates, as a class, all fathers who fail to comply with support orders, and punishes them in a wholesale manner by depriving them of their fundamental right to marry. The acceptable alternative would obviously be to deal with the offenders on a case-by-case basis.

There is no question that it is a desirable goal to pass laws which will force parents to live up to their responsibility to support their children. But this statute will not serve as a successful means toward that end. It is more likely that the effect of making it more difficult to marry will simply encourage cohabitation without benefit of marriage and do nothing to encourage fulfillment of support obligations. If anything, a more successful (though not necessarily valid) statutory scheme would be one that promoted and encouraged marriage between a father and mother of illegitimate children. Unfortunately, an additional infirmity of the statutory language is that it fails to distinguish between the marriage of the offending father to the mother of his unsupported children and marriage to an unrelated woman.

57. CRIMINAL PROCEDURE

Denton's attorney can state a much stronger case for suppression of the evidence seized in the two searches conducted on December 15 than he can with respect to Denton's statement to the detectives about his role in the murder case. Both searches were unconstitutional as unreasonable and unjustified warrantless searches. The Defendant's December 16 confession was an admissible voluntary statement in response to a proper interrogation.

To uphold the admissibility of evidence seized during a warrantless search, law enforcement officers must demonstrate the search to be valid by reason of one of the several recognized exceptions to the requirement of a warrant. Patrolman Palmer's initial search of Denton was a pat-down search. A police officer may only stop and frisk a suspect if he has some reasonable and articulable suspicion of criminal activity; and if so, he may proceed to frisk the suspect, or patdown the outer layer of his clothing, but only if he has reason to believe the suspect may be armed and dangerous. During the frisk, the officer may seize any item the officer reasonably believes is a weapon or contraband.

There was nothing about Denton's conduct on the night of the burglary that would serve as a reasonable or articulable basis for suspicion of criminality. Walking toward an automobile in the vicinity of a crime, in and of itself, cannot reasonably support such a suspicion, particularly at the not unreasonable hour of 9 p.m. Even if one argues that the officer had the right to stop Denton and inquire about the nature of his activities, there is nothing in the factual record which supports that such an inquiry was ever made. There is also nothing in these facts that could support a reasonable belief in the mind of the officer that Denton might be armed and dangerous. The whole episode appears most likely to have been a fishing expedition.

Once the officer did proceed with the frisk, he felt only a glass-cutting tool and car keys in the jacket. There is a real question as to whether either of these items might feel sufficiently like a weapon or contraband to justify a further intrusion. The further search produced the glasscutter and the keys, but this disclosure was not sufficient to rehabilitate the State's case with respect to the pat-down search, and certainly did not justify the violation of constitutional rights that was to follow. A search of inaccessible areas of an automobile, not in plain view, requires sufficient probable cause. Denton was not an occupant of the automobile and appears to have identified himself as a local resident. The mere fact that a person is carrying a glasscutter in the vicinity of a burglary does not give rise to sufficient probable cause to justify a warrantless search of an automobile.

The conduct of the two interrogating detectives the next morning, however, was more reasonable, and in no way amounted to a violation of either Denton's Fifth Amendment right against self-incrimination, or his Sixth Amendment right to counsel. The State had honored Denton's request to remain silent, after being advised of his *Miranda* rights during the previous interrogation. In this instance, the officers were interrogating Denton about his knowledge of a different, unrelated crime. As to this second offense, he was not yet an actual suspect or the focus of an investigation or prosecution.

This time, Denton was given a fresh set of *Miranda* warnings and simply asked some questions. In response, he knowingly waived his *Miranda* rights and offered a voluntary confession for reasons that he apparently believed were in his own interests.

The motion will probably be denied as to the inadmissibility of this confession, and Denton will probably have to stand trial on the felony murder charges. The suppression motion should be granted as to the evidence needed for the State's case on the burglary charge. The stop and frisk was an unjustified violation of the Fourth Amendment's prohibition of unreasonable searches and seizures. Even if, for the purpose of discussion, a judge believed that the suspect's possession of a glass-cutting tool constituted sufficient probable cause to proceed to search his car for further evidence, the evidence should be suppressed anyway as the "fruits of the poisonous tree." If the initial frisk was an unreasonable search and seizure, then the taint should extend to all subsequent evidence produced as a direct result of the initial unlawful search.

58. TORTS

Linda is entitled to recovery of substantial damages from Kingston University, for the severe permanent injuries she sustained as a proximate result of the school's negligence, under one or more theories. The University is responsible, as the owner of the undergraduate dormitory, for the existence of the dangerous condition; that is, the concrete stairway without side railings. It had taken no steps to correct the situation despite prior notice of the condition, *i.e.*, the report of the student falling in the previous semester. Furthermore, the school has reason to know that young children would be likely to be on the premises encountering the risk, because it sponsors and encourages participation by students in the "Little Sibling" program.

Linda, being only seven years old, cannot be expected to apprise the hazard and appreciate the risk of injury. The facts and circumstances of the accident therefore support her theory of liability on the part of the University under the attractive nuisance doctrine. All of the requisite elements are present, including:

(i)   The existence of a dangerous condition,

(ii)   The knowledge of the landowner of the existence of the dangerous condition,

(iii) The knowledge of the landowner of the likelihood of young children playing in a dangerous area,

(iv)   The resultant likelihood of injury as a consequence of the child's inability to appreciate the risk, and

(v)   The fact that the cost of remedying the condition would not be overly burdensome when weighed against the appreciable risk of injury.

Even if Linda could not sustain her burden to factually establish all the elements necessary for a case based on attractive nuisance, the University would still be liable under a theory of landowner's negligence. Linda enjoys the status of an invitee by reason of the school's invitation to her to participate in the adoption program. The University therefore owes her a duty to use reasonable and ordinary care to keep the property safe, and repair dangerous conditions, in order to protect invitees from any foreseeable risk of injury.

The University might contend that Linda is merely a licensee because she was on the premises for her own benefit and not that of the University. Even if this were the case, which is not likely, a landowner still has a duty to warn a licensee of a known dangerous condition, that the licensee might not be aware of (because of her age). This the University failed to do. While the University might also raise a defense of contributory negligence to bar her action or reduce her recovery, a jury would probably minimize the fault attributable to Linda by requiring a much more lenient standard of care for a child of such tender years.

Perri would be likely to also sue the University seeking recovery of damages for her psychoneurotic injury. She would allege that her depression proximately resulted from the trauma of watching an incident that caused a severe injury to a child. However, in most jurisdictions, a cause of action does not lie for purely emotional injuries resulting from negligence. In those few states where such an action is recognized, it is normally limited to extreme situations, as where a mother witnesses the death of her child in a horrible accident.

The facts of this case, where a young woman witnessed a five-foot fall by a child that she merely related to "like a sister," do not support such a result. Additionally, Perri would have a much weaker case for damages than Linda, since the cost of her psychotherapy is probably picked up by the University, and as a scholarship student, she probably suffers no pecuniary loss as a result of the withdrawal from her courses.

The University would probably implead Perri as a third-party defendant, seeking contribution from her as a joint tortfeasor in the defense of an action brought by Linda. They would allege that Linda was under Perri's immediate supervision; that, by her own admission, Perri was aware of the hazard; and accordingly she was more comparatively negligent than they. Though I personally believe such a defense lacks merit, it would ultimately be a matter for factual determination by the jury. It would have to be specifically proved that Perri breached some duty of reasonable care. There is no relationship between Perri and Linda that would allow for imputation of the negligence of the little girl to the older student, or any other sort of vicarious liability.

59. CONTRACTS
(a) Burgerama vs. Slo-poke Builder
MEMORANDUM OF LAW

The damage most clearly recoverable by Burgerama (hereinafter "Plaintiff") in this action would be compensatory damages. The aim of an award of compensatory damages is to place a nonbreaching party in the position he would have been in had the contract been fully performed. Ideally, the award would compensate Plaintiff for all of his lost profits attributable to delay in completion of construction. However, the law requires that such damages be established by competent evidence to a reasonable degree of certainty.

The trier of fact could find a Plaintiff's claim of lost profits to be hypothetical and speculative, particularly with regard to the anticipated profits of a new business without a track record. In this case, Plaintiff must argue that the restaurant in question was not a brand new business, but rather was an expansion of an ongoing business, with an established record of success.

Plaintiff will offer the testimony of Harry Heartburn, as an expert witness, in support of his position. While it is clear that, based on his prior experience, Mr. Heartburn would qualify to testify about restaurant operations, he might not qualify as an expert for purposes of testimony as to facts about the market area, notwithstanding his preparation of a market study, and his experience in site selection. If the Plaintiff is successful in establishing the admissibility and the competence of Mr. Heartburn's testimony based on his market research, then perhaps his case for damages can be based on proof of typical profits in comparable restaurants.

To guard against the possibility of the trier of fact rejecting his claim for lost profits as too speculative, Plaintiff should be prepared to argue for an award of compensatory damages under two alternative theories of recovery. He might prove the loss of the fair rental value of the premises by the testimony of a qualified real estate expert. Finally, if he prevails on no other grounds, he should certainly be able to prove the loss of a reasonable return on his invested capital.

Plaintiff may be additionally entitled to an award of consequential damages if he can prove certain other facts. Plaintiff may have hired employees in anticipation of a certain date of operation. These labor costs would not be offset by the return of income during that period. The same reasoning would apply to wasted expenses for advertising.

It should be noted that Plaintiff is not entitled to recovery of all costs expended. Plaintiff's claim is for damages attributable to a delay in performance, vis-a-vis a failure of performance. Sooner or later, Plaintiff would be faced with the expense of his capital investment and his operating overhead in any event. Normal operating expenses must be distinguished from any unnecessary costs incurred in connection with the delay. Only the latter would be recoverable.

In order to prevail on a claim for consequential damages, Plaintiff would have to establish that such damages were foreseeable to the Defendant, or at least to an ordinary person. In this case, Defendant was on notice of the importance of the completion date, and the adverse consequences that would be likely to result from delay by reason of the time is of the essence provision in the contract. Moreover, it is likely that Defendant has prior experience in the construction of fast food restaurants, a specialized type of construction, and would, therefore, be familiar with the nature of the business.

Defendant would have little success in asserting, as a defense, Plaintiff's failure to mitigate damages. Removing Defendant from the job and finding and engaging a substitute contractor to complete the work started by Defendant would have been cost prohibitive, even if such a substitution were possible.

Punitive damages are ordinarily not recoverable in contract actions. The thrust of the law of contract damages is compensatory and remedial. Unless Plaintiff could prove that Defendant's unjustified actions were wanton, willful, or even tortious (for example, Defendant building for a competitor of Plaintiff during the contract period), which appears unlikely on the facts of this case, punitive damages would not lie.

(b)   Questions for Harry Heartburn

(1)   Describe in detail your employment experience in the fast food industry. Include the various positions you have held, the years of service at each position, and the description of the duties each position involves.

(2)   Describe with particularity, if not already set forth in your previous answer, any employment-related experience you have had in site selection or market research.

(3)   Describe in detail your study of the market area in which this Burgerama is located; include in your answer the geographical area included in the study, the number of fast food restaurants in the area, prospects of future growth in the area, major access roads and related traffic patterns, and any demographic data you deem pertinent to the restaurant business.

(4)   On the basis of either your prior experience in the restaurant business, or your study of comparable restaurant facilities in this market area, were you able to arrive at a conclusion as to the probable amount of profits that Burgerama might have earned had they been in operation between July 1 and October 1, 1983? If so, state the amount of lost profits and discuss the basis for your conclusion.

(5)   What was the total amount of money that had been invested by the Burgerama chain in this restaurant as of October 1, 1983?

(6)   Based on your years of experience in the employ of Burgerama, what is the average net profit per month in a typical Burgerama restaurant, expressed as a percentage or ratio per dollar of cost? Can you offer a profit and loss statement, or similar documentation, in support of your opinion?

(7)   In the course of your employment-related activities devoted to site selection, have you had occasion to become familiar with the cost of commercial rental space in the market area?

(8)   To your knowledge, does Burgerama lease any of its facilities?

(9)   Based on your answers to either of two previous questions, are you able to determine with reasonable certainty the monthly rental income that could be derived from leasing this facility, if it were offered for rent?

(10)   How was the construction of this Burgerama restaurant financed?

(11)   If funds were borrowed for the construction of this facility, at what interest rate; and what change, if any, was there in the interest rate between July 1983 and October 1983?

60.   CONTRACTS

Dear Ms. Porter:

After a careful review of the facts and circumstances of your dealings with Leisure, Inc., I recommend that a suit for damages against Leisure be started promptly. In my opinion, your cause of action is meritorious because the agreement between Leisure and Export Co., the terms of which were set forth in John Lee's February 1984 letter, and as modified in your subsequent conversation with Mr. Lee, was a valid, binding, and enforceable contract.

Under the terms of the contract, Export was to exclusively market Leisure's products abroad and was entitled to a commission on all sales made. Leisure was obligated to produce the merchandise and pay Export a commission on sales. When John Lee advised you that he was discontinuing production and not filling your orders, he was breaching the contract in three ways: (i) refusing to fill the orders submitted which exposed you, as an independent sales representative, to liability to your customers; (ii) failing to pay commissions due on sales already made; and (iii) stating an intention not to further perform, without having first given 30 days' notice, as required for cancellation under the contract.

The third breach is a more complicated matter than the first two. In addition to the notice requirement, the parties' right of cancellation was subject to a condition subsequent, that sales did not reach anticipated levels. Because Leisure discontinued production, it is impossible to determine what level sales might have reached. Leisure is certainly not entitled to benefit by the satisfaction of a condition which was within its control and which it brought about by its nonperformance of the contract. Another distinction between the third breach and the others is that it might be considered an anticipatory repudiation because it warned of nonperformance, as to future orders, before performance was actually due. In other situations, an anticipatory repudiation might create an election of remedies for the nonbreaching party, and duty to mitigate his damages by covering or obtaining the goods to fill his orders elsewhere. Obviously, there was only one source of Frivia so the distinction in this case is not meaningful.

With respect to damages, I would argue that Export was entitled to a sum equivalent to lost income for the entire five-year term of the contract, for the reasons I have already stated in my comments on Leisure's right to cancel. The object of an award of damages in a contract action is to put the nonbreaching party in the same position as if the contract were fully performed. To expect a recovery that large would be optimistic, because the measure of damages sought would be speculative and very difficult to prove.

At a minimum, however, I would expect to recover an award of damages consisting of the following:

(a)   Lost commission income, assessed at least at the minimum rate of 10% of sales, or at a higher rate if you could prove that the higher rate would be reasonable, according to the customs of trade in the industry. You will recall that under the contract, the exact rate of commission was to be agreed on upon acceptance of the first order. The law provides that a reasonable price term can be implied when omitted by the parties.

(b)   Reimbursement of expenses incurred for promotion of the product, travel and entertainment, etc. These expenses would have been Export's responsibility, as a cost of doing business had the contract been performed, but are properly recoverable from Leisure as damages resulting from the breach; and possibly

(c)   Lost income from commissions that would have been earned on sales orders taken during the 30 days following the breach, using figures based on sales performance for a similar period preceding the breach, as if required notice had been given.

You can expect that the attorneys for Leisure will raise several issues in defending the matter, all of which I would deal with in the following manner.

They may allege a lack of consideration, necessary to form a binding contract, because the agreement did not create any firm duty of performance by you. First, I would argue that there is an implied promise that you would use your best efforts to market the product in consideration of the exclusive agency. Second, even if Lee's letter were only an offer, you accepted the offer and formed the contract by performance. Third, you relied, to your detriment, on Lee's promises, in expending considerable sums of money and efforts on promotion. Under any of these theories, there was a valuable consideration or a legally sufficient substitute.

They may allege an infirmity in the contract by reason of vague, missing, or illusory terms such as the undetermined rate of commission, the undefined "anticipated level" of sales, or the broad discretion afforded Leisure to reject orders. As I previously mentioned, the law will imply a reasonable price term. The standards for rejection of orders were narrowed to serious credit risks, and the anticipated level of sales was specifically stated during the discussions that took place upon delivery of the letter. To a contention by Leisure that testimony as to those statements would be inadmissible under the parol evidence rule, I would respond that the rule did not apply to subsequent modification or clarification of terms of a contract that was not yet fully integrated. If they contended that the Statute of Frauds required all terms of this contract, which could not be performed within a year, to be in writing, I would respond that the right of cancellation after less than a year took the contract out of the purview of the Statute of Frauds.

They may attack the contract on the grounds of illegality of its terms, *i.e.,* the provision concerning bribery of purchasing agents. That particular provision is neither a material nor essential term of the contract and therefore is severable from the rest of the contract, and not destructive of its validity.

Finally, they may attempt to exercise a right to submit the issue of wrongful rejection to arbitration, and allege that the arbitration provisions bar suit. The issue in controversy is the repudiation by Leisure of the entire agreement; not an unreasonable rejection of any particular order. The arbitration provisions therefore do not apply.

For the foregoing reasons, I would proceed to recover judgment before Leisure, Inc. has an opportunity to dispose of all of its assets.

Very truly yours,

61. REAL PROPERTY
(a) Separate Defenses

(1) Plaintiff's claim is barred by the applicable Statute of Limitations, more than 20 years having elapsed since the construction by defendant of the encroaching improvements.

(2) Plaintiff's claim is barred, under the doctrine of laches, because he delayed pursuing his rights for an unreasonable time, to the extreme prejudice of defendant.

(3) Plaintiff's claim is barred, under the doctrine of waiver, in that Jones, his predecessor in title, objected to the encroachment, but thereafter abandoned his rights and acquiesced in defendant's continued use and encroachment, and plaintiff could acquire no greater rights or interests than Jones in purchasing the property.

(4) Plaintiff's claim is barred, under the doctrine of estoppel, in that defendant relied, to his detriment, on the inaction and apparent consent of Jones, in making substantial investments and improvements in the property.

(5) Plaintiff's injury, if any, is the result of his sole negligence in purchasing the property without first having same surveyed.

(b) Counterclaim:
Defendant and counterclaimant Smith (hereinafter "defendant"), resident of the Borough of Suburbia, State of New Jersey, by way of counterclaim against Plaintiff Dally (hereinafter "plaintiff"), alleges and says:

(1) He is the owner of one of two adjoining properties that are the subject matter of this action, the other being owned by plaintiff.

(2) In or about 1960, defendant raised the level of his home to minimize the possibility of damage by flooding.

(3) At that time, the elevation of the building necessitated replacement of the existing stairway to the dwelling's side yard entrance with a longer stairway.

(4) At that time, defendant inadvertently constructed the required longer stairway in such a way that it encroached slightly on the adjoining property of the neighbor, Jones.

(5) At that time, Jones knew, or should have known, of the encroachment but failed to object to same.

(6) In or about 1965, defendant undertook, at his considerable expense, to replace the wooden stairs with more water-resistant concrete stairs of similar dimensions.

(7) At that time, the said Jones knew, or should have known, of the continuing encroachment on his property, and of the improvements which rendered the encroachment to be of a more permanent nature, but failed to object to same.

(8) Since 1960, and for the more than 20 years that have passed to the present date, defendant has used the encroaching stairs, and has traversed a narrow strip of the aforesaid adjoining property, as a way of access to said stairs openly, notoriously, continuously, exclusively, and under claim of right, adverse to that of plaintiff.

(9) In or about 1966, Jones objected to the encroachment, but took no further action to pursue any rights or remedies with respect thereto.

(10) In or about 1970, plaintiff acquired title to the premises from Jones.

(11) At that time, and all during the next 14 years that followed, plaintiff knew, or should have known, of the encroachment and of defendant's use of his property as a way of access thereto, but plaintiff failed to object.

(12) In or about 1984, plaintiff commenced construction of a fence along the common boundary with defendant's property, thereby interfering with defendant's use of, and denying defendant access to, the stairs to his side entrance.

(13) The local fire code requires that defendant's dwelling have an additional entrance besides the front door, and defendant cannot remove his steps and renovate to create another entrance, except at great expense and hardship.

WHEREFORE, defendant demands judgment, as follows:

A. Adjudging and declaring that defendant has acquired an easement by prescription across plaintiff's property, of a reasonably sufficient width to grant him access to his side entrance; or in the alternative

B. Adjudging and declaring that defendant has an irrevocable license, coupled with an interest, which the plaintiff is estopped to deny;

C. Permanently enjoining plaintiff from constructing a fence or other barrier in such a way as to impair or interfere with defendant's use and enjoyment of his interest in the premises, whether that interest be adjudged to be a prescriptive easement or executed license.

62. CRIMINAL LAW

(a) State v. Betty and Claude—Indictments

(1) First degree felony murder;

(2) Attempted murder;

(3) Involuntary manslaughter;

(4) Aggravated assault;

(5) Attempted extortion;

(6) False imprisonment;

(7) Illegal possession of firearms;

(8) Conspiracy to aid and abet the escape of a convicted felon.

(b)(1) I would conduct a thorough investigation of the management of the situation by the mayor and police chief to determine whether their decision to use the incendiary device was warranted or ill-advised under the circumstances. Were police personnel qualified in the use of such weapons? Was the decision made prematurely, before other less onerous alternative courses of action were fully considered?

(2) I would investigate the preparations for the holdout by Betty and Claude, such as their obtaining of firearms and making renovations of their home, and interrogate other members of the group to obtain evidence that would support the conspiracy charge.

(c) There is little doubt that indictments would be returned and convictions obtained on the firearms and aggravated assault charges. The suspects were captured with the arms in their possession and there were many eyewitnesses to the use of the weapons, which resulted in serious bodily harm to six people. It is also very likely that a jury would draw an inference of specific intent from the actions of the defendants, which were clearly substantial steps toward the commission of the crime of murder, sufficient to support a conviction on the attempted murder charge. If they did, the aggravated assault charge might be held by the judge to merge into the attempted murder charge, because of the common identity of the elements of both offenses which the state needs to prove.

The state should make a strong case on the conspiracy charge based on evidence of the preparations for the siege made by Betty and Claude, combined with the documented demand for the release of the prisoners. A conspiracy conviction requires proof of an agreement between two or more people, to carry out a criminal enterprise. The case can be proven entirely on the basis of circumstantial evidence, because of the difficulty of obtaining direct evidence of a secret pact.

The state will attempt to obtain a conviction on the charge of attempted extortion by proving the basic elements of the offense; that is, that the defendants attempted to obtain large sums of money and other considerations, by employing threats of violence, harm, and disruption. But this is not a typical case of extortion, because neither the threats nor the demands were directed toward the victims, or to others concerning the victims.

The state's false imprisonment case has similar problems. It can be proven that the defendants pinned down and detained many people for many hours at Gotham Station under threat of death or bodily harm. But it was probably not the purpose of the suspects to confine any particular individuals. If the deprivation of freedom was only an incidental consequence of defendants' action and not the objective, then they are probably not guilty of the imprisonment charge.

The felony murder charges and involuntary manslaughter charges are probably mutually exclusive; that is, the state may get a conviction on either one but not both. The felony murder case would be based on the state's contention that five people died in a fire as a direct and proximate result of, and in the course of, the commission of a felony by the defendants. Even if the state were successful in obtaining a conviction of one or more of the several felonies charged, this theory will not hold up. First, none of these offenses are any of those normally associated with felony murder, such as robbery, burglary, rape, etc. Second, it would be hard to prove the element of causation, because the intervening act of bombing by the police, which was the direct and proximate cause of death, was independent of any action by the defendants.

With respect to the deaths of three of the victims, the children, Claude and Betty can be convicted of involuntary manslaughter. By placing their children in the environment during the commission of the crime, they negligently or recklessly exposed them to a foreseeable and appreciable risk of harm.

63. TORTS/CONTRACTS

Paul Plaintive has a cause of action for wrongful discharge against his employer. Having no written employment agreement providing for a stated term of employment, he is an employee at will. But the common law of this state limits the right of an employer to fire an employee at will. An employer may act to reasonably protect his business interest, and may terminate an employee at will with or without cause, but it must be under circumstances which are reasonable. If the employee is fired for a reason, or under circumstances which violate public policy, then his termination is actionable.

Paul Plaintive was fired as corporate counsel of the Widget Corporation for failure to comply with an order of Barry Businessman, president of Widget, directing him to submit altered documents to an attorney in compliance with a discovery request. Thus, his continued employment was conditioned on his cooperation in an illegal scheme. The employer's conduct was clearly a violation of public policy and, therefore, amounted to a wrongful discharge.

The action for wrongful discharge may be maintained in tort or contract. In a tort action, the plaintiff must prove an intentional act by defendant which violates a duty to plaintiff, proximately causing him to sustain damages. In the contract case, the plaintiff has to prove a breach by defendant of the terms of the employment contract. In reality, these are technical distinctions of pleading and procedure. The only meaningful differences between the two actions is the availability of punitive damages in the tort action. Proof of the same facts will sustain either cause because the essence of the case is the unreasonable interference with an employee's protected interest in being employed, in violation of public policy. Plaintive should proceed in both tort and contract, naming Widget Corporation and Businessman individually and as president of the company, as defendants. It is most likely that the corporate employer will be held liable for compensatory contract damages, and the individual, who is capable of malice, will be held liable for punitive damages.

Plaintive also has a cause of action against Vanessa Veep for malicious interference with contractual relations. The element that he needs to prove is unjustifiable interference with the contract of another. It was Veep who suggested to Businessman that Plaintive be fired. The motive for this advice was apparently her self-interest and not the best interest of the employer, as it was, coincidentally, her husband that succeeded to Plaintive's position with the company.

The liability is clear as a matter of law. The extent of damages is an unliquidated amount, left to the sound discretion of the trier of fact. The proofs present the only serious hurdle to recovery. Plaintive must meet his burden almost entirely on the basis of circumstantial evidence.

Unless some interoffice memoranda is obtained, which is very unlikely, there is no direct proof of the reason for termination, which the defendants never admitted, or the remarks by Veep which constituted the interference. The circumstantial evidence, however, is very persuasive. Plaintive was a successful employee for 12 years. The employer had no problem or complaint until he refused to break the law at the employer's request. The inference that his firing was without good cause is undeniable. Similarly, Veep was the person who advised Businessman on personnel matters in the ordinary course of business. She was directly involved in the firing, and treated Plaintive harshly and abruptly at the time. As previously stated, she stood to gain personally by his firing. The testimony of any of the many eyewitnesses to Plaintive's outrageous and insensitive treatment on his last day of employment would go to support a large award of damages.

This treatment of Plaintive would also give rise to actions for defamation and for intentional infliction of emotional distress. A prima facie defamation case requires the publication of defamatory language of and concerning the plaintiff and damages to plaintiff's reputation. Conduct may constitute a defamatory statement in a case such as this, where the security guard escort of Plaintive in full view of the staff falsely implied some dishonest conduct on the part of Plaintive. This imputation of dishonesty is actionable per se (so damage to reputation is presumed) and does not fall within the scope of a qualified privilege. Intentional infliction of emotional distress may be established by extreme and outrageous conduct on defendants' part (having a security guard escort an honest longtime employee to his car), intent (which includes knowing that such conduct is substantially certain to cause severe emotional distress), causation, and damages. Proving that defendants' conduct caused Plaintive's physical injury will be the most difficult element to establish for this tort.

Mrs. Plaintive should pursue a cause of action against all of the tortfeasors for loss of earnings, cost of medical services, and loss of consortium as a direct and proximate result of the tort. She has a difficult case. She must establish by expert testimony a causal connection between the tortious conduct of defendants and her husband's physical injury. If she prevails, she will be entitled to a very large recovery to compensate her for her lost earnings, as well as her husband's, and the cost of medical care and related services.

64. CONSTITUTIONAL LAW

Article XX of the state constitution is invalid insofar as it can deny any individual the right to run for an elective office, simply because he was appointed a judge, even after he resigns his judgeship. The right to run for office is a constitutionally protected right under the Fourteenth Amendment.

As a matter of substantive due process, no state law can arbitrarily impair or diminish such rights, unless it carries out some valid governmental interest or purpose. States may pass laws which regulate access to the ballot as a means of preserving the integrity or promoting the efficiency of the electoral process. States may require officials to resign a government office before running for another office. But such regulations must be reasonable and not arbitrary. The fact that we are dealing with a state constitution rather than a statute does not make a difference. If it conflicts with the clear mandate of the federal Constitution, it must fail.

The law in question, which prohibits Johnson from running for the state legislature simply because he is a former judge, serves no valid governmental interest. It could be argued that the law assures full staffing of the courts and helps prevent openings that must be filled in the middle of a term, but this interest seems tenuous.

Aside from being an unreasonable deprivation of a right, the law is also discriminatory, in that it singles out certain individuals to be affected by the restriction. This is violative of the guarantee of equal protection of the laws under the Fourteenth Amendment.

The First Amendment guarantee of freedom of association has been held to apply to state regulation of political activity through the Fourteenth Amendment. To place any restriction on one's freedom of political activity, there must be some compelling state interest, which is not the case with Article XX of the state constitution.

The provision must be struck down as unconstitutional to protect not only the members of the immediately affected class of judges, but also to protect the interest of the voting public. The franchise must be vigorously protected, not only as to the right to vote itself, but as to the process which insures free access to the ballot for all qualified candidates.

65. CRIMINAL LAW

MEMORANDUM

TO: Assistant Prosecutor
FROM: County Prosecutor
RE: State v. Dave Dickson
Investigation File #1234-85

Please be advised that the State may bring the following homicide charges against Dickson: Felony murder, vehicular homicide (involuntary manslaughter and/or criminal negligence). The State cannot press charges of voluntary manslaughter because the mens rea requires an intentional killing and adequate provocation. Dickson did not intend to kill Viola Victors.

I.   FELONY MURDER

Dickson may be charged with felony murder. The killing of a nonparticipant—even an accidental one—during the commission, flight from the commission, or attempted commission of a felony is murder. When fleeing from the commission of a bank robbery, Dickson's car jumped the sidewalk and narrowly missed hitting Viola. Thereafter, Viola suffered a heart attack. The requisite elements of felony murder are most likely present.

II.   INVOLUNTARY MANSLAUGHTER—CRIMINAL NEGLIGENCE AND VEHICULAR HOMICIDE

Dickson may be charged with criminal negligence and/or vehicular homicide. Criminal negligence requires a greater deviation from the "reasonable person" standard than is required for civil liability. Dickson's driving during his flight must have been so reckless as to cause the injury and ultimately death. Since a causal connection may exist between Dickson's driving in a reckless manner and Viola's heart attack (and death), criminal negligence or vehicular manslaughter may be charged.

III. EVIDENCE PROBLEMS

A. Causation: In *all* homicide charges the defendant's conduct must be the cause-in-fact of the resultant death of the victim. Causation is not a defense. It is an element of every homicide charge to be proved by the prosecution.

Causation has two components: Cause-in-fact and proximate causation. It must be shown that Dickson's reckless driving was the actual cause, or the cause-in-fact of Victors's death. Victors could not have died "but for" Dickson's reckless driving. It may be argued by defense that considering the victim's age, on that date, at that time, Victors could have had a heart attack anyway. However, as in torts, the thin skull theory applies and defendant takes his victim as he finds her. Any "age" defense would prove weak.

Under common law, Dickson could not be convicted because of the "year and a day rule." The victim died on July 15, 1986. The alleged cause of death occurred on July 1, 1985. Since more than a year and one day had expired between the two, no homicide charge could have been filed. However, New Jersey law is currently following the modern trend and disregarding this requirement. This rule is not a bar to prosecution anymore.

Dickson is responsible for all results that occur as a "natural and probable" consequence of his conduct, even if he did not anticipate the precise manner in which they would occur. Dickson was driving in a reckless manner. He may not have anticipated that death would result therefrom; however, it was a foreseeable consequence. The chain of proximate causation between Dickson's driving and Victors's heart attack and her resultant death could only be broken if a "superseding factor" intervened. The nursing care received during the year prior to death could not break the chain of proximate causation unless the care was grossly negligent and grossly negligent care or lack of care caused the death.

B.   Prior Convictions: A defendant's prior conviction is usually proved by checking an admission on cross-examination or by admitting his record of conviction into evidence. The admissibility could go only to impeachment. The federal robbery conviction is admissible. The municipal court conviction is not admissible because a traffic infraction does not constitute a crime. New Jersey follows the majority view, which states that ***any felony*** conviction is admissible for impeachment purposes. Misdemeanors and traffic infractions are not felonies and therefore are inadmissible.

IV.   DEFENSES: DOUBLE JEOPARDY

The Fifth Amendment right to be free of double jeopardy has been incorporated into the Fourteenth Amendment [Benton v. Maryland, 395 U.S. 784 (1969)], and is applicable in state courts. Generally, if jeopardy attaches, the defendant cannot be retried for the same offense.

Dickson will argue that he was convicted in federal court of robbery and therefore cannot be retried in state court for homicide. The constitutional protections against double jeopardy do ***not*** apply to trials by separate sovereigns. Thus, Dickson may be tried for the same conduct by both a state and federal court. [United States v. Lanza, 260 U.S. 377 (1922)] Furthermore, for double jeopardy to attach, the crimes must constitute the same offense. If each crime requires proof of even one additional fact which the other does not, then double jeopardy does not apply. Homicide, which necessitates death, has an element which robbery does not, and they are consequently two separate crimes.

Dickson will also allege that double jeopardy attaches because of his guilty plea to reckless driving in municipal court. Municipal and state courts are not separate sovereigns. [Waller v. Flonda, 397 U.S. 387 (1970)] It would appear that double jeopardy should attach, but it does not. As an exception to the double jeopardy rule, if a defendant is convicted in municipal court of a traffic infraction and the victim thereafter dies, the defendant may be tried again in the state court on a murder charge.

V.   CONCLUSION

The following charges may be brought by the State against Dickson: felony murder; criminally negligent homicide, and/or vehicular homicide. Evidence problems include causation and the admission of prior convictions into evidence. Dickson would likely raise the defense of double jeopardy.

66. CONTRACTS

MEMO TO: Scientific University General Counsel
FROM: Staff Attorney
RE: Scientific v. Microchip Corporation

You have requested a memorandum evaluating Scientific's claims and damages and Microchip's defenses in connection with Scientific's purchase of Microchip's Mother Nature computer and its subsequent failure.

The threshold issue to be determined is whether a contract was formed between the parties and, if so, its terms. Because a sale of goods is involved, this discussion shall focus on the controlling provisions of the Uniform Commercial Code. When a breach of contract suit is commenced, the court must decide if a contract was formed and will ask three basic questions in that regard: (i) was there mutual assent? (ii) was there consideration or some substitute? and (iii) are there any defenses? Here, Microchip's brochure could not reasonably be considered an offer, which requires a promise, undertaking, or commitment to enter into a contract, with certainty and definiteness in the essential terms, all communicated to the offeree. Advertisements, catalogues, circular letters, and the like containing price quotations are usually construed to be mere invitations for offers. They are announcements of prices at which the seller is willing to receive offers. That being the case, the next question is whether Scientific's purchase order was an offer. It was an offer as it met the foregoing requirements, being an express promise to enter into a contract, communicated to the offeree, and definite in its essential terms by specific reference to Microchip's brochure. Microchip's acknowledgment was an acceptance of Scientific's offer but the critical issue is the terms of the contract thus formed.

Between merchants, additional proposed terms in the acceptance that differ from the offer automatically become part of the contract unless they materially alter the contract, the offer expressly limits acceptance to the terms of the offer, or the offeror has already objected to the additional terms. Here, Scientific is not a merchant, so the general rule would apply, *i.e.,* that an expression of acceptance or a confirmation creates a contract even though in the same communication the offeree adds terms different than those in the offer. If the new terms materially change the bargain, the person accepting is bound to a contract on the offeror's original terms. Since a disclaimer of warranties is a material term, they will not be a part of the contract.

As to warranties, it must be determined what warranties, if any, were created. The brochure's representation that the computer's useful life would be five years was an express warranty. Any affirmation of fact or promise made creates an express warranty if it is part of the basis of the bargain, meaning if the buyer could have relied upon it when entering into the contract. There was also an implied warranty of merchantability, meaning that the goods are fit for the ordinary purpose for which such goods are used. If Microchip had reason to know the particular purpose for which the computer was to be used and that Scientific was relying on Microchip's skill and judgment to select a suitable computer, a warranty of fitness for a particular purpose would also exist.

As to damages, a buyer may reject the goods prior to acceptance, revoke acceptance of the goods, replevy, sue for specific performance, or sue for damages and recover the loss resulting in the normal course of events from the breach. This latter choice would be Scientific's remedy and would be the difference between the value of the goods delivered and the value they would have had if they had been according to contract plus incidental and consequential damages. Incidental damages include expenses reasonably incurred in inspection, receipt, transportation, care and custody of goods rightfully rejected, and other expenses reasonably incident to the breach, such as the amount spent trying to get the MN to function properly. Consequential damages include any loss resulting from the buyer's general or particular requirements and needs of which the seller had reason to know at the time of contracting and which could not be prevented by buying substitute goods or otherwise.

Microchip will raise various defenses to Scientific's lawsuit, beginning with a claim that since its brochure described the computer as "experimental," it is obvious no warranties would be given. All implied warranties are disclaimed by expressions such as "as is" or other expressions which in common understanding call the buyer's attention to the fact that no implied warranties exist. Microchip would liken "experimental" to "as is." Microchip may also argue that Scientific is a merchant and that, therefore, the disclaimer of warranties in the acknowledgment was a part of the contract. As to damages, Microchip will claim no recovery is possible for the $3 million lost research because it was not reasonably foreseeable. It will also claim that Scientific's resale of the computer for $50,000 was not commercially reasonable.

67.   REAL PROPERTY

Plaintiff's interest does not amount to a lease: Volt's interest in the subject property cannot be a lease because no estate in land was given. All that was given was a right to install a machine on another's property. A lease implies that a tenancy must exist giving a right of possession to the tenant for either a fixed period or at will. In either case, a right of possession is involved and, here, nothing was granted to Volt other than the right to maintain his video machine on the premises. Furthermore, even if a lease was created, Volt's claim of notice on the part of Bravo must fail because the agreement between Volt and Whipple, Bravo's predecessor in interest, was never recorded.

Plaintiff's interest does not amount to an easement in gross: An easement is a liberty, privilege, or advantage which one may hold in the lands of another. It is a nonpossessory interest. The holder of an easement has the right to use a tract of land (the servient tenement) for a special purpose, but has no right to possess and enjoy the tract of land. Unlike an easement appurtenant, which benefits the holder in his use and enjoyment of another tract of land, an easement in gross is created where the holder of the easement interest acquires his right of special use in the servient tenement independent of his ownership or possession of another tract of land. Typically, easements are created in order to give their holder the right of access across a tract of land. At common law, an easement in gross was deemed to be personal to its original holder and inalienable. That rule has been limited to some extent today, as for commercial purposes such as telephone and power lines, etc. Such is not the case here and no such necessity exists for the continuation of any easement.

Plaintiff's interest amounts to a mere revocable license: A license is a revocable privilege to enter upon the lands of the licensor, *i.e.,* the servient tenement, and is not considered an interest in land. An essential characteristic of a license is that it is personal to the licensee and, therefore, not alienable. But more importantly to the instant case, it is revocable by nature. It may be revoked at any time by a manifestation of the licensor's intent to end it. This manifestation may be by a formal notice of revocation, as was sent by Bravo, or it may consist of conduct which obstructs the licensee's continued use. A license also ends by operation of law in that a conveyance of the servient tenement by the licensor terminates the licensee's privilege. It should be noted that it was, in fact, a license that was created by the agreement between Volt and Whipple.

Plaintiff's interest does not amount to a real covenant: A covenant running with the land is a hybrid concept lying somewhere between an interest in the land, such as an easement, and a mere personal agreement to do or refrain from doing some action. A covenant runs with the land when the burdens, benefits, or both, of the covenant pass to succeeding holders of the estates of the original covenanting parties. For the creation of a covenant, there must be a writing which satisfies the Statute of Frauds, an intent that the covenant run with the land, and the covenant must "touch and concern" the land. In addition, breach of a covenant at law is remedied by an award of money damages, not by specific performance. Even if the agreement were deemed an equitable servitude, which is a restriction on the use to which an owner may put his land, it would be unenforceable here against Bravo because he had no notice of the covenant, an essential requirement.

68. TORTS

Oxide: Tilly can assert a claim of negligence against Mr. Oxide for the loss of her home, possessions, and possibly for any emotional distress she suffered as a result of viewing the destruction of her possessions.

To establish her negligence claim against Oxide, she must show that Oxide owed her a duty of care, that he breached that duty of care, and that his breach was the actual and proximate cause of the losses and injury she sustained.

To show that Oxide owed her a duty of care, Tilly must establish that she is a foreseeable plaintiff. Two theories, the Cardozo view and the Andrews view, are used to determine who is a foreseeable plaintiff. Under the Cardozo view, Tilly is a foreseeable plaintiff only if a reasonable person could have foreseen a risk of injury to her or her property under the circumstances. Here, one could argue that Oxide's demonstration of the "fireworks" effect of sodium presented a risk that the students would be harmed but not that Tilly's apartment away from the school would be harmed. However, harm of the type Tilly suffered was a likely result of Oxide's failure to lock the lab. Even more, the two actions in conjunction created the risk that a student, impressed with the demonstration, would attempt to take some of the unsecured metal and use it for its "fireworks" effect, creating the likelihood of a fire such as that which consumed Tilly's home and possessions. Under the Andrews view, Tilly would be a foreseeable plaintiff if Oxide breached a duty to any potential plaintiff and as a result any other person, such as Tilly, was harmed. Under this view, Tilly is clearly a foreseeable plaintiff because Oxide's demonstration of the "fireworks" effect and failure to lock up the sodium created a foreseeable risk that someone or something would be injured by the dangerous substance.

Because Tilly was a foreseeable plaintiff, Oxide owed her a duty of care. The ordinary standard of care is that which an average, reasonably prudent person would exercise given the circumstances. Here, the serious risk of injury created by Oxide's acts indicates that he negligently failed to exercise ordinary care. Even if Oxide was found to have exercised ordinary care in the handling and storage of the sodium, as a teaching professional he would have exercised a higher standard of care consistent with the knowledge and skill a member of his profession would have concerning the dangerous properties of metallic sodium.

Oxide's negligence was clearly the actual cause of Tilly's injuries because if he had not demonstrated the "fireworks" effect and then left the metal where it could be taken, Tilly's home would not have been destroyed by fire. Therefore, Tilly's damages would not have occurred but for the negligence of Oxide. However, Oxide's negligent conduct must also be shown to be the proximate cause of Tilly's damages. Here, the chain of events leading to the harm was indirect because it involved the theft of the sodium by a third party and the unsafe disposal of the explosive metal in a building without adequate fire safety equipment. However, where the intervening events were reasonably foreseeable, such intervening events will not break the chain of causality.

The theft and unsafe disposal of the sodium by Bunny and Clyde was clearly foreseeable because Oxide's negligence invited those acts. However, a close issue of fact is presented by Paul's failure to fireproof the building and the subsequent failure of the sprinkler system. It is likely that a trier of fact would find that Paul's failure to install adequate fire-proofing as required by statute was merely negligent and was therefore foreseeable. The failure of the sprinkler system would also likely be found to be a foreseeable risk. Oxide's warning to Bunny and Clyde does not cure his initial breach of duty. Bunny's and Clyde's failure to heed the warning was a foreseeable consequence of Oxide's negligent acts. Only if their failure to heed the warning was an unforeseeable intentional tort act would the chain of causality be severed.

Damages: Tilly may recover damages for the destruction of her home and the fair market value of her possessions or the cost of their repair if some are merely damaged. Oxide will also be liable for consequential damages such as temporary shelter and locating and reletting an apartment. It is unlikely that she will be able to recover for the emotional distress she felt when she watched the fire. The majority view holds that to recover for emotional distress caused by negligence, the Plaintiff must be within the zone of danger created by the negligent act. Because Tilly was not in the burning apartment, she was not within the zone of danger. Some courts have found that where the negligent act creates an unreasonable risk of great emotional harm, a plaintiff may recover. However, that limited exception does not seem to apply here because the destruction of a plaintiff's possessions by fire does not present an extraordinary risk of extreme emotional distress.

Rural High School: Rural High School can be held liable to Tilly on the principle of respondeat superior. An employer, who stands in a master/servant relationship with his employee, will be held vicariously liable for the torts of the employee where those torts are committed within the scope of the employment relationship. Here, there is nothing to suggest that Oxide was not within a traditional master/servant relationship while teaching and supervising the lab. Oxide's negligent acts were also directly within the scope of his employment as a high school teacher.

Paul: Paul also breached a duty to Tilly through his failure to install fire-retardant insulation as required by the Rural ordinance. The majority rule is that violation of an ordinance is evidence of negligence with respect to the class of people who are to be protected by the ordinance. Here, the purpose of the ordinance was to prevent fire, and it is reasonable to conclude that the residents of apartments above restaurants were within the class of people to be protected. However, it may be difficult to establish that the harm would not have occurred but for the failure to insulate. It may be easier to establish that damage from the fire would have been less severe had the insulation been in place and to hold Paul liable for the additional fire damage due to lack of insulation.

Rural Water Company: Rural Water Company owes a duty to all plaintiffs who may rely on it to provide adequate water pressure for fighting fires. If the failure to supply water was the result of a negligent act or omission by the company, it will be liable for damages to Tilly's property which resulted therefrom. Even if Rural Water Company is a municipal entity, it will not be given municipal governmental tort immunity because its function, providing water, is proprietary as opposed to providing a governmental service.

Bunny and Clyde: Clyde can be held liable to Tilly because he breached a duty of reasonable care to Tilly when he stole and improperly disposed of the sodium causing a fire. The damage to Tilly's apartment was clearly a foreseeable consequence of his act because he attended the lecture which demonstrated the explosive property of sodium mixed with water. Here, the chain of causation was more direct because his negligent act caused the fire which resulted in the damage. As discussed above, the lack of fireproof insulation and adequate water pressure were both foreseeable intervening events.

Bunny, however, presents a closer case because she did not participate in negligently disposing of the sodium. However, she did have sole possession of the sodium after she and Clyde stole it. It could be argued that her failure to safeguard the metal, and prevent it from falling into Clyde's or anyone else's hands, constituted a breach of duty rendering her liable. At issue here is the appropriate standard of care given her age. Although children are generally held to lesser standard of care commensurate with their experience and knowledge, here Bunny, a senior in high school at 16, and having attended the demonstration by Oxide, should be aware of the danger her handling of the metal caused and therefore should be held to an adult standard of care.

Bunny's mother: Ordinarily a person is not liable for the tort of another except where they have the authority and actual ability to control that person and they know of or should know of circumstances which would require them to exercise control. Here, Bunny's mother knew Bunny was a hard-to-handle teenager and additionally was informed by Bunny of the explosive chemical. In this circumstance, Bunny's mother, who as her parent had authority to control her, was also under a duty to exercise control. Her retreat without a word, after being informed of the way the dangerous chemical was to be used, constitutes a breach of her duty to protect Tilly and others like her from unreasonable risk.

Early Alertco, Flamco: Tilly does not have a viable cause of action against either Early Alertco or Flamco. There are no facts which indicate that Early Alertco was in any way negligent or under a duty to supply water. Flamco might be liable to Tilly on a theory of strict liability, which holds a commercial supplier strictly liable for the harm caused by any unreasonably dangerous product. However, it is unlikely that metallic sodium would be considered unreasonably dangerous because there is no alternative substance which has sodium's exact properties. It is possible but not likely that a court might impose liability on the theory that supplying the metal to a high school class is negligent given the potential hazards the element presents.

Conclusion: A lawsuit should be instituted against Oxide, Rural High School, Paul, Rural Water Company, Bunny, Clyde, and Bunny's mother.

69. CONSTITUTIONAL LAW

To: Judge
From: Law Clerk
Re: Sierra Toxics

Commerce Clause: The Commissioner of Ecological Preservation's (CEP's) order violates the Commerce Clause. At issue is whether a state may prohibit hazardous waste disposal facilities within the state from accepting hazardous wastes from outside the state.

The Commerce Clause gives Congress plenary power to regulate commerce among the states. This power is not exclusive; the states may also regulate commerce. However, state regulation that discriminates against interstate commerce usually will be stricken as violating the Commerce Clause unless the regulation is necessary to an important state interest.

Here, the CEP's order clearly discriminates against interstate commerce since it prohibits disposal of out-of-state wastes but allows disposal of wastes generated within the state. The Commission would no doubt argue that the state's interest in the safety of residents around Sierra's disposal facility necessitates the limitation, but this argument will fail. A nondiscriminatory regulation (*e.g.*, limiting the amount of hazardous waste that may be disposed of at Sierra's plant, regardless of where the hazardous waste was generated) could provide the same protection as the prohibition here. Thus, the regulation discriminates against interstate commerce without valid justification and so violates the Commerce Clause.

Contracts Clause: The order of the CEP might also violate the Contracts Clause. At issue is whether a state order that prohibits a waste disposal facility from accepting wastes from certain customers violates the Contracts Clause.

The Contracts Clause generally prohibits states from acting to retroactively and substantially impair existing contracts rights. However, the bar is not absolute; even if a state act substantially impairs existing contract rights, it still will be upheld if the impairment serves an important public interest and the law is reasonable and narrowly tailored to promote that interest.

Here, it is not clear whether the CEP's order substantially impairs any existing contract rights—although we are told that the order prohibits Sierra from accepting hazardous wastes from outside the state, and that Sierra has contracted with out-of-state customers in the past, we are not told whether Sierra has any continuing contracts that would be impaired by the CEP's order. Assuming such contracts exist, the order would violate the Contracts Clause. Since the CEP is a state agency, there is action by the state. And while safeguarding the community from toxic wastes is clearly an important interest, as discussed above, the order here is not reasonable to deal with the problem because it does nothing to prevent wastes generated within the state from jeopardizing the community's safety. Accordingly, the order violates the Contracts Clause.

Privileges and Immunities Clause of Article IV: The CEP order might violate the Privileges and Immunities Clause of Article IV, at least with respect to the citizens of State Beta. At issue is whether a state may prohibit nonresidents from contracting for commercial services in the state.

The Privileges and Immunities Clause of Article IV prohibits states from discriminating against nonresidents in matters concerning fundamental rights, which includes important commercial activities and civil liberties. However, even if a state discriminates against nonresidents, the discrimination can be upheld if the state has a substantial justification for the different treatment and there are no less restrictive means to accomplish the state's goal. In any case, the Privileges and Immunities Clause is available only to natural persons; corporations cannot take advantage of its protections.

Here, we are not told whether any of Sierra's customers are natural persons; they might all be corporations. If Beta is allowed to represent the interests of natural persons who are being discriminated against by the CEP's order, the order probably violates the Privileges and Immunities Clause. Contracting for commercial waste disposal services probably is an important commercial activity, and the CEP's order discriminates against nonresidents by completely prohibiting them from contracting on an equal basis with residents of Alpha. And while there probably is substantial justification for the order (to protect the community from hazardous wastes), as discussed above, the order is not the least restrictive means of protecting that interest. Thus, the order could violate the Privileges and Immunities Clause of Article IV.

Procedural due process: Finally, it could be argued that Sierra was denied its right to procedural due process. At issue is whether Sierra had an adequate opportunity to present its case.

The Due Process Clause of the Fifth Amendment, made applicable to the states through the Fourteenth Amendment, provides that the government shall not take a person's life, liberty, or property without due process of law. Due process contemplates fair procedures, which requires at least an opportunity to present objections to the proposed action and a fair and neutral decisionmaker. The timing and scope of the hearing due depends on the circumstances of the deprivation. In most cases, the person being deprived of life, liberty, or property should receive notice of the government's proposed action and have an opportunity to respond before the deprivation.

Here, the CEP has limited Sierra's right to contract, a liberty interest. The facts state that a public hearing was held, but we are not told whether Sierra was given individual notice of the meeting or was given an opportunity to speak. Presumably, sufficient notice and an opportunity to respond were given, and thus Sierra was afforded adequate procedural due process.

70. CONSTITUTIONAL LAW

In response to your request for my opinion regarding your proposed termination of Esther's employment and the consequences that may result in connection with Eden's statute, I hereby submit the following:

Initially, I believe that Esther will have no success in claiming any violation of her constitutional rights of due process and/or equal protection. These rights are guaranteed to all citizens, but can only be applied to governmental action. The Fourteenth Amendment, therefore, prevents states from depriving any person of life, liberty, or property without due process of law and equal protection of the law. The Supreme Court has consistently refused to extend the Fourteenth Amendment limitation to purely private acts of discrimination. The sole issue present in the context of your proposed action is whether or not the fact that your students receive free busing from the local school district transforms your acts into "state action." In my opinion, it does not because to do so the state must be "significantly involved" in the private entity. Merely providing essential services, such as busing, is insufficient to change the nature of your actions from "private" to "state."

Two constitutional provisions bear on whether the law is violative of your rights. The first, called the "Establishment" Clause, essentially bars governmental sponsorship of religion, financial support of religion, and active involvement of government in religious activities. In order not to violate this clause, a statute must (a) have a secular purpose; (b) have a principal or primary effect that neither advances nor inhibits religion; and (c) not produce excessive government entanglement with religion. As applied to you, the statute might be found unconstitutional in that it inhibits your practice of religion in being able to hire and terminate only those employees who share your religious beliefs, and would probably produce excessive government entanglement, specifically in the area of enforcement of the statute. In essence, although the statute appears valid on its face, it can be argued that it is unconstitutional on the specific facts of your case.

The second constitutional provision of concern is the First Amendment right to the free exercise of religion. In cases such as yours, a distinction is drawn between statutes which interfere with religious belief and those which interfere with conduct engaged in because of religion. While the freedom to hold religious beliefs is absolute, conduct undertaken because of religious beliefs may be regulated or prohibited by the state unless it can be shown that the state's action was motivated by a desire to interfere with religion. Here, the state statute prohibits sexual discrimination by employers. Nothing in the statute indicates that it was adopted to interfere with any religious practices; it appears to be a general conduct regulation well within the state's police power that just happens to interfere with the church's practices. Indeed, states have a substantial interest in preventing sexual discrimination. Thus, the church is not likely to succeed in an argument that the statute interferes with free exercise rights of church members.

In the final analysis, I believe that your actions will be upheld and that the statute will be found unconstitutional under the Establishment Clause because it forces a religious organization to retain in its employ an employee not subscribing to the belief of that organization.

71. CONTRACTS

Celestial's claims and damages would be governed by the Uniform Commercial Code, Article 2, since the present situation involves a sale of goods. Celestial will sue Gaze for breach of contract, claiming that a contract was reached between the parties for the production and manufacture of the telescopes. Celestial will claim, first, that this was a sale between "merchants," thereby dispensing with the Statute of Frauds requirement that a contract for the sale of goods over $500 must be in writing. Between merchants, if one party, within a reasonable time after an oral understanding has been reached, sends a written confirmation to the other which binds the sender, it satisfies the Statute of Frauds requirement against the recipient as well if he has reason to know of its contents unless he objects to its contents within 10 days of receipt. Celestial would claim Gaze's purchase order confirmed the oral understanding reached over the telephone earlier.

A second argument Celestial would advance is that since the telescopes were imprinted with Gaze's name, they were specially manufactured goods. If goods are to be specially made for the buyer and are not suitable for sale to others in the ordinary course of the seller's business, the contract is enforceable if the seller has, under circumstances which reasonably indicate the goods are for the buyer, made substantial beginnings in their manufacture or commitments for their purchase before notice of repudiation is received.

Celestial will also claim that Gaze is liable for the delivered and finished telescopes and the parts in inventory as well, arguing that the discussion on the telephone as to a quantity of 100,000 units is part of the contract. There is no method for the introduction into evidence of this claim, however, except parol evidence, since none of the written memoranda between the parties refer to any quantity other than 20,000 units.

As damages, Celestial is entitled to recover incidental damages plus either the difference between the contract price and the market price or the difference between the contract price and the resale price. In this case, since the purchase order was for 20,000 units and Celestial was paid for 15,000 units, the damages could only be based on the remaining 5,000 units. In addition, since they were imprinted with Gaze's name, they could probably not be reasonably resold. Therefore, the measure of damages would be the difference between the contract price of $7 per unit and the market price, measured as of the time and place for delivery. It should be noted, however, that if this measure of damages does not put Celestial in as good a position as performance would have, Celestial may recover lost profits, as measured by the difference between cost of manufacturing, purchase price, and contract price.

Gaze will defend the lawsuit claiming, first, that no contract was formed on the telephone, there being no firm offer and acceptance but mere negotiations. Second, Gaze will claim that he is not a "merchant," defined in the Uniform Commercial Code as one regularly dealing in goods of that kind. Therefore, the Statute of Frauds would apply and the contract would be limited to Gaze's purchase order and encompass all its terms. This is crucial because if Gaze were deemed a merchant, the terms in Celestial's acknowledgment would automatically be a part of the contract unless they materially altered the contract, Gaze's offer expressly limited acceptance to the terms of the offer, or if the offeror had already objected to those terms. Since Gaze arguably is not a merchant, Celestial's additional acknowledgment terms do not become a part of the contract.

The liquidated damages clause would probably be held inapplicable. Parties may liquidate damages at any amount which is reasonable in view of the actual or anticipated harm caused by the breach, the difficulties of proof of loss and the inconvenience or feasibility of otherwise obtaining an adequate remedy. Unreasonably large liquidated damages are considered penalties and are void.

Celestial should deposit the check and endorse it "under protest" so it will not act as an accord and satisfaction, thereby barring Celestial from a possible future recovery of amounts still in honest dispute.

72. CONSTITUTIONAL LAW/REAL PROPERTY
MEMORANDUM OF LAW

The first issue presented by the instant motion and cross-motion is the standing of Watchful to seek an injunction staying further construction and revoking the building permit. As a neighboring property owner, assuming he will be aggrieved or affected in some manner by the contemplated construction, he would have standing to enforce the ordinance or have its constitutional validity passed upon. Reference should, however, be had to the specific ordinance in question.

Having passed the threshold issue of standing, we come to the subject of the validity of the zoning ordinance itself. The state may enact statutes to reasonably control the use of land for the protection of the health, safety, morals, and welfare of its citizens. This power to zone is based on the state's inherent police power but is not unlimited in scope. The constitutional limitations on such power stem from the Due Process and Equal Protection Clauses of the Fourteenth Amendment and the "no taking without just compensation" clause of the Fifth Amendment. The clear trend, however, is to uphold such statutes against challenges on constitutional grounds. Federal courts have consistently applied a "rational relation" test to determine whether zoning classifications are invalid.

Generally, if the statute produces an arbitrary or unreasonable result, it is considered invalid. Zoning ordinances can be held invalid if any of the following is true:

(a)   The ordinance bears no rational relation to the public health, safety, morals or general welfare. In a similar case, the United States Supreme Court upheld such an ordinance because it was rationally related to permissible goals of preserving family values and quiet seclusion. [Village of Belle Terre v. Boraas, 416 U.S. 1 (1974)]

(b)   The ordinance is so restrictive that it deprives the land of virtually all economic use, rendering it essentially without value. While the instant ordinance does not go quite that far, it does adversely impact the land from an economic point of view.

(c)   The ordinance is discriminatory, affecting one parcel in a way that does not affect surrounding parcels and with no rational basis for the difference in treatment. This is inapplicable to the case at bar because the subject parcel is not the only affected parcel.

(d)   The ordinance is beyond the grant of authority given to the municipality by the state enabling act. Reference must be had to the enabling act itself, but this situation rarely exists.

(e) The ordinance was adopted without procedural due process of law. This is likewise inapplicable to the instant case, because rezoning is typically deemed a legislative act rather adjudicatory in nature and thus not subject to the due process requirement.

In essence, the statute appears to be valid on its face under this test. However, New Jersey law applies strict scrutiny where a particular class may be excluded by a restrictive zoning ordinance. In this case, prohibiting all multi-family dwellings arguably has the effect of excluding low-income persons from living in the area, which would make the ordinance invalid under New Jersey law. In the event that the ordinance is upheld, the resolution of the issue will depend on whether the proposed construction is deemed a multi-family dwelling. The amendment prohibiting mother-daughter dwellings, if valid, would render the construction, if completed, a nonconforming use. A use that exists at the time of passage of a zoning act which does not conform to the statute cannot be eliminated at once. Some statutes provide for the gradual elimination of such nonconforming uses, such as terminating the use upon the death of the mother, for example.

Since the statute's definition of "single family" does not limit it to blood relatives, it passes constitutional muster in that regard, since such a restrictive definition has been held invalid. It can be argued that because of Homeowners' reliance on the issuance of the building permit and the absence of a separate entrance, the proposed structure would not be deemed a multi-family dwelling. In any event, because additional fact issues need to be resolved, summary judgment should not be granted to either party.

73. CRIMINAL PROCEDURE
DEFENDANT'S BRIEF
THE GOVERNMENT WIRETAPPING, BUGGING, AND PLACEMENT OF CONCEALED TELEVISION CAMERAS WAS ILLEGAL, AND EVIDENCE GAINED BY THESE METHODS MUST BE SUPPRESSED.

Defendant's instant motion centers on the applicability of the exclusionary rule to the facts of the instant case. Briefly stated, the exclusionary rule states that not only must illegally obtained evidence be excluded from a criminal trial but all evidence obtained or derived from exploitation of that evidence must also be excluded. The courts have deemed such evidence the tainted fruit of the poisonous tree. The government herein may claim that their investigator was only seeking to enforce an internal rule of the Department of Defense. While it is true that the exclusionary rule does not apply to a violation of only internal agency rules, the defendant is now on trial for espionage as a result of the evidence obtained by the investigator, so the exclusionary rule must apply. The government may also claim that their investigator was not a law enforcement agent; however, he was assigned to monitor the activities of the defendant and all evidence now in issue was obtained by or through his efforts, so, again, the exclusionary rule definitely applies. The exclusionary rule is a remedy for violations of a defendant's Fourth and Fifth Amendment rights, both of which were grievously and recklessly violated herein.

This defendant clearly had a Fourth Amendment right against unreasonable searches and seizures. He has standing, an initial requirement, by virtue of the fact that his home and office were intruded upon and that he had a reasonable expectation of privacy in both locations. The court must evaluate the totality of the circumstances to determine whether such a reasonable expectation existed. Certainly, such an expectation is reasonable in one's own home and in one's "private" office. None of the devices used by the investigator were used out of doors or in any public place, where it would be unreasonable to have the same expectation of privacy. Where a reasonable expectation of privacy does exist, a warrant should have been issued to render the evidence legally obtained, but none was gotten in this case, nor, for that matter, could one have been issued even if requested. This defendant was not suspected of having committed any crime nor was there any "probable cause" to have suspected him of same. Nor would any of the standard exceptions to the warrant requirement (*e.g.*, consent, plain view, hot pursuit) be applicable under these facts.

Specifically regarding the eavesdropping and wiretapping, the Supreme Court has indicated that this form of surveillance, when violating a reasonable expectation of privacy, constitutes a search under the Fourth Amendment, requiring a warrant. In fact, no warrant could have been issued herein because the first requirement for the issuance of a valid warrant authorizing a wiretap is a showing of probable cause to believe that a specific crime has been or is being committed. Here, the defendant was suspected of nothing more than being a homosexual, which is certainly no crime. The only exceptions to this rule in this context are (i) the "unreliable ear" exception, stating that a speaker assumes the risk that the person to whom he is speaking is unreliable and may be wired for sound, or (ii) if the speaker makes no attempt to keep the conversation private. Obviously, both of these possible defenses are inapplicable to the instant facts.

Due to the reasonable expectation of privacy in defendant's home and office, it is abundantly clear that an illegal warrantless search was conducted by the surveillance employed and any evidence obtained thereby must be suppressed.

THE DEFENDANT'S ORAL AND WRITTEN CONFESSIONS ARE INADMISSIBLE AND MUST BE EXCLUDED FROM THE TRIAL.

It is now well settled that as a protection against compelled self-incrimination under the Fifth Amendment, the *Miranda* warnings and a valid waiver are prerequisites to the admissibility of any statement made by the accused during custodial interrogation. Although the government will no doubt argue that no custodial interrogation occurred since the defendant was not under arrest, it seems apparent that the circumstances surrounding the defendant's statements indicate a custodial interrogation. The questioning lasted for several hours, the interrogator was a government agent who barged into the defendant's home without a warrant and uninvited, and the defendant was badgered, humiliated, and taunted, all leading to the inescapable conclusion that the confession was made under severe duress and coercion. Given the totality of these circumstances, it was entirely reasonable for the defendant to have felt himself in custody and unable to come and go freely. Furthermore, because the written confession was prepared immediately following the oral statements, the written confession was fruit of the poisonous tree and just as illegal as the oral statements.

74. TORTS/CONTRACTS

The uncontroverted facts herein indicate that Pipeco, the defendant, manufactured and installed a defective water pipe in a building designed for lawyers and well known for its state of the art central-ized electronic support facilities and, in which, plaintiff Lawfirm leased a third floor suite of offices. As a result of the bursting of a water pipe, the centralized support facilities were rendered inoperable for several weeks and plaintiff lost substantial business as a result. Plaintiff seeks to recover its eco-nomic loss on the grounds of negligence, strict liability, and breach of implied warranties. We are now presented with defendant's motion for judgment on the pleadings.

As to negligence, a prima facie case is established by showing (i) the existence of a duty on the part of the defendant to conform to a specific standard of conduct for the protection of a foreseeable plaintiff against an unreasonable risk of injury; (ii) breach of that duty by the defendant; (iii) the breach of the duty was the proximate and actual cause of plaintiff's injury; and (iv) damage to plain-tiff's person and/or property. Here, the defendant very obviously had a duty to manufacture and install a pipe that would not burst. By its bursting, it was defective, indicating a breach of duty by the defen-dant. As a tenant, Plaintiff was certainly a foreseeable plaintiff and, had the pipe not burst, the support system would not have been rendered inoperable, allowing Lawfirm to complete its work in a timely fashion. Lawfirm's failure to do so resulted in its economic injury, thereby satisfying the damages requirement. Plaintiff also may rely on the theory of res ipsa loquitur, a legal doctrine that deals with those situations where the fact that a particular injury has occurred may itself establish a breach of duty. Plaintiff has met the essential elements by showing that the bursting of the pipe would not normally occur without negligence, that the pipe was in the defendant's sole control, and that plaintiff was free from negligence. Based upon the foregoing, defendant's motion as to the negligence claim must be denied.

To establish a prima facie case for strict liability, the following elements must be shown: (i) the existence of an absolute duty on the part of the defendant to make safe; (ii) breach of that duty; (iii) the breach of that duty was the proximate cause of plaintiff's injury; and (iv) damage to plaintiff's person or property. Since the defendant both manufactured and installed the defective pipe, it would be liable for a defect that existed when the product left its control. In this court's opinion the pipe was in a defective condition unreasonably dangerous to users. However, following the majority rule, recovery must be denied on the ground of strict liability when the sole claim is for economic loss. For this reason, defendant's motion as to the strict liability claim is granted.

Regarding the implied warranties theory of recovery, the general rule is that if a product fails to live up to the standards imposed by an implied warranty, the warranty is breached and the defendant will be liable. When a merchant who deals in a certain kind of goods sells such goods, there is an implied warranty that they are "merchantable," meaning that the goods are of a quality equal to that generally acceptable among those who deal in similar goods and are generally fit for the ordinary purposes for which such goods are used. The pipe's unfitness for its ordinary purposes has been shown by the fact of the pipe bursting and that, therefore, the warranty had to have been breached.

The implied warranty of fitness for a particular purpose arises when the seller knows or has to know: (i) the particular purpose for which the goods are required and (ii) that the buyer is relying on the seller's skill or judgment to select or furnish suitable goods. Here, Pipeco knew the purpose for the pipe as they themselves installed it. The buyer was obviously relying on Pipeco's skill in choosing whatever pipe it felt was best suited for the job, absent evidence that the buyer specified a particular pipe to be used.

The only significant issue, applicable to both implied warranties, is whether this plaintiff, not being the buyer of the pipe, can recover. The Uniform Commercial Code has given the states three alternatives on the issue of horizontal privity between plaintiff and defendant. Most states have adopted the first alternative, extending implied warranty protection to a buyer's family, household, and guests. In the instant case, Plaintiff cannot reasonably be said to fall under any of these categories and so defendant's motion as to the implied warranties claim must be denied.

75. CRIMINAL PROCEDURE

After examination of the issues raised by Harry ("H") and Wilma ("W") (discussed below), the appeals court should reverse the lower court convictions and send the case down for retrial.

H and W: The strongest issue H and W could raise on appeal concerns the ineffective assistance of their counsel, Barry Starr ("BS"). The right to effective assistance of counsel is constitutionally guaranteed under the Sixth Amendment. There is a presumption of effective assistance unless it can be shown that (i) counsel's representation was deficient for reasons other than inexperience, complexity of charges, trial tactics and the like, and that the results of the trial would have been different had there not been a deficiency; or (ii) there is a conflict of interest for counsel representing co-defendants.

Under this set of facts, the interests of H are adverse to those of W because of the existence of the written statement and the differences in culpability for each defendant. When an attorney represents co-defendants with conflicting interests, the defendant is entitled to an automatic reversal. Here, H and W's interest are conflicting and, thus, they are deserving of reversal on appeal based on a claim of ineffective assistance of counsel due to a conflict of interest.

The prosecutor committed prejudicial, reversible error in his closing statement to the jury. The Fifth Amendment, through the Fourteenth Amendment, guarantees that the defendant has a privilege against self-incrimination. Such privilege means that a defendant need not take the witness stand at trial or be asked to do so. If a defendant does not testify, the prosecutor may not bring that fact to the jury's attention because of fear of negating the presumption of innocence in the mind of the jurors. Here, the defendants, H and W, invoked their constitutional right and did not testify at trial. The prosecutor, in his closing statements, told the jury that H and W must be guilty because they did not testify. The prosecutor's statement is prejudicial and violates the defendants' constitutional rights against self-incrimination.

The judge's charge to the jury, citing the criminal code, violates the basic component of a fair trial, the presumption of innocence until proven guilty. Under the Due Process Clause, the prosecution has the burden of proving the guilt of the defendants "beyond a reasonable doubt." Except in the case of an affirmative defense, the defendant does not bear any burden to prove his innocence. It is for the State to lay down a case in which each and every element of the crime is proven so that no doubt as to the defendants' guilt fills the jury's mind.

Here, the judge's charge that fraud is "presumed" if a check is not made good within 10 days of its rejection, places the burden of proof on the defendants. This is unconstitutional because it would lead a reasonable jury to conclude that proof of guilt may be inferred from the nonaction of the defendants unless the defendants can prove otherwise. Thus, the charge to the jury violates the defendants' constitutional rights and the verdict should be reversed.

W's Issues: W was charged with having "fraudulently issued bad checks." This crime involves the obtaining of another's property by making fraudulent misrepresentations with the intent to defraud. Additionally, "bad check" legislation makes it a crime to pass false or insufficiently funded checks with the intent to defraud.

W wrote a check for $200 to the supermarket believing that her account contained a balance of $900. W's intention was to pay her grocery bill of $200. Her honest belief that there were sufficient funds to cover the check and that the supermarket would be paid the $200 negates the element of "intent to defraud." Also, because of a mistake in fact, W did not fraudulently misrepresent the validity of her check because she honestly believed that there was enough money in her account to cover it. Though W may have negligently misrepresented the validity of the check because she had a duty to keep abreast of her finances, this is not a criminal offense. Thus, on appeal, the verdict against W should be reversed because the prosecution did not prove the elements of the crime as against W.

H's Issues: W's written statement should not have been admitted into evidence. Generally, when one co-defendant makes a confession or statement, it may not be used against the other co-defendant unless: (i) all references to the other defendant are omitted; (ii) the defendant making the statement takes the stand; or (iii) it is used to rebut the claim of the testifying defendant that a nontestifying defendant's statement was obtained by coercion. Merely because the co-defendants are joined as parties to the action does not allow the admission to be brought in against the other defendant.

In this case, W and H were co-defendants, and W made a statement which implicated H. Over the objections of BS, the judge allowed W's statement into evidence. Because the above mentioned exceptions to the "non-admission" rule existed at trial, BS's objection should have been sustained. Thus, H's conviction should be reversed on appeal because it was an error to allow W's written statement into evidence without removing the portions pertaining to H.

Additionally, there may be an argument for not allowing W's written statement into the record based on the "confidential marital communications" privilege. The general rule is that either spouse has a privilege to refuse to disclose or to prevent the other spouse from disclosing confidential communications made during the marriage. In this situation, H informed W of his acts in confidence while they were husband and wife and is thus entitled to the benefit of the privilege.

Therefore, the written statement should not have been admitted into evidence because a co-defendant's admission which implicates the other defendant is not admissible and because of the confidential marital communications privilege.

76. REAL PROPERTY

Dear Attorney:

Please be advised that the undersigned has been retained for the purpose of representing Mr. Byer in the purchase of real property from your client Mr. Owens.

As you are aware, there exists a controversy between Owens and Byer as to the date of the closing. According to the contract, the closing is to take place "on or before September 1, 1986." The contract does not state that "time is of the essence." You will note that when time is not of the essence, failure to close on the date specified in the contract does not constitute a breach. The contract is still enforceable if compliance is completed within a reasonable time. The courts have generally held that one or two months is considered a reasonable time. My client has asked for an extension to September 8, 1986, in order to secure the funds needed to close this deal. Since that date is within only eight days of the contract date, I do not feel that it is unreasonable.

Though your client stated in a letter dated August 25, 1986, that "time is of the essence," this does not act to alter the terms of the contract. Since there was no new consideration passed, Owens's "time is of the essence" statement does not become a contract and is not enforceable. Understanding that your client desired to have the closing on that date in order to make payment on another parcel, he should have made his intentions known at the signing of the contract, incorporated it into the contract, or at least have given reasonable notice to Byer. Your client's response on August 25, five days prior to the closing, does not constitute sufficient notice to establish Owens's desire to make "time of the essence," especially when Owens's statement was merely in response to Byer's letter of August 20, 1986.

While my client understands that he is liable for any incidental damages caused by the delay in the closing date, he is still interested in closing the sale. Byer will have all the financing needed by September 8, and we expect you to confirm a closing for that date.

Upon examination of the deed, I have noted a number of problems which should be brought to your attention so that we may clear them up.

The metes and bounds description of the property as stated in the deed does not match the description that Byer obtained through a recent survey of the property. The discrepancy is in the measurement from Main Street to Babbling Brook. The deed which you present at closing should reflect the difference. As you know, when property abuts a body of water the owner of land is entitled to any additions to his property through accretion and is subject to any losses through erosion. Here, Babbling Brook over the years has deposited an additional 20 feet of soil. The correction should be noted in your deed. This should not affect the marketability of title.

According to the terms of the contract, Owens is to deliver "good and marketable title, free and clear of all liens and encumbrances." To be "good and marketable title" means that it must be free from reasonable doubt that there is a risk of litigation. The deed to Owens from Sellalot is signed by Sellalot but notarized by Owens. As a notary, Owens should have been aware that it is not proper for him to affix his seal to a document in which he has an interest. Owens's notary on the deed may give rise to doubt as to the validity of the transfer. However, since the title was passed in 1952 to Owens, and Owens claims this to be his residence, if there is a defect in the title by deed, Owens is still entitled to title in the property through adverse possession. This means that Owens was in possession of the land for 10 years or more under the conditions of it being open, notorious, continuous, hostile, and under claim of right.

Therefore, we request that your client produce, at closing, the proper documentation and affidavits and furnish us with a Bargain and Sale Deed with Covenants against Grantor's Acts.

Additionally, there are two easements on the premises. One is held by the prior owner, Sellalot, and the other by Powerful Electric Company.

Sellalot, upon his sale to Owens, expressly reserved his right to use a portion of the property to reach Babbling Brook. My client does not wish for this easement to continue if he is to take title to the property, as is specified in the contract.

To remove this cloud on title a number of measures may be taken. The property was transferred in 1952. The status of the easement at this point may be questionable because of abandonment or prescription. If the grantor has ceased to use the easement with intent to permanently abandon it, then the easement no longer exists. If Owens has used the property adversely to the grantor's easement over a period of 10 years or more and under the same conditions as adverse possession, the easement is extinguished. In either case, we request that the proper documentation be filed with the appropriate court and the order of said court extinguishing the easement be presented at closing.

Also, unless Sellalot owns the land adjacent to Owens's, then all he has is an easement in gross. An easement in gross is personal to the holder of the easement and cannot be assigned or devised. Therefore, if Sellalot is no longer living, the easement is terminated. If this should be the case, then we request that a certified copy of the death certificate for Sellalot be produced at closing.

If the easement is still in use by Sellalot, a release of his easement, duly recorded, must be presented at closing.

The easement to the Powerful Electric Company is also an easement in gross. Commercial easements in gross are assignable and devisable. However, my client realizes that he must take the property subject to PEC's easement.

In light of the foregoing, we respectfully request that you furnish all of the above documentation so that we may properly close in accordance with the terms of the contract.

Byer's Attorney

77. CONSTITUTIONAL LAW

The Anti-Pornography Tax Act would not be upheld if brought to court because it is in violation of the United States Constitution.

Congress has plenary power to regulate commerce among the several states. Local or state governments may regulate local aspects of interstate commerce if Congress has not legislated in that area or if local regulation is not in violation of existing federal regulations and it: (i) does not discriminate against out-of-state competition; (ii) does not require nationally uniform regulation; and (iii) does not unduly burden interstate commerce.

It is considered discriminatory against out-of-state competition to place a tax on out-of-state goods while not taxing the same goods produced in state. Here, the state legislature has placed a $.05 tax on out-of-state pornographic magazines and not on those produced in state. This tax obviously favors in-state as opposed to out-of-state publishers of pornography. On this basis, the Act is in violation of the Constitution.

A state may tax a company, foreign or domestic, which engages in local commerce, for the privilege of doing business within the state. The activity being taxed must have a substantial nexus to the taxing state, it must be fairly apportioned, it must not discriminate against interstate commerce, and it must fairly relate to services provided by the state.

In this case, the 10% tax on the gross annual revenues of publishers of child pornography is constitutionally invalid. The tax discriminates against out-of-state companies by taxing not just the revenues produced within the state but the annual gross revenues produced worldwide.

It should be noted that the government may prohibit the sale or distribution of visual depictions of sexual conduct involving children below a specific age group even though the material could not be found obscene if it did not involve children. However, this does not allow a state to impose a tax of this sort. Because the Act fails to apportion the tax based on income derived within the state, it is a violation of its taxing and spending powers.

The Act also fails because of "vagueness." The statute does not define that which is and is not "sexual activity." Failure to do so is a violation of the First Amendment right of freedom of expression. Without any guidelines to follow for its application, the Act is too vague, and, thus, unconstitutional.

The Establishment Clause prohibits government sponsorship of religious activities. A government program that is suspected of violating the Establishment Clause must pass a three-part test. First, the law must have a secular purpose. Second, the law must have a primary effect that neither advances nor inhibits religion. Third, the law must not produce excessive government entanglement with religion.

Under the Act, all revenues raised by the tax are to be applied to a program for runaway teenagers run by religious organizations. If the runaway program has a secular purpose, has a primary purpose that does not aid a religious purpose, and does not create excessive entanglement between government administrators and religious authorities, that portion of the Act will be upheld. In light of the religious organization's exclusive control over the program, the likelihood of the promotion of religion within the program is great. A better alternative would be for the government to organize its own teenage runaway program so as not to run afoul of the constitutional guarantees of separation of church and state.

Therefore, the Act will not withstand challenge on constitutional grounds because it is discriminatory on its face and in its application; it unconstitutionally taxes corporations engaging in business within the state; and it violates the constitutional policy of separation of church and state.

78. TORTS

Mrs. Jones ("P") may recover against her husband, Mr. Jones ("J"), if she can show that he was negligent in his actions. To do this, she must prove that J owed her a duty of care, that he breached that duty, and that his breach was the proximate cause for her injuries.

Traditionally, a husband and wife could not sue one another under intra-familial tort immunity. However, today most jurisdictions have eliminated the immunity as it pertains to suits for personal injuries. Thus, P is free to sue her husband for her alleged injuries.

J violated a regulatory rule and a statute. His violation of the regulatory rule, driving without a license, does not give rise to negligence per se. It is not a valid presumption to say that a person was driving negligently simply because he did not possess a license. To do so would mean that the inverse must also be true; everyone who has a license does not drive negligently. Thus, violation of this regulation does not give rise to a presumption of negligence. Violating the statute against stopping a vehicle on the highway, however, would be held by a majority of courts as negligence per se. Other jurisdictions hold that violation of a statute is either a presumption of a duty and breach thereof or it constitutes merely prima facie evidence of negligence. Even in the absence of the statute, the driver of an automobile owes a duty to his passengers to exercise reasonable care in the active operation of his automobile. According to the facts in this case, J entered onto the turnpike and into the speed lane even though he knew or should have known that his car was low on gas. Additionally, when the car ran out of gas, he left it on the highway, in the speed lane, with P sleeping inside. It is a question of fact for the jury to determine whether such acts by J were a breach of his duties. Under these facts, a jury would most likely find that J breached his duty of care. This now leads to the next element of the negligence case: causation.

Factual causation is proven by using either the "but for" or "substantial factor" test. Using the "but for" test, a plaintiff must show that "but for" the first act of the defendant the second act would not have occurred. Under the "substantial factor" test, when there is more than one cause for a plaintiff's injury, defendant will be found negligent if his conduct was a "substantial factor" in causing the injury.

In this case, "but for" (i) J's failure to monitor his fuel gauge and take proper actions to prevent it from running out of fuel; (ii) his taking the risk of bringing his car, which was dangerously low on fuel, onto the speed lane of a turnpike; and (iii) leaving it there with his wife sleeping inside when it subsequently ran out of fuel, the resulting injuries would not have occurred.

In the alternative, were J's actions a "substantial factor" in causing W's injuries? Given these facts, it seems reasonable to believe that a jury would find that J's actions were the factual cause for W's injuries.

The next issue to determine is whether J's actions were the proximate cause of plaintiff's injuries. It may be argued that J's actions were only an indirect cause of P's injuries because Trooper Smith's ("S") failure to use his warning flashers is an intervening force in the causal chain. However, rescuers are deemed to be foreseeable intervening forces and a defendant is liable for their negligence. Thus, S's appearance on the scene as a rescuer does not take away liability from J for P's injuries.

P claims that she suffered from J's negligent infliction of emotional distress due to a miscarriage which she claims was caused by the accident. A majority of courts hold that there is no duty of care to avoid causing emotional distress to another unless the emotional distress was brought about by physical injury to the plaintiff or if the plaintiff was within the "zone of danger" of the defendant's negligent conduct. It would appear that P, by being in the car, was within the "zone of danger." The majority of jurisdictions also require that there be some sort of physical injury or that a physical injury be produced from the shock in order for there to be recovery. However, it is not evident that P's miscarriage was caused by the accident. This is a question of fact to be determined by the jury after hearing the facts and the opinions of experts in the field. That the miscarriage occurred a month after the accident leads to some doubt as to the extent that the accident caused the miscarriage. If the accident was not the cause for the miscarriage, J will not be liable for P's claim of emotional distress.

S may recover some of his damages against J even though he himself was negligent in not using his warning flashers while parked on the turnpike because J's negligence was still a proximate cause of the accident. However, S's recovery against J in comparative negligence jurisdictions will be reduced by the percentage of fault attributable to S.

79. CRIMINAL PROCEDURE

Double jeopardy: The Constitution prohibits one from being tried or "put in jeopardy" for the same offense more than once. Simply, double jeopardy is the exposure to two trials for the same substantive offense.

Two crimes do not constitute the same offense for purposes of double jeopardy if **each** crime requires proof of an additional fact that the other crime does not require. "Attempting to cause or knowingly causing bodily injury to another" does **not** contain the same elements as "committing an act of sexual contact with a victim who is less than 13 years old." There is no requirement for a simple assault conviction that the "touching" be sexual and there is no requirement contained in sexual assault that the touching result, or be intended to result, in bodily injury. (*Note:* Defendant's plea of guilty to the simple assault has the same effect as a trial on the merits.)

Thus, Defendant will not be successful on the double jeopardy issue. The doctrine of merger also does not apply. Merger occurs when a lesser offense contains only elements of that contained in a greater offense. Such merger precludes a trial for both offenses. Since the two charges of simple assault and sexual assault contain differing elements, the merger doctrine does not apply.

Defendant's right to confront witnesses: Defendant has a constitutional right to confront adverse witnesses. The issue arises as to whether defendant was denied his constitutional right to confront witnesses against him when he was not present during the testimony of Pureheart in chambers.

Defendant in fact was afforded the right of cross-examination although not in person, but through his lawyer. Such a manner of cross-examination is proper where the purpose is to protect societal concerns.

Under the facts, it was proper for Pureheart, a three-year-old child, to be "examined" outside of the courtroom and only in the presence of the judge, the prosecutor, and defense counsel. The facts show that if such procedure were not followed, Pureheart would have suffered irreparable psychological damage. In addition, the presentation of the interview on videotape is sufficient to allow the jury, as trier of fact, to evaluate Pureheart's testimony in terms of demeanor so they can assess truthfulness and competence. There is an issue of the competence of a three-year-old child and her ability to understand the need to tell the truth.

Rejection of Defendant's psychiatrist: The court improperly excluded evidence offered to show that Defendant was psychologically incapable of committing sexual assault, on "ultimate issue" grounds. It was highly relevant evidence that was more probative than prejudicial. The exclusion of evidence based on ultimate issue grounds properly applies only where mental capacity is the ultimate issue, as when the defense of insanity is raised. Since sanity is not an issue, evidence from Defendant's psychiatrist on his psychological incapability was improperly excluded.

Admittance of former plea of guilty: Evidence of Defendant's plea of guilty is more prejudicial than probative. Since the conviction was for acts arising out of the same criminal conduct in issue at trial, it was clearly prejudicial. (*Note:* Where a defendant takes the stand, thus putting his character in issue, prior convictions may be admissible to rebut character. Such is not the case here.)

Prosecutor's summation: The duty of a prosecutor is to present the case, not to advise the jury as to his personal opinions. In addition, it is improper for the prosecutor to personally attack the defendant by calling him names. Such conduct was clearly prejudicial.

Consecutive sentencing: For double jeopardy reasons, consecutive sentencing would be improper only if the simple assault were a lesser included offense of sexual assault. Since the two charges do not contain the same elements and, specifically, since simple assault does not have the same elements as sexual assault, such sentencing is not improper.

80. CONTRACTS

To: Seller-Client
From: Attorney
Dear Seller,

The following is my opinion concerning your legal position with respect to your exposure to liability in the action for indemnification brought against you by Starco and Clearvu.

The main issue to discuss is whether your indemnification liability extends to Clearvu. Paragraph 10(c) is the clause that is called into question with respect to any liability you may have. Specifically paragraph 10(c) states that you will indemnify and hold Starco harmless with respect to any liabilities it may have arising out of your manufacture of Plexiglas display cases, including any liability incurred by Starco from its sale of such goods. This paragraph is clear on your indemnification liability to *Starco*. Paragraph 13 permitted Starco to direct you to deliver the bill of sale for the assets to any Starco subsidiary designated by Starco which raises the issue of whether your liability for indemnification is extended to the subsidiary. It is my opinion that your liability would *not* be extended to a Starco subsidiary based on the clear meaning of this paragraph. Paragraph 13 simply authorized Starco to direct you to *deliver* the bill of sale to an appointed subsidiary, it did *not* extend paragraph 10(c) to encompass indemnification liability to anyone other than Starco.

In addition, there is no evidence that Clearvu was intended as a beneficiary of the contract entered into between yourself and Starco. Oral evidence will be inadmissible to alter the terms of the otherwise clear contract language.

Clearvu is a separate legal entity from Starco. Thus, based on the clear meaning of paragraph 10(c), you do not owe them any indemnification.

Starco has not incurred any liability with respect to the sale to VIP and thus is not entitled to indemnification from you. Even though Clearvu had Starco join in the indemnification action against you, this was done simply because Clearvu by itself has no viable action against you.

If the court should find that Clearvu is entitled to indemnification from you, we still have meritorious defenses to the action. First, we can argue that liability did not arise out of the manufacture of Plexiglas, but by the negligent packaging by Clearvu. In rebuttal to Clearvu arguing that paragraph 10(c) applies to "any liability incurred by . . ." we would claim that paragraph 10(c) was intended to mean that you would be liable only for damages flowing from manufacture of the cases. Since the U.C.C. states that a writing that was intended to be the final expression of the parties cannot be contradicted or supplemented by prior or contemporaneous statements or writings but will allow evidence to help clear up any ambiguity, we will argue that "any liability" is ambiguous.

As a last resort we will claim that Clearvu was grossly negligent so as to invoke the final sentence of paragraph 10(c) (excluding liability for gross negligence). "Gross negligence" is basically a conscious or reckless form of negligence. We would need to show that Clearvu knew when it packaged the display cases that they would be cracked and scratched when delivered.

The 180-day limitation of your liability applies only to paragraphs 10(a) and (b). Unless we can show that there was a mutual mistake in not including 10(c), the limitation will not be helpful to you.

If we are unable to show gross negligence and our other defenses are not successful, then we must examine the damages to determine only those that were foreseeable, since you would only be liable for foreseeable damages. We would argue that VIP's loss of business was not foreseeable, and the damages should be limited to VIP's good faith cover (*i.e.,* the costs of buying replacement display cases).

81. REAL PROPERTY

Bank v. Mr. Spender: Mr. Spender is the sole debtor in the amount of $10,000 with Bullion Bank as creditor.

Assuming that Mr. Spender has no assets or income to satisfy his loan obligation, there is an issue of whether the bank may look to Greenacre to satisfy the amount outstanding.

Even though the loan application stated that the loan was for a down payment on Greenacre, Mr. Spender waited more than two months to enter into a contract to purchase Greenacre. In addition, only $5,000 was used as a down payment. There is an issue whether the money borrowed from Bullion Bank was legally connected to Greenacre.

The important issue is that even if the loan is legally connected to the property, Mr. Spender is not the title owner of Greenacre. The fact that Mr. Spender paid for the property does not change this.

Bank v. Mrs. Spender: However, if it can be shown that Mrs. Spender's name was used solely to defraud the bank, the bank may be able to attach a lien on the property. This result is unlikely to be reached at law, simply because the facts are that Mrs. Spender has legal title to Greenacre and Mr. Spender is the sole debtor on the loan.

Bank v. Prosperity Mortgage Company: Prosperity Mortgage Company is not subject to any action by Bank since there was no lien against Mrs. Spender or Greenacre at the time of giving the mortgage to Mrs. Spender. Thus, Prosperity had no knowledge of any impediments on the property. Additionally, Prosperity was not required to search the judgment records or lien records as against anyone other than Mrs. Spender, including Mr. Spender. Therefore, Prosperity had no actual, constructive, or inquiry notice of the previously recorded judgment/lien placed on Greenacre.

Bank v. Ms. View: As an attorney, Ms. View's primary obligation is to represent her client's best interests. Ms. View only suggested the idea of putting the property in Mrs. Spender's name, she did not actively engage in a fraudulent or deceptive practice.

82. TORTS

Al Kaholl v. Private University: A claim can be brought against Private University, alleging its negligence for failure to properly secure the stadium and enforce its "no alcoholic beverages" policy in the stadium.

For Kaholl to recover he must show that he is a foreseeable plaintiff, that the defendant owed him a duty, that this duty was breached, and that such breach was the proximate cause of his injuries.

Private University had the duty to protect their students from the unreasonable risk created by the consumption of alcohol at games. By establishing security checks for this purpose, they affirmatively undertook this duty.

The University is vicariously liable for the actions of its security officers under a theory of respondeat superior, as the officers were acting within the scope of their employment when they were working during the football game. The security personnel themselves could be sued in negligence as well, for their failure to properly inspect all containers at the gate, specifically Kaholl's container. They were negligent in keeping alcoholic beverages out of the stadium and protecting individuals like Kaholl from having accidents of the sort that occurred when Kaholl became intoxicated.

In addition, a claim of negligence can be brought directly against the officer Kaholl had an encounter with while acting rowdy. Aside from the security personnel's job of inspecting containers at the gates, they also had a duty to escort visibly intoxicated people from the stadium. If this security guard would have escorted Kaholl from the stadium, Kaholl would not have climbed on the wall and injured himself.

There is also an issue of whether the University was negligent in not having gates or bars to prevent persons from being able to jump over the wall only to land on concrete steps 20 feet below. Al Kaholl clearly would not have been injured had the University and its security personnel not been negligent.

Further, the University and its security personnel would also be liable for Kaholl's paralysis. Even though the medical treatment was an intervening act, it was not a superseding, intervening act that will relieve the original tortfeasors (University and security personnel) for aggravation of Kaholl's injuries. Subsequent medical malpractice-aggravation of an injury is considered to be foreseeable. An intervening foreseeable action will not cut off the initial tortfeasors' liability; thus, liability would extend to the full range of Kaholl's injuries.

Defenses the University and its security personnel may assert: If contributory negligence applies in this jurisdiction, Kaholl's negligence could bar his action against the University and the security personnel. If comparative negligence controls, then his negligence would only go to reduce his recovery by his percentage fault.

Another defense that may be asserted against Kaholl is that he assumed the risk of harm when he jumped over the wall. Assumption of risk is established when it can be shown that the plaintiff voluntarily undertook the risk of harm and placed himself in danger. It may be difficult to prove he voluntarily assumed any risk due to his intoxication.

Kaholl v. Emergency Room Physician: Kaholl would have a claim for medical malpractice against the doctor. The facts are clear that he was in an obviously intoxicated state at the time of injury and thus at the time of his arrival in the emergency room. The physician will be held to the standard of care applicable to such a doctor in the locale of his practice. Since the antibiotic had an adverse effect on Kaholl due to his intoxicated state, the physician acted negligently in administering the drug that resulted in Kaholl's paralysis if doctors in the locale would not have administered the antibiotic knowing that Kaholl was intoxicated.

Kaholl v. Three Drug Manufacturers: Strict products liability would be the theory Kaholl should use for recovery against the three drug manufacturers. If the manufacturers created an unreasonably dangerous drug and the cost/utility of making the product safe was feasible, then the manufacturers would be strictly liable to the recipient of the drug for any injuries.

This drug should have been properly labeled with a warning of possible side effects to an intoxicated individual.

As to which drug manufacturer would be liable to Kaholl, Kaholl can proceed against all three on a market-share liability theory whereby each defendant would contribute to the damage award according to the percentage of their market share. If possible, the defendants could try to show that they individually were not liable for plaintiff's injuries and thus would not have to share liability under the market-share liability theory.

83. CONSTITUTIONAL LAW

Boozine's essential argument is that Eden's statute, as applied, imposes an impermissible burden on interstate commerce under the Commerce Clause of the Constitution.

The free flow of goods without barriers is part of the plan to provide a healthy national economy.

Although the statute on its face purports to regulate only in-state transportation and to promote pricing fairness to in-state purchasers, the statute as applied impermissibly proscribes and punishes out-of-state competition. Regardless of whether the competitor was subject to Eden licensing, Eden is interfering with out-of-state conduct by those who also do an in-state business.

Eden has the constitutional power under the Twenty-First Amendment to regulate alcohol within its borders. The Eden statute has not sought solely to regulate alcohol within the state, but has unreasonably interfered with interstate commerce.

Eden's interests to protect fair pricing within the state is outweighed by other states' rights to compete and the national interest in unimpeded interstate commerce.

The Eden statute also might deny Boozine equal protection under the law, as is granted by the Fourteenth Amendment. When states classify according to economic regulation, the "rational basis" test is applied. Any statute that is reasonably related to furthering a legitimate state interest would survive this test. The Eden statute classifies out-of-state distillers and treats them differently than in-state distillers. Since this is an economic classification, the rational basis test would apply. Eden could show a legitimate interest in controlling the flow of alcohol. However, if Boozine could show that Eden is not interested in controlling consumption, but is interested in controlling prices, then a non-legitimate state interest would be shown.

The events of December show that the statute with which Boozine partially complied (by maintaining its filed price of $9.00 within Eden) is actually self-defeating. Since, the apparent purpose of the statute was to maintain low prices for the benefit of Eden buyers, which in reality had the opposite effect (maintaining the $9.00/liter price rather than the $7.50/liter price), Boozine can argue that the statute is *not* rationally related to the legitimate state interest of assuring fair or low prices to in-state buyers. This argument, however, will probably be unsuccessful, because the Equal Protection Clause in cases such as this, does not require the best law, but only a rational law, and the law here is probably rational.

84. CRIMINAL LAW; CRIMINAL PROCEDURE

Memorandum of Law
To: Senior Equity Partner
From: Junior Associate
Re: Paul, his rights, claims, defenses, and assertions

CRIMES

The crimes Paul can be charged with are larceny, burglary, conspiracy to commit burglary, conspiracy to commit larceny, and receipt of stolen property. It will be most difficult to overcome the burglary and conspiracy charges, with respect to Paul, even though we can put forth challenges based on his mental state and possible lack of mental capacity.

A solicitation charge against Paul will not be tenable since solicitation punishes asking another to commit an unlawful act and Paul did not ask anyone to burglarize the house. In any event, the crime of solicitation merges into the crime of conspiracy after the party solicited agrees to act.

Paul will be charged with conspiracy. At common law, a conspiracy was defined as a combination or agreement between two or more persons to accomplish some criminal or unlawful purpose, or to accomplish some lawful purpose by criminal or unlawful means. There must be an intent to enter into the agreement which is the subject of the conspiracy.

Paul can also be charged with the crime of burglary, which is the breaking and entering of a dwelling house of another at night with the intent of committing a felony or larceny therein. When Paul agreed to act with Tony to get money, he agreed to become a participant in a burglary. The definition of burglary has been expanded in most states to include daytime breaking and entering. Here, all of the elements of a burglary exist: Tony broke into and entered the residence. The intent of the parties (to steal money) is the larceny (the taking and aspiration of property from the possession of another person, without consent or with consent obtained by fraud, with the intent to steal or permanently deprive the owner).

Furthermore, a co-conspirator can be charged with the underlying crime where the act committed by a confederate or partner was a reasonable and foreseeable event during the course of the conspiracy. The nature of Paul's guilt will be analyzed as an accomplice; *i.e.,* one who works with and takes part in the performance of the criminal act.

Paul can also be charged with the receipt of stolen property; *i.e.,* the credit cards and the cash. It is obvious from the facts and from Paul's own statements that he knew that these items were stolen and not rightfully in his possession.

The finders of fact must determine whether Paul had the requisite state of mind required for conspiracy. It is questionable whether Paul had the necessary mental state, or state of mind, to perform and complete the crimes with which he has been charged. Paul can raise both the insanity and diminished capacity defenses.

According to our information, Paul is slightly retarded. We could argue that Paul had a disease of the mind, which caused a defect of reason, such that he lacked the ability at the time of his actions to either know the wrongfulness of his actions or understand the nature and quality of his actions (the *M'Naughten* rule). The diminished capacity defense applies where the defendant may assert that as a result of a mental defect (neurosis, obsessive compulsiveness, or dependent personality) short of insanity, he did not have the particular mental state (purpose, knowledge, recklessness, or negligence) required for the crime charged.

If Paul is proven to have either been insane or suffering from diminished capacity, it would eliminate the element of intent needed for him to be found guilty of the crimes charged. It is worth repeating that Paul was regarded as slightly retarded, he was allowed to attend special classes at school and take part in most traditional activities. As such, he most likely knew the resultant consequences of his actions, which mitigate his defense of insanity and diminished capacity.

Paul might be able to claim withdrawal as a defense, at least as to the larceny charge. Since the crime of conspiracy is complete upon the agreement, most states do not recognize withdrawal as a defense to conspiracy. However, a co-conspirator can withdraw from the conspiracy to avoid liability for the target crime and other crimes committed in furtherance of the conspiracy. To withdraw, the conspirator must perform an act that notifies the other members of the conspiracy of the withdrawal at a time when the other members have an opportunity to abandon their plan. Here, Paul attempted to leave the house after breaking in, but before the larceny was committed. It is unclear whether he made his intention known to Tony. If Paul did inform Tony, this may be sufficient for withdrawal, so Paul will not be liable for the subsequent larceny. He would still be liable for the burglary, however, because the crime of burglary is complete upon the breaking, and Paul's withdrawal came after the breaking.

SEARCHES

With respect to the locker search and the gym bag found therein, a motion should be made to suppress its introduction, since no warrant was obtained. However, it has been held that school searches are valid without a warrant if conducted by school officials and reasonable grounds exist for the search.

The Fourth Amendment to the United States Constitution provides that all persons are entitled to be free from unreasonable searches and seizures. A search is unreasonable when it is not based on probable cause. Probable cause is present when a reasonable person, supplied with information, would believe that an illegal act has occurred. Ordinarily, a warrant for the search must be obtained from a neutral and detached magistrate reviewing the facts to determine if probable cause exists. The warrant should list the time to search, the place to search, and all specifics with respect to the search. Here, the police did not obtain a warrant before having the principal search Paul's locker. As stated above, school searches do not require a warrant.

Normally, school officials have the right to search the lockers of students to enforce safety provisions within the school and to make the area safe.

The general rule is that locker searches can take place only where reasonable suspicion exists that a crime or violation of safety rules exists. Here no violation of school rules was alleged. However, the facts suggest that the principal had a legitimate concern for safety, given the fact that Paul's school ID was found at the scene of a burglary. Thus, the warrantless search should be challenged, but it is doubtful that the challenge will be successful.

CONFESSIONS

We should move to suppress Paul's confession on grounds that Paul did not knowingly and voluntarily waive his rights, but it is doubtful that this will be successful.

Once a defendant is in custody, he must be given his so-called *Miranda* warnings; a confession made in response to interrogation by the police while a defendant is in custody will be not be admissible into evidence unless the defendant was given *Miranda* warnings and knowingly and voluntarily waived his right to remain silent and right to counsel. We should argue that as a result of Paul's age and slight retardation, his waiver was neither voluntary nor intelligent. However, we are not likely to succeed in this argument for two reasons. First and foremost, although Paul was in custody at the time of the confession, there was no interrogation—Paul blurted out his confession spontaneously—and so *Miranda* is inapplicable. Even if the confession were made in response to interrogation, Paul might still be found to have voluntarily and intelligently waived his rights. The decision is made on a case-by-case basis, but the Supreme Court has found that juveniles can waive their rights without parents or counsel [Fare v. Michael C., 442 U.S. 707 (1979)], and even severe mental illness does not make a waiver involuntary [Colorado v. Connelly, 479 U.S. 157 (1986)].

CONCLUSION

We have little chance of having Paul's confession or the materials found in his locker excluded from evidence.

85. CONTRACTS

To: Karen Client

Re: The contractual breach associated with the building of your new home.

I am writing in response to your request for information regarding your contract for the building of a one family house and the associated breach by the contractor.

As you are well aware, you entered into a binding contract for the erection of a house. This contract is not for the sale of goods, but rather for the performance of a service, and so the Uniform Commercial Code does not apply to your situation. Instead, this contract will be enforced and supported based on issues of equity, fairness, and detrimental reliance. As you know, a contract is an agreement between two or more parties to act, or perform a service, which they are otherwise not obligated to perform. It is an agreement which the law will enforce.

The March 2, 1989, contract that you and Contractor signed lists the house, the price, the specifications, and the date the residence is expected to be completed. Normally, the date of completion is not specifically listed on building contracts, but here it was, making it an essential part of the contract. Any deviation from that time or date would result in a contractual breach.

The contract had a completion date of May 30. On April 2, the job superintendent suffered his eighth heart attack and died. Contractor notified you of the job superintendent's death and that he, Contractor, would not be able to complete the job on the date specified in the contract. Contractor hereby notified you that he was breaching the contract with you. As such, you were correct in believing that the contract was breached on the date of notification rather than having to wait until May 30. On April 3, you rightfully fired Contractor.

The house was to be built at a cost of $1 million. When the job was stopped, the house was not yet completed. When Contractor was fired he submitted a bill for $600,000, including $200,000 for Taper. Taper was hired by Contractor, and approved by you, to put up the frame and sheetrock on the house.

After you fired Contractor, you contracted with Expensive Construction Co. to finish the house for an agreed price of $1.1 million. This, as you know, was only for the charge of completion of the project already under construction. Your question, as I understand it, is who must be paid under the various contracts.

First, Contractor was not excused from performing as per the contract due to the death of the job superintendent. Valid excuses would include: completion was impossible; a mutual mistake in the contract; or frustration of purpose; *e.g.,* a tornado destroyed your home and the entire area. It was not impossible for the contractor to continue performance of the job. He could have, and should have, hired a new job superintendent to supervise and complete the job. The contractor had notice of his employee's poor health by virtue of the fact that he had already suffered seven prior heart attacks. This health condition is something which should have been considered by Contractor prior to his agreeing to take the job with the specified completion date.

Obviously, you do not want to pay the $600,000 to Contractor in addition to the $1.1 million to the new builder. Accordingly, we need to look at the reasonableness and validity of the $600,000 claim. This claim is for the work done by Contractor as well as Taper. Taper did not contract with you to do the job, nor were you his supervisor on the job. However, if no payment is made to Contractor, Taper might sue you for the value of the services he performed for your benefit. He would most likely not be successful in this pursuit, since he was only an incidental third-party beneficiary of the contract between you and Contractor. You were the intended third-party beneficiary in the contract between Taper and Contractor. In the unlikely event you pay Taper, his payment amount should be deducted from any figure paid to Contractor. I seriously doubt that you can or will be held liable for the fee to be paid to Taper.

The $600,000 figure for a partially completed house is possibly too high. The contract was breached by Contractor, and the basic remedial goal is to put the nonbreaching party in as good a position as if the contract had been performed by virtue of the partially completed house. Thus, we need to figure out the value of the benefit conferred on you by Contractor and hold you responsible for only this figure and no more. The amount of the benefit is termed quantum meruit, which can be established as being at least $200,000, the cost of the framing and sheetrocking.

Until a detailed itemization of the expenses incurred by the contractor can be established, you should make no payment to Contractor over the $200,000.

In any event, you can maintain an action for contractual breach against Contractor. Contractor's failure to perform as directed cost you money. Contractor can be shown to be responsible for all costs over $1 million, the original contractor price.

As always, the basic goal is to put the nonbreaching party into as good a position as if the contract had been performed. If there had not been a contract breach, then there would have been no charges over $1 million, the maximum amount you should have had to spend for your home. All sums over $1 million that need to be paid should be paid by Contractor, the party responsible for the additional charges. Virtually all courts would agree with this.

If you would like to initiate legal proceedings over this matter, please feel free to contact me at the phone number indicated on my letterhead.

86. TORTS

Memo to Judge X

Re: Theory of liability and possible defenses of the fathers of both Brenda and Jody in the case at bar.

This case deals with the liability of the fathers of Brenda and Jody, two five-year-old girls who were hurt when a toy they were playing with exploded. The toy, which was given to Brenda for her birthday by Jody, John's daughter, was an edition of "Barbie's and Freddie's Real Life Hawaiian Volcano Kit." This kit, which was purchased by John as Jody's gift for Brenda, stated on the box that the toy should not be used by children under the age of five. The instructions also contained information which stated that the kit contained volatile liquids that should not be shaken prior to their use, since such activity could cause a major explosion. There was an explosion and the girls were injured.

The available theories on which you can find liability in this case are based on the negligence and fault of the fathers.

Hank, Brenda's father, will be liable to both Brenda and Jody for their injuries.

Jody was an invited guest to the party, and as such is deemed a licensee. A licensee is one who enters property with permission, which can be revoked at anytime, *i.e.,* a social guest. Hank had a duty to protect all licensees against concealed dangerous conditions he was or should have been alerted to, including the volatility of the volcano kit. He breached this duty and his carelessness was the cause in fact for Jody's disfigurement. Thus, he is liable to Jody.

Hank is also liable to both girls for negligent supervision. He had a duty to observe all the children who came to his daughter's party. Not only did he not keep a proper vigil, but he also failed to read the instructions on the toys. A responsible, prudent adult charged with the care of five-year-old children certainly would have read and followed the instructions of a dangerous toy like a volcano kit. Since Hank did not safeguard the children from the reasonable foreseeable harm, he is liable to both Brenda and Jody.

Along the same vein, Hank was also negligent by not watching his 17-month-old son, especially in light of the dangerous nature of the volcano kit.

Hank can raise several defenses on his own behalf, including parent-child immunity. The traditional view is that this immunity insulates a parent from any claims his child might raise against the parent, based upon a breach of a duty the parent owes to that child. This defense can be raised with respect to Brenda, but not Jody, since she is not Hank's daughter. The defense will probably fail, however, because the current trend is to hold parents responsible for the injuries to their children as a result of the parents' negligence.

Hank might also assert as a defense that his 17-month-old son's playing with the chemicals was an unforeseen event. An unforeseeable event, causing injury, cuts off liability stemming from the event. In this case, however, the intervening cause was clearly foreseeable. It is obvious that a small child's curiosity will cause him to play with things left around the house. Thus, since it was foreseeable that the infant permitted to roam unsupervised would get into the volcano kit, the unforeseeable intervening cause defense will fail.

Hank may also assert that his conduct of answering the telephone was reasonable. A party acting reasonably under the circumstances will not be liable. This defense should fail, inasmuch as it was unreasonable to leave the children unattended in the presence of a dangerous volcano kit. It is not unreasonable to expect Hank to remove the kit before he answered the telephone.

Hank can raise the defense of contribution and indemnification from John, Jody's father. If Hank is successful, the amount of money he would be required to pay in damages to Brenda and Jody would be reduced by John's equitable liability. Contribution and indemnification are not real defenses, but rather are methods of sharing liability.

As alluded to, John, the purchaser of the toy, may be liable to Jody and Brenda. A reasonable and prudent person would think about the nature of a volcano kit, the possible consequences of its use, and the fact that the girls were under the manufacturer's age recommendations. By purchasing such a toy, it should have been foreseeable to John that improper use could cause injury.

John may be found liable for the injuries to Jody based on the legal duty to take care of his child. While it is true that Jody was in Hank's zone of control at the time of the injury, and not in John's control, John is not absolved of responsibility to his daughter. It was foreseeable that injury would occur following use of the volcano kit. The toy was highly dangerous and should not have been purchased for use by the children.

John can raise the defense of parent-child immunity with respect to the injuries sustained by his daughter, but he will be unsuccessful because, as was stated earlier, there is no parent-child immunity.

John's defense of intervening cause may be availing, since the baby playing with the test tubes filled with chemicals was not clearly foreseeable to him. It was also not foreseeable to John that Hank would not watch the children or read the instructions or would fail to observe warning labels with respect to the usage of the kit.

CONCLUSION

Your Honor, many of the issues I have presented are questions that can only be resolved by a finder of fact. Thus, I respectfully submit that a trial should be held. I will provide you with any additional research that you desire.

87. REAL PROPERTY
MEMORANDUM
To: Mr. Lestor

As per your request, this memorandum outlines the legal rights and possible liabilities regarding the dwelling originally leased to Leslie Lost on January 1, 1981.

The property was rented to Leslie Lost by a lease dated January 1, 1981 (hereafter "Lease") for a period of five years at a rate of $900 per month. The lease contained an option to renew for an additional five-year period with rent to remain at $900 per month. The lease was scheduled to expire on midnight December 31, 1985. Ms. Lost paid rent on January 1, 1986.

The initial issue is whether Lost's action constituted a renewal of the lease. Under the holdover doctrine, when a tenant continues in possession after the termination of her right to possession, the landlord has two choices of action: eviction or creation of a periodic tenancy. Under eviction, the landlord may treat the holdover tenant as a trespasser and evict her under an unlawful detainer statute.

Since you, as landlord, accepted the rent presented by Lost on January 1, 1986, it appears that you waived the eviction and created a periodic tenancy. Generally, in a holdover situation, the terms and conditions of the expired tenancy (*i.e.,* rent, covenants, etc.) apply to the new tenancy. If the original lease term was for a year or more, as here, where the lease was for five years, a year-to-year tenancy results from holding over. While it could be argued that Lost's attempt to renew the lease in April created a month-to-month tenancy, the law does not appear to take the tenant's intent four months after the creation of the new tenancy into account.

A question still exists as to whether the holding over constituted a renewal of the lease for the full five-year extension period. Differences of opinion surround the question whether a tenant's act of holding over and paying rent amounts to an election to renew or extend in cases where the clause in the lease does not specify the manner in which she shall elect. The terms of renewal of the lease are unknown.

The general principle is that the lessee must reasonably manifest her election; the difference concerns whether holding over meets the test. As Ms. Lost did not reasonably manifest an election to renew and actually asked for a renewal of the lease in April, 1986, for a period of one year (less than the stated five years), it appears that Lost did not renew the Lease according to its terms. In some instances it has been determined that accepting any payments after the lease expires automatically renews the lease at the same rate and provisions as existed in the prior lease. Here, however, the evidence supports the conclusion that Lost did not intend to renew the lease in the proper fashion and for the requisite time.

Another issue exists as to the breach of the lease by Lost when she paid her April rent on April 30. The lease stated that if the rent was not made timely, by the seventh day of the month, Lost would be in violation of her agreement and in default. Thus, Lost was in default.

At common law, a breach (*i.e.,* failure of the tenant to pay rent) resulted only in a cause of action for money damages. The breach neither terminates the landlord-tenant relationship (the lease) nor gives rise to a right to terminate. However, if the lease grants a nonbreaching party the right to terminate upon breach, such a forfeiture or termination clause is recognized. While virtually all modern leases give the landlord such a right, it is unclear whether your lease included such a termination clause.

Also, under unlawful detainer statutes enacted in most states, a landlord may terminate the leasehold interest of his tenant for the tenant's failure to pay rent. If the lease had a forfeiture clause or was in a state with an unlawful detainer statute, you, as landlord, would have an action for eviction.

The final issue involves Lost's attempt to purchase the house after you rejected the one-year renewal and notified Lost that she had 30 days to vacate the property. Leases frequently grant purchase options for only a stated period. If the lease does not limit the time when the option may be exercised, it endures during the term of the lease, plus any extensions or renewals.

Here the question is whether the Lease was still in existence after you gave the 30-day notice to vacate. It appears it still is. As noted previously, in a holdover situation, the terms and conditions of the expired tenancy apply to the new tenancy. This new tenancy does not end upon notice of eviction, but the eviction itself. Thus, the lease had not terminated as of the day Lost attempted to pick up the purchase option on the dwelling property and you were incorrect in refusing to sell.

88. REAL PROPERTY

Dear Ms. Seezun:

You requested an analysis of your rights and liabilities. You have a remedy with respect to all three parties involved in this series of transactions.

There was a valid contract of sale with Dee Feezence ("DF"). The issue is whether DF has breached, because she has not yet failed to make the payments called for by the contract. We are now in late February and the first $40,000 is due March 1. The contract does not say that full payment is a condition precedent to delivery of the deed, but this condition can be implied from the fact that both parties entered into an escrow agreement containing those exact terms. It would have been pointless to have an escrow if DF could have paid after accepting the deed. When DF accepted delivery of the deed, without concurrently paying in full, she broke the implied condition. This places her in breach.

The remedy available is damages (an action for the price) in an amount calculated to give you the benefit of the bargain. While this is usually stated as the difference between the contract price, and the market value of the land on the date of the breach, this method only works where the vendor is the breaching party. Where the purchaser breaches, the correct measure is the contract price ($100,000, less what has already been received ($20,000), *i.e.,* $80,000. In effect, specific performance is granted to the seller.

Another alternative is to rescind the contract and petition for specific restitution. Under this theory, DF would return the land and you would return the $20,000 down payment. This is preferable to a damages action because the value of the land is higher than the contract price.

You may also proceed against Barry Sterr ("BS"), the escrow agent, under a tort theory. BS is liable for negligence because he failed to perform his duties with reasonable skill and care under the circumstances. His total disregard of your instructions may amount to willfulness or recklessness, subjecting him to liability for exemplary or punitive damages, as well as consequential damages.

I advise that both DF and BS be sued. Thus, they will be jointly and severally liable and you will have a greater likelihood of recovering a judgment.

Bonnie Fyde's ("BF") demand that you vacate your home is without basis in law. The issue is who has superior title to the property. For a deed to convey title it must be properly delivered. Delivery is primarily a question of the intent of the grantor. Here your intent is clearly expressed by the instructions you gave to BS. Since BS did not comply with those conditions, the delivery was defective and title did not pass to DF. Therefore, as between yourself and DF your interest is superior.

Your rights are also superior to BF's. The recording acts in the majority of states protect a subsequent bona fide purchaser. The purchaser must have purchased for value, in good faith, and without notice of prior adverse conveyances.

Notice may be actual or constructive (*e.g.,* imputed from the records or imputed from the appearance or possession of the land). Where possession is unexplained by the record, the purchaser is obligated to make an inquiry and is charged with the knowledge she would have obtained. Since you were in possession of the home at the time BF purchased the property, she had notice and cannot be a bona fide purchaser.

BF may claim that the recording by DF raises a presumption of proper delivery of the deed. The presumption, however, may be rebutted by a showing that the conditions of the escrow were violated. She may also claim that you are estopped to deny the delivery of the deed because you were negligent in selecting BS as your escrow agent, or that you delayed in asserting your title. The facts do not reveal anything to support these claims.

A plaintiff can only gain one recovery, *i.e.,* you can either have quiet title to the property or damages from DF and BS pursuant to the conveyance and tort actions. It would be most advantageous to get quiet title because this would allow you to sell the property for $130,000. This is $30,000 more than you would get in an action against BF and DF, and you will not have the problems associated with enforcing a judgment.

I recommend that we institute an immediate action to quiet title and keep the other possible suits in abeyance, to be pursued only if this action fails.

89. CRIMINAL LAW; CRIMINAL PROCEDURE

MEMORANDUM

To: Prosecutor
From: Assistant Prosecutor
Date: 7-26-90
Re: John, David, and Mary

POTENTIAL CHARGES

John and David can potentially be charged with conspiracy, embezzlement or larceny, and possession of stolen property. Since there is no evidence that Mary was a party to the agreement other than that her house was being used, a conspiracy charge will not lie against her. However, if Mary is found guilty of conspiracy, she can be liable for any crimes committed by the other conspirators if the crimes were committed in furtherance of the conspiracy and were foreseeable.

John and David can be charged with conspiracy. For a conspiracy to exist, there must be an agreement between two or more persons to commit a crime, an intent to enter into an agreement, and an intent to achieve the objective of the agreement. A majority of states also require that an act in furtherance of the conspiracy be performed. The agreement can be express or implied. An agreement may be inferred from sufficiently significant circumstances showing that the parties were aware of the purpose and existence of the conspiracy and agreed to participate in the common purpose. It appears from the statements made by John to David that John and David had an implied agreement. Intent to agree can be inferred from the existence of an agreement. Additionally, mailing of the diamonds to the summer house was an act in furtherance of the conspiracy. Finally, there must be intent to achieve the objective of the conspiracy. This intent must be established as to each individual defendant. While the evidence is sufficient to support the charge against John, it may not be sufficient to support the charge against David.

John and David might be charged with embezzlement. Embezzlement is the fraudulent conversion of property of another by a person in lawful possession of that property. Whether possession is sufficient for embezzlement depends on the scope of control. Mere custody over another's property is not sufficient. Most employees have only custody of an employer's property, but John and David might have had possession, depending upon the nature of their jobs. John's statement to David about moving "the merchandise," coupled with finding the diamonds in Mary's basement labeled for shipment to Florida, supports a charge of embezzlement against John and David. John and David can also be charged with larceny. Larceny is the unlawful taking and immediate asportation of the personal property of another without consent with the intent to permanently deprive the person of his interest in the property. John and David can be charged with taking the diamonds from Totally Magnificent Diamond Conglomerate and transporting them to the secluded house. The property (diamonds) did not belong to them, the company did not consent to the taking, and since the diamonds had shipping labels to Florida, they likely had no intention to return them.

John and David can be charged with possession of stolen property. The diamonds were located in a house owned by John's ex-wife which he had access to, and John was on his way there, and almost inside the house when he was stopped. These facts support a charge of possession of stolen property. David, being a co-conspirator, is liable for all of the crimes committed in furtherance of the conspiracy that were foreseeable. Possession of the diamonds is both in furtherance of the conspiracy and foreseeable.

AVAILABLE DEFENSES AND ANTICIPATED PRETRIAL MOTIONS

Motions and defenses against admission of the telephone conversation: The defendants will likely make a motion to suppress the phone conversation, asserting a violation of their Fourth Amendment right to be free from unreasonable search and seizure. The motion will seek to suppress the conversation on two grounds. First, that it was illegally obtained without a search warrant. Second, that the statement is hearsay, not within any exception.

To suppress the telephone conversation, the defendants must establish a violation of their Fourth Amendment rights. A violation is shown when there is (i) police conduct; (ii) a reasonable expectation of privacy; and (iii) unlawful police action. The defendants' motion to suppress the telephone conversation should be denied, since there was no governmental conduct in monitoring the telephone conversation. No warrant was needed since the wiretapping was performed solely by Conglomerate security officers who were not acting as agents of the police or with any governmental authority. Since the Fourth Amendment generally protects only against governmental conduct and not against searches by private citizens, the defendants' motion to suppress the phone conversation will be denied. It should be noted that the defendants may have a tort action against the security guards and the Magnificent Diamond Conglomerate for invading their right to privacy.

The defendants may move to suppress evidence of the telephone conversation on the ground that it is hearsay. Evidence will be considered hearsay if it is an out-of-court statement used to prove the truth of that statement. However, any testimony by the security officer concerning John's recorded statement to David "They are on to us," is admissible under the hearsay exception for admissions by a party.

Motions and defenses to the search: The defendants will move to suppress the evidence found in Mary's home based on three theories. First, that the diamonds are inadmissible because they are fruits of the poisonous tree. Second, that the stop and frisk of the defendant was unlawful. Third, that the search of Mary's home was unlawful.

The defendants will argue that the evidence found at Mary's home is inadmissible as fruit of the poisonous tree. They will contend the tracking device was unlawfully placed on their vehicle. Therefore, the stop and frisk and search of Mary's home were unlawful and the diamonds are inadmissible as fruit of the poisonous tree. A motion to suppress the evidence based on these grounds should be denied. Again, there must be governmental conduct, a reasonable expectation of privacy, and a failure of the police to obtain a search warrant or come within any of the exceptions to the warrant requirement. In this case, the tracking device was placed on the defendants' vehicle by the Conglomerate security guard, who was not acting on behalf of the police or with any police authority. The police played no part in placing the tracking device on the defendants' vehicle. Therefore, there was no government conduct. Even if the police did place the tracking device on the defendants' vehicle, they did not violate the defendants' reasonable expectation of privacy. The police do not need a warrant to attach an electronic tracking device to a car unless they are doing so in a private residence, because a person does not have a reasonable expectation of privacy in objects held out to the public, such as the location of one's car. Thus, the defendants' motion to suppress the diamonds as fruit of the poisonous tree will be denied.

The defendants will also make a motion to suppress the evidence based on an illegal stop and frisk. This motion should be denied since a police officer may stop a person without probable cause for arrest if she has an articulable and reasonable suspicion of criminal activity. The scope of the frisk is generally limited to a pat down of the outer clothing for concealed instruments of assault or contraband. The admissibility of evidence obtained during a stop and frisk depends on whether the officer could have reasonably believed it to be a possible instrument of assault or contraband. [Sibron v. New York] If the officer feels something during the initial pat down that could be an instrument of assault or contraband, she may reach into the clothing, and the evidence discovered will be admissible. The facts show that the police officers had reasonable suspicion to stop the defendant. This was based on the security guard's information that the defendant was going to move "the merchandise." If the officer reasonably suspected that John had a weapon, the frisk was proper. It is irrelevant that the pat down discovered a set of keys rather than a weapon since the officer may have reasonably believed the keys to be an instrument of assault. Thus, the defendants' motion to suppress the evidence based on an illegal stop and frisk should be denied.

The defendants will also make a motion to suppress the evidence based on an illegal search and seizure of Mary's home. The police officers' search of Mary's home was illegal since there was no warrant and none of the exceptions to the warrant requirement applied. Any contention by the police that the search was incident to a lawful arrest is without merit. The police could lawfully search the defendant's grab area as a search incident to a lawful arrest, but the basement was not within the defendant's grab area since he was stopped outside of the house. Nevertheless, a motion to suppress the diamonds by John and David will likely be denied since they do not have standing to contest the illegal search of Mary's home. A person has standing to assert a Fourth Amendment violation if he owned or had a right to possession of the place searched or the place searched was in fact his home, whether or not he owned or had a right to possess it. The facts indicate that the home belonged to John's estranged wife. Unless it was also John's home or he owned or had a right to possess it, he will be unable to contest the illegal search of Mary's home and the evidence of the diamonds will be admissible against him and David. In addition, if the security guard was not acting with police authority when discovering the diamonds, then the defendant could not assert a Fourth Amendment violation, since there would be no government conduct. Mary would be able to contest the illegal search by the police officers. She has standing and a reasonable expectation of privacy since it was her home that was illegally searched. Therefore, any evidence of the diamonds would be suppressed as an unreasonable search and seizure and a violation of Mary's Fourth Amendment rights.

90.   CONSTITUTIONAL LAW

Introduction: The first issue to be determined is whether Anna Applicante's challenge to the licensing procedure is ripe for adjudication. An issue is ripe for review if there is the immediate threat of harm. In the case at hand, Ms. Applicante has yet to submit her application for casino employment and the immediate threat of harm is in the future. The courts will refuse to review an issue where subsequent events may sharpen the controversy or remove the need for decision. It is advised that Ms. Applicante submit her application leaving the objectionable questions, release form, and consent form blank. Upon the Casino Watchdog Commission ("CWC") rejecting the application because of the missing information, the issue will be ripe for adjudication.

Right to privacy: The first cause of action that will be raised is that the questionnaire is unconstitutional because it violates the fundamental right to privacy. Where government action jeopardizes an individual's right to privacy, it will be invalidated unless the government can demonstrate that the action is necessary to promote a compelling interest. The concept of substantive due process rests on the belief developed by the courts that certain rights are so fundamental to our concept of liberty as to require constitutional protection under the Due Process Clause. This holds true even though such rights or individual freedoms cannot be readily found within the text of the Constitution. Disclosures in the area of sexual preference, physical and mental history, and marital status would fall under the realm of the right to privacy. Impinging on an individual's right to privacy in this particular case greatly outweighs the need to regulate the gambling industry and is, therefore, unconstitutional.

In defense of its regulation, New Jersey must demonstrate under strict scrutiny analysis that its licensing procedure requiring the disclosure of sexual preference, marital status, and physical and mental history is necessary to promote a compelling interest. The compelling interest it will be claiming to promote is a corrupt-free gambling industry.

Right of freedom of association: The second cause of action that will be raised is that the questionnaire is unconstitutional because it violates the First Amendment's right to freely associate. Freedom of association under the First Amendment is a fundamental right. Where a fundamental right is limited by government action, the action in question must be necessary to promote a compelling state interest pursuant to strict scrutiny analysis.

The state of New Jersey must defend that their licensing procedure is necessary to promote a compelling state interest. Gambling has historically been a suspect activity, prone to abuse and controlled by organized crime. Questions as to professional and personal associations will give the CWC invaluable insight into a prospective applicant's integrity and background. Thus, the licensing procedure promulgated by the CWC is necessary to promote the compelling state interest of a corrupt-free gambling industry.

Unreasonable search and seizure: The final cause of action that the CWC requirement of signing a consent to warrantless searches in a casino facility is violative of the Fourth Amendment right to be free from unreasonable searches and seizures. This cause of action will be premised on the theory that the warrantless search goes far enough to invade upon the fundamental right to privacy. Where government action impinges upon a fundamental right, the governmental action is subject to strict scrutiny analysis. The governmental action in question must be necessary to promote a compelling interest. If there is no compelling state interest, the governmental action is unconstitutional.

In defense of this consent requirement, the CWC will argue that no fundamental right is involved, and therefore, strict scrutiny analysis would be inapplicable. In the alternative, the CWC would defend that the rational relationship test is the appropriate standard of review. Under the rational relationship test, the government action in question need only be rationally related to a legitimate government interest.

If, however, the courts decide that a fundamental right is indeed impinged upon, the CWC will defend that the consent to search requirement is necessary to promote a compelling state interest. The compelling state interest at hand would be the maintenance of a corrupt-free gambling industry, as stated above.

It should also be noted that the Fourth Amendment protection from unreasonable searches and seizures applies to government action only. In the case at hand, the searches and seizures would probably be conducted by private casino officials. However, the consent requirement is at the direction of the CWC, a statutorily created commission, and therefore, the Fourth Amendment protection is applicable.

91. TORTS
GASH AND GIMPY V. TOWN TAVERN

Causes of action: Town Tavern will be liable to Gash and Gimpy for the injuries they received under the doctrine of respondeat superior. Under this doctrine, an employer is vicariously liable for the tortious acts committed by her employee if the tortious acts occur within the scope of employment.

Gash and Gimpy must establish a prima facie case in negligence against Bartender. To establish their prima facie case they must prove: (i) Bartender owed a specific duty of care to Gash and Gimpy; (ii) Bartender breached this duty; (iii) the breach of the duty by Bartender was the proximate cause of Gash and Gimpy's injuries; and (iv) damages.

Bartender owed Gash and Gimpy the duty to act as a reasonable person. A reasonable person would know that a drinker would become intoxicated after being served many rounds in a bar and likely would attempt to drive upon leaving the bar. Therefore, a reasonable person has a duty to cut off the drinker. Bartender breached this duty of care owed to Gash and Gimpy.

Gash and Gimpy must show that Bartender was the proximate cause of their injuries. They can show this because but for Bartender continuing to serve them, they would not have become intoxicated. It was clearly foreseeable they would drive home in an automobile and get into an accident.

Town Tavern will argue that Bartender is not the proximate cause of the injuries suffered by Gash and Gimpy. Getting into Crash's car and having an accident was an intervening act. Thus, the bar will contend it should not be held vicariously liable. However, Town Tavern will be held liable for Bartender's negligence because Gash and Gimpy's getting into a car and having an accident after drinking is a foreseeable intervening force that is a normal incident of, and within the increased risk caused by, Bartender's negligence.

Finally, Gash and Gimpy must show damages. Gash and Gimpy simply have to prove the personal injuries they suffered as a result of the accident. In the case at hand, Gash suffered a wound to his arm and Gimpy suffered a broken leg.

Based on the negligence of Bartender, Town Tavern is vicariously liable to Gash and Gimpy under the doctrine of respondeat superior.

Defenses: Town Tavern will raise the defenses of contributory negligence and assumption of the risk. These defenses overlap and have a considerable area in common.

Town Tavern will first argue that the plaintiffs, Gash and Gimpy, assumed the risk. Under the assumption of risk defense, the plaintiff will be denied recovery if he assumed the risk of any damage caused by the defendant's acts. To have assumed the risk the plaintiff must have known of the risk and voluntarily assumed it.

In the case at hand, Town Tavern will have to prove that Gash and Gimpy assumed the risk of any damage upon entering the automobile of an intoxicated driver. While Town Tavern will have no difficulty in proving the "voluntary" requirement, it will have a difficult time in proving that Gash and Gimpy had full knowledge of the risk at hand. Gash and Gimpy were intoxicated, and thus were unable to realize fully the extent of the risk.

Town Tavern will then argue that Gash and Gimpy were contributorily negligent in failing to wear their seat belts. Contributory negligence is conduct on the part of the plaintiff which falls below the standard of care of a reasonable person and contributes as a legal cause to the harm he has suffered. If the plaintiff is found to be contributorily negligent, he is barred recovery. Town Tavern must argue that the reasonable person would wear a seat belt.

Gash and Gimpy breached the duty of reasonable care by failing to wear their seat belts. It was foreseeable that failure to wear a seat belt could result in personal injury in the event of an auto accident. Thus, Gash and Gimpy were contributorily negligent in their failure to wear seat belts.

It should be noted that Gash will be able to counter-argue that had he been wearing his seat belt, he probably would have received additional injury. Therefore, Gash may not have been contributorily negligent and the defense may not apply to him.

It is important to note that a substantial majority of states now permit a contributorily negligent plaintiff to recover a percentage of his damages under some type of comparative negligence system. In cases where a defendant has proven that a plaintiff has been contributorily negligent, the trier of fact weighs the plaintiff's negligence against that of the defendant and reduces plaintiff's damages accordingly.

In partial comparative negligence jurisdictions, the plaintiff will be barred from recovering if his negligence passes that jurisdiction's particular threshold level. In some states, a plaintiff may recover only if his negligence was less serious than that of the defendant. In other jurisdictions, a plaintiff may recover if his negligence was no more serious than that of the defendant. In jurisdictions that use a pure comparative negligence system, a plaintiff may recover no matter how great his negligence is.

GASH AND GIMPY V. CRASH

Causes of action: Gash and Gimpy have a cause of action against Crash in negligence for driving while intoxicated. As passengers in Crash's car, Crash owes Gash and Gimpy the duty to act as a reasonable person in the active operation of an automobile. A reasonable person would not become intoxicated and then drive an automobile. This duty was breached when Crash got behind the wheel of the automobile and drove. Crash was the proximate cause of Gash and Gimpy's injuries, as it is clearly foreseeable that a person operating an automobile while intoxicated is likely to have an accident. As a result of Crash's negligent operation of his automobile, Gash and Gimpy suffered personal injuries.

Defenses: Like Town Tavern, Crash will raise the defenses of assumption of risk and contributory negligence. Crash will argue that Gash and Gimpy assumed the risk when they got into Crash's car. However, Gash and Gimpy will argue that they were so intoxicated that they were unaware and did not have full knowledge of the risk at hand.

Similarly to Town Tavern, Crash will also argue that Gash and Gimpy were contributorily negligent in failing to wear their seat belts. In failing to act as a reasonable person, they should be barred recovery. However, as pointed out above, had Gash been wearing his seat belt, his injuries would have been exacerbated and the defense of contributory negligence might not apply to him.

GASH V. GIMPY

Cause of action: Gash has a potential cause of action against Gimpy under social host liability pursuant to a negligence theory of recovery. As a social host, Gimpy is held to the standard of ordinary negligence. A reasonable person would not serve alcohol to guests and then send them from his house in an apparently intoxicated state. Gimpy breached this duty. Gash must then argue that Gimpy was the proximate cause of his injuries since it was clearly foreseeable that sending an intoxicated person from your residence is likely to result in harm. As a result of Gimpy's negligent conduct of sending Gash from his house in an intoxicated state, Gash was injured.

Defenses: Gimpy will be able to argue that he was not negligent and acted as a reasonable person. Gimpy served only four beers over a period of three to four hours. Consumption of four beers over a period of three to four hours by an average male will most likely not result in intoxication. Thus, Gimpy may assert that he acted as a reasonably prudent social host and was not negligent.

CONCLUSION

Our firm should not handle both cases. Gash and Gimpy have a possible cause of action against one another. It is virtually never proper in a litigation context for a lawyer to represent two clients whose interests are in present, actual conflict. Lawyers within a firm are treated as a single unit for conflict of interest purposes. Therefore, different lawyers in the same firm must not represent opposing parties in a civil case. Our firm should not handle both cases.

92. CONTRACTS

To: Senior Partner
From: Associate
Re: Possible causes of action by the Smiths

Smiths v. Joneses: The Smiths will be unsuccessful against the Joneses for a cause of action based on breach of the 1986 sales contract. The Smiths are likely to succeed in an action against Contractor for breach of contract. The issue is whether the contract for sale was valid and whether the Joneses made any implied warranties of fitness on the house.

The Joneses 1986 contract to sell their home to the Smiths was valid. The contract between the Joneses and Smiths was subject to a condition precedent, requiring a satisfactory engineering inspection of the premises based on the value of the land. A condition precedent is a condition that must occur before an absolute duty of immediate performance arises in either party. Upon satisfaction of this condition, the Smiths' duty to purchase and the Joneses' duty to sell the house was triggered. Since the Smiths purchased the house, it can be inferred that the engineering inspection based on the value of the house was satisfactory. The contract for sale was therefore valid.

The Smiths are not liable for the subsequent defects in the patio since there were no express or implied warranties made concerning the house. The rule is that contracts of sale of real property carry no implied warranties of quality or fitness. The exception of implied warranties for contracts of sale of a building under construction does not apply here. Thus, the Smiths had to make a reasonable inspection of the premises and discover any defects in the patio. Moreover, there is no evidence that the Joneses made any misrepresentations to the Smiths concerning the patio so there were no express warranties. In addition, the contract contained a merger clause expressly stating that the parties made no representations except as set forth in the contract. Since there were no warranties made on the house, the sale of the premises was "as is." The Smiths therefore have no cause of action against the Joneses for breach of an implied warranty and cannot recover damages from them for the defects in the patio.

Smiths v. Contractor: The next issue is whether the rights under the contract between the Joneses and Contractor were assignable to the Smiths. The general rule is that all rights under a contract may be assigned. However, there are several exceptions. The rights under a contract may not be assigned where: (i) assignment of the rights would substantially change the obligor's duty; (ii) the rights assigned would substantially alter the obligor's risk; (iii) the rights under an employment contract are expected to rise in the future; (iv) the law prohibits assignment; or (v) the contract provides that contractual rights may not be assigned.

Under the facts of this case, the rights that the Smiths had under the contract with Contractor are assignable since none of the exceptions stated above apply. Thus, the Smiths have all the rights under the contract with Contractor that the Joneses had.

Because the rights of the contract have been assigned to the Smiths, they may sue Contractor for breach of contract. The basis for this action is Contractor's negligent design and installation of the patio.

To be successful in their action, the Smiths must establish a prima facie case in negligence. They must prove: (i) the existence of a duty to conform to a specific standard of conduct; (ii) breach of that duty; (iii) actual and proximate cause; and (iv) damages.

Contractor had a duty to design and install a patio. The Smiths will be able to prove breach of this duty by demonstrating the faulty design and installation. Further, they can show that it was clearly foreseeable that the improper design and installation would result in the buckling of the patio floor. The Smiths also will sue for incidental and consequential damages.

Contractor may raise any defenses against the Smiths that he could have raised against the Joneses. Contractor will not have many defenses available to him. He may argue, however, that he was not negligent in his design and installation of the patio; *i.e.,* that he conformed to the standard of conduct of proper design and installation of the patio. He might also argue that the damage to the patio was caused by either the Smiths' or Joneses' misuse.

Contractor might also argue contributory negligence on the part of the Smiths. Contractor would argue that the Smiths had a duty to inspect the house upon their purchase. By hiring an incompetent engineering firm that failed to detect the defective design and installation, the Smiths were contributorily negligent. If a competent engineering firm were hired, it would have discovered the defects.

Smiths v. the engineering firm: The Smiths also have a cause of action against the engineering firm for its negligent inspection and the Smiths' subsequent reliance on it. To establish this cause of action, the Smiths must prove a prima facie case in negligence. This will include proving the existence of a duty of care owed to the Smiths, breach of this duty, proximate cause, and damages. The Smiths will argue that the engineering firm had a duty to discover any defects in the house and patio. The engineering firm breached this duty by failing to discover the defective design and installation. Because of the firm's negligence, the Smiths relied to their detriment. It was clearly foreseeable the Smiths would rely on the firm's inspection and that the resulting damage would occur. Thus, the engineering firm was negligent in their inspection of the patio by failing to discover the defective design and installation.

The only defense the engineering firm will be able to assert is that they were not negligent in their inspection. They will argue that upon making their inspection, the defective design and installation was not apparent and could not be detected.

93. CONTRACTS

Electro will have an action for $10,000 against Able, and Able will remain bound by his bid to Developer.

Electro v. Able: Electro submitted a timely response to Able's solicitation of bids. However, the total cost to Able, itemized in the bid to be $22,500, was in fact $10,000 below the price that Electro had intended. This mistake was based on a mathematical error in the computation of the cost and was evident in the bid itself. Thus, the issue in an action between Electro and Able would be whether Electro will be held to the mistaken figure of $22,500.

Generally, where a promisor induces reliance by a promisee on the basis of a promise lacking in consideration and the promisee relies on that promise to his detriment, the promisor is estopped from denying the enforcement of the promise on a theory of promissory estoppel. Thus, a subcontractor would be bound by a bid for a proposed contract if he had reason to believe that the contractor will be relying on that bid in putting together the calculations for his own bid on a project.

However, it is also well settled that if a nonmistaken party to an agreement is or should reasonably be aware of a mistake in the other party's understanding of the agreement, the agreement is voidable at the mistaken party's option. Note that if the mistake is not readily apparent to the nonmistaken party, the agreement will not be voidable.

In the instant case, if the mathematical error in the bid had not been readily apparent, Electro would have been bound by his erroneous bid to Able on a theory of promissory estoppel. Even though the bid was never formally accepted by Able and Electro was unaware that Developer awarded the contract to Able prior to attempting to rescind the bid, the common practice in the construction industry is that bids are held open for a reasonable time in order to allow contractors an opportunity in which to formulate their own bids. In this case the time period of 11 days is clearly reasonable.

However, Able is not without fault in this matter. The computational error made by Electro in calculating the cost of his services to Able was readily apparent in the telegram sent to Able, and Able should reasonably have been aware of it. Therefore, as the mistaken party in this matter, Electro will be successful in an action to conform his agreement with Able to the figure he had originally intended.

Able v. Developer: Developer awarded Able a project for $230,000, with no reason to suspect that there was an inaccuracy in this figure. The $10,000 dispute between Able and Electro is negligible in light of the total cost of the project. Therefore, Able will be bound by his bid to Developer. Any refusal to perform on his part would constitute a breach of contract entitling Developer to all consequential damages. Note that there is a minority trend toward canceling bids where in actuality no detrimental reliance has occurred.

94. CRIMINAL LAW

MEMORANDUM

To: Senior Partner
From: Attorney
Re: Potential Charges Against Al and his Defenses Thereto

Upon my review of Al's file, I have determined as follows with respect to his case:

1)   Al may be charged with the crime of conspiracy. To establish the elements of a conspiracy, the prosecution would have to establish that Al entered into an agreement to commit an illegal act, and that an overt action in furtherance of the goals of the conspiracy was performed by any one of the co-conspirators. The overt act does not in and of itself have to be illegal. The mere preparation to perform a conspiracy will be deemed sufficient. If the conspiracy is established, all co-conspirators will be held liable for acts foreseeably committed in furtherance of the conspiracy.

In this case, the prosecution would argue that Al entered into an agreement with Chuck to steal the money they had lost gambling. The fact that they both went to Ben's house to achieve this end would constitute the requisite overt act in furtherance of the conspiracy.

Al's belief that he was cheated out of the money in question would be no defense to the conspiracy charge. The defense of justification will prevail only in situations where the use of force was necessary. Clearly, Al's recourse in this situation was judicial rather than one of self-help.

However, in his defense, Al could assert that he never entered into an agreement with Chuck to commit an illegal act. The facts indicate that he merely agreed to go to Ben's house to retrieve the money that he had lost. There was no discussion of retrieving this money in an illegal manner. In support of this argument, note that Al and Chuck verbally demanded their money before grabbing it from the table. It is plausible that Al and Chuck grabbed the money in the heat of the moment, never having agreed to do so prior to arriving at Ben's house.

2)   Al may be charged with the crime of larceny. The elements of larceny are the taking and carrying away of the property of another with the intent to permanently deprive that person of his interest in the property. Clearly the elements of larceny can be established in the instant case since Al took and carried away money which belonged to others (the players at Ben's house) with the intention of depriving them of it.

3)   Al may be charged with the crime of robbery. The elements of robbery are a taking of the personal property of another from the other's person or presence by force or intimidation with the intent to permanently deprive him of it. The force must be used either to gain the possession of the property or to retain possession immediately after possession has been achieved. The prosecution would argue in this respect that Al took the money from Ben's presence with the intent to permanently deprive him of it and, in concert with Chuck, used force to retain it.

Al's defense to this charge can be formulated in two ways. Initially, if, as discussed above, Al had no intention of entering into an agreement with Chuck to commit an illegal act, he would not be deemed to be acting in concert with Chuck and therefore would not be responsible for Chuck's actions. Thus, if it is found that the money was stolen in the heat of the moment, without any prior planning, Al will not be found guilty of robbery. Moreover, even if there did exist a conspiracy between Chuck and Al to forcibly take money from Ben, it can be argued that Al was not aware that Chuck was armed and that the use of force was not reasonably foreseeable to further the conspiracy. Since co-conspirators will only be liable for the acts of other co-conspirators if the acts were reasonably foreseeable for the furtherance of the conspiracy, the jury would have to determine the validity of this argument.

As stated above, justification would not constitute a valid defense in this situation. The use of force in taking the money was not necessary.

4)   Finally, Al may be charged with battery and attempted murder. Battery is the unlawful application of force to the person of another causing an injury. To establish attempted murder, the prosecution would have to show that the defendant took an overt action beyond mere preparation in furtherance of his intent to commit a murder or to inflict serious bodily harm.

In the instant case, the prosecution would argue that Al, acting in concert with Chuck, is liable for the crimes that Chuck committed in shooting the player. Chuck is clearly guilty of battery in that he injured the player by an unlawful application of force when he shot him. Chuck will also be found guilty of attempted murder if it can be shown that he had the intent to kill or seriously injure the player. This will not be difficult since Chuck shot the player with a gun.

Al's defense to these charges will be similar to his defense to the conspiracy charge. If he can initially establish that he never entered into an agreement to recover his money from Ben by criminal activity, he will not be deemed to have acted in concert with Chuck when Chuck shot the player. Thus, he will not be liable for Chuck's crimes in doing so. Moreover, even if a conspiracy is deemed to have occurred, Al may argue that he was not aware that Chuck was armed and that the resultant injury to the player was not foreseeably within the scope of his agreement with Chuck.

95. REAL PROPERTY

Dear Mr. Vent:

On July 1, 1987, you entered into a binding mortgage agreement with Holden. The acceleration clause therein was not unusual. Such clauses have been recognized as valid methods of protecting lenders from sale to a poor credit risk or allowing the lender to change the terms of the mortgage when the property is actually sold. Moreover, in recording your mortgage you guaranteed its priority as against any mortgage subsequently taken on the property.

Upon executing a contract of sale with Holden and moving into Holden's home, Broke acquired equitable title to the premises. Although under the Holden-Broke contract the deed was put into escrow and so legal title did not pass to Broke, courts have recognized similar transactions as passing equitable title since the buyer takes on all of the characteristics of an owner. Since equitable title in the property has been transferred to Broke, the acceleration clause in your mortgage with Holden has been activated.

Consequently, you now have the option of invoking the acceleration clause. Although Broke assumed your mortgage, he never entered into an assumption agreement with you and is therefore only secondarily liable to you. Holden will remain primarily liable on the mortgage note. Also, note that your receipt of payments from Broke will not constitute a waiver of the acceleration clause since you were unaware that the ownership of the property had changed hands when you accepted payment from Broke.

You also have the option of satisfying your mortgage from the proceeds of the foreclosure on the property. Your mortgage will be satisfied prior to the satisfaction of the $25,000 purchase money mortgage extended by Holden to Broke. A purchase money mortgage arises when a seller extends a loan to the buyer, retaining an interest in the property until it is paid off. Generally a purchase money mortgage will have priority over a recorded mortgage extended at around the same time. However, in this case, your mortgage was extended and recorded on or about July 1, 1987, well before the date upon which Holden executed the contract with Broke in April of 1988. Remember that Holden will remain primarily liable and Broke will remain secondarily liable on the mortgage note for any amount that is not satisfied from foreclosure on the property.

You also have a claim against Holden for damages arising due to her willful attempt to circumvent the terms of your mortgage. Inasmuch as the interest rate has risen to 13% from the 8% rate extended to Holden originally, you are entitled to recover from her the difference in interest on the three payments made to you by Broke. Since you were never informed of the transfer of ownership, you never had the option of collecting your investment by enforcing the acceleration clause and investing your capital in another project at a 13% interest rate.

96. TORTS

To: Senior Partner
From: Attorney
Re: Potential Liability of Glowco

There are several legal theories pursuant to which ARC can attempt to recover its damages from Glowco, assuming of course that Glowco is not judgment proof. Each action is discussed below.

Negligence: The elements of an action in negligence are the existence of a specific standard of conduct or duty, breach of that duty, and the causation of damage to the foreseeable plaintiff as a result. The major issues in establishing a case rooted in negligence against Glowco will be the demonstration of Glowco's duty with respect to disposition of the radium and the foreseeability of ARC as a plaintiff.

In establishing Glowco's duty to properly dispose of the radium, note that the facts of this case are vague as to Glowco's specific awareness of the dangers of improper disposition of radium. Since Glowco was only in business for five years, it is unlikely that Glowco knew from experience that radium releases the radioactive gas radon over time. Further, the sterility of Glowco's chief engineer is irrelevant to the instant case since there is no indication that this condition was caused by the engineer's handling of the radium, much less from radon. Finally, the fact that two of Glowco's employees developed cancer is also not helpful because there is no indication that Glowco knew that the radium they handled was carcinogenic at the time they were employed by Glowco.

Despite the lack of specificity in the facts as to what Glowco actually knew about radium, it is clear that Glowco was on notice that radium was a dangerous substance since its employees wore protective aprons. Therefore, acting in a reasonable manner, Glowco had a duty to properly dispose of the radium rather than just dumping it on vacant property.

The determination of ARC as a foreseeable plaintiff is also problematic. ARC, a successor on Glowco's property, has been injured as a result of Glowco's failure to properly dispose of radium. However, the injury sustained was of a nature that was not anticipated at the time of Glowco's breach, since it does not appear that Glowco was aware that radium would emit radon.

Thus, prior to determining Glowco's liability in this case, the foreseeability of ARC as a plaintiff must be established. There are two schools of thought on this issue. The Andrews view is that a defendant will be held liable whenever he breaches a duty of care causing subsequent damage, whereas the Cardozo view is that the defendant is liable only to plaintiffs located in the foreseeable zone of danger. The distance in time would not be relevant in finding liability once it is established that the plaintiff was in the foreseeable zone of danger. Although Justice Cardozo's rule is the majority rule, this issue is far from resolved.

ARC would be a foreseeable plaintiff under Justice Andrews's view that all plaintiffs damaged by the breach of Glowco's duty are foreseeable. ARC would not prevail under Justice Cardozo's view because the damages it sustained cannot be deemed within the zone of danger contemplated by Glowco's deposit of radium on its vacant property.

Strict liability: To establish a case in strict liability, it must be shown that the plaintiff had an absolute duty to make safe, and caused damage to the plaintiff when he failed to do so. Strict liability would be appropriate in situations involving abnormally dangerous activities that involve a risk of serious harm, cannot be performed with complete safety, and are not commonly engaged-in activities. Whether the use of radium by Glowco was an "ultrahazardous activity" at the time Glowco was in business would be a question of fact for the jury. Further, the issue of ARC as a foreseeable plaintiff would also arise, as discussed above, in establishing a case in strict liability.

Damages: If ARC recovers under either of the theories discussed above, the damages recoverable will include the cost of the property and all consequential damages sustained by ARC, including the cost of remedial action it took to decrease exposure to radon; *i.e.,* costs of the ventilation system, reduction in work hours, the outside engineering firm, construction of the enclosure, and relocating.

97. CONSTITUTIONAL LAW

To: Senior Partner
From: Attorney
Re: Eyeway Cinema

The Flick City ordinance is unconstitutional, but construction of the concrete center median is not a violation of the Due Process Clause in the Fourteenth Amendment. The facts raise two issues that must be addressed in determining Eyeway's likelihood of success in a lawsuit against Flick City. These issues are: (i) does the ordinance enacted by Flick City infringe on Eyeway's First Amendment rights? and (ii) does the construction of the concrete center median along the highway adjacent to Eyeway violate the fourteenth amendment's Due Process Clause or the Fifth Amendment's Taking Clause?

The ordinance: The First Amendment guarantees protection from restrictions on speech by governmental agencies and is extended to the states by the Due Process Clause of the Fourteenth Amendment. However, freedom of speech is not absolute and can in many instances be regulated. The Supreme Court has determined that obscenity is not protected speech and has defined it as a description of sexual conduct which, if taken as a whole by the average person applying contemporary community standards, appeals to the prurient interest in sex, portrays sex in a patently offensive manner, and does not have serious literary, artistic, political, or scientific value using a national reasonable person standard. The determination of whether material is obscene is a question of fact for the jury. If the ordinance bans nonobscene speech, it will be upheld only if it is narrowly drawn to achieve a compelling state interest. If the regulation is merely a content-neutral time, place, and manner regulation, it will be upheld if it is narrowly tailored to serve a significant governmental interest.

Any contention by Flick City that the ordinance in question seeks to regulate obscenity and is therefore constitutional would fail. The regulation is overbroad because it completely bans certain types of speech out of the context of the films in which they are being shown. A determination of obscenity must be made on a case-by-case basis and cannot be extended to speech out of the context of the circumstances in which it occurs.

Since the ordinance in question is clearly not content-neutral, Flick City must establish the existence of a compelling state interest in its enactment, and demonstrate that the ordinance is narrowly tailored to achieve that end. Although Flick City would argue that its ordinance is geared toward easing the traffic problems around Eyeway Cinema and the congregation of teenagers in adjacent parking lots, it is highly unlikely that these concerns would constitute a "compelling" state interest. More importantly, Flick City has not demonstrated how, if at all, the prohibition of the speech set forth in the ordinance would resolve these problems. Presumably, the same problems would still arise if movies that did not show bare buttocks, genitalia, and breasts were projected from Eyeway. Therefore, the ordinance would be declared unconstitutional if challenged in court.

The median: Eyeway's strongest argument against the construction of the concrete center median would be that this state action violates the Due Process Clause of the Fourteenth Amendment because it has resulted in a reduction of Eyeway's economic interests without due process of the law. In support of this allegation, Eyeway would argue that its ticket sales have decreased by 25% since the construction of the median.

Where a fundamental right is restricted by a governmental action, it must be established that the action was necessary to promote a compelling interest. Fundamental rights include all First Amendment rights. However, in the instant case, Eyeway's First Amendment rights have not been infringed by the construction of the concrete median. Unlike the enactment of the ordinance, which restricted the type of speech in which Eyeway could engage, construction of the median merely made access to the theater more difficult. Therefore, the high standard applicable to situations where governmental actions infringe upon a fundamental right is inapplicable in this case.

State action that has an effect on economic interests will be upheld as long as it is rationally related to a legitimate governmental interest. Since Flick City has a legitimate interest in regulating traffic congestion around Eyeway and in preventing the congregation of teenagers in deserted parking lots, and erection of the center median is rationally related to the state's interest in controlling these conditions, erection of the median does not constitute a violation of the Fourteenth Amendment.

Also, note that the resulting reduction of revenue to Eyeway would not constitute "a taking of private property" within the meaning of the Fifth Amendment's prohibition against the taking of private property for public use. Government regulations that decrease the value of property do not result in a "taking" as long as an economically viable use for the property remains.

98. CONSTITUTIONAL LAW
To: Partner
From: Associate
Re: Coach's Causes of Action

Coach v. AAA: AAA has informed State University that it will be subject to sanctions unless Coach is suspended for two years. The first issue is whether the action of AAA constitutes state action.

To find state action, an actor must perform public functions or have significant state involvement. It appears, under this standard, that AAA is not a state actor; regulating sports at public and private institutions is not a function traditionally reserved to the states and neither are its activities so involved with the state so as to rise to the level of state action.

Furthermore, AAA has given State University a choice of what to do, albeit a coercive choice. State University does not have to suspend Coach; it could choose to accept further sanctions and not suspend Coach. Therefore, no causes of action will lie against AAA because it merely made findings and left it to State University to decide what actions to take. [*See* National Collegiate Athletic Association v. Tarkanian, 488 U.S. 179 (1988)]

Coach v. State University: The actions of State University through its president, however, do constitute state action. The University is an institution of the state, as indicated by its name, and President is a state actor. The question, then, is what constitutional rights Coach has, and whether these rights were infringed by the University.

We must ascertain whether Coach was removable for cause. An employee removable only for cause has a property interest in his job, and thus is entitled to due process before the state deprives him of his job.

Assuming Coach is removable only for cause, due process requires that he be given notice of the charges against him, as well as a pretermination opportunity to respond to the charges. An evidentiary hearing regarding the termination decision must be provided either before or after the termination, with reinstatement if he prevails. If no cause is required for removal, Coach is an employee at will and is not due any process before or after termination.

We should move to secure the above procedural safeguards for Coach. While Coach participated in the AAA hearing, he appeared only as a witness, and not as a party. Coach is entitled to a more substantial opportunity to respond to the charges against him. Coach has received notice of the decision to suspend him. He may respond to President's notification of suspension and is entitled to an evidentiary hearing regarding his termination.

University may assert that a two-year suspension is not the same as a termination. However, our position is that a two-year loss of job and salary is an infringement of Coach's property rights serious enough to warrant a hearing.

Should we bring this claim, University may institute a defense of ripeness. They could claim that no action has been taken against Coach and that his claim is premature. However, an action is ripe for review when there is the immediate threat of harm. Here, President has notified Coach of its intent to suspend him. Thus, Coach will not fail for lack of ripeness.

Coach's First Amendment claim: Coach feels silenced by the refusal of the school newspaper to print the views he expressed in his interview. However, Coach's constitutional rights probably have not been violated. First, the contents of a school-funded newspaper can be regulated because the Supreme Court has found that such papers are not public forums, but merely are educational devices.

Even if the newspaper were a public forum, it would not give rise to a cause of action by Coach. Generally, a party cannot assert the constitutional rights of others. To have standing, the claimant must have suffered a direct impairment of his own constitutional rights. Here, a prior restraint has been placed on the newspaper. This is a burden on the newspaper's rights. And while Coach is affected, it is not a direct impairment of his rights. Thus, he lacks standing to bring a suit based in the First Amendment.

99. TORTS

Dear Mr. Media:

Assuming that the anonymous derogatory letter can be traced to its authors, Creep, Crawl, and Conniver ("defendants"), Media has a cause of action for defamation by libel. Libel is a defamatory statement recorded in writing or some other permanent form.

A prima facie case of defamation is made if the following elements are met: First, there must be defamatory language on the part of the defendant. Second, the language must be of or concerning the plaintiff so as to identify the plaintiff to a reasonable reader or listener. Third, there must be publication of the defamatory statement by the defendant to a third party. Finally, there must be a showing of damage to the reputation of the plaintiff.

The letter to Pretendo assailing your work as "juvenile" and a "costly flop" is defamatory on its face. No interpretation is needed to recognize the derogatory nature of these terms.

Furthermore, the letter sent by the defendants claimed to report the status of Media's reputation in the advertising industry. Since these allegations were made as statements of fact, they are more actionable than a mere statement of opinion. The element of defamatory language is thereby satisfied.

Because the letter to Pretendo specifically discussed Media, there is no doubt that the plaintiff was identified to the reader. Nor is there any question that the defamatory statement was published.

There are two types of damages that can be recovered in an action for defamation: general and specific. In most jurisdictions, general damages are presumed by law in libel actions and need not be proved by the plaintiff. They are intended to compensate the plaintiff for the general injury to his reputation caused by the defamation. It is of no consequence that Media is a corporation and not a natural person. Media may receive general damages from the defendants, but specific damages may be hard to prove.

To receive specific damages, a plaintiff has to prove a specific monetary loss as a result of the defamation. Here, Media would have to show that it did not get the Super Maria Sisters account because of defendants' letter.

Media could introduce the Pretendo memo stating that all advertising work should go to Media, and that the defendants' defamatory letter interfered with this arrangement.

However, defendants could assert that Media was simply outbid by Conniver and that the only factor involved in Pretendo's decision was economic. Indeed, Pretendo's internal memo expressly stated that one of the reasons Media would not receive a contract was because of substantial economic reasons and, in fact, Conniver submitted a substantially lower bid than Media.

The reasons why the contract was awarded to Conniver should be explored nevertheless to see if Pretendo based its decision in whole or in part on the defamatory letter from the defendants. This factor will decide the issue of specific damages.

Media may also have a cause of action against the defendants for interference with prospective economic advantage.

To prove this action, it must be shown that there was a special relationship between two parties and that a third party interfered with their relationship with the intent to do so. The linchpin of such cases is evidence of the defendant's motive.

The internal memo at Pretendo evidences a special relationship between Media and Pretendo; there was a strong bias to award future work to Media. Furthermore, defendants' motive for writing the derogatory letter is obvious. Conniver was seeking the Super Maria Sisters advertising account from Pretendo; Creep and Crawl are his friends. If Media, as plaintiff, can make out a prima facie case that defendants' letter played a material and substantial role in Pretendo's decision not to award Media the contract, then Media will succeed on this cause of action.

Creep, Crawl, and Conniver can be sued jointly or severally on these causes of action. Since all three acted in concert to bring about Media's injury, they can be sued together or separately. If Media prevails in its action, any judgment awarded could be obtained from any one of the defendants.

100. CONTRACTS

Dealer,

I have analyzed the possible claims and defenses arising out of the sale on May 1, 1989, of the car to Buyer and subsequent return of the car and its resale by you. Discussed below are the claims you have against Buyer, the claims he has against you, and the probable success of each claim.

Your sale of a car to Buyer is a sale of goods, and therefore your rights and liabilities are governed by the Uniform Commercial Code.

Buyer breached his contract with you when he returned the car to the lot after it had ostensibly been repaired. This gave you the right to resell the car in a commercially reasonable manner.

You may recover from Buyer the difference between the resale price (which is not necessarily market value) and the contract price. [U.C.C. §2-706] Thus, you would be entitled to the benefit of your bargain (60 installments of $350), less the installment payments you have received from Buyer and the money you received from the resale of the car. You may also recover consequential damages. These are defined as losses that fairly and reasonably arise naturally from the breach of contract itself. In effect, courts will hold the breaching party liable for any further losses resulting from the breach that any reasonable person would have foreseen would occur from a breach at the time of entry into the contract. This would include the costs of storage, advertising, and any other foreseeable costs resulting from Buyer's breach. Buyer, however, will probably claim that he was entitled to return the car because you breached his warranty.

Buyer may claim that he had the right to revoke acceptance of the purchase of the car. Under the U.C.C., a buyer may revoke his acceptance of goods that have a defect which materially impairs their value to him. Buyer has the duty of revoking within a reasonable time of the discovery of the defects and before any substantial change in the goods not caused by their own defects. A proper revocation of acceptance has the effect of a rejection.

The failure of the car's electrical system and cruise control was a defect that materially impaired the value of the car to Buyer. Nevertheless, Buyer's revocation was wrongful. He accepted the car with a warranty that assured him that any defect of materials or workmanship arising within 12 months would be cured. While it is unusual that the car developed the same problem four times, Buyer was wrong for revoking the contract and returning the car merely because he feared a recurrence of the same problem, since the car had no defect at the time it was returned. Buyer had no right to return a functioning car.

Buyer may want to sue you to recover the money he paid in installments for the car that he has since rejected. However, as was discussed above, Buyer does not appear to have any grounds on which to base his revocation. Thus, such an action is unlikely to succeed.

101. REAL PROPERTY

To: Senior Partner
From: Associate
Re: Wy Knott

This memorandum will address the possible discharge of Wy's mortgage obligation or a partial reimbursement from the estate of her late husband in light of the facts presented.

At issue is the effect of Blanche's transfer of the mortgage to her father, Ty. If the assignment is effective, then Ty's estate is entitled to enforce the mortgage. If the assignment is ineffective, Wy may be totally or partially discharged of the debt. Factors to be considered are the assignment of the mortgage from mortgagee to mortgagor, the mutual disinheritance of Wy by Ty, and the failure to record the assignment.

After Ty's death, Wy succeeded to sole ownership of the house. As tenants by the entirety, both Wy and Ty had an undivided interest in the property and the right of survivorship. The right of survivorship provides that upon the death of one tenant, the surviving tenant enjoys the estate free of the decedent's interest. This right is unaffected by the fact that the couple's relations had soured. It is also unaffected by Ty's attempt to disinherit Wy. Thus, Wy became the sole owner of the house upon Ty's death. The issue is who is liable for the $40,000 due at the end of the two-year period.

Wy could argue that the transfer of the mortgage from Blanche to Ty completely discharged her mortgage obligation. Although Blanche lent her parents $40,000, she assigned the mortgage to her father for $4,000. She kept this a secret from her mother and the assignment was not recorded. Wy could claim that this is a fraudulent transfer because $4,000 does not seem like reasonable consideration for the right to receive $40,000 plus interest. However, the $4,000 paid by Ty probably will be seen as sufficient consideration to support the assignment. Courts are extremely reluctant to rule on the sufficiency of consideration. Thus, since it was not fraudulent, Wy will not be discharged from her obligation.

It is more likely, though, that Wy will get a partial reimbursement from Ty's estate. Ty became mortgagee to himself and his wife when the mortgage was transferred to him by Blanche in 1987. This gave him the right to receive mortgage payments, but it did not excuse him from paying his share of these payments as provided in the note.

Furthermore, although Ty attempted to disinherit Wy, she would still receive some of his estate under the intestacy laws of the state. Thus, she would be entitled to partial reimbursement from the estate of her late husband to pay her share of the mortgage.

102. CRIMINAL LAW/CRIMINAL PROCEDURE

To: Senior Partner
From: Associate
Re: William and Robert criminal case

Charges: Based on the facts presented, William and Robert will most likely be charged with robbery, conspiracy, and felony murder.

Robbery is defined as a taking of personal property of another from the other's person or presence by force or intimidation with the intent to permanently deprive him of it.

Here, if it can be proven that William and Robert committed the acts set forth, both can be charged with robbery. They took cash and a bracelet from the liquor store by force by brandishing weapons and firing one of them. Their intent was indicated by the statement of one of the defendants who yelled, "Give me all the cash from the register!" On these facts it seems certain that they meant to permanently deprive the store owner of his money and property.

Insofar as defendants acted in concert with one another, they can be charged with conspiracy. Conspiracy arises from an intentional agreement between two or more persons to achieve an unlawful objective.

The agreement and intent elements of this crime are substantially met by the act of robbing the liquor store. Note that a charge of conspiracy will not merge with the robbery charge and stands as a separate offense.

Defendants will also be charged with felony murder. A felony murder is a killing committed during the course of a felony. The element of malice is implied from the intent to commit the underlying felony.

The facts establish that Ed was shot by one of the defendants because he startled the defendants when he emerged from the back room. The fact that one of the defendants fired his gun (actus reus) and may have had the requisite intent (mens rea) for murder is of no consequence; both defendants will be charged with felony murder despite the fact that only one of them killed Ed, since Ed's death was foreseeable and occurred during the commission of the robbery.

Pretrial motions: We should move to suppress the gun and bracelet found in the apartment leased by William's fiancée. It was the fruit of an unconstitutional warrantless search. Furthermore, the actions of the police do not seem to fall under any good faith exception to the Fourth Amendment warrant requirement.

To constitutionally search the premises, the police needed a properly executed search warrant. Here, they searched the apartment without first obtaining a warrant even though it seems they had information that would have supported the issuance of a warrant—probable cause in the form of a reliable witness who described the item sought and its location with particularity.

The police may try to rebut this motion by claiming that they did not need a warrant because they had been given permission to enter the premises by Philip, the 11-year-old boy. For the police to conduct a valid warrantless search, though, they must receive voluntary and intelligent consent to do so. Philip may not have had knowledge of the right to withhold consent. Such knowledge, however, is not a prerequisite to establishing voluntary and intelligent consent; it is merely a factor to be considered. Nevertheless, it is unlikely that Philip knew of this right and it is unlikely that his consent would be considered voluntary given his age and the fact that there were several detectives at his door. It is also likely that Philip was incapable of making an intelligent decision regarding consent. At age 11, Philip most likely did not have the capacity to consent to the officers' search request. Taken together with the fact that Philip probably lacked knowledge of his right to withhold consent, we will probably succeed on our motion to suppress the gun and the diamond bracelet as the products of an illegal search.

Both defendants, however, may have problems in asserting standing to bring this motion. A person has standing to raise a Fourth Amendment claim if he owned or had a right to possession of the place searched, or if the place searched was in fact his home whether or not he owned or had a right to possession of it.

William may have standing if he lived with his fiancee, but if he lived elsewhere, he lacks standing to bring this claim.

It is unlikely that Robert could claim that the apartment of William's fiancee was his home. Thus, lacking any reasonable expectation of privacy in her apartment, Robert has no standing to bring a Fourth Amendment claim. Therefore, no motion should be brought on these grounds on his behalf.

Robert's confession: We should move to suppress Robert's confession on the ground that it violates his Fifth and Sixth Amendment rights, but the facts given are insufficient to determine whether the motion will be successful.

The Fifth Amendment provides defendants with a right to remain silent, and since *Miranda*, this right has also been held to include a right to counsel whenever there is custodial interrogation by someone known to be a police officer. The Sixth Amendment provides a right to counsel at all critical stages of a prosecution, including any post-charge interrogations. The facts indicate that Robert was in custody at the time he made his statement and apparently had been charged with the robbery, but nothing indicates that his rights were violated. His Sixth Amendment right to counsel was not violated since that right is charge-specific and the officers to whom Robert confessed were not investigating the robbery for which he was charged. It is unclear whether Robert's Fifth Amendment rights under *Miranda* were violated. The facts indicate that Robert was advised of his rights upon arrest but nothing indicates whether he waived his rights. If Robert requested an attorney, all questioning had to stop. If he invoked the right to remain silent, the subsequent questioning two days later about unrelated crimes was probably permissible, but Robert should have been rewarned of his rights. It is also unclear whether Robert's confession was in response to police interrogation. Interrogation includes anything likely to elicit a response. While it could be argued that the police should have known that any questioning relating to ownership of a gun would cause Robert to respond regarding the crime for which he was charged, Robert's response might also be found to be spontaneous since it went beyond what the police were looking for. On balance, Robert's motion to suppress probably will not succeed.

Difficulties in representing both defendants: It is most likely unethical for us to represent both William and Robert. Since one defendant could inculpate the other, zealous representation of one defendant could likely lead to damage to the case of the other. Therefore, I recommend that we represent one defendant, but not both.

103. EVIDENCE

(a)   The court should probably rule the transcript of Oats's testimony inadmissible. Although Oats's testimony is relevant to prove that Dick possessed and disposed of drugs during the high-speed chase (*i.e.,* it tends to prove that Dick stole the dangerous drugs), it is hearsay. Hearsay is any statement, other than one made by the declarant while testifying in the current proceeding, offered in evidence to prove the truth of the matter asserted. Oats's testimony is being offered to prove that Dick possessed and disposed of the drugs during a high-speed chase; thus, it is being offered for its truth and is hearsay.

The testimony of a now-unavailable witness, given at another proceeding, under oath, is admissible under the former testimony exception to the hearsay rule as long as there is sufficient similarity of parties and issues so that the opportunity to develop testimony or cross-examine at the prior hearing was meaningful. Here, Oats is deceased and, thus, clearly unavailable. His prior testimony was under oath and the parties were identical. Dick was represented by counsel and had an opportunity to cross-examine Oats.

The problem in trying to apply this exception to these facts involves the requirement of identity of subject matter. While the cause of action in both proceedings need not be identical, the party against whom the testimony is offered must have had a similar motive to develop the declarant's testimony at the prior proceeding. Since the statement regarding the bottles was not really material to the reckless driving case, Dick did not have the same motive to cross-examine Oats on this point as he does in the drug case. Therefore, the transcript should probably be excluded.

(b)   Phil's testimony should be admitted, provided the proper foundation is laid. Phil has personal knowledge of the facts to which he is testifying. The only question arises with respect to the labels on the bottles. The best evidence rule (or the original document rule) requires that where the knowledge of a witness concerning a fact results from having read it in a document, the original writing must be produced, if possible. Secondary evidence in the form of oral testimony regarding the contents of the writing is permitted only after it has been shown that the original is unavailable for some reason other than the serious misconduct of the proponent. Any evidence that the bottles were thrown into the river should suffice to satisfy the requirement that the original be unavailable.

Phil's testimony about the labels is relevant, circumstantial evidence that there were dangerous drugs in the bottles that were in Dick's possession.

(c)   The court should take judicial notice of the fact that DLD is an opium derivative. A fact that is capable of accurate and ready determination by resort to sources whose accuracy cannot reasonably be questioned (*i.e.,* a manifest fact) can be judicially noticed at any time whether or not requested. If a party requests judicial notice and supplies the court with the necessary information, notice is mandatory. Thus, if the pharmacological dictionary qualifies as a source whose accuracy cannot reasonably be questioned, the court must judicially notice that DLD is an opium derivative.

(d)   Win's testimony should be admitted.

Although extrinsic evidence of other misconduct is inadmissible against a criminal defendant if offered solely to establish criminal disposition or bad character, it is admissible if relevant to some other issue. Purposes for which other acts of misconduct are admissible include to show motive, opportunity, intent, lack of mistake, and identity. Here, Win's testimony that Dick was a narcotics user is highly relevant on the issue of motive (and, if mistake was offered by the defense, absence of mistake). Thus, Win's testimony should not be excluded on the basis that it is inadmissible character evidence.

The fact that Dick attempted to conceal his narcotics use from Win is relevant on the issue of whether he can prevent her testimony because of the privilege for confidential marital communications. Either spouse has a privilege to refuse to disclose, ***and to prevent another from disclosing***, a confidential communication made between the spouses while they were married. Divorce will not terminate the privilege. To apply, the communication must have been made in reliance upon the intimacy of the marital relationship. The communication may be by conduct and need not be spoken. Here, Dick could argue that his conduct with respect to his narcotics use constituted a confidential marital communication. The fact that he attempted to conceal the use, however, is strong evidence against application of the privilege. If he did not want Win to know of his drug use, he could not have been relying on the intimacy of his marital relationship or intending his conduct to be a communication to his wife. Thus, Win should be permitted to testify despite Dick's assertion of this privilege.

Note that spousal immunity does not apply in this case. First, it may be asserted only during marriage. Second, under the Federal Rules, the privilege belongs to the witness-spouse.

104. EVIDENCE

(a)   For evidence to be admissible, it must first be relevant. Evidence is relevant if it tends to prove or disprove a fact in issue. Sam's testimony is relevant because it tends to prove that Dave was pouring gasoline over the building lobby immediately before the fire. This tends to prove Dave was guilty of arson.

The major objection to Sam's testimony is that it is hearsay. Hearsay in an out-of-court statement offered to prove the truth of the matter asserted. Hearsay is generally inadmissible because of its lesser degree of reliability and because there is no opportunity to cross-examine the out-of-court declarant.

Here, Sam's testimony is hearsay. Sam is testifying as to what Bart said immediately prior to the fire. The testimony is being offered to prove the truth of what Bart said. There are, however, several exceptions to the hearsay rule. The exceptions generally involve out-of-court statements that have their own indicia of trustworthiness.

Statements made during or shortly after a startling event are admissible under the excited utterance exception. The statement must relate to the startling event and must be made so shortly after the event that there is no opportunity for the declarant to reflect or fabricate a statement. Here, Bart's statement was an excited utterance. The statement was made as soon as Bart saw Dave spilling gasoline over the lobby of the building. Seeing someone douse an occupied building with gasoline is certainly a startling event. Bart's comments were directly related to the event in that Bart asked his co-workers to call the police.

(b)   Ellen's testimony is relevant because it tends to show that Dave had previously engaged in similar conduct, thus making it more likely that he committed the crime in this instance.

The proper objection would be that the prosecution is attempting to prove Dave's bad character to show that he was more likely to have committed the crime in this case. The general rule is that the prosecution cannot use a defendant's prior act of misconduct to show his propensity to commit the crime in this instance.

Even though character evidence is not admissible to show criminal propensity, it is admissible for other purposes, such as to show absence of mistake, motive, or common plan or scheme. Here, there is a good argument that Ellen's testimony is admissible either to show common plan or scheme or to show absence of mistake or accident. Given Dave's testimony that the fire occurred as a result of an accident, Ellen's testimony was proper to show that Dave was aware of the flammable quality of gasoline and to show that the fire was not an accident.

(c)   Dave's testimony on direct was relevant to disprove his intent to set the fire. Further, Dave's testimony tends to prove that he was not the cause of the fire because a patron flipped a lit cigarette butt, causing the gasoline to ignite. The questioning of Dave was relevant because it tends to impeach his credibility by suggesting that he is dishonest.

A party can impeach an adverse witness by cross-examining the witness as to any prior bad act that calls into question the veracity and trustworthiness of the witness. The cross-examination must be conducted in good faith. Here, the cross-examination of Dave was proper. The fact that Dave was expelled from college for cheating certainly calls into question his credibility. Moreover, the cross-examination was clearly conducted in good faith since Dave had in fact been expelled for cheating.

The only other possible grounds for exclusion is that the evidence elicited on cross-examination was unduly prejudicial. Such an argument is unlikely to be successful. Trial courts have broad discretion in this area. Although the evidence is prejudicial to Dave, it is not ***unduly*** prejudicial given its probativeness on the issue of Dave's veracity and trustworthiness.

(d) Dr. Hix's testimony was relevant because it tends to support Dave's defense that the fire occurred as a result of an accident.

The objection here would be that this was improper expert opinion testimony. The general rule is that expert opinion testimony is permitted where the expert is properly qualified and where the expert testimony would be helpful to the trier of fact.

Here, there may be an argument that Dr. Hix was not qualified as an expert. However, as a chemist, he probably has sufficient expertise to testify regarding the use of gasoline as a cleaning solvent. Moreover, this is an area where expert testimony would be useful to the trier of fact in that most people would not be familiar with the chemical qualities of gasoline. Finally, there appears to be a proper basis for the expert testimony. An expert is allowed to rely on any type of information reasonably relied upon by an expert. Here, Dr. Hix's reliance on standard scientific treatises and his own experimentation was clearly proper. Dr. Hix's testimony was properly admitted.

(e) A court may take judicial notice of matters of common knowledge, those matters which well-informed people generally accept as true. It is well known that gasoline vapor is extremely combustible and, thus, it was proper for the court to take judicial notice of this fact.

However, it was improper for the court to take judicial notice of the legal conclusion that the use of gasoline was gross and reckless. Particularly in a criminal case, it is improper for a court to give conclusive weight to a judicially noticed fact. To do so violates a defendant's Sixth Amendment right to a fair trial.

105. EVIDENCE

(a) For any item of evidence to be admissible it must be relevant, competent, and material. Materiality exists when the evidence relates to one of the substantive legal issues in the case. Relevancy exists when the evidence tends either to prove or disprove a material fact.

In this case, Mang's testimony was clearly material. One of the critical issues in the case against Dale was whether the rental car was wrongfully obtained. Mang's testimony was related to that issue in that it demonstrated that the car had not been rented. Mang's testimony was also relevant because it tended to prove that Dale had not obtained possession of the car in a legal manner. The general rule is that evidence that a business or firm had an established business routine is relevant to show that a particular event occurred or did not occur. Mang certainly was competent to testify regarding Acme's computerized system of tracking automobiles. His testimony indicated that he is a "supervisory employee of Acme" who is "thoroughly familiar with the (company's) computerized system." Thus, Mang's testimony is admissible unless some other rule of evidence requires that it be excluded.

Here, Dale could have raised a best evidence rule objection to Mang's testimony, but such an objection, if raised, was properly overruled. In general, the best evidence rule provides that the original of a writing be produced whenever the terms of the writing are material. Here, Mang was testifying based on computerized records of rental transactions. Because his testimony was based on his review of the records and not his own direct observation, the best evidence rule would ordinarily require that the original records be produced or some satisfactory explanation be given for their nonproduction. Here, Mang testified that he had reviewed the computer records and found no record that the car in question had been rented out. The nonexistence of a record can be offered as proof that an event did not occur. The best evidence rule can be avoided by demonstrating that the records in question are too voluminous to bring to court. The prosecution could successfully argue that it would be unreasonable to require Mang to bring the computerized records to court. This argument would be less convincing if Dale could demonstrate that the records could be printed out and brought in printed form to the court.

Dale could also have raised a hearsay objection to Mang's testimony. Hearsay is an out-of-court statement offered to prove the truth of the matter asserted therein. The general rule is that hearsay is inadmissible because of its lack of trustworthiness. Numerous exceptions to the hearsay rule exist.

These exceptions involve types of evidence that have sufficient indicia of trustworthiness. In this case, Mang's testimony involved hearsay because Mang was testifying as to what other employees recorded in the computerized records. The out-of-court statements by the other employees were offered to prove that the 1985 Buick Skylark was not rented out. Any hearsay objection, however, should have been overruled. Mang's testimony clearly fell within the business records exception to the hearsay rule. Under this exception, records maintained within the regular course of business are admissible if the person making the entry in the records had personal knowledge and was required to make the entry as part of her employment. The entrant need not be unavailable for the exception to apply. In addition, under the Federal Rules of Evidence and the modern trend, business records can be used to prove the nonoccurrence of an event if it was the regular practice of the business to record all such events. Thus, no hearsay objection could be raised to Mang's testimony that Acme's records indicated that the 1985 Buick Skylark had not been rented.

(b)   Gum's testimony was properly admitted as circumstantial evidence that Dale had been in the car before it was wrecked. Again, to be admissible, testimonial evidence must be material and relevant.

Here, Gum's testimony was both material and relevant. Again, one of the key issues in the case was establishing that Dale was wrongfully in possession of the automobile. Gum's testimony was probably relevant because it may have tended to prove circumstantially that Dale was in possession of the automobile. The issue of relevancy is difficult to determine based on the information supplied. The evidence was certainly relevant if additional evidence was introduced linking the shirts with Dale. For example, relevancy would be indisputable if the prosecution had introduced evidence that Dale's initials were DAL or that the laundry which washed the shirts routinely identified shirts with the first three letters of a customer's first name.

(c)   The denial of the motion for a directed verdict was well within the trial court's discretion. While a criminal defendant can be convicted only upon proof that is beyond a reasonable doubt, that quantum of evidence can consist of both direct and circumstantial evidence. Here, the prosecution offered sufficient circumstantial evidence linking Dale with the theft of the rental car. Although the prosecution did not specifically prove that the rental car was worth more than $100, the automobile was maintained in good working order as a rental car. Thus, it would be proper for the court to take judicial notice of this common knowledge and not require direct proof.

(d)   In general, all of a defendant's statements are inadmissible in a criminal case unless the prophylactic *Miranda* warnings were given. However, several exceptions to this general rule exist. One of the principal exceptions is that voluntary statements taken in violation of *Miranda* may be admitted to impeach the credibility of the witness. Involuntary statements are presumed to be untrustworthy and are therefore inadmissible for any purpose.

In this case, no *Miranda* warnings were given prior to Dale's 1979 confession, but the confession was apparently voluntary. Thus, the confession was admissible to impeach Dale's statement that he had never stolen a car in his life.

Dale might nevertheless argue that the confession should have been excluded because of its remoteness and because of the fact that Dale was acquitted of the charges. This argument should be rejected. While remoteness of a criminal act is relevant in determining the admissibility of a conviction, there is no time limit on prior inconsistent statements offered for impeachment.

Dale might also try to argue that the prior confession should be excluded because its probative value was outweighed by its potential for prejudice. The trial court generally has broad discretion to rule upon such objections. Here, the confession was potentially prejudicial because it involved a confession to a similar crime that had occurred many years before. However, the confession was also probative because it tended to demonstrate that the defendant was untruthful. For these reasons, the trial court could properly overrule the objection.

106. EVIDENCE

(a)   Paul's testimony is logically relevant to prove that Don was in a hurry, and thus negligent. Don's fault is necessary to Paul's suit against Cabco under a vicarious liability theory.

Paul stated his opinion that Don was "hurting real bad." Normally, lay opinions are inadmissible unless based on the witness's perception and unless the information is helpful to the trier of fact. Here, Paul saw Don after the accident and his observation is helpful to determine Don's condition. Paul's opinion is admissible lay opinion, similar to other admissible observations regarding speed or intoxication.

Paul testified to Don's out-of-court statement, offered to prove that Don was in a hurry and caused the accident. Paul's testimony would be inadmissible unless a hearsay exclusion or exception applies.

An admission is a statement made or act done that amounts to a prior acknowledgment by one of the parties to an action of one of the relevant facts. Although traditionally an exception to the hearsay rule, an admission by a party-opponent is not hearsay at all under the Federal Rules. Here, however, Cabco is the party and Don is the declarant. Statements made by an agent concerning any matter within the scope of his agency, and made during the existence of the employment relationship, are vicarious admissions, not hearsay, and are admissible against the principal. Therefore, since Don was Cabco's agent, his statement concerned a matter within the scope of his agency (driving the cab), and the statement was made while he was an employee of Cabco, it is a vicarious admission and is admissible nonhearsay. Note that under the traditional admission exception to the hearsay rule, an agent's declarations were admissible against the principal only if making statements was within the scope of the agent's authority. If that rule still applied, Don's statement would probably be inadmissible, since it is unlikely that a company would give a cab driver authority to speak for the company.

Even if the statement did not qualify as an admission (*e.g.*, if the jurisdiction did not follow the Federal Rules approach), it could probably be admitted under the excited utterance exception to the hearsay rule.

Statements made under the stress of a startling event are admissible. Here, Don's statement related to the accident, a startling event. However, it is not clear whether Don made the statement immediately after the accident to insure its trustworthiness. Don made the statement "after the accident." Paul would successfully argue that Don's statement is reliable because Don was still hurting from the accident and would not have been able to fabricate a statement.

If Don is unavailable, the statement would be admissible under the statement against interest exception to the hearsay rule since Don's statement would be against his pecuniary interest.

Paul's testimony was properly admitted.

(b)   Paul would argue the question regarding a traffic accident was beyond the scope of direct, unless there was questioning beyond what Don had said in (a), above. In addition, Paul would assert evidence of prior accidents is inadmissible to prove conduct in conformity with character.

While the question asked may be objectionable, evidence of the conviction itself is admissible if the court determines that its probative value as impeachment evidence is not substantially outweighed by the danger of unfair prejudice.

Under certain circumstances, a witness may be impeached by proof of a conviction of a crime. The fact of the conviction is proved by either eliciting an admission on cross-examination or by the record of the conviction. This type of impeachment requires an actual conviction; an arrest or indictment is insufficient. A witness may be impeached by *any* crime (felony or misdemeanor) involving dishonesty or false statement. The court has no discretion to exclude this type of impeachment. A witness may also be impeached by *any felony*, even if it does not involve dishonesty, but if the felony does not involve dishonesty, the court may exercise discretion to exclude it. Vehicular manslaughter is a felony that does not involve dishonesty; thus, the court has discretion to exclude Paul's prior conviction. When, as here, the witness being impeached is someone other than the accused in a criminal case, the court should exclude the conviction if its probative value as impeachment evidence is substantially outweighed by the danger of unfair prejudice. Given the nature of the incident involved in this case, a court should probably exclude Paul's conviction. Its probative value with respect to Paul's veracity is quite weak, and the danger that the jury will be misled and consider this as substantive evidence that Paul was at fault is high.

(c)   Doc's testimony is relevant because it tends to prove that Paul was contributorily negligent, a defense to Paul's suit.

Confidential communications between patient and doctor are privileged if made for the purpose of diagnosis and treatment. Here, the communication was confidential since Vicky told Doc, "Don't tell anybody. . . ," but her statements relating to the joint and Paul's looking down are not necessary to treatment. Furthermore, even if the privilege did apply to any of Vicky's statements, the privilege does not survive the death of the patient. Thus, the privilege will not bar Doc's testimony.

The biggest hurdle is the fact that Vicky's statement is hearsay. Doc is restating Vicky's out-of-court statement to prove Paul was at fault; *i.e.,* it is being offered to prove the truth of the matter asserted.

The statement could be admissible, however, as a statement against interest. Being deceased, Vicky is clearly unavailable. To qualify, the statement must be against the declarant's penal, proprietary, or pecuniary interest. Here, Vicky's statement would be against her penal interest since marijuana possession and usage is likely a criminal offense. In the alternative, her statement would be against her pecuniary interest since it would expose her to civil liability.

Vicky's statements relating to her physical condition that are relevant to Doc's diagnosis and treatment are admissible as an exception to the hearsay rule. It could be argued that Vicky's condition of having smoked marijuana would likely affect her surgery. Thus, that part of her statement would be relevant to diagnosis and treatment.

Doc's testimony was properly admitted.

107. EVIDENCE

(a)   Ward's testimony was properly admitted. It is relevant because it helps to prove that Parks fell because of a tear in the carpet. Delta may object that Ward's testimony is inadmissible hearsay because Ward repeats the statement of an unknown bystander, and the statement is offered to prove that what it asserts is true—that the carpet was torn.

The statement is probably admissible, however, as an excited utterance. The bystander was apparently startled when Parks tumbled down the stairs. The bystander's statement was apparently spontaneous, and it appears to have been made while the bystander was under the stress of excitement produced by the startling event. Thus, it should be admitted under the excited utterance exception to the hearsay rule.

I see no tenable argument for discretionary exclusion of Ward's testimony. The trial judge did not err in admitting the testimony.

(b)   The court could have properly admitted Carter's testimony, but it is a close call.

Parks will argue that Carter's testimony is relevant in two ways. First, the fact that Delta ordered a new carpet shortly after Parks's accident is some circumstantial evidence that the old carpet was dangerous. Second, the fact that the old carpet had been removed before Carter arrived could be a type of "spoliation evidence." If Delta disposed of the old carpet right after the accident, hoping to deprive Parks of a chance to prove that the carpet was torn, that act of spoliation could itself be circumstantial evidence that the carpet was torn.

Public policy favors the repair of dangerous conditions; therefore, evidence of a subsequent repair is not admissible when offered to prove that the prior condition was dangerous. Thus, the mere fact that Delta replaced the old carpet is not admissible as circumstantial evidence that the old carpet was dangerous. But Parks can avoid the subsequent remedial conduct exclusion by arguing that Carter's testimony is relevant for the second purpose noted above—to prove Delta destroyed evidence. Under the doctrine of limited admissibility, the trial judge could admit Carter's testimony; if this is a jury case, the trial judge could instruct the jury as follows: "If you believe Carter's testimony, and if you believe that Delta disposed of the old carpet in order to deprive Parks of the opportunity to prove that it was torn, then you may infer that the carpet was in fact torn."

If Parks uses this argument to avoid the subsequent remedial conduct rule, then Delta's lawyer should argue for discretionary exclusion. Carter's testimony may prejudice Delta because the proposed jury instruction asks the jury to perform difficult mental gymnastics. The jury may be baffled by the limiting instruction and may use Carter's testimony as evidence that the carpet was torn, even if they don't conclude that Delta was trying to hide evidence.

The discretionary exclusion point is a close one. If the trial judge did exercise discretion and did give the jury instruction described above, then the appellate court ought to sustain the trial judge.

(c)   Adams's testimony with respect to Parks's intoxication was properly admitted, but his testimony regarding the cause of the fall should have been excluded. Adams's testimony is relevant to prove that Parks was intoxicated and that his intoxication, not the carpet, was the cause of the accident.

Parks will probably object to Adams's testimony as inadmissible lay opinion. Generally, lay witnesses must testify to *facts,* not opinions. But a lay witness may express an opinion if two conditions are satisfied. First, the opinion must be rationally based on what the witness has himself perceived. Second, the opinion must be helpful to the trier of fact in its effort to understand what the witness has perceived. To satisfy the first condition, Delta's lawyer will need to question Adams about his opportunity to perceive Parks's drunken condition. How long was Adams sitting next to Parks? Did Parks smell like a rum barrel? How was Parks behaving during the movie? When Adams followed Parks down the stairway, how was Parks walking? If Adams gives suitably detailed answers to these background questions, the trial judge will probably find the first condition is satisfied. To satisfy the second condition, Delta's lawyer will have to convince the trial judge that it would be helpful to hear Adams's *conclusions* as well as his more detailed observations about Parks's condition. A person's apparent intoxication is hard for a witness to explain without resorting to conclusory terms. For this reason, judges have traditionally allowed lay witnesses to express an opinion about intoxication.

As noted above, to be admissible, lay opinion must be helpful to the trier of fact in understanding the testimony or determining a fact in issue. It is for the trier of fact to decide what caused Parks's fall. Adams's opinion on the cause is not helpful to the trier of fact. Therefore, even though the Federal Rules no longer exclude opinions that embrace the ultimate issue, this portion of Adams's testimony would still be excluded.

(d)   Martin's testimony is relevant in two ways: First, it helps prove that the stairway was not dangerous. If thousands of patrons used it without incident or complaint, that suggests that there was nothing wrong with it. Second, Martin's testimony helps prove that Delta had *no notice* of any danger and that Delta was, therefore, not negligent with respect to plaintiff Parks. Under either of these two theories, Delta's lawyer will need to ask Martin some foundational questions to prove that if any patron had fallen or had complained about the stairway, theater manager Martin would have heard about it.

Many courts are reluctant to admit absence of similar accidents to show absence of negligence or lack of defect. However, where a structural condition is involved and that condition is unchanged, the court may admit the evidence of absence of other complaints to show lack of defect. Thus, for Delta to succeed in introducing this testimony for the first purpose (to show that the stairway was not dangerous), it will need convincing evidence that the condition of the stairway when Parks fell was *substantially identical* to its condition when prior patrons used it without incident or complaint. Delta will have a difficult time here. The condition of a carpet changes over time. It wears out gradually, and if it wears out enough, it tears. Thus, the experience of prior patrons seems of questionable relevance if offered to prove lack of dangerousness. Prior safety history and absence of complaints is always admissible to show the defendant's lack of notice or knowledge of the danger. Thus, Martin's testimony was properly admitted to show that Delta was unaware of any defect in the carpet.

(e)   The court properly admitted Attorney Nate's testimony.

Attorney Nate's testimony is relevant to help prove that Parks was intoxicated, that his intoxication caused his fall, that the theater carpet was not torn, and that Parks's tort claim against Delta is without merit.

Parks's lawyer will probably not bother to make a hearsay objection to Nate's testimony because Parks's statements to Nate are clearly admissions of a party-opponent.

Parks's lawyer might object on the ground that Parks's communications with Nate are protected by the attorney-client privilege. Assuming that Parks spoke with Nate in confidence, the privilege would apply; even though Nate eventually decided not to represent Parks, the communication was clearly in contemplation of an attorney-client relationship, and that is enough to bring the privilege into play. The client holds the privilege. Thus, in the absence of an exception to the application of the privilege, Parks could prevent Nate from testifying.

There is no privilege if the services of the lawyer were sought as an aid in planning or commission of something the client knew, or should have known, was a crime or fraud. Delta's lawyer will argue that Parks's statements to Nate demonstrate Parks's intent to assert a baseless tort claim against Delta, and his knowledge that it was fraudulent.

Although Parks's statements to Nate suggest that he was not certain about the cause of his fall and was not certain about the condition of the carpet, I think there is enough here to justify applying the crime-fraud exception to the privilege.

108. EVIDENCE

(a)   Adam's testimony was properly admitted.

Adam's testimony passes the first test of admissibility in that it is relevant. The basic test of relevance is whether the evidence tends to prove or disprove a fact of consequence. Here, those facts are: (i) that Tess was raped; and (ii) that the rapist had a blemish on his left arm. These facts would help establish that the crime was committed and the identity of its perpetrator.

Although the testimony is relevant, it is hearsay (*i.e.*, an out-of-court statement offered to prove the truth of the matter asserted). Here, it is offered to prove that a rape was committed by a man with a blemish on his left arm. Hearsay is inadmissible unless it falls within a recognized exception to the hearsay rule. Adam's testimony would almost certainly be admissible under modern interpretations of the "excited utterance" exception. To fall within this exception, there must have been a startling event, the statement must have been made under the stress of the excitement and before the declarant had time to reflect, and the statement must relate to the startling event. Here, the rape was a startling event and the statement relates to the rape. Roe will no doubt argue that the five-minute lapse between the rape and the statement was sufficient to give Tess time to reflect. However, a modern court would be unlikely to accept Roe's argument, as Tess's apparent physical condition (sobbing) would indicate that Tess was still under the shock of the startling event and that sufficient time had not elapsed for Tess to fabricate a story.

(b)   Cable's testimony should have been excluded.

If the prosecutor is offering this evidence to prove that, having raped once, Roe is likely to have raped Tess, the evidence should be excluded. Evidence of prior acts of misconduct is not admissible to prove a person's character as circumstantial evidence of his conduct on the occasion in question. Prior misconduct evidence can be admitted to prove some relevant fact *other than character* (for example, modus operandi or lack of mistake), but no such relevant fact is apparent here. A prior felony conviction can be used to impeach Roe's testimony (*see* (e), below), but apparently Roe has not testified yet and this would not be the proper way to prove a prior conviction. Furthermore, the court would probably have to exclude the conviction if offered for impeachment purposes. If offered to impeach the accused in a criminal case, the felony (not involving dishonesty) will be admitted only if the prosecution shows that its probative value as impeachment evidence outweighs its prejudicial effect.

This showing appears to be impossible in this case. The judge should sustain Roe's character evidence objection.

Cable's testimony also violates the best evidence rule. Cable's knowledge concerning the facts in his testimony results from having read the police record, a document. Before his testimony is admitted, it must be shown that the report is unavailable. There is no indication of such a showing. The judge should sustain Roe's best evidence rule objection.

Cable apparently has no personal knowledge of Roe's prior rape conviction or of the blemish on Roe's arm. Cable is simply repeating what is said in the police record, and the record is an "out-of-court statement." The record is hearsay if used to prove that Roe was convicted and that he has a blemish on his arm. If the record *itself* were offered in evidence, it might be admissible as a business record, assuming it were properly authenticated and shown to be trustworthy. But Cable's oral repetition of the record is bald hearsay, not admissible under any hearsay exception.

Even if this evidence did not violate the rules discussed above, the judge should exclude it because its probative value is outweighed by its danger of unfair prejudice. The police record would be both cumulative and highly prejudicial to Roe. The jury would be too likely to misuse it as evidence of Roe's bad character.

(c) Tess's testimony was properly admitted.

Tess's testimony is admissible, nonhearsay identification evidence under the Federal Rules of Evidence. An out-of-court identification by a witness available for cross-examination at trial is admissible as substantive evidence.

(d) Mrs. Roe's testimony was properly admitted.

Roe will try to assert the spousal privilege to prevent his wife from testifying against him. In some jurisdictions, this privilege belongs to the party-spouse (Mr. Roe) and may be invoked by him. However, under federal case law and in about half the common law courts, the privilege belongs to the witness-spouse. Although the prosecution could not *compel* Mrs. Roe to testify against Roe, she *may* so testify if she wishes. The facts indicated that Mrs. Roe is testifying voluntarily; thus, Mrs. Roe's testimony is admissible, unless the jurisdiction still maintains the common law ban prohibiting one from testifying against his or her spouse.

Roe may also try to assert that Mrs. Roe's testimony is inadmissible because it reveals a confidential marital communication. Either spouse has a privilege to refuse to disclose, and to prevent another from disclosing, a confidential communication made between the spouses while they were husband and wife. Roe's agitated state and scratches, however, cannot constitute a communication. Thus, Roe cannot prevent Mrs. Roe from testifying.

(e) The shoe and the expert's testimony were properly admitted.

Roe will argue that the shoe is the fruit of an illegal search and, as such, should be barred under the exclusionary rule. Generally, that assertion would be correct. However, there are recognized exceptions to the exclusionary rule, and one of them applies here. Roe has testified that he was never near Tess's house. The prosecution is offering the shoe to *impeach* Roe's testimony. Such use of the shoe is constitutionally permissible, despite the illegal seizure.

The testimony of the expert indicates the relevance of the shoe; *i.e.,* it tends to establish that Roe was near Tess's house, despite Roe's testimony to the contrary. Shoe print identification would seem to be an appropriate subject matter for expert testimony in that it is an area where scientific, technical, or other specialized knowledge would assist the jury to understand the evidence. Assuming that the prosecution has properly qualified the witness as an expert, and that the expert is testifying from a proper basis, the testimony should be admitted.

(f) The prosecutor's argument was properly permitted.

The constitutional right to be protected against self-incrimination under the Fifth and Fourteenth Amendments applies to testimonial evidence. A request to bare one's arm for purposes of identification does not constitute an attempt to elicit self-incriminating testimonial evidence, nor is it an intrusive procedure that shocks the conscience. Because Roe's refusal was not within the ambit of the constitutional protections, the prosecutor was free to comment upon it in his closing argument.

109. CRIMINAL LAW/CRIMINAL PROCEDURE

To: Senior Partner
From: Associate
Re: *State v. Frankie and Johnnie*

CHARGES AND DEFENSES

Johnnie: Johnnie may be charged with conspiracy, battery, false imprisonment, kidnapping, and/or murder. The issue is whether Johnnie's conduct constitutes the elements that make up these crimes, and if so, whether there are any possible defenses which he may assert.

Conspiracy: Although Johnnie may be charged with conspiracy, it seems unlikely that he would be convicted of the crime, because the State may not be able to establish all elements of the crime. Conspiracy is an agreement between two or more people to accomplish some criminal purpose. The elements of conspiracy are as follows: (i) an agreement between two or more parties; (ii) an intent to enter into an agreement; and (iii) an intent to achieve the objective of the agreement. Most states require an overt act in furtherance of the conspiracy, but mere preparation will suffice.

It is very difficult to separate the intent to agree from the act of agreement. Intent to agree can be inferred from conduct, in this case, Johnnie's nod to Frankie in response to Frankie's statement that "you know how to handle this problem." Frankie's statement and Johnnie's nod appear to evidence both the act and the intent of agreement. The intent to achieve the objective must be established as to each defendant. This will be a bit tougher, because it is difficult to determine exactly what the objective was: assault, battery, false imprisonment, kidnapping, or murder? Unless there is an intent to *achieve the same purpose*—a "meeting of guilty minds"—there can be no conspiracy.

The problem the prosecution will have in establishing an intent to achieve an objective will be Johnnie's best chance to avoid a conspiracy conviction. On the given facts, it seems almost impossible for the State to prove that Frankie and Johnnie agreed to the same objective; perhaps Frankie only wanted Johnnie to give Chad a lecture on proper morals. Johnnie may also assert in his defense that his nod was not an indication of agreement in response to Frankie's statement about "handling the problem" and that, therefore, there was no agreement.

Battery: Johnnie may also be charged with battery. Battery is the unlawful application of force to the person of another resulting in either bodily harm or an offensive touching. The facts indicate that Johnnie struck and "continually beat" Chad, ultimately breaking his arm. Thus, Johnnie can be charged with battery. It does not appear that Johnnie has any defenses available to him under the given facts.

False imprisonment/kidnapping: Johnnie may be charged with false imprisonment and/or kidnapping. False imprisonment is the unlawful confinement of a person without that person's valid consent. Kidnapping is defined as the confinement of a person which involves either movement of the victim or concealment of the victim in a secret place, without that person's consent. In most jurisdictions, kidnapping is treated as a form of aggravated false imprisonment; therefore, the State may charge Johnnie with both, but he may not be convicted of both.

In the present case, either charge would be proper: Chad was taken against his will, as evidenced by his being thrown into the van after having a burlap sack thrown over his head, and was moved to a location some 10 miles away.

Johnnie's only possible defense would be that the taking and asportation were not a separate crime in itself, but were simply part of a larger set of circumstances, and occurred only as part of the battery. Some courts have held that it is only kidnapping if the movement of the victim substantially increases the risk to the victim over and above that necessarily involved in the other crime committed. This defense is not likely to succeed in Johnnie's case, because the movement of Chad to another location—*i.e.,* the interstate, put Chad directly in the path of the motorist that struck and killed him.

Murder: Finally, Johnnie may be charged with murder. Murder is the unlawful killing of a human being with malice aforethought. Malice aforethought exists if the defendant either: (i) intends to kill; (ii) intends to inflict great bodily injury; (iii) has a reckless indifference to an unjustifiably high risk to human life; or (iv) intends to commit a felony (*i.e.,* felony murder). Under the facts of the case, either a charge of murder based on reckless indifference or a charge of felony murder would be the State's best chance for a conviction.

Johnnie beat Chad and left him standing in the interstate with a sack over his head. These circumstances probably do not indicate an intent to kill or inflict great bodily injury, as required for a murder charge under (i) or (ii). However, the State could establish that Johnnie acted with reckless indifference to an unjustifiably high risk to human life, because there is a high probability that a person standing in the middle of an interstate highway without the ability to see would be struck by a car. In addition, a foreseeable death resulting from the commission of a felony is punishable as a felony murder. If Johnnie is charged with kidnapping, a felony, he could be also be charged with murder for the death which followed.

If Johnnie is charged with murder based on reckless indifference, he could assert that the interstate was not a very busy place at 11 p.m. or so, and that Chad was still standing when he was left in the road, so that there was not such a high risk to Chad's life. This argument is likely to fail, in light of the fact that Chad could not see to get out of the road, and could not remove the sack from his head because his arms were broken and bound.

If Johnnie is charged with felony murder, he could argue that, as discussed above, the movement of Chad was not a kidnapping but part of the battery, a misdemeanor. For the reasons discussed above, however, Johnnie's defense probably will not succeed.

Frankie:

Conspiracy: Frankie may be charged with conspiracy, but the State may have trouble obtaining a conviction because it is not evident what objective each party had in mind when Frankie said "you know how to handle this problem," and Johnnie nodded. (*See* above.) If Frankie is found to be a co-conspirator, he can also be charged with all other crimes committed by the other co-conspirators that are foreseeable and are committed in furtherance of the objectives of the conspiracy.

Accomplice liability: Frankie may be charged as an accomplice to battery, false imprisonment and/or kidnapping, and murder. An accomplice is one who ***intentionally*** aids, counsels, or encourages the person who actually engages in the act that causes the criminal result (the principal) before or during the commission of a crime. An accomplice is liable for the crimes he committed or counseled and for any other foreseeable or probable crimes committed in the course of committing the crime contemplated.

In this case, Frankie is likely to be viewed as an accomplice, because he encouraged Johnnie's conduct when he told Johnnie to "handle the problem," and he aided Johnnie by giving Johnnie the keys to the van. Although the exact intent behind Frankie's statement is not clear, Chad's death is a foreseeable result of the actions Johnnie took in response to the statement. Therefore, even if there was no conspiracy, Frankie may be charged with battery, false imprisonment and/or kidnapping, and murder under the doctrine of accomplice liability. His only defense would be that he did not ***intend*** to aid the crimes against Chad, but this is not likely to succeed in light of Frankie's actions in giving Johnnie the van keys and suggesting that Johnnie "handle the problem."

PRETRIAL MOTIONS

Johnnie and Frankie should move to suppress Frankie's statement to Lolita (*i.e.,* "If you don't want the same thing . . ."). At issue is whether the statement was obtained in violation of either party's rights. However, neither Johnnie nor Frankie will be successful.

Our clients might first attempt to have Frankie's statement suppressed on Fourth Amendment grounds. The Fourth Amendment to the United States Constitution provides that people shall be free from unreasonable searches and seizures. To ensure that this edict is carried out, the Supreme Court has adopted an exclusionary rule generally prohibiting the use of evidence in a criminal trial if the evidence was obtained in violation of the defendant's constitutional rights. The motion will not succeed, however, as to Johnnie, because he lacks standing to challenge the admission obtained from Frankie.

Only persons with standing are allowed to challenge the admission of evidence on Fourth Amendment grounds. A defendant will have standing only if the evidence was obtained in a manner that violated that defendant's constitutional rights. Here, the evidence was elicited from Frankie; Johnnie simply had no rights with respect to Frankie's statement. Therefore, Johnnie may not successfully move to suppress the statement on this ground.

Frankie, of course, does have standing to challenge the statement he made to Lolita, since he was the one who made it. However, Frankie's motion will likely fail because the statement was not taken in violation of Frankie's constitutional rights.

Frankie should argue that his confession was "seized" from him in his home, that he has a privacy interest in his home, and that therefore the police should have obtained a warrant to "wire" Lolita before sending her into Frankie's home to transmit their conversation. However, while it may be true that Frankie had a privacy interest in his home, the Supreme Court has held that speakers assume the risk that persons to whom they speak are unreliable, and if a person to whom another speaks turns out to be an informer wired for sound, the speaker has no Fourth Amendment right to object to the transmitting of the conversation without a warrant. [United States v. White, 401 U.S. 745 (1971)]

Frankie could raise Fifth Amendment grounds in support of his motion, but this too would be futile. The Fifth Amendment provides a right against self-incrimination. To protect this right, the Supreme Court has adopted a number of prophylactic rules—generally called *Miranda* rights— regarding custodial interrogations. These rules, however, are not applicable here because they apply only when a defendant is in custody (*i.e.*, not free to leave) and is being subjected to interrogation by someone known to be a government agent. Here, Frankie was not in custody; he was in his own home and was free to come and go as he pleased. Moreover, there was no interrogation by someone known to be a government agent; rather, the "questioning" was by Frankie's wife and Frankie did not know that she was working as a government agent.

Similarly, Frankie could raise Sixth Amendment grounds in support of his motion. The Sixth Amendment prohibits obtaining confessions from a defendant in the absence of his attorney. However, the Sixth Amendment does not come into play until the defendant has been charged, and here Frankie still has not been charged with any crime let alone when Lolita spoke with him. Thus, this motion will be unsuccessful.

110. CRIMINAL LAW/CRIMINAL PROCEDURE

To: County Prosecutor
From: Attorney
Re: *State v. Al, Steve, and Frank*

CHARGES AND DEFENSES

Al and Steve: The facts do not indicate which acts were committed by Al, which were committed by Steve, and which were committed by both. Therefore, the discussion of possible charges and available defenses will be the same as to both defendants.

Al and Steve can be charged with conspiracy, battery, kidnapping, larceny and/or robbery, and felony murder. The issue is whether Al and Steve's conduct constitutes the elements of these crimes, and if so, whether either defendant has any defenses he may assert.

Conspiracy: Both defendants can be charged with conspiracy. Conspiracy is an agreement between two or more people to commit a crime. There must be agreement between the parties, intent to enter into the agreement, and intent to achieve the illegal objective of the agreement. Intent to agree can be inferred from conduct, and is usually not treated by courts as separate from the act of agreement itself.

It appears from Al and Steve's conduct that they had an agreement to steal a car and to commit whatever additional illegal activity was necessary to obtain a car and deliver it to the strip shop. There is no indication from the facts that either defendant was unaware of the objective of the enterprise or was unwilling to participate. Therefore, there does not appear to be any defense available to either defendant against this charge.

Battery: Al and Steve can also be charged with battery. Battery is the unlawful application of force which results in an offensive touching or bodily injury. John's being blindfolded and bound certainly amounts to such an offensive touching. Al and Steve do not have any defenses to this charge.

Robbery/larceny: Al and Steve can be charged with robbery and/or larceny, but may not be convicted of both. Robbery is the taking and carrying away of property from the presence of another by force or the threat of force, with the intent to permanently deprive the person thereof. Larceny is the taking and carrying away of the property of another with the intent to permanently deprive the owner of the property. Therefore, larceny is a lesser included offense of robbery, and Al and Steve may be convicted of only one of these crimes.

Al and Steve appear to have intended to permanently deprive John's fiancee of her car; they left John by the side of the road, took off with the vehicle, and brought it to a strip shop where it was destroyed. Nothing in the facts indicates that the taking of the vehicle was a temporary joyride. In addition, the two clearly obtained the car by the threat of force, *i.e.,* by threatening John's life. Thus, either a charge of larceny or robbery would be proper. Their only defense would appear to be that they did not have the requisite intent when they took the car; however, for the reasons discussed above, this defense is likely to fail.

Kidnapping: Both defendants can be charged with kidnapping, which is the unlawful confinement of a person that involves either movement of the victim (asportation) or concealment of the victim in a secret place. Here, Al and Steve forced John to drive to a particular location against his will, where he was then bound, blindfolded, and left on the roadway. John's movement was restrained because of the threats to his life made by Al and Steve.

Al and Steve's only possible defense would be that the taking and asportation were not a separate crime in itself, but were simply part of a larger set of circumstances, and occurred only as part of the robbery. Some courts have held that it is only kidnapping if the movement of the victim substantially increases the risk to the victim over and above that necessarily involved in the other crime committed.

Murder: Al and Steve can also be charged with murder for the death of Tommy. Murder is the unlawful killing of a human being with malice aforethought. For malice aforethought, there must be: (i) intent to kill; (ii) intent to commit great bodily injury; (iii) reckless indifference to an unjustifiably high risk to human life; or (iv) intent to commit a felony (felony murder).

Murder based on (i) through (iii) would not apply in this case, because it was John's action that proximately caused the death of Tommy, rather than the acts of Al or Steve. However, charges against Al and Steve based on felony murder would be proper.

Felony murder is a murder committed during the perpetration of a specified felony. The defendant must be guilty of the underlying felony, and the felony must be a distinct transaction from the murder itself. Finally, the death must be a foreseeable result of the felony. Courts tend to find most of such deaths foreseeable.

Tommy was killed while John was being kidnapped and robbed by Al and Steve. It is certainly foreseeable that a child chasing a ball in the street could be killed by a person who is speeding because he is in fear for his life. Thus, both Al and Steve may be charged with felony murder. Their only defense would be that they are not guilty of any of the underlying felonies. For the reasons discussed above, however, this defense will not succeed.

Frank: Frank can be charged with conspiracy; as an accomplice to battery, kidnapping, robbery and/or larceny, and felony murder; and with receiving stolen property.

Conspiracy: Frank may be charged with conspiracy. (*See* discussion above.) If Frank is found to be a co-conspirator, he can also be charged with all other crimes committed by the other co-conspirators that are foreseeable and are committed in furtherance of the objectives of the conspiracy.

Under the given facts, it is not clear whether Frank was part of the agreement to steal the car, or if he simply pays people for vehicles without knowing where they were obtained. Since the facts say that Frank paid Al and Steve for their "services," it appears that there was an agreement to pay the two for stealing cars. Frank's best defense, of course, is that he had no involvement in the transaction until the vehicle was brought to him; therefore, he would have no liability for any of the crimes committed by Al and Steve.

Accomplice liability: Frank may be charged as an accomplice to battery, kidnapping, robbery and/or larceny, and murder. An accomplice is one who *intentionally* aids, counsels, or encourages the person who actually engages in the act that causes the criminal result (the principal) before or during the commission of a crime. An accomplice is liable for the crimes he committed or counseled and for any other foreseeable or probable crimes committed in the course of committing the crime contemplated.

Under the given facts, it is not clear whether Frank aided or encouraged the theft of the vehicle or any of the related crimes except for the cryptic statement that he paid Al and Steve for their services. Again, his best defense is that his involvement did not begin until Al and Steve brought the vehicle to his shop.

Receiving stolen property: Frank can be charged with receiving stolen property, which is defined as receiving possession and control of stolen personal property which is known to have been obtained in a criminal manner by another person with the intent to permanently deprive the rightful owner of the property.

Frank's best defense is that he was unaware of the nature of the property (*i.e.*, that it was stolen) at the time he acquired it. This defense will probably fail; because a large number of cars that are disassembled in strip shops are stolen, he should certainly be held liable for knowing that a car brought to him by two 17-year-old boys is likely to be stolen.

PRETRIAL MOTIONS

The defendants are likely to move to suppress Al's statement ("I hope the kid with the basketball is OK"), Steve's confession, and the money found in Al's locker. At issue is whether any of this evidence was obtained in violation of the defendants' constitutional rights.

As a preliminary matter, it should be noted that one has standing to object to unconstitutional seizures of evidence only if the seizure violated one's own constitutional rights; a co-felon has no right to complain that a seizure violated another's constitutional rights. In the light most favorable to the defendants, Al might have a claim that his rights were violated by Officer Ruthless's eavesdropping and by the search of his locker, and Steve might have a claim that his confession was obtained unconstitutionally, but Frank has no personal claim that his constitutional rights were violated and so will be unsuccessful in having any of the evidence excluded. Similarly, Al will not be able to successfully argue for exclusion based on any violation of Steve's rights and Steve will not be able to argue for exclusion based on violations of Al's rights.

It should also be noted that the Constitution prohibits unconstitutional searches only by persons employed by the government; persons acting in a private capacity cannot violate a defendant's constitutional rights. Here, we clearly have governmental conduct: Officer Ruthless and the principal were both working for the public school here.

Al could move that his statement regarding the "kid with the basketball" be excluded on Fourth Amendment grounds; however, such a motion will be unsuccessful. At issue is whether Al had a legitimate expectation of privacy in his statement.

The Fourth Amendment prohibits unreasonable searches and seizures of evidence. In most cases, seizure of evidence requires a warrant if the defendant has a reasonable expectation of privacy in the place searched or the item seized. Here, Al made his statement while in the boys' locker room. Since the locker room is accessible by other students, coaches, etc., Al could not have a reasonable expectation of privacy there. Thus, he may not successfully complain that Officer Ruthless unconstitutionally seized his statement.

Al could move that the money was illegally seized from his locker on Fourth Amendment grounds; however, this motion, too, will be unsuccessful. At issue is whether a public school principal may search a student's locker without a warrant.

As discussed above, the Fourth Amendment prohibits unreasonable searches and seizures, and searches of places where a person has a legitimate expectation of privacy generally are unreasonable unless a warrant is first obtained. However, the Supreme Court has relaxed this standard with regard to searches of public school students. Due to the nature of the school environment, searches of students are allowed if there are reasonable grounds for the search. [New Jersey v. T.L.O., 469 U.S. 325 (1985)] The Supreme Court has not held that this relaxed standard applies to searches of students' lockers as well as their person, but such an application is likely since a student would appear to have less of an expectation of privacy in his locker than in his person. Assuming this lower standard applies, Steve's confession would surely give the principal reasonable grounds for the search here, and this is true even if Steve's confession was obtained illegally, since, as discussed above, Al would have no standing to complain about how Steve's confession was obtained. Thus, Al's motion would fail.

Steve could move to have his confession suppressed on Fifth and/or Sixth Amendment grounds. At issue is whether Steve's confession was obtained in violation of his right against self-incrimination or his right to counsel.

An argument for exclusion of Steve's confession directly under the Sixth Amendment will fail. The Sixth Amendment provides a right to counsel at all critical stages of a prosecution. However, the right does not apply until adversary judicial proceedings against the defendant have begun. Here, Steve had not even been charged at the time the principal questioned him; thus, Steve's Sixth Amendment right had not yet attached.

Steve could argue that his Fifth Amendment rights to counsel and against self-incrimination were violated by the principal's interrogation. In *Miranda v. Arizona* and its progeny, the Supreme Court has held that a person being interrogated while in police custody must be warned that he has a right to remain silent and a right to an attorney. Moreover, if the person in custody requests counsel, all questioning must cease. Confessions obtained in violation of these rules must be suppressed.

Here, Steve was clearly in custody. He was not free to leave the principal's office; in fact, Officer Ruthless was standing guard to prevent Steve's departure. However, *Miranda* speaks about custody by law enforcement officers, and it has never been decided whether custody by a school official is sufficient custody to trigger *Miranda* rights. Considering that the underlying rationale of *Miranda* is to offset the coercive nature of police-dominated interrogation, the Supreme Court could very well find custody by a public school official sufficient to trigger *Miranda* since such custody is very similar to police custody, especially when an off-duty police officer is standing guard outside of the interrogation room.

If the custody element was sufficient, it is clear that the principal interrogated Steve apparently without giving Steve any *Miranda* warnings. Thus, Steve's confession could be inadmissible on this ground alone.

If *Miranda* warnings were given, Steve could argue that his rights were violated because questioning did not cease on his "request" for counsel. Such an argument would fail, however, because Steve's statement ("why should I answer any questions from you without a lawyer?") was ambiguous, and requests for counsel must be honored only if they are clear.

Thus, it is unclear whether Steve's statement should be suppressed. On a narrow interpretation of *Miranda* and its progeny, Steve's motion should be denied because there was no police interrogation. Under a slightly broader interpretation, Steve's motion could be successful because he was not given *Miranda* warnings.

111. REAL PROPERTY

To: Partner
From: Associate
Re: Windswept Easement

Brown will probably prevail in a suit to compel the state to terminate its use of the Windswept property as a public bathing beach. The issue is whether Adam created a valid easement.

An easement holder has a right to use land possessed by someone else for a special purpose, but does not have the right to possess the land; the owner of the servient tenement (the land on which the easement is located) continues to have the right of full possession and enjoyment subject only to the limitation that he cannot interfere with the right of special use created by the easement. Since the state does not own land appurtenant to Windswept, the easement created (if any) would have to be an easement in gross. A holder of an easement in gross acquires a right of special use in the servient tenement independent of his ownership or possession of another tract of land. In an easement in gross, the easement holder is not benefited in his use and enjoyment of a possessory estate by virtue of the acquisition of that privilege. Easements are created by express grant, by reservation, by implication, or by prescription. Given this background, I would suggest that Brown make the following arguments:

No easement created by express grant: The facts state that there has been no instrument other than deed to Brown purporting to convey an easement to New Jersey. The language in the deed speaks of an "easement to be given," which suggests that the easement would be granted in the future. Obviously, after the deed is delivered to Brown, Adam has no interest left in Windswept and, thus, would have no right to convey an easement to the state.

No easement created by reservation: An easement by reservation arises when the owner conveys title but reserves the right to continue to use the land for a special purpose after the conveyance. Under the majority view, an easement can be reserved only for the grantor; an attempt by the grantor to reserve an easement for anyone else is void. Here, Adams, the grantor, attempted to reserve an easement in a third party, the state. Under the majority view, the easement is void. Note that there is a growing trend (though still a minority view) to permit reservations in third parties.

No easement created by implication: An easement by implication cannot arise with respect to an easement in gross. This type of easement can arise only as a result of a division of a single tract into smaller parcels.

No easement created by prescription: An easement is acquired by prescription when someone other than the owner's use of the property is open and notorious, adverse (Brown did not give permission and Adam had no power to), and continuous for the statutory period. Here, the state's use of the property is open and notorious, adverse, and continuous, but it has not continued long enough to satisfy the statutory period. Although the creation of the easement was attempted in 1985, the use that would give rise to a prescriptive easement has continued for only one year. The statutory period for adverse possession, and thus prescription, varies from five to 21 years depending on the jurisdiction; the common law period is 20 years. In no jurisdiction is the period only one year.

License did not exist: A license gives the holder the right to go upon the land of another, but unlike an easement, it is not an interest in land. Often courts will construe a failed attempt to create an easement as a license. This would not work in this case for one important reason: A license terminates when the licensor (here, Adam) conveys the property. Thus, Adam could not both create a license and convey the property in the same instrument; the license to the state will not survive the conveyance of Windswept.

In summary, I think Brown's chances of success in arguing that no easement was created are excellent. However, we must consider our course of action should the court rule against us, such as by determining that New Jersey will recognize easements created by reservation in a third party. In such a case, the following arguments could be made:

Easement was terminated: Since the easement did not provide for termination, it is deemed perpetual. Thus, the only plausible arguments for termination are abandonment and prescription. Neither argument, however, has much chance of success. An easement can be extinguished without conveyance if the easement holder demonstrates an intent to permanently abandon the easement. In this case, New Jersey waited from 1985 until last year before taking any action with respect to the easement. This, however, is not sufficient to extinguish the easement; to work an abandonment, there must be *physical* action that shows the intent to abandon. No such physical action was taken by the state here; therefore, the abandonment argument is unlikely to succeed. Brown could then argue that he terminated the easement by prescription. Continued possession and enjoyment of the servient tenement in a way that would indicate to the public that no easement right existed will end the easement right if done for the requisite period (*e.g.*, 20 years). To so terminate an easement, the owner must so interfere with the easement as to create a cause of action in favor of the easement holder. Here, Brown has done nothing to the beach area that would give rise to a cause of action in the state. Thus, this argument too will probably fail.

Easement is limited to original boundaries: Brown can argue that the easement created is limited to the original boundaries, which in effect, means that the easement is worthless since it is now completely under water. This is Brown's best argument in the event that a court finds an easement was created.

The state's argument will be two-pronged: First, the state will argue that the intent of the parties controls, and clearly Adam's intent was that New Jersey should have use of dry land for a bathing beach. Second, the state will argue that the general rule is that any additions to land caused by accretion will benefit the current owner and/or the one with the right to the waterfront property. Moreover, most courts hold that it does not matter whether the accretion was due to natural or manmade forces. These arguments are sound and would succeed but for one fact: New Jersey built the jetty that caused the accretion. Generally one owner is not allowed to acquire another's land by causing accretion to occur. Brown will argue that, by analogy, this principle should extend to holders of beachfront easements, such as the state in this case. Since New Jersey did not construct the jetty merely for the purpose of increasing its rights to the Windswept property, the state may succeed in overcoming Brown's argument, but it is still Brown's best shot at reclaiming the beach area for his exclusive use.

Easement is not exclusive: Even if Brown cannot succeed in shutting down the public beach, he probably can succeed in forcing the state to remove the fence and allow his private operations to function in conjunction with the public beach. Absent an express restriction in the original easement agreement, the owner of the servient estate may use the land in any way he wishes so long as his conduct does not interfere with performance of the easement. Thus, assuming there is useful beach area beyond the western boundary of the state's easement, Brown should be able to operate a private beach area, and the state cannot deny his customers access to the water.

112. CRIMINAL LAW/CRIMINAL PROCEDURE

To: File
From: Public Defender
Re: *State v. Ted*

CHARGES AND DEFENSES

Ted can be charged with burglary, battery, false imprisonment, attempted larceny and/or attempted robbery, and felony murder. The issue is whether Ted's actions constitute the elements of each crime, and if so, whether he has any defenses which he may assert.

Burglary: Ted may be charged with burglary. Burglary is the breaking and entering of a dwelling of another, at night, with the intent to commit a felony therein. "Breaking" occurs when one creates an opening with the use of at least minimal force. "Entering" occurs when any portion of a body or instrument used to commit the crime is placed in the structure. A "dwelling" is a structure used for the sleeping purposes of one other than the defendant. The felony within the structure need not be carried out, but the intent to commit the felony must be present at the time of entry.

In this case, Ted entered John and Mary's home, a dwelling, at 2:30 a.m., seeking money and jewelry. Thus, he fulfilled the requirements of breaking and entering at night with the intent to commit a felony therein, *i.e.*, larceny or robbery. It is irrelevant that Ted ended up taking nothing, because the facts indicate that the requisite intent was present at the time of the breaking. Ted does not appear to have any defenses to this charge.

Battery: Ted also can be charged with battery, which is the unlawful and intentional application of force to the person of another, resulting in bodily injury or an offensive touching. Here, Ted forced

Mary to bind and gag John, which resulted in an offensive touching and possibly bodily injury to John. It is no defense that it was Mary, not Ted, who did the actual touching; Mary will be seen as the instrumentality of the offensive touching of John by Ted. In addition, Ted struck Mary, causing her to fall. This action is clearly an offensive touching which resulted in bodily injury to Mary.

False imprisonment: Ted can be charged with false imprisonment. False imprisonment is the unlawful confinement of an individual without that person's valid consent. The confinement may be accomplished with actual force or by threat of force.

Here, Ted forced Mary to tie and gag John, and John remained that way for over an hour. Clearly, this action was without John's valid consent, and completely restricted his movement. Again, it is no defense that it was Mary who actually bound and gagged John (*see* discussion above).

Attempted larceny/attempted robbery: Ted can be charged with either attempted robbery or attempted larceny, but he cannot be convicted of both. In crimes of attempt, specific intent to commit the crime must be present, and the perpetrator must perform an overt act in furtherance of that intent. Larceny is the taking and carrying away of the property of another with the intent to permanently deprive the owner of the property. Robbery is the taking and carrying away of property from the presence of another by force or the threat of force, with the intent to permanently deprive the person thereof. Therefore, larceny is a lesser included offense of robbery, and Ted cannot be convicted of both.

In this case, Ted had the intent to steal money and jewelry when he entered the dwelling, and he never intended to return the property to John and Mary. Ted's acts of entering the house and assaulting the couple constitute the overt act in furtherance of the specific intent. In addition, Ted had the specific intent to steal John and Mary's money and jewelry by force or threat of force. This intent is manifested by Ted's simulation of the possession of a gun, his demand for money, and his assault of Mary. Thus, a charge of either attempted larceny or attempted robbery would be proper. Ted would not have a defense to either charge.

Murder: Finally, Ted may be charged with murder. Murder is the unlawful killing of a human being with malice aforethought. Malice aforethought exists if the defendant either: (i) intends to kill; (ii) intends to inflict great bodily injury; (iii) has a reckless indifference to an unjustifiably high risk to human life; or (iv) intends to commit a felony (*i.e.,* felony murder). Under the facts of the case, a charge of murder based either on reckless indifference or on a charge of felony murder would be the State's best chance for a conviction.

Ted assaulted Mary and she fell and struck her head, which caused her death. These circumstances probably do not indicate an intent to kill or inflict great bodily injury, as required for a murder charge under (i) or (ii). However, the State may be able to establish that Ted acted with reckless indifference to an unjustifiably high risk to human life, because there is a high probability that a person who is assaulted may fall and suffer a fatal head injury. In addition, a foreseeable death resulting from the commission of a felony is punishable as a felony murder. If Ted is charged with burglary, larceny, or robbery, all felonies, he could be also be charged with murder for the death which followed.

If Ted is charged with murder based on reckless indifference, he could assert that his actions in assaulting Mary did not amount to reckless indifference. This argument may succeed if the facts show that the severity of Mary's injuries from the fall was a fluke. If Ted were charged with felony murder, however, he would not have a defense unless he were ultimately acquitted of the underlying felony, *i.e.,* the burglary, larceny, or robbery.

PRETRIAL MOTIONS

Ted will make pretrial motions to exclude the lineup and the voice identification. However, it is unlikely that they will be suppressed. The issue is whether any of Ted's constitutional rights have been compromised in the carrying out of the procedures in question.

Ted will assert that the lineup violated his Sixth Amendment right to counsel. This right exists at all critical stages of a prosecution, which has been held to mean that the right takes effect after judicial proceedings have begun or formal charges have been filed. However, an accused person does not have a right to counsel at investigative lineups. Here, Ted was under arrest for a parole violation; no charges had been brought against him with regard to the home invasion until after the lineup. Thus, the lineup was a pre-charge investigative lineup. Thus, Ted's motion is unlikely to succeed.

Ted will also assert that the lineup violated his Fourteenth Amendment right of due process. Due process is violated when a lineup is unnecessarily suggestive or there is a substantial likelihood of misidentification. The fact that Ted was singled out by the police officer creates a prejudicial effect, perhaps stressing Ted in the mind of the victim. John did not hear anyone else in the lineup speak those words, which may have also created prejudicial effect. This argument may be successful, but it will not prevent John from identifying Ted at trial. Trial identifications tainted by an unconstitutional lineup will not be excluded if an independent basis for the trial identification can be shown. Here, the prosecution will argue that John's memory was triggered by Ted's voice, that he had 45 minutes to view Ted, and that he is likely to remember Ted's appearance and voice due to the traumatic events of the evening. Thus, the prosecution will assert that there is an independent basis for the identification and while the lineup identification may be suppressed, a trial identification will not be.

Lastly, Ted may assert that his Fifth Amendment right against self-incrimination was denied due to the voice identification. However, this argument will fail. The Fifth Amendment privilege against self-incrimination protects only testimonial evidence, not physical evidence. A suspect can be forced to give voice samples despite the Fifth Amendment. [United States v. Wade, 388 U.S. 218 (1967)]

113. EVIDENCE

To: Senior Partner
From: Associate
Re: *John v. Doctor*

The following memorandum outlines the areas in which the expected testimony of John's witnesses can be attacked, the legal basis for each challenge, and the likelihood that each challenge will succeed.

Testimony of Expert: A challenge to Expert's testimony regarding the x-rays will not succeed because the best evidence rule is satisfied. Any challenge to Expert's qualifications may or may not succeed since it seems at least somewhat questionable as to whether Expert has established himself to have special knowledge, skill, and experience on the subject to which his testimony relates. In addition, any challenge of the testimony regarding the emergency room nurse's statement is likely to succeed, due to the fact that this testimony is hearsay.

Expert's testimony concerning the x-rays may be attacked on the basis of the "best evidence rule," but this challenge is not likely to succeed. The issue is whether Expert's testimony regarding the x-rays satisfies the "best evidence rule" in light of the fact that Expert does not have a copy of the original x-rays. The best evidence rule requires that, when proving the material terms of a writing, including x-rays, the original writing must be produced, particularly where the writing is a legally operative or dispositive instrument or the knowledge of a witness concerning a fact results from having read it in the document. However, if the original writing cannot be produced in court, the proponent may offer secondary evidence of its contents, in the form of oral testimony concerning the contents of the original document, if a satisfactory explanation is given for the nonproduction of the original. For example, loss, accompanied by a diligent search, or good faith destruction of the original are sufficient explanations of nonproduction which will allow the proponent to testify to the contents of the writing.

In this case, Expert examined John's x-rays prior to their loss. It is not clear how the x-rays were misplaced. If Expert can show that he diligently searched for the x-rays and did not destroy them in bad faith, his oral testimony will likely be admissible in court. Thus, a challenge to this testimony probably will not succeed.

A challenge of Expert's ability to testify as an "expert" may succeed. The issue is whether Expert's listed qualifications are sufficient to establish him as an expert. Before testifying as an expert, a witness must demonstrate that: (i) the subject matter is appropriate for expert testimony; (ii) the witness is qualified as an expert (*i.e.*, that he possesses special knowledge, skill, experience, training, or education); (iii) the expert's opinion is based on a reasonable probability; and (iv) the expert's opinion is supported by a proper factual basis.

In order to be qualified as an expert, one must have special knowledge, skill, training, and experience sufficient to establish him as an expert on the subject matter to which his testimony relates. Here, Expert has attempted to establish himself as an expert by indicating that he has been licensed since 1990. However, since that time, Expert has remained in the hospital obstetrics clinic and has only viewed emergency care from time to time. Thus, it is unclear whether or not Expert's limited experience qualifies him to read x-rays of bone fractures. However, Expert's medical school experience and limited time in the emergency room may be deemed sufficient since a bone fracture diagnosis does not appear to be complicated. Thus, a challenge based on Expert's qualifications may or may not succeed, depending on how a court views Expert's ability and experience.

A challenge to Expert's testimony, relying on his interview with Adam, the emergency room nurse, is likely to succeed, due to the doctrine of hearsay. The issue is whether Adam's out-of-court statement falls within the definition of hearsay and, if so, whether or not it is covered by one of the hearsay exceptions. Federal Rule of Evidence 802 defines hearsay as "a statement, other than one made by the declarant while testifying at the trial or hearing, offered in evidence to prove the truth of the matter asserted." The reason such testimony is excluded is that the adverse party was denied the opportunity to cross-examine the declarant, the person making the out-of-court statement. If a statement is considered to be "hearsay," then it may still be admissible if it qualifies as one of the exceptions to the rule: (i) former testimony of a witness given at another hearing or in a deposition; (ii) statement by declarant against his interest; (iii) dying declaration made under a belief of impending death; (iv) statement of personal or family history; (v) statement showing the declarant's present state of mind; (vi) excited utterance; (vii) present sense impression; (viii) declaration of physical condition; (ix) business record; (x) past recorded recollection; (xi) official record or other official writing; and (xii) learned treatise.

In this situation, the statement made by the declarant, Adam, is being offered to prove the truth of the matter at hand, the fracture of John's wrist and Doctor's malpractice. Therefore, it is clear that the statement is hearsay. In addition, it does not appear that the statement falls within any of the hearsay exceptions delineated above.

However, Federal Rule of Evidence 703 allows an expert to base an opinion on facts supplied to him outside the courtroom, such as the reports of nurses and technicians. The facts relied upon do not need to be in evidence or of a type admissible in evidence. It is only required that the facts are of a kind reasonably relied upon by experts in the field in which the expert practices. Therefore, if the court determines that Adam's statement is of the kind that would be relied upon, Expert will be permitted to rely on Adam's statement in the formation of Expert's own opinion. However, it may be concluded that Adam's statement is not one which would be relied upon by experts: Adam merely stated that he did not see Doctor examine John's wrist. Such an observation is not necessarily definitive as to whether or not Expert did in fact make such an examination. Therefore, a challenge to Expert's testimony relying on Adam's statement is likely to succeed on the basis that it is hearsay and does not fall within the purview of Federal Rule of Evidence 703.

Written summary of John's medical bills: A challenge to the admission of John's medical bills will probably succeed since is it likely that the summary of bills will be considered hearsay. The first issue is whether the summary falls within the definition of hearsay and, if so, whether the summary can be admitted as an exception to the hearsay rule.

The summary of John's medical bills does appear to fall within the definition of hearsay. The summary is an out-of-court statement, being offered to prove the truth of the matter asserted, the cost of John's medical care. Faithful telephoned each of the doctors that had given John care and it is unclear whether she received the billing information over the phone or in writing. Therefore, it does appear that there are multiple layers of hearsay in this situation. It also does not appear that the summary falls within any of the hearsay exceptions.

The only plausible exception is the business records exception. This exception stipulates that any writing or record is admissible into evidence as proof of that act or occurrence if it is made in the regular course of any business, and if it was the regular course of such business to make it at the time of the act or occurrence or within a reasonable time thereafter.

In this case, Faithful did not take the records herself but received them from doctors, possibly over the phone. In addition, the recording of these records, although it is in the ordinary course of business of the doctors who treated John, is not in the ordinary course of Faithful's business—she is John's office manager. Therefore, the business records exception does not cover the summary of John's medical bills and a challenge to the admission of the summary is likely to succeed.

114. TORTS

To: Senior Partner
From: An Associate
Re: Robert Jones

Mr. Jones has several causes of action grounded in both negligence and strict liability in tort.

Negligence re: Z Corp.: Mr. Jones has a cause of action against Z Corp. based on negligence, providing there is no worker's compensation statute barring recovery. In order to maintain a negligence action, the plaintiff must demonstrate that the following elements are met: (i) existence of a duty on the part of the defendant to conform to a specific standard of conduct for the protection of the plaintiff against an unreasonable risk of injury; (ii) breach of that duty by the defendant; (iii) breach of duty by the defendant was the actual and proximate cause of the plaintiff's injury (causation in fact and legal causation); and (iv) damage to the plaintiff's person or property. A general duty of care is imposed on all people to act as an ordinary, prudent, reasonable person. If the defendant's conduct creates an unreasonable risk of injury to persons in the position of the plaintiff, the general duty of care extends from the defendant to the plaintiff. Z Corp. owes a duty of care to Mr. Jones since Z Corp. was his employer. As an employee, Mr. Jones may be categorized as an "invitee." Thus, Z Corp. owes a duty to Mr. Jones to use reasonable and ordinary care in active operations and in keeping its property reasonably safe for the benefit of the invitee, Mr. Jones. It is clear that Mr. Jones, as an employee, is a foreseeable plaintiff.

It appears that Z Corp. breached its duty of care since Mr. Jones did not receive any training from Z Corp. regarding the operation of the press. Z Corp. was aware that Mr. Jones, who was hired as a punch press operator, had no experience in the operation of the machine. Mr. Jones was not given instructions in the use of the press, nor were any such instructions included in the operator's manual. In addition, the area in which the press came down was always accessible and unprotected. Z Corp.'s deviation from the standard of care was an actual and proximate legal cause of Mr. Jones's injury: if proper care had been taken by Z Corp., the injury probably would not have occurred. Therefore, Mr. Jones may bring a negligence action against Z Corp.

Negligence re: Brown Manufacturing: Mr. Jones may have a products liability action based in negligence against Brown. In order to establish a prima facie case, the following elements must be proved: (i) the existence of a legal duty owed by the defendant to that particular plaintiff; (ii) breach of that duty; (iii) actual and proximate cause; and (iv) damages. In a products liability case, the plaintiff establishes breach of duty by showing (i) that the defendant acted negligently, and (ii) that the product was defective when the product left the defendant's control. In the case of a "design defect," all of the products of a line are made identically according to manufacturing specifications, but have dangerous propensities because of their mechanical features or packaging. Inadequate warnings may be considered to be a design defect since a product must have clear and complete warnings of any dangers that may not be apparent to users.

A duty of care arises if the defendant is considered to be a "commercial supplier." This term includes manufacturers of a chattel or a component thereof, assemblers, wholesalers, and retailers. The defendant's conduct must fall below the conduct expected of a reasonable person under like circumstances. In order to establish that a manufacturer's negligence has resulted in a design defect, a plaintiff must show that those designing the product knew or should have known of enough facts to put a reasonable manufacturer on notice about the dangers of marketing the product as designed.

This case is a products liability case since the press had a design defect—the absence of safety features on the machine, the open exposure of the foot pedal, and the lack of conformity to safety standards. In addition, there were no adequate warning labels on the machine that informed users of potential dangers or precautions to be taken. In addition, the press left Brown in a defective condition.

Brown rebuilt the press and made substantial modifications to it and, as such, the company may be considered a "manufacturer," even though it was not the initial manufacturer of the press. Therefore, Brown owed a duty of care to conform with industry standards. Brown did not add any protective components to the machine, nor did it change the foot-activating pedal—the portion of the press which led to Mr. Jones's injury—in any way. In 1988, the applicable statute was modified and subsequently required that foot pedals be replaced by hand-activating buttons. Brown did not make certain that the remodeled punch press was in conformity with statutory and safety requirements—an action that Brown should have taken, considering that it should have been aware of industry standards and developments. Thus, Brown, a supplier of the rebuilt press, should have known about the dangers of the product and breached a duty of care to Mr. Jones, a user of the press and foreseeable plaintiff. Brown's action, or inaction, was an actual and proximate cause of Mr. Jones's injury: his accident would not have occurred if Brown had properly remodeled the press.

If Brown is not considered to be a "commercial supplier," because it only remodeled the press, then Brown may still be liable under an ordinary theory of negligence, the elements of which are discussed in the prior section regarding Z Corp.

Therefore, Mr. Jones may bring a products liability action based on a theory of negligence or an ordinary theory of negligence against Brown.

Potential defenses of Z Corp. and Brown: Both Z Corp. and Brown will attempt to defend against the suits on the basis of the doctrines of contributory negligence, assumption of risk, and comparative negligence. However, the defendants are not likely to prevail with respect to any of these approaches.

Contributory negligence, requiring the same standard of care from the plaintiff as that for ordinary negligence, completely bars the plaintiff from recovery. Comparative negligence, the doctrine adopted by most jurisdictions, similarly involves fault on the part of the plaintiff. However, in such jurisdictions, if a "partial" comparative negligence approach is taken, the plaintiff will recover if his negligence does not pass a threshold level. If a "pure" comparative negligence approach is taken, the plaintiff may recover no matter how large his degree of fault may be. In such instances, a plaintiff's damages will be reduced by a percentage equivalent to his degree of fault. It is unlikely that these defenses will work since Mr. Jones does not appear to be negligent in his use of the press. He could have easily assumed that Z Corp. would have given him any instruction necessary to operate the machine. The slipping of his foot was inadvertent, and there was no reason for Mr. Jones to take extra precautions. Therefore, it is unlikely that the defenses would succeed.

Both Z Corp. and Brown may assert that Mr. Jones assumed the risk in his operation of the machine without any experience. Under the assumption of risk doctrine, a plaintiff must have known of the risk and voluntarily assumed it in order to be barred from recovery. In this situation there was no reason for Mr. Jones to be aware of the danger imposed by the exposed foot press on the machine. Therefore, it is unlikely that this defense would succeed.

Negligence re: AB Press Corp.: Jones may be able to sue AB under a products liability negligence theory, the elements of which are discussed in the section regarding the negligence of Brown.

Here, AB owed a duty to Mr. Jones, as AB is a "commercial supplier." It does not matter that Press Corp. manufactured the machine that caused the injury. A corporation acquiring the assets of another is liable for the torts of its predecessor if the purchasing corporation is a mere continuation of the selling corporation. In this case, AB purchased Press Corp.'s assets, equipment, goodwill, customer lists, and manufacturing plant. In addition, AB continued to manufacture punch presses at the same plant. Thus, it does appear that AB was a "continuation" of Press Corp. Press Corp. is not liable since the corporation was dissolved: claims of creditors are barred if not timely filed unless litigation is pending or the court allows the late claim. Since Press Corp. was dissolved in 1952, it is unlikely that it would be held liable for the tort in question.

However, not all of the elements necessary to be met in a products liability case based on negligence are found here. The product may be said to have been defective when it left AB's hands: the press machine was manufactured by Press Corp. to include such a hazardous design defect, thus leaving Press Corp.'s hands in its defective state. However, AB could argue that Press Corp. was not negligent when it first manufactured the press in 1949, and that the dangers of foot pedals did not become apparent until long after the product had reached the public. Thus, Press Corp. did not act negligently in its original design of the punch press. Therefore, Mr. Jones probably will not be able to bring a successful products liability action based on negligence against AB.

Strict liability: re AB Press Corp.: Mr. Jones may also assert a products liability claim against AB based on strict liability. To prove such a claim, the following elements must be met: (i) strict duty owed by a commercial supplier; (ii) breach of that duty; (iii) actual and proximate cause; and (iv) damages. Additionally, in a strict liability case, the product must be expected to, and must in fact, reach the user or consumer without substantial change in the condition in which it is supplied. A plaintiff must prove that the product was so defective as to be "unreasonably dangerous"; it does not matter whether the commercial supplier had an opportunity to inspect the product before sale. In addition, in such cases, to prove actual cause, the plaintiff must trace the harm suffered to a defect in the product that existed when the product left the defendant's control. As with negligence claims, the defendant is liable for all harmful results that are the normal incidents of and within the increased risk caused by his acts.

In this case, AB is considered a "commercial supplier." In addition, the press did meet the user, Mr. Jones, without substantial change in the condition in which it was supplied; while Brown rebuilt the press, it did not change the foot-activating pedals or add any protective components. The press may be considered "unreasonably dangerous" since the press did not include any protective device surrounding the foot pedal, an addition that was probably an inexpensive one. It appears that it was very easy for one to be unnecessarily injured by the device. Finally, the proximate cause requirement is met as well: the defect in the product existed when the product left Press Corp.'s control. Therefore, AB Press Corp. may be charged with a products liability claim based on a strict liability theory.

Defenses of AB Press Corp.: In strict liability products liability cases, contributory negligence does not serve as a defense where the plaintiff merely failed to discover the defect or guard against its existence, or where the plaintiff's misuse was reasonably foreseeable. Therefore, this defense would not apply in the strict liability action against AB since Mr. Jones was not actively a cause of his injury: he simply was not aware of the danger involved with the machine's operation. The same rule applies in many comparative negligence states: failure to discover or guard against a defect is not an acceptable defense. Assumption of risk may be used as a defense by AB with respect to the strict liability claim since it is a potential defense in such situations, and failure to discover a guard against a defect may be a defense in some comparative negligence states. However, as is the case with the other defendants, these defenses are not likely to succeed.

Potential cross-claims: All defendants are likely to cross-claim against each other. Thus, Brown will cross-claim against AB and Z Corp., AB will cross-claim against Brown and Z Corp., and Z

Corp. will cross-claim against AB and Brown. Where two or more tortious acts combine to proximately cause an indivisible injury to the plaintiff, each tortfeasor will be jointly and severally liable for that injury. Thus, each party is liable to the plaintiff for the entire damage incurred.

Since the plaintiff may recover the entire judgment from one defendant, any defendant required to pay more than his share of damages has a claim against the other jointly liable defendants for the excess. In this situation, if any one of the defendants is held liable for all of the damages paid to Mr. Jones, that defendant will cross-claim against the others in a contribution action.

115. EVIDENCE

To: Senior Partner
From: Associate
Re: Available Evidence For Case Concerning Life Support Removal

STANDARD OF PROOF

In this case, the requisite standard of proof will be by clear and convincing evidence. At issue is the standard of proof Marie must meet in order to show that her mother Joan, if competent, would decline further medical treatment. Most civil cases are governed by a preponderance of the evidence standard, in which the fact finder must be persuaded that the facts presented are more probably true than not. However, in some cases, where the consequences are severe, the mandated standard of proof is by clear and convincing evidence. This standard requires the trier of fact to be persuaded that there is a high probability that the facts in question are true. Since the resolution of this case will determine if Joan lives or dies (*i.e.*, a case where the consequences are severe), the higher standard of proof will be required. Therefore, Marie must show by clear and convincing evidence that Joan, if competent, would decline medical treatment.

AVAILABLE EVIDENCE

Joan's actions to keep Fred alive: Joan's actions to keep Fred alive will be admissible and weigh against Marie's claim. The issue presented is whether Joan's prior acts (*i.e.*, her authorization of a feeding tube and her order to resuscitate) regarding her husband are relevant as evidence of her wishes to remain alive under similar circumstances. Relevant evidence is evidence which has any tendency to make the existence of any fact more or less probable. Although evidence which relates to an event or person other than the event or person directly at issue must be closely examined to determine if it would prove or disprove the specific fact at issue, previous actions of a party under similar circumstances will generally be admissible as related, relevant evidence having probative value of the present issue. Accordingly, evidence of Joan's actions will be admitted and weigh against Marie's case.

It also should be noted that a hearsay objection to the admission of this evidence will be unsuccessful. Hearsay is defined as an out-of-court statement offered for the truth of the matter asserted. In this case, however, even to the extent that Joan's actions rose to the level of statements, they are offered not for the truth of the statements themselves, but rather to establish Joan's frame of mind or intent to remain alive under similar circumstances. In other words, the evidence is not being offered to prove that Joan ordered the resuscitation or the feeding tube. Consequently, there would be no hearsay bar to the admission of Joan's actions.

Joan's statements to the treating physician and Marie: Joan's statements to the treating physician and her daughter that "she regretted prolonging Fred's suffering" and "that she hoped to go peacefully when her time came" will most likely be admissible and helpful to Marie's case. The issue is whether these statements are hearsay and, if so, whether there is an exception under which these statements may be admitted. As previously stated, hearsay is an out-of-court statement offered to prove the truth of the matter asserted. Hearsay is not admissible evidence unless it falls into a recognized exception. The present state of mind exception allows a statement of the declarant's then-existing state of mind to be admitted into evidence when it is offered under circumstances of apparent sincerity. This exception is premised on the need to obtain evidence of the declarant's internal state of mind or emotion. Here, there is no question that the statements Joan made were out of court and will be offered to prove the truth of the matter asserted. However, the statements are certainly indicative of Joan's state of mind. The rationale for the state of mind exception is clearly established in this case. Specifically, Joan's state of mind is directly at issue in this situation, for which it is difficult to offer proof. Furthermore, Joan's statements are reliable and trustworthy. There is no problem with the accuracy of Joan's memory since the statement was made at a relevant time. In addition, there is no problem with perception, since there is no better person than the declarant to know the declarant's state of mind. Finally, the statement was offered under circumstances of apparent sincerity because there is no reason why Joan would have lied to the physician or her daughter about what she felt.

Joan's statements to her minister and attorney: Joan's conversations with her minister and attorney regarding the use of extraordinary means to prolong her life also will be admissible. The statements are hearsay; however, they can be admitted under the present state of mind exception. The relevant issue regarding these statements is whether the attorney-client and clergy privileges will bar the admission of this evidence. Generally, communications between an attorney and client, made during professional consultation, are privileged from disclosure and the client can prevent others from disclosing these confidential communications. Similarly, a person also has a privilege to refuse to disclose, and to prevent others from disclosing, a confidential communication by the person to a member of the clergy as long as it was conveyed to the clergy in his capacity as a spiritual advisor. Each of these privileges can be waived by the individual or representative authorized to act on behalf of the individual. In this case, the statements are helpful to Marie's case so she would want them to be admitted. Since she will be bringing an action on behalf of Joan, it can be inferred that she has representational capacity regarding matters concerning Joan and, accordingly, can validly waive the privileges. Therefore, the statements will be admissible to show that Joan did not want life support.

Dr. Peters's testimony: Dr. Peters's testimony will be admissible. The issue is whether Joan's treating physician can testify as to his opinion of Joan's medical condition. Ordinarily, a physician will be barred by the physician-patient privilege from providing evidence regarding the patient's physical condition. However, the privilege is not applicable when patients put their own physical condition at issue. Here, the question of Joan's medical condition is being placed directly at issue by Joan's representative, Marie. In order to be permitted to give expert testimony, an individual must have special knowledge, skill, experience, training, or education that is sufficient to qualify him as an expert on the subject to which his testimony relates. In addition, the expert opinion must be supported by a proper factual basis. In this case, it can be implied that Dr. Peters, as the treating physician, has the medical training and skill necessary to be qualified as an expert. Moreover, Dr. Peters's opinion will possess a proper factual basis since he has personally observed and tested Joan's condition. Therefore, Dr. Peters will be able to give his expert opinion as to Joan's medical condition.

Dr. Morgan's testimony: Dr. Morgan's testimony will be admissible. The issue is whether Dr. Morgan will be able to testify as an expert, and how reliable and trustworthy his testimony will be if admitted. As stated above, in order to give expert testimony, an individual must have special experience regarding the subject to which his testimony relates and the opinion must be supported by a proper factual basis. In this case, Dr. Morgan is stated to be "a neurologist renowned for his study of comatose patients." Based upon this description, Dr. Morgan will be considered an expert. Furthermore, Dr. Morgan's three-hour examination of Joan provides a proper factual basis for his testimony. Accordingly, Dr. Morgan will be permitted to testify.

However, Dr. Morgan's expert opinion may be considered untrustworthy and unreliable. Dr. Morgan may be attacked on cross-examination because of his failure to document his findings, but ultimately he should be a strong witness. The issue is to what extent may Dr. Morgan's testimony be impeached. Although the scope of cross-examination is subject to the discretion of the trial court, it is well-established that the opposing party may cross-examine on matters brought out on direct examination and matters affecting the credibility of the witness. In this case, Dr. Morgan's conclusions will be brought out on direct examination and, therefore, will be subject to cross. In addition, the fact that he will be testifying from memory may make his testimony ripe for attack if he is not able to recall specific details to support his conclusion. However, the fact that he is a leading expert on this condition will certainly weigh heavily against Dr. Peters, who does not appear to be a specialist of the same magnitude.

Unsigned handwritten note: The handwritten note also will be admitted into evidence. The issue is whether the unsigned, undated note can be sufficiently authenticated to be admitted. Documentary evidence must be relevant and, as part of relevancy, must be authenticated as actually being what it appears to be. In this case, there are two ways in which the note can be authenticated. First, a writing may be authenticated by evidence of the genuineness of the handwriting of the maker. Handwriting verification can be by the testimony of a lay witness who has personal knowledge of the handwriting of the supposed writer. Additionally, the note can be verified by circumstantial evidence, which would be by any proof tending to establish the genuineness of the writing. In this case, it is likely that Marie can verify, or at least provide witnesses who can verify, Joan's handwriting and testify that the handwriting in the note is Joan's. In addition, its authenticity can be verified circumstantially because the note was included in Joan's other papers and dealt with a subject in which it was known that Joan has expressed an interest. Accordingly, since the writing can be verified to be Joan's, it will be admitted.

CONCLUSION

Since there will be much evidence that demonstrates that Joan did not wish the use of extraordinary means to extend her life, Marie will likely be able to demonstrate by clear and convincing evidence that Joan should be allowed to die. Indeed, this evidence, including Joan's statements to her family, clergy, and attorney, as well as a document in her own handwriting establish that she did not want to be kept alive by artificial means. The evidence against Joan is not compelling and does not demonstrate her will.

116. TORTS

To: Judge
From: Law Clerk
Re: *Jones v. Toot, Martin and Brown*

This memorandum will identify each party, discuss the possible causes of action they may have, and examine all conceivable defenses and cross-claims that may be raised.

Tom Jones and Ed Jones ("Joneses") v. Frank Martin ("FM"): The Joneses have a cause of action in negligence against FM for failure to safely operate a train in a residential area. The issue is whether FM acted negligently in his operation of the train. Additionally at issue is the question of whether FM can be relieved of liability, even if he acted negligently, since he was acting within the scope of his employment when the incident which gave rise to the cause of action occurred.

The prima facie requirements for a defendant to sustain a cause of action in negligence are as follows: (i) duty to conform to a specific standard of care; (ii) breach of that duty; (iii) the breach of the duty by the defendant was the actual and proximate cause of plaintiff's injury; and (iv) damages to the plaintiff.

FM had a duty to operate the train as a reasonable, prudent train operator would in a residential zone. FM owes this duty to all foreseeable plaintiffs—all persons in the "zone of danger." This zone is the area in which the defendant could have reasonably foreseen the plaintiff to be. The Joneses probably are foreseeable plaintiffs, because it is foreseeable that two teenagers would take a shortcut across train tracks if it were available to them rather than walking all the way around to a railroad crossing.

A breach of duty occurs when a defendant, who has a duty, fails to meet this standard of care, and the harm predicted from the defendant's failure occurs. On these facts, the Joneses could argue that the train conductor breached his duty to drive at a reasonable speed in a residential area and as a result of his failure to stop, injuries occurred. Specifically, Tom Jones was killed and Ed Jones was exposed to extreme emotional anguish.

In order for the plaintiffs to prove negligence, they must show that the defendant's actions were both the actual and the legal cause of their injuries. Here, "but for" FM's failure to stop, the injury would not have occurred. With regard to the proximate cause of the plaintiff's injuries, the question is whether it is foreseeable that the defendant's conduct would have caused the injuries that were sustained. Both Tom Jones's death and Ed Jones's serious emotional distress from seeing his brother killed are consistent with the type that would occur based on the defendant's conduct.

The final requirement in the Joneses' cause of action is that damages must have been sustained. In this case, the damages are readily provable by showing Tom's demise in the prime of his life and Ed's emotional problems, which can be documented through medical records and testimony. In the wrongful death action of Tom's estate, the damages he sustained are for the loss of life. The measurement will be based on the pain and suffering Tom sustained and any actual lost earning that can be clearly established. No proof of speculative earning will be allowed. For Ed's cause of action for "negligent infliction of emotional distress," Ed's emotional harm must be severe enough to be manifested by physical symptoms, because as a general rule, recovery for negligent infliction of emotional distress is permitted only when the emotional distress results in physical injury.

FM can raise the defenses of "assumption of the risk" and "contributory negligence." These defenses, though not complete bars to recovery, can reduce the Joneses' damage award by the amount of fault attributable to them. With regard to the "assumption of the risk" doctrine, the defendant must show that the plaintiff had knowledge of the risk. This knowledge can be express or implied. The defendant must demonstrate that there was an alternative means that was safe and accessible, and, nevertheless, the plaintiff voluntarily chose a high risk course of action. "Contributory negligence" is established when the plaintiff fails to exercise that degree of care to protect himself from injury. This standard is subjective and is measured against how other children of like age, experience, and intelligence would act. On these facts, the Jones boys, ages 17 and 15, voluntarily crossed a working railroad track in an unsafe and unauthorized place. Arguably, the Joneses impliedly and voluntarily assumed the risk of their actions. Because the boys are both minors, however, it is a question of fact for the jury to determine, using a subjective standard, whether the boys could have assumed the risk or were contributorily negligent.

Although FM may be liable for negligence, he can cross-claim against Toot and/or Joseph Brown for contribution if FM is required to pay more than his share of damages, as long as Toot and/or Brown were also negligent.

Tom Jones and Ed Jones v. Toot ("T"): The Joneses have an independent cause of action in negligence against T for failure to repair its fence that paralleled the train tracks. The issue is whether T acted negligently with regard to its duty to maintain the fence and, thereby, whether T was the cause of the Joneses' injuries. If T is liable, the issue is whether T has any defenses or counterclaims.

For a defendant to be found liable in a negligence cause of action, the plaintiff must prove four basic elements. The elements are: (i) duty to conform to a specific standard of care; (ii) breach of that duty by the defendant; (iii) the breach of the duty by the defendant was the actual and proximate cause of the plaintiff's injury; and (iv) damages to the plaintiff.

Here, T, the railroad company, had a duty to act as an ordinary, reasonable, prudent railroad company when its trains were traveling in residential areas. The duty is measured by employing an objective test to determine possible harm to foreseeable plaintiffs. While the Joneses were trespassers on T's property, they may be foreseeable plaintiffs under the "attractive nuisance" doctrine. To maintain a negligence claim based on attractive nuisance, the plaintiff must show that: (i) the defendant landowner knew or should have known that a dangerous condition existed on his property; (ii) the defendant knew or should have known that young people frequent the vicinity of this dangerous condition; (iii) the condition is likely to cause injury; and (iv) the expense of remedying the situation is slight compared to the magnitude of the risk. On these facts, the Joneses' action of using the hole in the fence as a shortcut should have been foreseen by T. T should have discovered the harm upon reasonable inspection and remedied it. T's actual knowledge, or lack thereof, is no defense if it failed to conduct regular inspections. Rather, its failure to maintain its property in a manner consistent with its responsibilities goes to demonstrate that it breached its duty. To prove breach of duty, the plaintiff must show that the foreseen injury occurred, and that the defendant acted unreasonably by his action or inaction. T breached its duty by not routinely inspecting and repairing the fence and preventing holes in the fence that would provide a dangerous access through which unauthorized people could enter the railroad tracks and become injured.

The plaintiff must show that the defendant's breach was both the actual and the proximate or legal cause of the harm which occurred. Simply stated, the actual harm sustained would not have occurred "but for" the defendant's failure to repair the fence. Additionally, the complaining party must demonstrate that the harm that occurred was a normal result of, and within the increased risk caused by, the defendant's breach. Specifically, the plaintiffs must show that the defendant's failure to eliminate the hole in the fence increased the likelihood that this exact type of harm (death as a result of being struck by a train) might occur.

Lastly, the Joneses need to allege actual damages. Here, the ultimate personal injury occurred—death. In addition, Ed Jones sustained emotional trauma which can be an element of damages to the extent that it is manifested through physical symptoms.

The Joneses may have a second cause of action in vicarious liability because T, as FM's employer, is responsible for any negligent conduct by FM occurring within the scope of his employment. Here, FM was operating the train within the scope of his employment; hence, T would be liable for any negligence that can be established against FM.

In each cause of action mentioned above, however, T can raise the defenses of "assumption of the risk" and "contributory negligence." Both of these defenses and the likely outcome of their use are discussed earlier in this memorandum.

T has a possible cross-claim against FM for indemnity to the extent it is held vicariously liable for FM's negligence. Under indemnity principles, T can recover the full amount of damages it paid because of its vicarious liability. T may also maintain a claim against Joseph Brown for contribution if Brown is determined to be negligent and T is required to pay the Joneses more than its share of damages. In an action for contribution, a defendant found liable for monetary damages may seek monetary compensation or contribution from the other responsible party or parties.

Tom Jones and Ed Jones v. Joseph Brown ("JB"): The Joneses may have a cause of action against JB under the attractive nuisance doctrine. The issue is whether a landowner is liable to infant trespassers for a dangerous condition that is adjacent to his property if he knows that they cross his property to get to it. Because the dangerous condition (the hole in the fence) was not on JB's property, and the Joneses were not injured on JB's property, it will be difficult to establish that JB owed the Joneses a duty to prevent them from entering the tracks through his yard. If it is established that JB had a duty, the question would arise as to whether JB breached that duty. Here, by failing to notify the railroad company of the hole in its fence, he could have been in breach of his duty to the children.

The question then arises as to whether JB's breach was the cause of the injuries sustained by the Joneses. The test would be "but for" the defendant's breach, the injury would not have occurred. Next, the court would have to determine if JB's actions were the legal cause of the Joneses' harm. If each of these questions is answered in the affirmative, the Joneses would have to prove the existence of damages in order for the cause of action to be sufficiently established.

JB can raise the defenses of "assumption of the risk" and "contributory negligence." Additionally, JB has a cross-claim against both FM and T for contribution.

117. TORTS

To: Senior Partner
From: Associate
Re: Loveless & Lawsuit Actions

There are several causes of actions that may be pursued by Larry Loveless ("Loveless") and Linda Lawsuit ("Lawsuit"). I have outlined each cause of action with the defenses that are likely to be raised.

Loveless and Lawsuit v. Carnal College Newspaper: Loveless and Lawsuit can bring an action against the Carnal College Newspaper ("Newspaper") for placing them in a false light, thereby constituting an invasion of privacy.

The tort of false light is committed when one person attributes to another (i) actions he did not take or (ii) views he does not hold. To be actionable, the statement must be something that would be objectionable to a reasonable person under the circumstances. If the matter was in the public interest, the plaintiff must also show that the defendant acted with malice, at least when a public figure is involved. [*See* Time, Inc. v. Hill, 385 U.S. 374 (1967)] Malice is defined as knowledge that the statement was false or reckless disregard as to its truth or falsity.

On the surface, it looks like the plaintiffs could make out a prima facie case for false light. Newspaper published a photo of Loveless and Lawsuit captioned "your place or mine," strongly inferring that one of them solicited the other to engage in an adulterous relationship, when in fact, no such solicitation had occurred. It is safe to say that a reasonable person would find such an accusation objectionable. Nevertheless, the plaintiffs will not succeed on this claim because, taken in context, the caption does not really imply that such solicitation actually occurred. The photo and caption were among several similar photos and captions in Newspaper in a section called "The Lighter Side." A reasonable person would not assume that the captions were true; rather, a reasonable person would understand that they were intended to be humorous. Thus, the photo and caption do not really attribute to the plaintiffs actions that they did not take.

Loveless and Lawsuit v. Rude and Moon Magazine: Plaintiffs Loveless and Lawsuit will be more successful if they sue Rudy Rude ("Rude") and Moon Magazine ("Moon") for false light and defamation.

Loveless and Lawsuit will be able to make out a case for false light invasion of privacy. Rude and Moon republished the photo and caption concerning the plaintiffs on the magazine's cover with the headline "Prominent Activist Nabbed in Classroom Hanky Panky." Again, since no adulterous relationship actually occurred at the relevant time, this statement paints the plaintiffs in a false light. Moreover, the context of the headline here is different: The caption and photo are no longer in a humorous section of the campus newspaper but instead stand alone in the magazine, and so they will now be seen as intending to imply that such a relationship existed. As discussed above, a reasonable person would find this accusation offensive.

Since Loveless is a well known community activist and regularly appears on TV, he is probably a public figure. Furthermore, if Loveless were participating in an adulterous relationship, it would be a matter of public interest, given the fact that he frequently speaks on television regarding morality and family values. Thus, Loveless must show malice. Although Lawsuit is not a public figure, her adulterous involvement with Loveless is a matter of public interest because of his status.

Malice is clearly present here because Rude and Moon acted with reckless disregard for truth. The facts state that Rude and Moon published the photo, caption, and headline without making any attempt to verify the veracity of the photo and its caption. Moreover, given the photo and caption's original context, it is very likely that Rude entertained serious doubts as to the truthfulness of the caption and his headline. This suffices to establish reckless disregard.

Rude and Moon will probably raise truth as a defense, but this will be unsuccessful. Truth is a defense to a false light claim; so Rude and Moon might argue that because plaintiffs dated two years ago, the current photo does not present the plaintiffs in a false light. This argument will be unavailing.

The fact that the parties dated two years ago would not give Rude and Moon the right to falsely imply that they are having an adulterous relationship now.

Plaintiffs may also bring an action against Rude and Moon for defamation. The tort of defamation consists of (i) defamatory language on the part of the defendant; (ii) of or concerning the plaintiff; (iii) publication by the defendant to a third person; and (iv) damage to the reputation of the plaintiff. Where the defamation refers to a public figure or involves a matter of public concern, the plaintiff must also prove that the defamatory language was false and that the defendant acted with some degree of fault.

Loveless will likely succeed on a claim of defamation. The headline "Prominent Activist Nabbed in Classroom Hanky Panky" was language put forth by the defendants. It is defamatory language insofar as it implies sexual misconduct, and it will be taken to refer to the plaintiffs since their picture appears in the photo accompanying the headline. It obviously was published to third persons since it appeared in a magazine. Since the defamation was in a tangible form, it constitutes libel. Most jurisdictions presume damages in cases of libel. Thus, special damages need not be proved. Furthermore, as discussed above, even if Loveless is deemed to be a public figure, requiring him to show falsity and malice to prevail in a defamation action, he can probably do so.

Lawsuit also has a strong claim on the same grounds. Unlike Loveless, she does not have to prove malice since she is not a public figure. However, if the affair is considered to be a matter of public concern (because of Loveless's status), Lawsuit may have to show some lesser degree of fault (such as negligence) and actual injury. Here, given Rude's conduct and her reaction to the publication, she will be able to prove both elements. Furthermore, if she establishes malice on Rude's part (which is likely), she does not need to prove actual injury.

Loveless and Lawsuit v. Rude: Loveless and Lawsuit can bring a claim against Rude for malicious prosecution. Rude filed a citizen's complaint against Loveless and Lawsuit for violating Valhalla's public morals statute. To succeed on a claim of malicious prosecution, the plaintiff must show (i) institution of criminal proceeding against the plaintiff; (ii) termination of the action favorable to plaintiff; (iii) absence of probable cause; (iv) improper purpose of defendant; and (v) damages.

I believe that Loveless and Lawsuit can succeed on this theory. The facts state that Rude instituted criminal proceedings by accusing Loveless and Lawsuit of violating the state's infidelity statute. Thereafter a finding of no probable cause was issued; thus, the case was resolved on terms favorable to Loveless and Lawsuit. The third element is also met. It is not likely that Rude knew of the pair's infidelity two years ago. Fourth, there is a strong inference that Rude filed the complaint against Loveless to gain a competitive advantage. The facts state that Rude and Loveless are competitors in the software business. Rude probably filed the suit to legitimatize the magazine article. Whatever his purpose, this element is satisfied in a prima facie case when the plaintiff shows that the defendant's primary purpose in instituting the action was something other than bringing a person to justice. Since the infidelity occurred two years ago and it is doubtful that Rude knew of it, and since Rude was seeking (and got) a competitive advantage, this element is satisfied. Loveless and Lawsuit can recover damages, such as the cost of defending the suit and the embarrassment they experienced. The latter is likely to be great for Loveless since he is a community activist and a spokesman for family values. Since Rude's purpose was improper, Loveless and Lawsuit will be entitled to punitive damages.

Lawsuit v. Rude and Moon: Lawsuit can sue Rude and Moon for intentional infliction of emotional distress. To establish a prima facie case of intentional infliction of emotional distress, Lawsuit must show that Rude engaged in extreme and outrageous conduct with the intent to inflict severe emotional distress, or with recklessness with respect to the effect on plaintiff, and that such conduct caused severe emotional distress. A plaintiff's hypersensitivity generally is not taken into account in determining whether the defendant's conduct is extreme or outrageous unless it is known to the defendant. Here, it is safe to say that accusing someone of adultery on the front page of a magazine is extreme and outrageous conduct. Even a person who is not hypersensitive may be shocked. Although apparently Rude and Moon did not intend to inflict emotional distress on Lawsuit, they certainly acted with reckless disregard for how their headline might affect her. Finally, their conduct has caused damages—Lawsuit has required extensive psychiatric treatment. Thus, Lawsuit can recover her actual damages, *i.e.,* those incurred for treatment of deep depression.

118. CONSTITUTIONAL LAW
To: Senior Partner
From: Associate
Re: Client Bob

The order issued by Judge Gunne is partially valid and partially invalid: The issue is whether the order restraining PAAC from (i) demonstrating on the sidewalk immediately in front of the salon; (ii) waving placards in the faces of passers-by; and (iii) using a bullhorn to amplify "disturbing comments" is a violation of PAAC's First Amendment rights to freedom of speech and assembly.

The injunction: The First Amendment prohibits government from abridging the freedom of speech and from interfering with the right to assemble. The states are bound to the First Amendment through the Fourteenth Amendment. Nevertheless, government generally is allowed to regulate the conduct of speech in public places by content neutral time, place, and manner restrictions. However, injunctions that restrict speech in public places are judged more harshly because they pose a great risk of censorship and discriminatory application. The test depends on whether the injunction is content based. If it is content based, it will be upheld only if it is necessary to achieve a compelling purpose. If it is content neutral, it will be upheld only if it burdens no more speech than necessary.

Here part (i) of the injunction will be upheld. It is content neutral since it prohibits PAAC members from all demonstrations immediately in front of fur salons, not merely those directed toward the fur industry. Moreover, it appears to burden no more speech than necessary. There is a need to prohibit demonstrations immediately in front of businesses because such demonstrations impede access to the businesses, and the ban here is very narrow since it prohibits demonstrating only immediately in front of a fur salon. Apparently, demonstrating adjacent to a fur salon or several feet away is permitted. Thus, part (i) will be upheld.

Part (ii) of the injunction probably also will be upheld. It too is content neutral since it prohibits PAAC members from waving **any** placard in the face of a passer-by. It seems to restrict no more speech than is necessary; it only prohibits the dangerous and annoying practice of waving placards in a person's face. Thus, it is constitutional.

Part (iii) of the injunction will not be upheld. It is content based since it prohibits amplification only of "disturbing comments," and there is no apparent compelling interest being served by this part of the injunction. If noise were the compelling interest, the ban would be on amplification of any message. A ban only on "disturbing comments" obviously is based on the effect such comments might have, but the government does not have a compelling interest in censoring disturbing comments about fur. Moreover, restrictions on speech must not be vague. Here it is unclear what would constitute a "disturbing comment," and so the injunction is also void for vagueness. Thus, it should be stricken.

The court rule: The court rule prohibiting attorneys from making reckless statements concerning the qualifications of a judge is constitutional. The issue is whether the rule is a violation of the First Amendment right to freedom of speech. Generally, when the government regulates the content of speech, the regulation must be necessary to achieve a compelling state interest. Otherwise, the regulation will violate the First Amendment unless the speech falls into one of the recognized categories of unprotected speech. Here, the court rule [which incidentally is based on Rule 8.2 of the Model Rules of Professional Responsibility] is a content based restriction, since it prohibits attorneys from making statements concerning the qualifications of judges. It could be argued that the speech prohibited by the rule is unprotected defamation. Defamatory speech is not protected by the First Amendment, and an allegation that a person is not qualified to perform his job generally is considered defamatory. However, statements critical of public officials are not considered defamatory unless the statements are made by a person who knows the statements are false or who is reckless with regard to truth or falsity.

Here, the rule does not broadly prohibit criticism of a judge's qualifications, but rather prohibits only criticism that is made recklessly. Thus, it is limited to what would be considered defamatory speech. Therefore the rule is constitutional.

It could also be argued that the court rule is necessary to achieve a compelling interest. Protecting public confidence in the integrity of the judicial system is a compelling interest, and a rule that prohibits reckless criticism of the system is necessary to achieve that interest. Thus, the court rule could be upheld on this ground as well.

119. CRIMINAL LAW

To: File
From: CB Lawyer
Re: *State v. Doe*

The prosecutor has charged John Doe with burglary, simple assault, assault, and resisting arrest. John Doe may assert that he did not possess the intent necessary to commit burglary, simple assault, or assault. Mr. Doe is most likely to be found guilty of resisting arrest. However, he may argue voluntary intoxication as a defense to all of the charges.

Burglary of the clothing warehouse: The issue is whether John Doe committed burglary. Burglary is defined as the breaking and entering into the dwelling of another, at nighttime, with the intent of committing a felony inside. Burglary is a specific intent crime. Thus, the prosecution must show that John Doe broke into and entered the warehouse with the intent to commit a felony. Under the facts, John Doe did not possess the requisite intent to commit a felony. The facts state that it was getting late and Mr. Doe broke into the factory in order to find a warm place to sleep. Nothing in the facts indicates that he broke into the building with the intent to commit a felony inside.

The prosecution will likely argue that John Doe committed larceny by taking the ski jacket. Larceny is the taking and carrying away of tangible property of another by trespass, with the intent to permanently deprive the person of his interest in the property. The larceny argument is weak because the facts do not indicate that John Doe intended to permanently deprive the warehouse owners of the ski jacket. Further, the facts do not support the premise that John Doe entered the warehouse with the intent to steal the ski jacket. The facts merely state that John Doe felt cold, and so he wrapped one of the ski jackets around his shoulders. To obtain conviction on the burglary charge, the prosecution will have to establish that John Doe had the intent to commit larceny prior to breaking and entering the factory. Analysis of the facts suggests this result is unlikely.

Simple assault on the security guard: The simple assault charge stems from Mr. Doe's kicking the security guard. Most states would call this battery rather than assault. A battery is the unlawful application of force to the person of another resulting in bodily injury or offensive contact. The touching need not be intentional; negligence may suffice. Simple battery is a misdemeanor offense. Here, the issue is whether Mr. Doe's conduct was sufficiently culpable. The facts state that Mr. Doe was asleep when he was found by the security guard, the security guard then shook Mr. Doe to awaken him, and Mr. Doe kicked out his legs as a result, knocking the security guard down and causing his injury. It could be argued that Mr. Doe's reaction was not intentional or even negligent; it may have simply been a reflex from being shaken from his slumber. The prosecutor will no doubt argue that while Mr. Doe might not have intended any harm, he knew that he was kicking out at a person and that is sufficient for battery. We do not have the facts to determine which argument will succeed. Ultimately the trier of fact will have to decide.

Assault on the police officer: The assault charge arising from Mr. Doe's swinging his arms at the police officer probably will succeed. Again, the issue is Mr. Doe's culpability. Assault is defined as an attempt to commit a battery or intentionally placing a victim in reasonable apprehension of imminent bodily harm. Attempted battery is a specific intent crime, meaning that the defendant must have acted with the intent to cause a battery. Assault against a police office is a felony and carries a greater penalty than simple assault or battery. Here, it seems clear that Mr. Doe had the requisite intent. The facts say that the officer dragged Mr. Doe to his feet and Mr. Doe started swinging at the officer. Thus, it appears that Mr. Doe had the intent to cause a battery or at least intended to cause the officer to apprehend that Mr. Doe was going to hit him. Either intent is sufficient to support the assault charge. Mr. Doe might argue that having been dragged to his feet, he was swinging his arms simply in an attempt to maintain his balance. This would negate the required intent, but it does not seem very believable.

Resisting arrest: A person is guilty of resisting arrest when he intentionally resists a lawful arrest. Here, John Doe was wrongfully in the warehouse. Therefore, the officer had probable cause to arrest him. Mr. Doe may assert, however, that he was defending himself against a potential attacker. However, given that the officer was in uniform and that he told Mr. Doe that he was under arrest, this is a weak argument. As in the above assault charge, it is unlikely that Mr. Doe will escape conviction on this charge.

Intoxication as a defense: Considering the facts, Mr. Doe may assert voluntary intoxication as a defense to the charges. Intoxication is voluntary if it is the result of the intentional taking, without duress, of a substance known to be intoxicating. Voluntary intoxication is a defense when the defendant is charged with a crime that requires intent or knowledge and the intoxication prevented the defendant from formulating the requisite intent. Note also that voluntary intoxication is a defense only to specific intent, not general intent, crimes.

The facts indicate that Mr. Doe entered the warehouse in an intoxicated state. He was approached by the security guard within an hour of his entry. Thus, it is very likely that he was still intoxicated at the time the security guard awakened him. However, nothing in the facts indicates that Mr. Doe was so drunk that he could not form the requisite intent for any of the specific intent crimes charged. Thus, this defense is not likely to be successful.

120. REAL PROPERTY

Enforcement of the deed: The Barrys will succeed in enforcing the deed against the Smiths and can collect damages on either of two theories: (i) easement/profit or (ii) real covenant/equitable servitude.

Easement/profit: The Barrys will be able to enforce the deed against the Smiths and collect damages based on the first deed clause. At issue is whether that clause created an enforceable profit a prendre ("profit") and easement.

The first deed clause creates both a profit appurtenant and an easement appurtenant. A profit is a nonpossessory interest in land that allows its holder to remove something from another's land. An easement is a nonpossessory interest in land that gives the easement holder a right to enter the land of another for a particular purpose. Profits and easements are considered appurtenant when the reserved right to use the other's property (called the "servient tenement") benefits the use and enjoyment of another piece of property (called the "dominant tenement"). When this is the case, the burden on the servient tenement passes when the servient tenement is transferred if the transferee had: (i) actual notice of the profit or easement or (ii) constructive notice from recorded public records or from the visible appearance of the land.

Here, the deed gives the Barrys a profit to take water from parcel B and an easement of ingress and egress to maintain the wellhead and pipes on parcel B. The profit and easement were reserved to provide water to parcel A; thus the interests are appurtenant. The Smiths will also be held to have notice of the profit and easement. They were described in the Ables' deed to parcel B, that deed was recorded, and the Smiths took title from the Ables. Thus, the easement and profit are binding on the Smiths, and they will be liable for interfering with the Barrys' rights.

Real covenant/equitable servitude: The Barrys can also get damages and an injunction against further interference with the easement. At issue is whether a promise made in a deed is enforceable against subsequent buyers of the property when the promise was not mentioned in the subsequent buyers' deed.

The Barrys can collect damages because the Smiths' interference with the well breached a real covenant that is enforceable against the Smiths at law. A real covenant is a promise to do or refrain from doing something on land. A real covenant is binding and enforceable at law (*i.e.*, gives rise to a right to damages) against a subsequent landowner if the parties who originally made the covenant intended successors to be bound, the subsequent owner had actual or constructive notice of the covenant, there was horizontal privity between the original covenanting parties (*i.e.*, they shared some interest in the land other than the covenant, such as a grantor-grantee relationship), there is vertical privity between the successor and the original covenanting party (*i.e.*, the successor holds the entire interest that the original covenanting party held when the covenant was made), and the covenant touches and concerns the property (which means that the covenant requires the party to do something or refrain from doing something on the property).

All of the elements are present here. The second clause in the Ables' deed to parcel B included a covenant not to disturb the Barrys' profit and easement. The deed made it clear that the covenant was to be binding on successors. The Ables' deed was recorded, so the Smiths had constructive notice of the covenant because it was in the chain of title to parcel B. There was horizontal privity between the original covenanting parties—the Ables purchased parcel B from the Barrys. There is vertical privity since the Smiths own the entire interest that the Ables owned when they made the covenant. Finally, the covenant touches and concerns the land because it prohibits the owners of parcel B from interfering with the well that is located on their land. Thus, the covenant is enforceable at law against the Smiths. However, this will only give the Barrys a right to damages for violation of the covenant. To enjoin further violations, the Barrys will have to prove that there is an equitable servitude on the land.

An equitable servitude is a covenant that equity courts will enforce against assignees of the covenant. An equitable servitude requires proof of most of the same elements that are required to prove the existence of a real covenant, but proof of privity is not required. Thus, the Barrys' proof of the real covenant here is sufficient proof of an equitable servitude as well. Therefore, the Barrys may obtain an injunction against the Smiths prohibiting future interference with the well.

The cash: The Smiths have a right to recover the cash Mr. Barry found on the Smiths' land. At issue is ownership of mislaid property.

The Smiths have a right to recover the cash Mr. Barry found on their land because the money will be classified as mislaid property. Generally, the finder of lost property has a right to retain the property against the whole world except for the true owner. However, if property is mislaid, the owner of the real property where the personal property was found has a right to retain the property, except as against its true owner. Personal property will be deemed to have been mislaid where, judging from the place it was found, it can reasonably be determined that someone intentionally placed it there and then forgot about it. The common law recognized an exception to this rule for treasure trove, which is gold, silver, and paper representations thereof, but few states recognize this exception today.

Here, the cash will be treated as mislaid property. It was found wrapped in newspaper in a buried container. It clearly did not just fall out of the true owner's pocket. The container was found on the Smiths' land. Even though the container was found under one of the Barrys' well pipes, remember that an easement is nonpossessory; thus, the land under the well pipe belongs to the Smiths and not to the Barrys. Thus, the Smiths have a right to any remaining cash and can probably sue the Barrys for the amounts they spent. If the true owner of the cash comes forward, the Smiths will have to turn over the cash to him, but otherwise, the Smiths' right to the cash is superior to anyone else's.

121. CONTRACTS

To: President of Resale
From: Law Firm
Re: Bicycle light contracts

You have requested an opinion letter setting forth the causes of action that may be filed against your company. This letter addresses each possible lawsuit that may be filed, possible defenses, and the likely outcome of the lawsuits. Since the transactions here involve the sale of goods (*i.e.*, moveable things), they are governed by Article 2 of the Uniform Commercial Code ("U.C.C.").

Bikrite v. Resale: Bikrite will probably sue Resale for breach of contract and may be entitled to recover damages. At issue is whether the lights failed to conform to the contract.

Generally, under the U.C.C. "perfect tender rule," a buyer has the right to reject goods that fail to conform to the contract in any way. However, the right to reject goods is cut off by acceptance. Acceptance occurs when, after reasonable opportunity to inspect goods, the buyer: (i) indicates that they conform to the contract, (ii) fails to reject within a reasonable time after tender, or (iii) does any act inconsistent with the seller's ownership. Here, upon receiving the lights from Resale, Bikrite immediately determined that they were the wrong size and rejected them. Clearly the rejection came before any acceptance. The only issue is whether the lights will be deemed nonconforming. Although the contract between Resale and Lytco (discussed below) specifically provided that the lights were to fit Cyclone bicycles, the agreement between Resale and Bikrite merely provided for the sale of "bicycle lights." The lights that were delivered were bicycle lights, so arguably, there was no breach. However, we were not given the language of the entire contract between Resale and Bikrite. It seems likely that the contract somewhere specifies that the lights were to fit Cyclone bicycles. Even if the contract failed to include this specification, a court would likely allow Bikrite to argue that the course of dealing between the parties (*i.e.*, the conduct of the parties regarding the transaction at hand) makes it clear that the term "bicycle lights" in the contract really means bicycle lights suitable for use on Cyclone bicycles. Thus, the goods were nonconforming and the rejection was proper.

Where nonconforming goods are rejected by the buyer, the buyer is entitled to damages equal to the difference between the contract price and either the market price or the price of substitute goods (called "cover"), plus incidental and consequential damages. Incidental damages include costs reasonably incurred in inspection, receipt, transportation, care, etc., of the goods. Consequential damages include losses resulting from the particular needs of the buyer of which the seller was aware and which could not be prevented by buying substitute goods. Thus, if the $15 contract price here is below the current market price or Bikrite buys substitute lights that cost more than $15 each, Resale would be liable for those damages. Bikrite can also recover any incidental damages it incurred. However, Bikrite will not be able to recover its projected lost profits from Resale as consequential damages. There is no evidence that Resale knew that Bikrite was anticipating that inclusion of the bicycle lights would increase this year's profits by $100,000. Moreover, even if Resale had such knowledge, the profits still would not be recoverable because it seems likely that Bikrite could purchase suitable replacement goods. Finally, it should be noted that predicted profits as a result of a change in a product are highly speculative, and courts generally will not award damages based on such speculation.

Lytco v. Resale: Lytco will probably sue Resale for the profits it lost on the lights Bikrite returned. This claim will probably not succeed; instead Lytco may be liable to Resale for delivering nonconforming goods. At issue is whether a buyer may revoke acceptance of goods after the buyer has resold the goods.

Generally, if a buyer wrongfully rejects goods delivered under a contract, the seller may recover damages. The measure of damages generally is the difference between the contract price and the market or resale price, but if neither of these will put the seller in as good a position as performance would have (*e.g.*, because the seller lost sales volume), the seller may recover lost profits. Presumably, Lytco can manufacture as many lights as it can sell, so it falls into this "lost volume" category. Thus, if the lights were wrongfully rejected, Lytco's damages would be $25,000 ($10 contract price minus $5 cost of manufacture multiplied by 5,000 units under the contract). The only real issue here is whether the rejection of the lights was improper.

The rejection of the lights was not improper because they failed to conform to the contract and Resale had a right to revoke its acceptance. As discussed above, under the perfect tender rule, before acceptance a buyer may reject goods that fail to conform to the contract in any way. Here, the contract provided that Lytco was to supply lights for use on the Bikrite Cyclone, and the lights that were delivered do not meet this specification. However, Lytco will argue that Resale accepted the lights. Lytco has two plausible arguments: (i) Resale accepted expressly when its representative signed the receipt for "5,000 lights in as is condition" or (ii) Resale's subsequent delivery of the lights to Bikrite is an act inconsistent with Lytco's ownership of the lights and so constitutes an acceptance. The result of the first argument is uncertain. It is unclear whether the "as is" language meant that Resale was accepting the goods in whatever condition they happened to be in, or that Resale was merely acknowledging that the goods arrived. However, resolution of that issue is unimportant because clearly sending the goods on to Bikrite is inconsistent with Lytco's ownership and constitutes an acceptance. Nevertheless, Resale can revoke its acceptance.

A buyer may revoke acceptance of goods within a reasonable time after acceptance if the goods have a defect that substantially impairs their value and the goods were accepted: (i) under a belief that the defect would be cured, (ii) because it was difficult to discover the defects, or (iii) on the seller's assurance that the goods conformed to the contract. Here, the first enumerated condition is not relevant because Resale did not know of the defect. Neither was the third enumerated condition met— the receipt stated that the lights were in "as is" condition. Lytco will argue that the second enumerated condition also was not met. The facts indicate that had a carton been opened, it would have been readily apparent that the lights were too small. Resale could argue that while that defect was readily apparent to the people at Bikrite, no one at Resale could have made such a determination. Nothing in the facts indicates that Resale knew what size light was appropriate; indeed, Resale did not provide specifications for the light, but merely told Lytco it wanted lights suitable for the Cyclone bicycle. Thus, it seems reasonable to assume that Resale did not have any way of knowing that the lights were nonconforming. Therefore, Resale will probably prevail.

Since the revocation of acceptance was proper, Resale will be entitled to damages. As discussed above, where a buyer properly rejects goods, the buyer is entitled to damages equal to the difference between the contract price and either the market price or the price of substitute goods (called "cover"), plus incidental and consequential damages. Since Lytco probably knew that Resale would resell the lights to Bikrite, consequential damages here might very well include Resale's lost profits from the resale unless substitute goods were readily available.

Right to cure: It should be noted that this whole matter might be resolved without resort to any of the above remedies. Under the U.C.C., if a seller sends nonconforming goods and there still is time under the contract in which to perform, the seller may give notice to the buyer of its intent to cure by sending conforming goods. There is even a right to cure after the time for performance has passed if the seller had reason to believe the nonconforming goods would be acceptable or the seller could not have known of the defect despite proper business conduct (*e.g.*, where, as here in the resale to Bikrite, the goods were prepackaged from a supplier). The events here seem to have occurred recently, and nothing in the facts indicates that either contract had a hard and fast delivery date. Indeed, the sale of the bikes with lights was contemplated to occur over the course of the year. Thus, it appears that Resale has a right to cure with respect to its sale to Bikrite, and Lytco has a right to cure with respect to its sale to Resale.

122. EVIDENCE

To: Senior Partner
From: Law Clerk
Re: *Estate of George v. Top Notch Insurance Company*

A review of the evidentiary rulings reveals that the trial court improperly admitted certain items of evidence, which resulted in a ruling in favor of Top Notch Insurance Company. Therefore, our client, Jennifer, should appeal the ruling. On appeal, our client should assert that the court committed error by admitting the following evidence: (i) the testimony of George's attorney, Joseph Esquire, regarding his client's physical condition; (ii) the testimony of Joseph Esquire regarding George's diary statement, and (iii) the testimony of Sally, the autopsy physician's secretary, regarding information contained in the autopsy report.

Testimony of Joseph Esquire regarding George's physical condition: Any evidence admitted in a case must be relevant to the issues being discussed. An item of evidence is relevant if it tends to prove or disprove a material issue. A trial judge, however, has broad discretion to exclude relevant evidence if its probative value is substantially outweighed by the danger of unfair prejudice, confusion of the issues, or misleading to the jury. In the present case, the trial court admitted the testimony of Joseph Esquire, George's attorney, regarding his client's physical appearance and attitude during numerous consultations. Joseph Esquire testified that George "appeared anxious, distracted, and extremely depressed." Joseph Esquire's testimony was offered to prove whether George committed suicide. Although the testimony suggested that George was not well, it does not prove that he committed suicide. One could argue that many people act in the same manner on a daily basis and do not commit suicide. Thus, the testimony does not make the assertion that George committed suicide more or less true. Additionally, even if the court found that Joseph Esquire's testimony was relevant and material to the case, it should have been excluded because the probative value of Joseph Esquire's testimony was outweighed by the danger of unfair prejudice to the jury.

Testimony of Joseph Esquire regarding George's diary: The trial court permitted Joseph Esquire to testify to certain statements contained in George's diary. Joseph Esquire testified that he discovered an entry that stated, "I would rather die than go to trial." This testimony is being offered to help prove that George committed suicide. Although the diary statement may be relevant, it should have been excluded by the judge as hearsay. Hearsay is an out-of-court statement offered into evidence to prove the truth of the matter asserted. Joseph Esquire is testifying to what he read in George's diary; thus, it is hearsay. The statement should not have been admitted because it neither falls within any of the exceptions to the hearsay rule nor is it nonhearsay. Top Notch, however, may argue that the diary statement was appropriately admitted because it fell within the present state of mind exception to the hearsay rule.

Top Notch will assert that George's present state of mind is in issue because it demonstrates that he did what he intended to do, *i.e.,* commit suicide. However, one could reasonably argue that the diary statement should not have been admissible under the present state of mind exception because it was written several months prior to George's death. Thus, the diary statement may not be a sufficient representation of George's state of mind at the time of the car crash.

Second, the diary statement should have been excluded because it was subject to the attorney-client privilege. The attorney-client privilege provides that communications between attorney and client, made during professional consultation, are privileged from disclosure. George gave Joseph Esquire the diary after retaining him in the embezzlement suit. Since the diary was given to him in the course of his representation of George, it was privileged. The facts do not indicate that George waived the attorney-client privilege at any time; thus, Joseph Esquire was prohibited from disclosing the contents of the diary. However, the prosecution will likely argue that although communications between George and Joseph Esquire were privileged, the diary was not because objects and preexisting documents are not protected by the attorney-client privilege.

Testimony of Sally regarding autopsy report: Sally, Dr. Jones's secretary, testified to what she read in the autopsy report. The autopsy report is relevant to disprove Top Notch's claim that George committed suicide. The report tends to prove that George was in an accident because he was intoxicated. However, Sally's testimony regarding the autopsy report is hearsay. It is likely that the court admitted the testimony because it fit into the business records exception to the hearsay rule. However, Sally did not have personal knowledge of the autopsy; therefore, she should not have been permitted to testify to the contents of the autopsy report. Since Sally's knowledge of the report resulted from her having read the document, the court should have applied the "best evidence rule" to admit the report. Moreover, the statement of Dr. Jones's opinion should not have been admitted with the report. Dr. Jones's opinion was hearsay and does not fall within any of the exceptions to the hearsay rule. Furthermore,

Dr. Jones was not qualified as an expert witness; therefore, his opinion was that of a layperson, which is not admissible.

The prosecution may try to assert that as a lay witness, Dr. Jones was offering an opinion regarding intoxication, but that requires the witness to have observed the person and to be able to describe his actions and demeanor. Dr. Jones would not be able to testify to that. As a result, this argument fails.

The court erred in admitting Joseph Esquire's testimony regarding the diary, his testimony regarding his client's physical and emotional state, and Sally's testimony about the autopsy report. Thus, our client should appeal the trial court's decision.

123. TORTS

MEMORANDUM

Re: Defenses to Luckless claim.

Lack of causation: One of the prima facie case elements that Luckless will have to prove in all of her claims is causation. As a first defense, I would point out that preliminary medical reports are inconclusive regarding the precise cause of the miscarriage. In fact, the miscarriage occurred several days after she ingested both alcohol and fertility medication. The defendants should argue that Luckless's miscarriage was caused by her consumption of alcohol, not the use of Pro-Pregnancy. The defendants should argue that this was the cause of Luckless's injury. (Despite the fact that all the defendants have waived any conflicts, this may present a conflict of interest that would require separate representation because her doctor failed to warn her not to consume alcohol.)

Assuming that Luckless meets her burden of proving that Pro-Pregnancy was a cause of her miscarriage, she will face additional causation issues. The facts state that Luckless's lawyer filed suit against several drugstores where the device may have been purchased and that the identity of the store is impossible to determine because no invoices with this information exist at the present time. I would argue on behalf of each drugstore that it cannot be sued because Luckless cannot make out a prima facie case of negligence or strict products liability since she cannot state precisely who breached their duty of care.

This defense is not likely to work because the court may apply a "market share" or "enterprise" theory of liability. In questions of "but for" causation, courts allow the plaintiff to shift the burden to the defendants when all of them were negligent but it is impossible to determine which one caused the plaintiff's injury. It then becomes the burden of each defendant to prove that his or her negligence is *not* the actual (but for) cause of the plaintiff's injury. If a defendant cannot prove that he could not have caused the injury, then he will be responsible in part for the plaintiff's injuries. This theory has been applied in products liability cases to impose on all suppliers of the product (unable to prove their noninvolvement) liability equal to their market share.

Similarly, Pro-Pregnancy is sold by numerous manufacturers across the country and the facts state that it has become an almost generic product. This means that it will be difficult, if not impossible, to identify precisely which manufacturer sold the product to Luckless. Thus, an analysis similar to the one described above may be applied. Manufacturers will have to prove that they did not sell the product to Luckless or else bear a percentage of liability in proportion to their share of the Pro-Pregnancy market.

All defendants can argue that Luckless's nervous breakdown was not a foreseeable result of their breaches. Under the doctrine of proximate cause, a defendant will be liable for any harmful results that are the normal incidents of and within the increased risk caused by his acts. This test is based on foreseeability. The defendants can argue that there is no way that they could have known that Luckless had had several miscarriages. Luckless may counter this argument by noting that women who use Pro-Pregnancy are those who have had trouble carrying a pregnancy to term. Furthermore, the fact that the extent of the harm was not foreseeable does not affect liability, because a tortfeasor takes the victim as he finds her. Thus, this argument is not likely to succeed.

Comparative negligence: I would also argue on behalf of the defendants that Luckless's recovery should be reduced because she was negligent. Almost all jurisdictions have adopted comparative negligence, whereby the plaintiff's recovery generally will be reduced according to her degree of fault. Here, Luckless voluntarily became inebriated and forgot that she should not take fertility medication. Pro-Pregnancy specifically warns against simultaneous use with fertility medication—this prohibition was printed on the device in big red letters. Also, while her doctor did not specifically warn her not to consume alcohol, it could be argued that a reasonable person in her circumstances would have known not to drink. This negligent conduct by Luckless will almost certainly reduce the amount of her recovery in negligence. In failure to warn and other strict liability claims, most comparative negligence jurisdictions apply their comparative negligence rules. Becoming inebriated and forgetting a conspicuous warning label will reduce her recovery under these claims also.

No negligence by drugstores or middleman: Middleman and the drugstores can claim that they are not liable under a theory of negligence even if the product is defective. The majority view is that a dealer who buys from a reputable supplier or manufacturer with no reason to anticipate that the product is dangerous need make only a cursory inspection of the goods to avoid liability for manufacturing defects. The facts do not indicate that any of the drug manufacturers were anything but reputable. Thus, Middleman and the drugstores will not be liable for negligence as long as they inspected the product and found it in the condition it was in when shipped by the manufacturer. This defense does not apply to a strict liability claim.

Federal preemption: Plaintiff Luckless is proceeding against all defendants on common law causes of action in a state court action. All defendants should defend on the grounds that such claims are barred by the Supremacy Clause of the Constitution. A state or local law will be struck down if it commands conduct inconsistent with that required by the federal rule. Additionally, a state or local rule will be struck down even if it does not conflict with federally regulated conduct if it appears that Congress intended to "occupy" the entire field, thus precluding any state or local regulation. All the defendants will argue that the Food, Drug and Cosmetics Act ("FDCA") bars the suit by Luckless because the FDCA occupies the entire field of medical device labeling and safety. The defendants will argue that since the device used by Luckless was appropriately labeled, it was in fact safe and that any legal claim to the contrary is barred by the FDCA.

124. CONTRACTS

Breach of contract: The first claim you might bring is for breach of contract. At issue is whether Sam's promise is enforceable.

Sam made an offer to form a unilateral contract. A unilateral contract arises where an offeror promises to perform in exchange for performance by the offeree. The offeree cannot accept by making a promise; the offer can be accepted only by performance done with knowledge of the offer and motivated by the offer. Once performance has begun, the offeror may not revoke the offer until the offeree has had a reasonable time in which to perform. However, the contract is not truly formed until the offeree's performance is complete. If the offeror revokes before performance is complete, the offeree will be entitled to recover, at a minimum, the costs of his performance, but a court is likely to award damages needed to put the offeree is as good a position as performance would have put him.

Here, Sam promised to give you $200,000 if you would live with him until you turned 26. This promise for performance constitutes an offer to form a unilateral contract. Thus, your telling Sam that you would be happy to stay with him did not constitute an acceptance. However, you probably will be held to have begun performance under the offer, although this is a little uncertain. You said that you intended to live with your father and care for him before he made the offer, so it appears that your performance was not motivated by the offer. However, you could have changed your mind anytime during the years you cared for Sam. Moreover, you turned down a job offer shortly after Sam made his offer because you were expecting to be compensated by Sam. This shows that you were motivated to stay with Sam, at least in part, by the offer.

Sam might argue that he did not intend to form a contract, but rather was merely promising to give you a gift. An offer to make a gift generally is unenforceable. However, this argument will fail. Whether a party intends to make a contract is determined by an objective standard—whether a reasonable party would think a contract was intended. The difference between a gift and a contract is that with a contract, the promise is intended to induce a detriment—the price for the promise. With a gift, there is no similar bargained-for exchange. Here, Sam's promise clearly shows an offer for a bargained-for exchange—he would give you $200,000 if you care for him for six years. Thus, a contract was formed.

Sam's telling you that he would not give you the $200,000 can be construed as an attempted revocation of the offer. Since you clearly have begun to perform, completing five of the six years of the care sought, this attempted revocation would be invalid. As discussed above, the court may award you the costs of performance so far, or it may treat this as a breach of contract and award damages sufficient to place you in as good a position as performance would have put you.

Sam may raise the Statute of Frauds as a defense. Under the Statute of Frauds, a contract which by its terms cannot be performed within one year is not enforceable unless the material terms of the contract are evidenced by a writing signed by the party sought to be held liable. Here, the offer called for performance over the course of six years, and Sam did not put the offer in writing or sign any other memorandum containing the material terms of the deal. However, performance can take a contract out of the Statute of Frauds, either entirely or to the extent of performance. Thus, at a minimum, you would be entitled to five-sixths of the promised $200,000.

Sam might claim breach of contract as a defense. Since you began spending time with your girlfriend, you have not been spending much time with Sam. However, this argument is weak. The contract does not specify what duties you have other than living with Sam, and you are still doing that. Nevertheless, if this argument succeeds, you would still be entitled to some compensation under the doctrine of substantial performance. Where a party breaches a contract, but the breach is minor, the party is entitled to the price under the contract, but will have to offset any damages caused by his breach. In determining whether a breach is minor or material, the court will look to whether the promisor received the substantial benefit of his bargain.

Here, you performed about five-sixths of the contract before your purported breach. A court would likely find this to be substantial performance. Thus, it would award you the $200,000 contract price less damages cause by your breach. The simplest measure of damages here would be one-sixth of the $200,000, so again, you would receive five-sixths of $200,000.

Promissory estoppel: If the court finds that the contract failed for the Statute of Frauds, Sam might still be bound under a promissory estoppel theory. Under the theory of promissory estoppel, a contract will be enforceable to the extent necessary to avoid injustice where the promisor reasonably should have expected that his words would have induced action or forbearance of a definite and substantial character, and such action or forbearance actually occurred. Here, Sam should have expected that you would rely on his promise to pay you $200,000 if you lived with him for six years. You did in fact rely on the agreement and turned down a job offer in order to fulfill the duties under the offer. Thus, Sam would be liable to you to the extent of your detrimental reliance. This would be measured by what you would have made had you accepted the job offer minus expenses that you saved by not accepting the offer.

Quasi-contract: As an alternative to promissory estoppel, if your contract claims fails, you could also seek relief under a quasi-contract theory. Quasi-contract is an equitable remedy used to prevent unjust enrichment. It is available where parties attempt to enter into a contractual relationship, one party has performed in whole or in part, and the contract fails. The performing party may recover damages to prevent the unjust enrichment of the other party. Damages usually are measured by the benefit the defendant received, but they may be measured by the plaintiff's detriment, and may exceed the contract price, where the plaintiff's benefit is hard to measure and the plaintiff has not breached the contract.

Here, you would argue that Sam has been unjustly enriched because the contract failed. Sam received the benefit of having you live with him for five years. It would be unfair to allow him to retain that benefit without compensating you in some way. Thus, you would be entitled to recover the reasonable value of caring for Sam for that time. This probably would be less than the promised $200,000, so the breach of contract remedy should be your primary claim.

125. CRIMINAL LAW/PROCEDURE

To: File

Re: *State v. Perry*

In preparing Perry's defense, we should assert that our client's conduct does not satisfy the statutory requirements for murder. A motion for dismissal should be filed. A motion to suppress the statements Perry made regarding the air bag, as well as the articles unlawfully seized by the police officers in his apartment, should also be filed.

The murder charge: We may argue that Perry's conduct does not constitute murder under the statute for this jurisdiction. First, the statute defines murder as "purposely" causing death or serious bodily injury resulting in death. A person acts purposely when his conscious objective is to engage in certain conduct or cause a particular result. Given the facts presented, the prosecution will have difficulty showing that it was Perry's conscious objective to cause serious bodily injury, resulting in death, to Victor. The facts state that Perry decided to remove the air bag from Victor's car as a joke. Further, this was not unusual behavior since, according to the facts, both Victor and Perry engaged in practical jokes of this kind regularly. Perry did not possess the requisite intent necessary to prove murder under the statute.

Second, the statute defines murder as "knowingly" causing death or serious bodily injury resulting in death. A person acts knowingly when he is aware or knows that his conduct will necessarily or very likely cause a particular result. Perry did not know that his removing the air bag from Victor's car would result in Victor's death. Perry did not know that Victor would be involved in a car accident that might require deployment of the air bag to prevent serious injury. The prosecution will contend that Perry knew that driving in a car without an air bag could cause Victor to sustain serious injuries, were he to be involved in an accident. Further, it might argue that because Perry and Victor had a disagreement that ended their friendship, they were not friends. Therefore, Perry intended to cause Victor's death or serious bodily injury resulting in death. This is a very weak argument, however. Perry may have acted recklessly or negligently, but he did not remove the air bag believing that its removal would very likely result in Victor's death. He was merely playing a joke on Victor; thus, his conduct does not rise to the statutory standard.

Finally, the statute defines murder as causing death or serious bodily injury resulting in death during the commission of specifically enumerated felonies. Perry did not commit any of the felonies listed in the statute. The prosecution may contend that Perry committed robbery when he removed the air bag from Victor's car. Robbery is defined as a taking of the personal property of another, from the other's person or presence by force or threats of immediate death or physical injury, with the intent to permanently deprive him of it. When Perry removed the air bag, he did not do it in Victor's presence, by force or threat, nor did he intend to permanently deprive Victor of it. Perry was merely playing a practical joke on Victor, who was not even aware that the air bag was missing.

The prosecution may also contend that Perry committed a burglary. A burglary is a breaking and entry into the dwelling of another with the intent to commit a felony therein. It could be argued that Victor's car does not constitute a dwelling, but there are instances where the burglarized structure is expanded to include yards and cars. In this case, the prosecution might be able to prove burglary. However, Victor's death took place after the burglary, thereby making it impossible to prove murder, *i.e.,* that, beyond a reasonable doubt, the burglary directly resulted in his death.

Thus, although Perry was indicted for murder, it is unlikely that the prosecution will be able to prove, beyond a reasonable doubt, that Perry committed murder. The facts are unlikely to support a murder conviction because Perry does not meet the intent requirements of the jurisdiction's statute.

The air bag and newspaper articles: The Fourth Amendment provides that people should be free in their persons from unreasonable searches and seizures. A search is a governmental intrusion into an area where a person has a reasonable and justifiable expectation of privacy. In the present case, the police conducted an unlawful search of Perry's home. Perry had a reasonable expectation of privacy in his home. The police, who are considered government agents, entered his home without a valid warrant. Further, they did not conduct a valid warrantless search of his home.

To conduct a valid warrantless search, the officers needed to meet one of the six exceptions to the warrant requirement. Given the facts, consent is the only exception that would be applicable. The consent exception provides that the police may conduct a warrantless search if they obtain a person's voluntary and intelligent consent to enter his home. In this case, the police inquired if they could come in. Perry did not answer, he merely asked "what for?" and then tried to close the door. Perry did not voluntarily and intelligently consent to the police search of his apartment. Therefore, the police search of Perry's apartment was unconstitutional because it was in violation of his Fourth Amendment rights. Consequently, the air bag, newspaper articles, and Perry's statement regarding the air bag should be excluded from evidence. They are considered "fruit of the poisonous tree" under the exclusionary rule, because they were obtained in violation of Perry's Fourth Amendment rights.

The prosecution will argue that the police entered Perry's apartment because they believed there was evanescent evidence that would be destroyed. However, this argument fails since the officers were not aware of what Perry had in his apartment before they entered. Further, the prosecution may claim that the search was incident to a lawful arrest. However, the facts do not indicate that the police went to Perry's apartment to arrest him. Further, the facts do not state that they possessed an arrest warrant. Therefore, this argument also fails. Third, the prosecutors will claim that the newspaper articles and the air bag should be admissible because they were in plain view. However, this argument is weak because the police officers had unlawfully entered Perry's apartment when they saw the newspaper clippings and discovered him with the air bag. The officers did not glimpse the articles and air bag from the doorway prior to entering Perry's apartment.

The prosecution may also assert that the police were in hot pursuit of Perry and, therefore, it was permissible to arrest him without a warrant and conduct a warrantless search and seizure. Police in hot pursuit of a fleeing felon may make a warrantless search and seizure. The prosecution will likely assert that Perry's running into the bedroom gave the police probable cause to believe he was fleeing. This argument will likely fail, because the police did not enter Perry's dwelling while pursuing him as a felon. Likewise, they did not enter the apartment with the knowledge that Perry had committed any crime.

Finally, Perry's statement, "I found it on the street" regarding the air bag is inadmissible because the officers obtained this statement before informing Perry of his *Miranda* rights. Perry can argue that he was already in custody when the officers questioned him about the air bag because he reasonably believed that he was not free to leave. Thus, he should have been informed of his *Miranda* rights before the officers questioned him.

In conclusion, we should file a motion for dismissal on Perry's behalf because his conduct does not satisfy the definition of murder as defined by the statute of the jurisdiction. Likewise, a motion should be filed to suppress the statement Perry made regarding the air bag, the air bag itself, and the newspaper articles wrongfully seized by the police officers.

126. CONSTITUTIONAL LAW

Eleventh Amendment concerns: We may raise a number of arguments on Mike's behalf, but none are likely to be successful. It should be noted at the outset that the federal court would have jurisdiction to hear Mike's claims, and the Eleventh Amendment is not a bar. The federal courts have jurisdiction to hear cases and controversies arising under the Constitution, and as will be discussed below, all of Mike's claims arise under the Constitution. Moreover, Mike's claims are not barred by the Eleventh Amendment. The Eleventh Amendment bars federal courts from hearing claims against the states, but does not bar claims against municipalities. The claims here are against Olde City, a city. Thus, the Eleventh Amendment does not prevent the actions we might bring.

Equal protection: Mike's strongest claim is that the ordinance violates the Equal Protection Clause of the Fourteenth Amendment, but this claim will probably be unsuccessful. At issue is whether the ordinance is rational.

The Equal Protection Clause of the Fourteenth Amendment prohibits states from discriminating unreasonably among classes of persons. Whether a classification is reasonable depends on the nature of the right involved and the criteria on which the classification is based. An ordinance regulating economic activities and not involving any suspect or quasi-suspect classification (*e.g.,* race, religion, gender), will be upheld unless the challenger can show that the ordinance is not rationally related to a legitimate government interest.

Here, the ordinance prohibits peddling within any area designated a pedestrian mall, so it merely regulates economic activity. The ordinance classifies people by length of veteran peddler status. Such status is not a suspect or quasi-suspect classification. Therefore, the ordinance will be upheld unless Mike can show that it is not rationally related to a legitimate government interest. The facts say that the ordinance was adopted to revitalize the downtown commercial district, which is a legitimate government interest. The only real issue is whether the ordinance is rationally related to that interest. Mike could argue that it is not rational to allow some veterans to peddle within a pedestrian mall while prohibiting others from doing so. However, the city would argue that it is not required to adopt the best law to achieve its goal; a first step is permissible. Since the ordinance here would have the effect of cutting down on the number of peddlers who could peddle on the sidewalks in pedestrian malls, the ordinance seems to be rationally related to a legitimate government interest. Therefore, the ordinance will probably be upheld under the Equal Protection Clause.

Freedom of speech: Mike might claim that the ordinance violates his First Amendment right to freedom of speech, but this argument will probably be unsuccessful. At issue is whether the ordinance impinges upon speech.

The First Amendment to the United States Constitution, which is applicable to the states through the Fourteenth Amendment's Due Process Clause, provides that government shall not interfere with the freedom of speech. Laws interfering with the content of speech generally will be upheld only if the government can show that they are necessary to achieve a compelling interest. However, content neutral laws regulating the conduct related to speech (*i.e.,* the time, place, or manner of the speech rather than the content of the speech) will be upheld if they are narrowly tailored to serve a significant government interest and leave open alternative channels of communication. Here, Mike might argue that because he dispenses political commentary along with the food he peddles, the ordinance amounts to a time, place, and manner restriction. However, this argument is very weak. Although Mike may espouse his political views while he works, the ordinance here does not seem to restrict speech in any real way. Under the ordinance, Mike is free to go into the pedestrian mall and conduct any type of political speech he desires. The only conduct prohibited under the ordinance is peddling, which is not speech related conduct. Thus, this argument will fail.

Due process: Mike might claim that the ordinance denies him his right to due process, but this claim is also doomed. The Fourteenth Amendment prohibits states from denying a person life, liberty, or property without due process of law. Mike would face two hurdles here. First, he must show that he had a property interest in peddling in the pedestrian mall. The mere expectation of being allowed to peddle in the area is not enough; he must have some legitimate claim or entitlement. Here, Mike might argue that he had such a legitimate claim—his state peddler's license. To amount to a legitimate claim or entitlement, Mike will have to show that the license permits peddling in all public areas. We do not have sufficient facts to predict the success of this argument. However, even if Mike has a property interest here, the court will find that Mike received all the process that was due. Where government action is not directed toward an individual but instead is general, individuals are not entitled to an individual hearing. Here, the city adopted an ordinance prohibiting anyone from peddling within designated pedestrian malls and then modified the ordinance to exclude certain veterans. Since Mike's right to peddle within the zone was not determined on an individual basis, he would have no due process claim.

Bill of attainder: Mike might claim that the ordinance constitutes a bill of attainder. Bills of attainder are prohibited by the Constitution. An ordinance will constitute a bill of attainder if it inflicts punishment without a judicial trial on individuals by name or by past conduct. Here, Mike would argue that the ordinance as revised is punishing him for his speaking out against the city in the past. He would further argue that the veterans' exception to the prohibition against peddling was carefully structured to exclude him. However, there are two problems with this argument. First, it is doubtful that a court will view the denial of the right to peddle within a designated pedestrian mall as a punishment. Moreover, the ordinance is not singling out Mike for this treatment. Most persons are prohibited from peddling within a pedestrian mall; Mike simply is not within the small group that is excluded from the prohibition.

127. REAL PROPERTY
To: Senior Partner
From: Associate
Re: *Paul v. Frank*

Mr. Paul will likely be able to quiet title to the property. The issue is whether Mr. Paul took the property subject to an easement.

An easement allows the holder to use someone else's land for a special purpose, but not to possess or enjoy the land. An easement arises by express reservation when a grantor conveys title to land, but reserves the right to continue to use the tract for a special purpose. Easements are enforceable against subsequent purchasers who have constructive, actual, or implied notice.

An easement may be terminated by: (i) language in the grant creating the easement, (ii) merger of the estates, (iii) release by the owner of the easement, (iv) abandonment of the easement, (v) estoppel, (vi) prescription, (vii) necessity, or (viii) condemnation or destruction. When the same person acquires ownership of both the easement and the servient estate, the easement is terminated by merger. Later separation of the estates will not automatically revive the easement.

Assuming the language in Ms. Jones's deed reserved to Mr. Smith the right to maintain the grassy area and fence, then an easement was created by express reservation. Mr. Smith and his successors would have had the right to maintain the grassy area. This would explain why Mr. Smith, Ms. Jones, and Mrs. Frank all maintained the grassy area during their time of ownership of the house.

If an easement existed, then Mr. Paul took subject to it because he had record and actual notice of the grassy area. Mr. Paul obtained a survey of the parking lot property that clearly showed the easement and, had he conducted a record search, Mr. Paul would have found the easement language in Ms. Jones's deed.

However, no easement existed when Mr. Paul purchased the property. The easement was terminated by merger when Mrs. Frank owned both the single family home and the parking lot. If Mrs. Frank's interest in the parking lot was held as a conveyable interest (*i.e.,* a tenancy in common or a joint tenancy), then the estates merged and the easement terminated.

Mrs. Frank may argue that an easement was created by implication when Mr. Paul bought the parking lot. This argument will likely fail. An easement is created by implication if: (i) prior to division of a single tract, (ii) an apparent and continuous use exists on the servient part, (iii) that is reasonably necessary for the enjoyment of the dominant part, and (iv) the court determines the parties intended

170.

the use to continue after the transfer. An easement was not created by implication because the land was already divided when the use began.

Therefore, Mr. Paul will likely be able to quiet title to the property.

128. EVIDENCE
To: Judge
From: Law Clerk
Re: Evidentiary Rulings: *State v. Goodness*

An analysis of the evidentiary rulings in *State v. Goodness* indicates that the court committed error regarding several evidentiary items. The trial court incorrectly admitted testimonial evidence from Nancy Smith, Dr. Johnson, and the pastor in the sexual abuse trial of George Goodness.

Testimony of Nancy Smith: The issue is whether the trial court properly admitted Ms. Smith's testimony regarding George Goodness, the defendant. First, it is necessary to ascertain whether the testimony is relevant to the issue being discussed. An item of evidence is relevant if it tends to prove or disprove a material issue. The prosecution is trying to establish that George Goodness sexually abused his daughter, Mary Goodness. Ms. Smith's testimony that Mr. Goodness became "pale" and "visibly upset" when confronted is not relevant because it does not prove the issue being discussed. It would not be unusual for an individual, confronted in such a circumstance, to react as Mr. Goodness did. Therefore, the trial court should not have admitted this testimony. Furthermore, the court should have excluded the evidence because the danger of unfair prejudice and confusion of the issues substantially outweigh the probative value.

The prosecution likely contended that Ms. Smith's testimony was permissible opinion testimony by a lay witness. Opinion testimony by a lay witness is generally inadmissible. However, in most jurisdictions, opinion testimony is admissible if it is rationally based on the witness's perception and if it is helpful to create a clear understanding of her testimony or to the determination of a fact in issue. Opinions of lay witnesses are generally admissible to show the state of emotion of a person. Therefore, it was allowable for Ms. Smith to testify as to the state of emotion of Mr. Goodness. However, the testimony should still have been excluded by the judge because of its prejudicial value to the jury.

Second, Ms. Smith's testimony regarding Mary's description of the sexual assault was also admitted in error. This testimony is hearsay and cannot be admitted at trial without falling under a hearsay exception. Hearsay is a statement, other than one made by the declarant, while testifying at the trial or hearing, offered into evidence to prove the truth of the matter asserted. Ms. Smith's testimony was offered to prove the truth of the matter asserted therein, which is that Mr. Goodness sexually abused Mary. Thus, the testimony is hearsay, and because it does not fall within any exception, is inadmissible. Also, given that Mary was available and did testify, it is not necessary for Ms. Smith to state what Mary said.

Testimony of Dr. Johnson: The issue is whether Dr. Johnson should have been permitted to testify about the physical evidence and Mary's emotional response at the time of her medical examination. Dr. Johnson was competent to testify about the physical evidence because she had personal knowledge of the matter about which she testified. Her testimony was relevant because it was offered to prove that Mary was sexually abused. On the other hand, Dr. Johnson's testimony regarding Mary's emotional state may have been improperly admitted. The evidence regarding Mary's emotional state was relevant because it made it more likely that Mary was sexually abused. However, the facts suggest that Dr. Johnson was rendering an opinion regarding Mary's emotional state. Opinions by lay witnesses are generally inadmissible. Unless it was demonstrated that Dr. Johnson was an expert, her testimony regarding Mary's emotional state was inadmissible.

An expert may state an opinion or conclusion if the subject matter is appropriate for expert testimony, if the witness is qualified as an expert, and if the opinion is supported by a proper factual basis. To be qualified as an expert, an individual must have special knowledge, skill, experience, training, or education sufficient to qualify her as an expert on the subject to which her testimony relates. Because Dr. Johnson is a gynecologist in the Rape Crisis Unit, there is some indication that she may be an expert on sexual assault and abuse cases. If it is determined that Dr. Johnson is an expert, then her testimony regarding Mary's emotional state was properly admitted. If, however, the trial court did not qualify Dr. Johnson as an expert witness, the court erred in admitting her testimony on this issue.

Testimony of Mary: The issue is whether the judge's decision to permit Mary to testify via closed circuit television was proper. The Sixth Amendment to the Constitution gives defendants the right to confront adverse witnesses. However, the Supreme Court has upheld the use of special procedural protections for child witnesses and victims of sexual abuse. Closed circuit television is considered a protective device. Federal legislation has also been passed permitting the use of such devices upon a particularized finding that the child witness needs special protection to effectively testify. Taking the facts as given, the court acted correctly in permitting Mary to testify via closed circuit television.

Testimony of Pastor: The issue is whether the court correctly admitted evidence regarding the defendant's character during the direct and cross-examinations of the pastor. A review of the facts suggests that the court appropriately admitted pastor's reputation testimony on the direct examination; nonetheless, it should not have admitted the prosecution's cross-examination inquiry regarding the defendant's prior conviction.

In criminal cases, character evidence is admissible when offered by the defendant to show character not in keeping with the offense charged. This evidence is offered by calling another witness whose testimony is limited to opinion or reputation. Note, however, that character evidence is inadmissible if offered by the prosecution to show that the defendant has a propensity to commit the charged crime. In this case, Mr. Goodness placed his character at issue by having the pastor testify as to his reputation. Since the evidence was offered on direct examination, the court correctly admitted it.

Similarly, it was permissible for the prosecution to rebut the testimony of the pastor on cross-examination. The prosecution may rebut the defendant's character evidence on cross-examination by inquiring into specific acts of the defendant that would affect the opinion of the witness or the witness's knowledge of the reputation that he has testified about. The prosecution may inquire whether the witness knows of or has heard of, relevant specific instances of conduct involving the defendant. In the present case, the prosecution inquired whether the pastor knew that the defendant had been convicted of burglary 15 years earlier. This inquiry was irrelevant. Evidence is relevant if it tends to make a material fact more or less likely than it would be without the evidence. Also, to be relevant, the evidence must relate to the time, event, or person in controversy. In the instant case, although the defendant "opened the door" to allow questioning of his character, the prosecution should not have been permitted to inquire about a specific act unrelated to the specific instance of conduct being discussed. Moreover, the burglary conviction occurred 15 years ago, which subsequently detracts from its relevancy. Since the evidence regarding the burglary charge is not relevant, the court erred in admitting it.

Mr. Goodness has grounds for appeal because Nancy Smith's testimony was improperly admitted, as was the prosecution's inquiry on cross-examination about prior unrelated acts. Also, if the trial court did not qualify Dr. Johnson as an expert witness, her opinion testimony was improperly admitted.

129. TORTS

To: Senior Partner
From: Associate
Re: Professor Forgetful

Professor Forgetful v. Descend, Inc.: We should sue Descend, Inc. ("Descend") and possibly Astute Elevator Service ("Astute") on a theory of strict products liability. To succeed on this claim we will have to show that there was a strict duty owed by a commercial supplier, that such duty was breached, that the breach was the actual and proximate cause of the plaintiff's injuries, and that the plaintiff sustained damages.

Here it is apparent that Descend is a commercial supplier and that the safety interlock device which controls the operation of the elevator door did not work properly. Astute may be a commercial supplier because it installed the elevator and is arguably therefore an "assembler," but that argument may not succeed.

We will succeed against Descend if we can show that the malfunction was due to a manufacturing defect or a design defect. A manufacturing defect is one that is present in a product because of an error in the manufacturing process. The product emerges from the manufacturing process different from the other products and more dangerous than if it had been made properly. A design defect is one that is present in all products that are made according to manufacturing specifications. Here, the elevator's safety interlock device appears to have been defective—the burden would be on Descend to show that the failure was not due to a defect. Actual and proximate cause and damages can be established without difficulty.

Descend may also be sued in a products liability action based on negligence. To prove breach of duty, plaintiff must be able to show negligent conduct and the supplying of a defective product. To establish defendant's negligence, we could raise the doctrine of res ipsa loquitur. To succeed under res ipsa, we must show that (i) the accident would not occur unless someone was negligent; (ii) the instrumentality that caused the injury was in the sole control of the defendant; and (iii) the injury was not attributable to the plaintiff. Once this is established the defendant bears the burden of proving that they are not responsible. We do not know exactly why the elevator doors opened without the elevator being there; Descend will argue that Astute was in control of the elevator during its installation and that therefore res ipsa does not apply.

Professor Forgetful v. Astute Elevator Service: Forgetful can sue Astute Elevator Service ("Astute") on a theory of negligence. Descend contractually delegated the duty to install the elevator to Astute and Astute accepted this duty. To succeed on this theory, we will have to prove that the elevator malfunctioned because it was not installed properly. Again, we could try to use res ipsa loquitur, but Astute will argue that any negligence cannot necessarily be attributed to it because the failure may have arisen from an undetectable design or manufacturing defect. Astute owed a duty to all foreseeable users of the elevator, and Professor Forgetful was a foreseeable plaintiff. This duty was breached when the elevator doors opened improperly. This was the actual and proximate cause of the professor's injuries, and he sustained significant damages. Astute may argue that the proximate cause of the professor's injuries was the fact that he stepped into an open elevator shaft without looking. This claim will probably not succeed since it is reasonable for people to assume that the elevator doors only open when the elevator is on that floor.

If it is determined that the malfunction was caused by Astute, the Professor may have an additional claim against Descend for negligent selection. To succeed, Professor would have to show that Descend did not adequately review Astute's qualifications before delegating the duty to install the elevator to them. Even if Descend was not negligent in selecting Astute, it may be vicariously liable because it had a nondelegable duty to insure that its elevator was properly installed; the fact that Astute was an independent contractor would not relieve Descend of its duty.

If it is shown that the malfunction was partially due to the actions of both Descend and Astute, the professor will be able to recover jointly and severally. The defendants will then be able to seek contribution from each other so that each defendant pays only his proportional share.

Defenses: Descend and Astute will not be able to claim that the professor was contributorily negligent since this defense does not apply in cases of strict liability. They may be able to reduce the amount of damages they are liable for if they can show that the professor was partially liable (and assuming that they are in a comparative negligence jurisdiction). They will not succeed in all likelihood, since reading while entering an elevator is not really negligent behavior.

Professor Forgetful v. Up-State University: Professor Forgetful can sue Up-State for any negligence on the part of Descend or Astute on vicarious liability grounds. As discussed above, the general rule that a principal is not liable for the torts of its independent contractor has a broad exception for duties that are nondelegable on public policy grounds. Up-State's duty to keep its buildings safe for invitees is a nondelegable duty. Any tortious conduct by its agents in manufacturing or installing the elevator would make it vicariously liable.

Professor Forgetful v. Thomas: Professor Forgetful may file an action against Thomas for negligence, but it is not likely that such an action will be successful. For the professor to succeed, he would have to show that Thomas owed him a duty and that he breached that duty, as well as causation and damages.

Thomas owed a duty of ordinary care to all other elevator users. It is not clear how he breached this duty. Thomas returned to the building after it was closed. As a matter of security it may have been negligent *not* to lock the elevator. The purpose of the safety interlock device was security; only those with a key to the elevator could control its movement after-hours in the science building. Thus, when Professor Forgetful pressed the elevator button the door should not have opened. By locking the elevator on the third floor Thomas simply used it in a way that was intended and designed.

The Professor's greatest hurdle in bringing a case against Thomas is proximate causation. It is hard to see how Thomas could have foreseen that the elevator would malfunction. Thomas could also argue successfully that the malfunctioning safety switch was an unforeseeable intervening event that would relieve him of liability.

Potential cross-claims: Until the exact cause of the malfunction of the elevator is determined, it is hard to conclusively state which parties may bring cross-claims against the other parties. Several scenarios emerge based on the origin of the defect. Cross-claims are litigated by parties on the same side of the litigation, while counterclaims are litigated between opposing parties to the principal action. Descend and Astute will likely file cross-claims against each other, claiming that the malfunction of the elevator was the other's fault. If it is determined that the elevator was defective upon leaving the control of Descend, then all parties sued by the Professor will file cross-claims against Descend. If the accident occurred because Astute improperly installed the elevator, then the cross-claims will lie against Astute. Up-State will file a cross-claim for indemnity against Descend and/or Astute, since its liability arises from their tortious conduct.

130. REAL PROPERTY

To: Senior Partner
From: Associate
Re: Shopping Center

Lottery sales: Center likely cannot terminate Disco's lease or receive damages for breach of the covenant. The issue is whether Disco breached a covenant in their lease, and if so, whether Center waived its right to object to this breach.

A lease is a contract that governs the landlord-tenant relationship. A lease may contain covenants requiring either party to act or not act in some manner. Covenants in a lease are generally independent. Therefore, if one party breaches a covenant, the other party must still perform, but can collect damages. A landlord can reserve the right to terminate the lease if the tenant breaches any of the lease's covenants. A breach is material if, because of the breach, the nonbreaching party does not receive the substantial benefit of the bargain. To determine materiality, a court will consider: (i) the amount of the benefit received, (ii) the adequacy of compensation, (iii) the extent of part performance, (iv) hardship to the breaching party, (v) negligent or willful behavior, and (vi) the likelihood that the breaching party will perform.

174.

Disco and Center enjoyed a landlord-tenant relationship created by the 1988 and 1993 leases. The Disco-Center lease contained a covenant allowing Disco to use the rented space, "for the retail sale of records, tapes, compact discs, and allied products." Whether Disco violated this covenant depends on whether lottery tickets are considered "allied products." Assuming Disco did violate the covenant, Center may terminate the lease if Center reserved the right to terminate the lease for breach of a covenant. Disco will argue that there was no breach because lottery tickets fall within "allied products" and if there was a breach, then Center waived any objections to the breach. Disco's argument is bolstered by the fact that Disco has been selling lottery tickets continuously since 1989 and Center renewed Disco's lease in 1993 under the same terms as Disco's previous lease. Center may argue that it did not know Disco was selling lottery tickets as evidenced by the fact that Center entered a lease with News for the exclusive right to sell lottery tickets in the shopping center. Disco is likely to prevail on this issue.

News and Center enjoyed a landlord-tenant relationship created by the 1996 lease. The News-Center lease contained a covenant giving News "the exclusive right to sell newspapers, magazines, greeting cards, and lottery tickets in the shopping center." Center was violating the covenant because Disco was also selling lottery tickets in the shopping center. News may terminate the lease if the breach is material. It is not clear from the facts whether this is a material breach. Regardless of whether this is a material breach, News may seek damages from Center for breach of the covenant.

Loud music: News cannot terminate the lease because of the loud music. Center may be able to enjoin Disco from playing loud, obnoxious music, and News may be able to recover damages from Disco for creating a nuisance. The issues are (i) whether the covenant of quiet enjoyment has been breached by a constructive eviction, and (ii) whether Disco violated a covenant in its lease.

Every lease includes an implied covenant that neither the landlord nor someone with paramount title will interfere with the tenant's quiet enjoyment and possession of the premises. The covenant of quiet enjoyment may be breached in three ways: (i) actual eviction, (ii) partial actual eviction, or (iii) constructive eviction. Constructive eviction occurs when the landlord acts or fails to provide some service that he has a legal obligation to provide, and thereby makes the property uninhabitable. If the covenant of quiet enjoyment is breached, then the tenant may terminate the lease and may also seek damages. The covenant of quiet enjoyment is breached where: (i) the landlord's actions, or persons acting for the landlord cause the injury (acts of neighbors or strangers are not sufficient), (ii) the conditions must be so bad as to make the premises uninhabitable, and (iii) the tenant must vacate the premises within a reasonable amount of time, thereby demonstrating that the premises are uninhabitable.

The implied covenant of quiet enjoyment in News's lease has not been breached by a constructive eviction. The actions that News has complained about are not the actions of Center or someone acting for Center. Additionally, News has not vacated the premises, thereby demonstrating that the premises are habitable.

The Disco-Center lease likely contains a covenant requiring Disco not to interfere with the rights of other tenants. Center may terminate the lease for Disco's interference with News if Center reserved the right to terminate the lease for tenant breaches of the lease's covenants. Unlike the breach for the sale of lottery tickets, Center has not waived its right to enforce this covenant. The loud music is a condition about which Center only recently became aware. Center could also sue for damages for breach of the covenant.

131. CRIMINAL LAW/PROCEDURE
To: File
Re: *State v. Burt*

A careful review of the facts of this case suggests that Burt is unlikely to be convicted of armed robbery, or possession of a handgun with intent to use it unlawfully. However, Burt may be guilty of the illegal possession of a handgun. In Burt's defense, we should file a motion to suppress the use of the gun and any related statements regarding its location, as evidence against him.

Armed robbery: Robbery is the taking of personal property of another, by force or intimidation, with the intent to permanently deprive him of it, with a deadly weapon. A review of the facts implies that Al perpetrated an armed robbery against Chet. However, the question is whether Burt may be convicted of armed robbery as an accomplice. According to the facts, Burt did not have the intent to commit robbery; he merely accompanied Al who was going to "scare" Chet. For accomplice liability to attach one must aid, counsel, or encourage the principal before or during the commission of the crime. Further, a person must have given the aid, counsel, or encouragement with the intent to aid or encourage the principal in the commission of the crime.

In this case, Burt only agreed to help scare Chet. He did not agree to aid Al in robbing Chet, neither did he counsel Al with the intent to encourage him to commit a crime against Chet. The prosecution may argue that Burt did aid Al in the commission of the crime because he drove the car from the scene and disposed of the handgun. However, this argument will likely fail because Burt did not drive the car with the intent to assist Al in the commission of the crime against Chet. Further, he did not dispose of the gun with the knowledge that Al had used it to commit a felony against Chet. At most, the prosecution could assert that Burt was an accessory after the fact in this case. An accessory after the fact is one who aids another knowing that he has committed a felony. However, this argument fails as well, because again, Burt did not know that Al had committed a felony.

Possession of a handgun with intent to use it unlawfully: This charge requires the specific intent to use the weapon in an unlawful manner. To be found guilty, a person must form the requisite intent to use it unlawfully when he had possession of the weapon. Burt only had possession of the gun after Al had used it against Chet. Burt never possessed the gun with the intent to perpetrate a crime against Chet. He was aware that Al intended to use the gun to "scare" Chet into paying his debt. Burt only had possession of the gun with the purpose of getting rid of it. Since Burt did not possess the intent necessary to commit this crime, the prosecution is unlikely to succeed in convicting Burt on this charge.

Illegal possession of a handgun: This crime entails the possession of a handgun without the required license, registration, and authorization. The facts do not suggest that Burt had the legal documents necessary to authorize his handling and use of the handgun. Therefore, it is likely that the prosecution will succeed in achieving conviction on this charge.

Necessary pretrial motions: First, our office should file a motion to suppress the use of the gun and any related statements regarding the location of the gun as evidence against Burt. Burt may claim that the police violated his Fifth Amendment rights when seeking to obtain the gun. The Fifth Amendment protects a person from self-incrimination. According to the facts, when the police officers arrested Burt, they only advised him that he could remain silent or consult an attorney if he wished. The facts suggest that Burt was not informed of his full *Miranda* rights. By stating that they were really seeking to get Al and encouraging Burt to disclose the location of the gun, the police unlawfully interrogated Burt without informing him of his right against self-incrimination. Thus, the gun should be inadmissible against Burt in court.

Second, the facts do not indicate that Burt made a knowing, voluntary, and intelligent waiver of his *Miranda* rights, including right to counsel, while he was in custody of the police officers. Absent a clear waiver of his *Miranda* rights, the police did not have the authority to question Burt about the crime. Therefore, the gun should be inadmissible for any purpose except to impeach Burt's testimony if he takes the stand at trial.

There should also be a motion to suppress because home arrests require a warrant in a non-emergency situation. Home arrests are automatically presumed to be unreasonable unless the prosecution can show sufficient exigent circumstances to overcome the presumption. Thus, any evidence obtained without the warrant would be considered "fruit of the poisonous tree," such as the information Burt gave the officers about the location of the gun.

176.

As discussed above, the facts do not support a conviction for our client on charges of armed robbery and possession of a handgun with intent to use it unlawfully. There are indications, however, that Burt may be found guilty of the illegal possession of a handgun. In defense of our client, we should immediately file a motion to suppress the gun as evidence as well as Burt's statements regarding the location of the gun.

132. EVIDENCE

To: Judge
From: Law Clerk
Re: *Jones v. Adams*

A review of the evidentiary rulings of the trial court suggests that the court committed error because it incorrectly admitted certain items of evidence. In particular, the trial court should not have admitted the photographs of the accident scene submitted by the plaintiff. Similarly, the court should not have admitted the opinion testimony of Dr. Neurologist without qualifying him as an expert.

Admission of photographs of the accident scene: Generally, documentary evidence must be relevant to be admissible in court. An item of evidence is relevant if it makes a material fact more or less likely. In addition to the general test of relevancy, photographs must be properly authenticated in order to be received into evidence. Photographs are admissible only if identified by a witness as a portrayal of certain facts relevant to the issue and verified by the witness as a correct representation of those facts.

In the present case, the trial court permitted Mr. Jones to admit photographs of the accident scene taken just over a year following the accident. The photographs were offered to show that Ms. Adams was required to stop prior to entering the intersection, which according to Mr. Jones, she did not do. Despite their relevance, the photographs should not have been admitted into evidence because they were not a fair and accurate representation of the accident scene. The facts specifically state that since the accident, the intersection had been widened, repaved, and the stop sign was placed in a different location than it had been on the date of the accident. Since the pictures depicted the stop sign in a different location, they were not a correct representation of the facts, and therefore not relevant. In addition, the photographs should have been excluded because their probative value was greatly outweighed by the confusion they would cause the jury.

Cross-examination of Mr. Jones: A review of the evidentiary ruling regarding the cross-examination of Mr. Jones indicates that the court appropriately admitted testimony regarding the careless driving summons. According to the facts, Mr. Jones did not sign a summons for any stop sign violation. This evidence is relevant because it tends to disprove Mr. Jones's assertion that Ms. Adams ran the stop sign. Mr. Jones did sign one summons regarding careless driving, but he failed to do so for the stop sign violation.

Testimony of the police officer regarding Ms. Adams: The officer testified that Ms. Adams stated that she "was in a rush" at the scene of the accident. Testimony is relevant if it tends to prove or disprove a material issue or fact. The officer's testimony was relevant because it tends to prove that Ms. Adams was driving in a careless manner when the accident occurred. Additionally, the officer's testimony is considered nonhearsay. Hearsay is an out-of-court statement being offered into evidence to prove the truth of the matter asserted. Hearsay is not admissible unless it falls within an exception to the hearsay rule or fits the definition of nonhearsay. Although the officer is testifying to a statement made by Ms. Adams outside of court, it is not hearsay because the statement made by Ms. Adams was an admission by a party-opponent. An admission is a statement made or act done that amounts to prior acknowledgment by one of the parties to an action of one of the relevant facts. This could also be considered an excited utterance and fall within that hearsay exception. An excited utterance is a declaration made by a declarant during or soon after a startling event and it is admissible. Thus, the court properly admitted this testimony.

The police officer also testified that Ms. Adams stated that she had ignored the "no through street" sign. This testimony was offered to prove that it was more likely that Ms. Adams ignored the stop sign at Rose Avenue and Ash Road, thereby causing the accident with Mr. Jones. Ms. Adams's attorney objected to this testimony. The trial court sustained the objection. This evidence should not have been admitted at trial because it is not relevant. The fact that Ms. Adams disregarded one sign does not establish that she ignored the second sign at the accident scene. Furthermore, the evidence should have been excluded because its probative value was substantially outweighed by the danger of unfair prejudice. Mr. Jones's attorney likely argued that the evidence of Ms. Adams's prior conduct should be admitted because it demonstrated habit. However, one occasion is not sufficient to establish a pattern of behavior in order to constitute a habit. The trial court correctly ruled on this issue.

Testimony of Dr. Neurologist: Dr. Neurologist testified to the injuries Mr. Jones sustained as a result of the accident with Ms. Adams. Dr. Neurologist testified that Mr. Jones sustained a convulsive disorder because of the accident. The doctor's testimony was relevant because it tended to prove that Mr. Jones's injuries were caused by the accident with Ms. Adams. However, the court should not have admitted the doctor's opinion regarding what caused the convulsive disorder because it was rendered as a layperson. The facts do not state that the doctor was qualified as an expert in the field, and thus, his opinion was not admissible in court.

Testimony of Mr. Ace: Mr. Ace is an engineer who testified, as an expert, to the reasonableness of Mr. Jones's speed at the time of the accident. His testimony was relevant because it tended to prove that Mr. Jones was driving at a reasonable speed at the time of the accident, and thus Mr. Jones did not cause the collision. Mr. Ace was qualified as an expert over the objection of Ms. Adams's attorney. The court correctly qualified Mr. Ace as an expert because there is no requirement that an expert possess a university certification. All that is required for qualification is that the expert have the specialized knowledge, skill, experience, training, or education sufficient to qualify him as an expert on the subject matter to which his testimony relates.

An expert may state an opinion or conclusion if the subject matter is appropriate for expert testimony, if the witness is qualified as an expert, and if the opinion is supported by a proper factual basis. In the present case, the subject matter is appropriate for expert testimony because it would assist the jury in understanding the evidence or determining a fact in issue. Therefore, since Mr. Ace was qualified as an expert, it was appropriate for the court to permit his testimony.

Furthermore, Mr. Ace's testimony that was based on a mathematical formula not recognized by the majority of engineers in the accident reconstruction field was properly admitted by the court. Some jurisdictions require, as a condition of admissibility, that the methodology or explanatory theory have achieved "general acceptance" in the appropriate scientific field. However, unless this jurisdiction recognizes that standard for admissibility, the court did not commit error by permitting Mr. Ace to testify using a less popular methodology.

The trial court incorrectly admitted the unauthenticated photographs and the unqualified opinion testimony by Dr. Neurologist. However, a review of the file does not suggest that Mr. Jones should be granted a new trial, since the incorrect evidentiary rulings would not necessarily lead the trier of fact to a different result.

133. CONTRACTS

To: Senior Partner
From: Associate
Re: *Bumbler v. Ajax*

Breach of contract: The first claim Bumbler may make is that Ajax breached its contract with Smallco. At issue is the interpretation of contractual terms. Since the agreement here involves the sale of goods, it is governed by Article 2 of the Uniform Commercial Code ("U.C.C.").

Under the U.C.C., where a buyer refuses to accept goods under a contract of sale, the seller may recover damages equal to the difference between the contract price and the market or resale price, but if neither of these will put the seller in as good a position as performance would have, the seller may recover lost profits. The seller may also recover incidental damages, which include all expenses reasonably incurred in performing under the contract. Here, the normal measure of damages will not put Smallco in as good a position as performance because as a result of Ajax's conduct, Smallco was forced to liquidate and is no longer manufacturing parts to sell. Therefore, it would be able to recover its lost profits plus its incidental damages. Here, the incidental damages would probably include any costs incurred in installing the special equipment needed to perform under the contract with Ajax.

Smallco's best claim for breach is that the second contractual provision, that Ajax would purchase a minimum number of parts per month to cover Smallco's debt service, impliedly meant that Ajax would be required to make purchases until the entire debt Smallco incurred in order to produce parts for Ajax was paid. Ajax would no doubt counter that the fourth contract clause provided that either party could terminate the contract at any time on 30 days' notice, and Ajax invoked that right.

To buttress Smallco's claim over Ajax's claim, Smallco could raise two basic rules of contract construction. First, when contracts are interpreted, they are construed as a whole, so specific clauses will be subordinated to the contract's general intent. The general intent of the parties seems to have been that if Smallco would take on the expense of upgrading to manufacture parts for Ajax, Ajax would see to it that Smallco's expenses and a small profit would be covered. Second, ambiguities in a contract generally are construed against the party that drafted the contract. Since the meaning of the second clause is unclear and Ajax drafted the contract, it should be interpreted in favor of Smallco.

Ajax's best defense to the above arguments is that the agreement is not a binding contract. Under the U.C.C., a contract for the sale of goods is not binding unless it contains a quantity term. Here, the agreement does not contain a clear quantity term. It merely provides that Ajax will purchase a "minimum number of parts per month." The U.C.C. recognizes good faith output of a manufacturer or requirements of a buyer as valid quantity terms, but the term here does not appear to be either. It might be argued that the quantity here is sufficient because it is based on specific criteria (a minimum number at a price sufficient to cover Smallco's costs, debt service, and a reasonable profit), but this argument will probably fail because the stated criteria appear to go to price rather than quantity.

Unconscionability: If it is found that there is a contract between the parties, Smallco may claim that it is unconscionable to allow Ajax to exercise its option to terminate the contract upon giving 30 days' notice. Under the U.C.C., a court may refuse to enforce a provision of a contract, or may modify the contract, to avoid unconscionable terms, *i.e.*, terms that were so unfair and one-sided at the time the contract was made that the court in good conscience cannot enforce them. The concept is often applied where the parties were in greatly unequal bargaining position. Here, Ajax, an international company, was dealing with Smallco, a small machine shop. Ajax drafted the contract which provided that Smallco should bear a great expense to manufacture parts for Ajax and yet reserved the right to allow Ajax to back out of the deal at almost any time. Given the sophistication of Ajax's legal department and the apparent lack of sophistication on the part of Bumbler, Smallco's sole owner and operator, the 30-day cancellation provision should be found to have been unconscionable. That would make Ajax's cancellation a breach, and Smallco would be entitled to recover damages as discussed above.

Promissory estoppel: If the court finds that the quantity term here was not sufficient to form a contract, Ajax might still be bound under a promissory estoppel theory. Under the theory of promissory estoppel, a contract will be enforceable to the extent necessary to avoid injustice where the promisor reasonably should have expected that its words would have induced action or forbearance of a definite and substantial character, and such action or forbearance actually occurred. Here, Ajax should have expected that Smallco would rely on the written agreement and would incur great expense to produce the tractor parts for Ajax. Smallco did in fact rely on the agreement and incurred great expenses. Thus, Smallco is entitled to damages in an amount sufficient to, at least, pay for any amounts left owing on the equipment that Smallco installed to manufacture the parts for Ajax.

Quasi-contract: Where a contract fails, a party might still recover damages under a quasi-contract theory. Quasi-contract is an equitable remedy used to prevent unjust enrichment. Damages usually are measured by the benefit the defendant received, but they may be measured by the plaintiff's detriment, and may exceed the contract price, where the plaintiff's benefit is hard to measure and the plaintiff has not breached the contract.

Here, Smallco would argue that Ajax has been unjustly enriched because the contract failed. Ajax received the benefit of having a steady parts supply for six months, the value of which is hard to quantify. Since Smallco did not breach, it would therefore be entitled to recover the money it spent to supply the parts. Since Smallco already has been paid for some of this expense, damages should be the amount of debt remaining on the equipment Smallco purchased to produce the parts for Ajax.

Two-year prohibition: If the court finds that the agreement between the parties did not create an enforceable contract, the third contractual provision, prohibiting Smallco from producing similar parts for other manufacturers, of course, would not have been binding and Smallco would have been free to sell parts to others had it not liquidated. If the court finds that a contract was formed, it might still find this provision unenforceable. This is a type of noncompetition clause, and courts will not enforce noncompetition clauses unless they are reasonable as to geographic scope and duration. The clause here prohibits Smallco from selling similar parts to anyone, apparently anywhere in the world, for the next two years. Given that Ajax has curtailed production, it does not seem reasonable to prohibit Smallco from selling to Ajax's competition for the next two years. Therefore, this provision should be stricken.

134. CONSTITUTIONAL LAW

Helen and Joe have standing to bring their suit, and they will succeed under the Fourteenth Amendment's Equal Protection and Substantive Due Process Clauses, although their procedural due process claim will not succeed.

Standing: Helen and Joe have standing to challenge City's anti-nepotism ordinance. The issue here is whether Helen and Joe can demonstrate that they have a sufficient stake in the controversy. To have standing, Helen and Joe must show that they have suffered an injury (or that injury is imminent) caused by the government conduct, and that a ruling in their favor will eliminate the injury/harm. Here, Helen and Joe meet their burden, as they have suffered an injury (they had to choose between actual harms: postponement of their wedding or loss of employment) caused by City's ordinance, and if they succeed in convincing the court to invalidate the ordinance, they will be able to marry without having to resign. Therefore, Helen and Joe have standing to bring this claim.

Substantive due process: Helen and Joe should prevail on a substantive due process claim. The Fourteenth Amendment's Substantive Due Process Clause applies here. The issues here are whether the ordinance infringes on a fundamental right, and, if so, whether the ordinance overcomes the burden of meeting the strict scrutiny test for interfering with fundamental rights.

The Fourteenth Amendment provides that states shall not deprive persons of life, liberty, or property without due process of law. This Due Process Clause has been broadly interpreted to include not only a right to fair procedures, but also a substantive right to reasonable laws. What is needed to be reasonable depends on the nature of the right involved. If a law limits a fundamental right, a strict scrutiny analysis will be applied: the government action will only be upheld if it is necessary to promote a compelling or overriding state interest. The right to marry is among the penumbra of rights found to be included in the fundamental right to privacy.

Here, the anti-nepotism ordinance is interfering with the right to marry, a fundamental right. The facts do not state what the government's interest is in the ordinance. Presumably it is to prevent a supervisor from favoring a relative. This might constitute a sufficiently compelling interest, but the ordinance is broader than necessary to achieve its purpose. Where, as here, relatives are both supervisors of their own units, there is little chance that one can favor the other. Thus, the ordinance is unconstitutionally overbroad.

Procedural due process: Helen and Joe will not succeed on a procedural due process challenge. The issues here are whether Helen and Joe fit within the Fourteenth Amendment's Procedural Due Process Clause, and, if so, whether they were afforded the process that was due.

As discussed above, the Fourteenth Amendment provides that the government shall not take a person's life, liberty, or property without due process of law. Whether a person has a property interest in a government job depends on whether the person has a legitimate expectation of continued employment. There must be a contract or practice that justifies the expectation of continued employment. If there is such a property right, a person may not be dismissed without a hearing to determine whether the grounds for dismissal have occurred. Here, we don't know whether there is a contract or practice that would justify Helen's and Joe's beliefs in a right to continued employment. However, even if there were, they still could not make out a procedural due process claim because neither one has yet been fired without a hearing. In essence, this claim is not yet ripe for review.

Equal protection challenge: The ordinance appears to discriminate against women as applied and therefore is unconstitutional. At issue is whether the ordinance violates the Fourteenth Amendment's Equal Protection Clause.

The Fourteenth Amendment provides that states shall not deny persons the equal protection of the laws. Under this prohibition, if an ordinance discriminates against persons on the basis of gender, the Supreme Court has held that the ordinance is unconstitutional unless the government can show that the ordinance is substantially related to an important government interest. Discrimination can be on the face of the ordinance or can be shown through discriminatory application of the ordinance or through discriminatory purpose.

Here, the ordinance is neutral on its face. It merely provides that the relative with less seniority must resign. The fact that this usually results in women being forced to resign or transfer probably will not be sufficient to prove that the ordinance was passed with a discriminatory purpose. Such statistical evidence generally is held not sufficient to show a discriminatory purpose. However, Helen has a good chance in showing that the ordinance is applied in a discriminatory manner. Even though the Chief knew that Helen and Joe had identical seniority, he called Helen in and told her to "do the right thing." This seems like a clear attempt to encourage her to resign rather than Joe. If this is the common practice, then the ordinance is being applied in a discriminatory fashion. No important government interest that would justify favoring men to women in such situations is apparent from the facts. Thus, the ordinance is being applied in a way that violates the Fourteenth Amendment.

NEW JERSEY ESSAY SUBJECT BREAKDOWN

SUBJECT	ESSAY NUMBER
CRIMINAL LAW/PROCEDURE	3, 8, 14, 17, 21, 26, 32, 36, 46, 51, 57, 62, 65, 73, 75, 79, 84, 89, 94, 102, 109, 110, 112, 119, 125, 131
CONSTITUTIONAL LAW	4, 10, 11, 20, 23, 27, 34, 39, 41, 47, 54, 56, 64, 69, 70, 72, 77, 83, 90, 97, 98, 118, 126, 134
CONTRACTS	5, 9, 13, 16, 24, 25, 29, 30, 35, 40, 43, 45, 49, 52, 59, 60, 63, 66, 71, 74, 80, 85, 92, 93, 100, 121, 124, 133
EVIDENCE	32, 44, 51, 55, 103, 104, 105, 106, 107, 108, 113, 115, 122, 128, 132
REAL PROPERTY	2, 7, 15, 19, 25, 30, 33, 37, 45, 50, 53, 61, 67, 72, 76, 81, 87, 88, 95, 101, 111, 120, 127, 130
TORTS	1, 6, 12, 18, 22, 28, 31, 38, 42, 48, 58, 63, 68, 74, 78, 82, 86, 91, 96, 99, 114, 116, 117, 123, 129